Melville Madison Bigelow

Elements of the Law of Torts

Melville Madison Bigelow

Elements of the Law of Torts

ISBN/EAN: 9783743347656

Manufactured in Europe, USA, Canada, Australia, Japa

Cover: Foto ©ninafisch / pixelio.de

Manufactured and distributed by brebook publishing software (www.brebook.com)

Melville Madison Bigelow

Elements of the Law of Torts

ELEMENTS

OF

THE LAW OF TORTS.

London: C. J. CLAY AND SONS,
CAMBRIDGE UNIVERSITY PRESS WAREHOUSE,
AVE MARIA LANE.

Cambridge: DEIGHTON, BELL, AND CO.
Leipzig: F. A. BROCKHAUS.

ELEMENTS

OF

THE LAW OF TORTS

A TEXT BOOK FOR STUDENTS.

BY

MELVILLE M. BIGELOW, Ph.D.

LECTURER IN THE LAW SCHOOL OF THE UNIVERSITY OF BOSTON, U.S.A.

CAMBRIDGE:
AT THE UNIVERSITY PRESS.
1889

[*All Rights reserved.*]

Cambridge:
PRINTED BY C. J. CLAY, M.A. AND SONS,
AT THE UNIVERSITY PRESS.

TO MY FRIENDS

F. W. MAITLAND AND R. T. WRIGHT

OF THE

UNIVERSITY OF CAMBRIDGE

TO THEM THIS BOOK IS DUE

PREFACE.

IT chanced some time ago that my Elements of the Law of Torts found favour in the instruction of the Law School of the University of Cambridge, and that not long afterwards a suggestion came to me over sea, from those who had been using the book there, to prepare an English edition of it. More to say were needless. The University Press undertook the work; the result is here.

The present differs from the American edition in that it is a book of the law of England instead of the law of America. American cases are, indeed, cited here and there; but that has always been done with a view to throwing light upon the student's work. In the changes made, English authorities and illustrations have been substituted very generally for American, and the English statutes have been referred to wherever they fall within the scope of the book. Some chapters have been almost wholly re-written; chapter fourth, of Part I, appears here for the first time; the Introduction is a new one.

To be a little more specific in regard to the use of American cases, these have been referred to (1) where there appeared to be doubt concerning the state of the English authorities, (2) where they served to fill a gap now and then left, and (3) where they afforded particularly good illustrations of the law. In one or two instances, indeed, American cases not always accepted in the United States have been noticed for the instructiveness of the principles involved. An instance may be seen on pp. 326—328, in regard to the Sunday laws.

It is proper to repeat the statement made in the American edition, that the object of the book is to answer the question, as far as answer may be given, What is the legal conception of tort? and then more definitely the question, What constitutes the specific torts of the English law? Nothing else is attempted; a book for the beginner should, I think, stop there.

The end in view is sought by presenting and considering three or four fundamental duties, in which are found the 'elements of the law of torts.' These are (1) the duty to refrain from fraud and malice, (2) certain absolute duties—duties, that is to say, independent of any real or nominal attitude of mind, and (3) the duty to refrain from negligence; a train of duties extending from positive attitudes around to negative. The order, it should perhaps be said, is entirely academic; but it is believed to be natural.

The cases made use of have been presented with special reference to their instructiveness. The fact cannot be too strongly urged upon the student's attention that the cases are the authorities, and that a mastery of the more important ones is indispensable to a competent knowledge of the law.

M. M. B.

BOSTON, MASS.,
Aug. 2, 1888.

CONTENTS.

	PAGE
CASES CITED	xvii
INTRODUCTION	3

PART I.

BREACH OF DUTY TO REFRAIN FROM FRAUD OR MALICE.

CHAPTER I.

DECEIT		17
§ 1.	Introductory	17
§ 2.	Of the Representation	18
§ 3.	Of Defendant's Knowledge of Falsity	32
§ 4.	Of Plaintiff's Ignorance of Falsity	37
§ 5.	Of the Intention that the Representation should be acted upon	43
§ 6.	Of Acting upon the Representation	45
§ 7.	Of Slander of Title and Trade Marks	47

CHAPTER II.

MALICIOUS PROSECUTION 52
§ 1. Introductory 52
§ 2. Of the Termination of the Prosecution . . . 53
§ 3. Of the Want of Probable Cause 58
§ 4. Of Malice 67
§ 5. Of Damage 68
§ 6. Of Analogous Remedies 69

CHAPTER III.

CONSPIRACY 72
§ 1. Introductory 72
§ 2. Of the Nature of Conspiracy 74
§ 3. Of Damage 76

CHAPTER IV.

MALICIOUS INTERFERENCE WITH CONTRACT . . 76
§ 1. Introductory 76
§ 2. Of Malice 76
§ 3. Of Damage 79
§ 4. Conclusion : Contract not Property . . 80

CHAPTER V.

SLANDER AND LIBEL 81
§ 1. Introductory 81
§ 2. Of the Interpretation of Language . . . 82
§ 3. Of the Publication of Defamation and Special Damage 84
§ 4. Of the Imputation of having Committed a Crime . 86
§ 5. Of the Imputation of having a Contagious or Infectious Disease of a Disgraceful Kind . . 87
§ 6. Of an Imputation affecting the Plaintiff in his Office, Business, or Occupation 88
§ 7. Of an Imputation tending to Disinherit the Plaintiff 90
§ 8. Of an Imputation conveyed by Writing, Printing, or Representation; that is, of Libel . . . 91
§ 9. Of the Truth of the Charge 92
§ 10. Of Malice and Privileged Communications . . 93

PART II.

BREACH OF ABSOLUTE DUTY.

CHAPTER I.

	PAGE
ASSAULT AND BATTERY	115
§ 1. Introductory	115
§ 2. Of Assaults	115
§ 3. Of Batteries	118
§ 4. Of Justifiable Assault: Self-defence: 'Son Assault Demesne'	123
§ 5. Of Violence to or towards One's Servants	126
§ 6. Of Felony	129

CHAPTER II.

FALSE IMPRISONMENT	131
§ 1. Introductory	131
§ 2. Of the Nature of the Restraint	131
§ 3. Of Arrests with Warrant	134
§ 4. Of Arrests without Warrant	150

CHAPTER III.

ENTICEMENT AND SEDUCTION	157
§ 1. Introductory	157
§ 2. Of Master and Servant ex Contractu	158
§ 3. Of Master and Servant ex Gratia	160
§ 4. Of Parent and Child	162
§ 5. Of Guardian and Ward	168
§ 6. Of Husband and Wife	169

CHAPTER IV.

TRESPASSES UPON PROPERTY	176
§ 1. Introductory	176
§ 2. Of Possession	176
§ 3. Of what constitutes Trespass to Property	189

CHAPTER V.

	PAGE
CONVERSION	198
§ 1. Introductory	198
§ 2. Of Possession	199
§ 3. Of what constitutes Conversion	204

CHAPTER VI.

INFRINGEMENT OF PATENTS AND COPYRIGHTS	217
§ 1. Introductory	217
§ 2. Of Patents for Invention	218
§ 3. Of Trade Marks	228
§ 4. Of Copyrights	228

CHAPTER VII.

VIOLATION OF RIGHTS OF SUPPORT	240
§ 1. Introductory	240
§ 2. Of Lateral Support	240
§ 3. Of Subjacent Support	247

CHAPTER VIII.

VIOLATION OF WATER RIGHTS	251
§ 1. Introductory	251
§ 2. Of Usufruct and Reasonable Use of Streams	251
§ 3. Of Sub-surface Water	255

CHAPTER IX.

NUISANCE	256
§ 1. Introductory	256
§ 2. Of what constitutes a Nuisance	256

CHAPTER X.

DAMAGE BY ANIMALS	266
§ 1. Introductory	266
§ 2. Of Notice of Propensity to do Damage	266
§ 3. Of Escape of Animals	269

CHAPTER XI.

ESCAPE OF DANGEROUS THINGS	270
§ 1. Introductory	270
§ 2. Of the Nature of the Protection Required	270

PART III.

BREACH OF DUTY TO REFRAIN FROM NEGLIGENCE.

	PAGE
NEGLIGENCE	279
§ 1. Introductory	279
§ 2. Of the Legal Conception of Negligence	279
§ 3. Of Innkeeper and Guest	284
§ 4. Of Bailor and Bailee	285
§ 5. Of Professional Services	291
§ 6. Of the Liability of Agents, Servants, Trustees, and the Like	295
§ 7. Of Public Bodies and Public Officers	302
§ 8. Of the Use of Premises	304
§ 9. Of Notice	322
§ 10. Of Contributory Negligence	323
§ 11. Of Intervening Forces	331
STUDIES IN PLEADING	345
INDEX	355

ABBREVIATIONS OF AMERICAN REPORTS CITED.

[Unless otherwise indicated below, the Reports are of cases decided by courts of last resort.]

Ala. ....Alabama.
Barb. ....Barbour, New York, intermediate.
Blackf. ....Blackford, Indiana.
Conn. ....Connecticut.
Cowen ....New York, intermediate and of last resort.
Cush. ....Cushing, Massachusetts.
Denio ....New York, intermediate and of last resort.
Duer ....New York (City), intermediate.
Dutch. ....Dutcher, New Jersey, intermediate and of last resort.
Eng. ....English, Arkansas.
Gratt. ....Grattan, Virginia.
Halst. ....Halstead, New Jersey.
Heisk. ....Heiskell, Tennessee.
How. ....Howard, Supreme Court of United States.
Humph. ....Humphreys, Tennessee.
Ill. ....Illinois.
Ind. ....Indiana.
Ired. ....Iredell, North Carolina.
Johns. ....Johnson, New York, intermediate and of last resort.
Kelly ....Georgia.
Keyes ....New York.
Ky. ....Kentucky.
Lans. ....Lansing, New York, intermediate.

Mason ....Circuit Court of United States, intermediate Federal Court.
Mass. ....Massachusetts.
Met. ....Metcalf, Massachusetts.
Met. (Ky.) ....Metcalf, Kentucky.
Mich. ....Michigan.
N. H. ....New Hampshire.
N. J. ....New Jersey. See Dutcher; Halstead.
N.Y. ....New York.
Ohio St. ....Ohio State.
Penn. St. ....Pennsylvania State.
Pick. ....Pickering, Massachusetts.
R. I. ....Rhode Island.
Rob. ....Robertson, New York (City), intermediate.
Scam. ....Scammon, Illinois.
Smedes & M. ....Smedes & Marshall, Mississippi.
Smith, E. D.......New York (City), intermediate.
Story ....Circuit Court of United States, intermediate Federal Court.
Strobh. ....Strobhart, South Carolina.
Tenn. ....Tennessee.
U. S. ....United States.
Vt. ....Vermont.
Wall. ....Wallace, Supreme Court of United States.
Wall. C. C. ......Wallace, Circuit Court of United States, intermediate Federal Court.
Wend. ....Wendell, New York, intermediate and of last resort.
Wheat. ....Wheaton, Supreme Court of United States.
Wis. ....Wisconsin.

OTHER ABBREVIATIONS.

Div. (Ch. Div., Q. B. Div., &c.) = decision by Court of Appeal.
D. (Ch. D., Q. B. D., &c.) = decision by Divisional Court or by single judge.
L. C. Torts = Bigelow's Leading Cases on Torts.

NOTANDA.

Mr Herbert Stephen strongly urges that the effect of the decision in Abrath v. North-eastern Ry. Co., 11 App. Cas. 247, is to give to the jury the right to determine what constitutes probable cause (in cases, of course, not settled by law) in suits for malicious prosecution or for false imprisonment. Stephen, Malicious Prosecution, ch. 7; to which a reference should be made on pp. 67 and 153 of this book.

The reader is requested to substitute the word 'fraudulent' for 'artful', in line 2, p. 17; to insert the word 'distinctively' between 'be' and 'proved', end of middle paragraph, p. 70; and to add to note 2, p. 82, the following: As to libel see Fox's Act, 32 Geo. III. c. 60. The case of Whalley v. Lancashire Ry. Co., 13 Q. B. Div. 131, may be added to note 4, p. 259.

LIST OF CASES CITED.

	PAGE
Abrahams v. Kidney .	164, 165
Abrath v. North-eastern Ry. Co.	xvi, 68, 94
Absor v. French	195
Albany Sav. Inst. v. Burdick	40, 41
Albert v. Strange	231
Albro v. Jaquith	317
Aldred v. Constable	205
Alexander v. Southey	216
Allen v. Crofoot	196
v. Wright	156
Alton v. Midland Railway Co.	128, 334, 335
Ames v. Union R. Co.	335
Amick v. O'Hara	269
Andre v. Johnson	123
Andrews v. Marris	142
Arkwright v. Newbold	31, 32
Armistead v. Wilde	284
Armory v. Delamirie	201
Armstrong v. Lancashire Ry. Co.	336, 337
Arundell v. White	55
Ash v. Dawnay	195
Ashby v. White	303
Ashwell's Case	204
Aston v. Blagrave	90
Atkinson v. Matteson	138

	PAGE
Austin v. Dowling	146
v. Great Western Ry. Co.	335
Ayer v. Bartlett	183
Ayre v. Craven	89
Bacon v. Sheppard	188
v. Towne	56, 64
Badger v. Nichols	22
Badische Anilin Fabrik v. Levinstein	226
Baglehole v. Walters	42
Baird v. Williamson	272
Baker v. Bolton	129
Ball, Ex parte	130
Balston v. Bensted	255
Bamford v. Turnley	258, 259
Barfield v. Nicholson	233
Barker v. Braham	146
Barley v. Walford	34
Barnes v. Allen	172
v. Ward	307
Barnett v. Guildford	187
Barnstable v. Thacher	179
Barratt v. Price	137
Bartonshill Coal Co. v. Reid	318, 319
v. McGuire	319
Batchelor v. Fortescue	305, 306

b 2

LIST OF CASES CITED.

	PAGE
Batson v. Donovan	288
Baum v. Clause	87, 93
Baxendale v. McMurray	261
Baxter v. Taylor	181
Baynes v. Brewster	154, 155
Beach v. Hancock	117
Beal v. Robeson	66
v. South Devon Ry. Co.	287, 288, 302
Beattie v. Ebury	29
Beckwith v. Philby	153
Bellamy v. Burch	90
Bellefontaine & I. R. Co. v. Snyder	339
Benjamin v. Storr	263, 264
Bennet v. Bullock	187
Bennett v. Allcott	127
v. Smith	170, 171
Bernina, The	337, 340
Besébé v. Matthews	54
Bibley v. Carter	242
Bigaouette v. Paulet	170
Bird v. Holbrook	269, 305, 326
v. Jones	133
Birdsey v. Butterfield	27
Blackham v. Pugh	107
Blake v. Barnard	116
v. Lanyon	159, 334
Bliss v. Hall	259
Bloodworth v. Gray	87
Bloxam v. Hubbard	215
Blyth v. Birmingham Waterworks Co.	260
v. Topham	308
Bolch v. Smith	310
Bonomi v. Backhouse	240, 241
Bostick v. Rutherford	64
Bosworth v. Swansea	327
Boucicault v. Chatterton	234
Bowditch v. Balchin	154

	PAGE
Bowen v. Hall	5, 77, 78, 79, 160
Bovill v. Pimm	226, 227
Boyle v. Brandon	165
Bradbury v. Hotten	235, 236, 237
Bradlaugh v. Newdegate	71
Bradley v. Fisher	304
v. Fuller	46, 47
Bradt v. Towsley	84
Bramwell v. Halcomb	235, 236
Brannock v. Bouldin	75
Brass v. Maitland	289, 333
Bridge v. Grand Junc. Ry. Co.	328
Bridges v. Hawkesworth	203
Briggs v. Taylor	287
Brinsmead v. Harrison	212
Bristol v. Wilsmore	28
Broad v. Ham	52, 60, 62
Broadbent v. Imperial Gas Co.	258
v. Ramsbotham	254
Bromley v. Coxwell	212
v. Wallace	170, 175
Brooks v. Curtis	246
Broughton v. Jackson	59
Brown v. Boorman	283
v. Kendall	121, 122
v. McGregor	337
Brownlie v. Campbell	18, 33
Brushaber v. Stegemann	132
Buck v. Aiken	184
Buckley v. Gross	180, 202
Bulmer v. Bulmer	129
Burke v. Broadway	339
Burroughes v. Bayne	216
Burrows v. March Gas Co.	335, 336
Burt v. Place	61, 63, 64
Bushel v. Miller	204
Busst v. Gibbons	59

LIST OF CASES CITED. xix

	PAGE
Butcher v. Butcher	178
Butterfield v. Forrester	328
Byne v. Moore	56, 69
Bywater v. Richardson	42
Bywell Castle, The	328
Caffrey v. Darby	299
Caird v. Sime	231
Calder v. Halket	143
Caledonian Ry. Co. v. Sprot	242, 250
Callahan v. Bean	338
Campbell v. Spottiswoode	93, 110, 111
Cann v. Willson	315, 332
Capital Bank v. Henty	82
Card v. Case	266
Cardival v. Smith	55
Carleton v. Franconia Iron Co.	312, 313
Carpenter v. Hale	205
v. Tarrant	86
Carr v. Hood	110
Carratt v. Morley	142, 143, 145, 146
Carroll v. Hayward	34
v. Staten Island R. Co.	327
Carslake v. Mapledoram	87
Carstairs v. Taylor	273
Carter v. Kingman	200
v. Towne	331
Cary v. Longman	233
Case v. De Goes	187, 188
Cashill v. Wright	284, 285
Cass v. Boston & L. R. Co.	287
Castrique v. Behrens	54
Caswell v. Worth	328
Cavey v. Ledbitter	258
Central Ry. Co. v. Kisch	31, 32, 39

	PAGE
Chambers v. Bedell	194
v. Caulfield	174
v. Donaldson	178
v. Robinson	68
Chapman v. New Haven R. Co.	337
v. Rothwell	312
Chappell v. Boosey	234
Charitable Corp. v. Sutton	299
Chasemore v. Richards	5, 255, 271
Chauntler v. Robinson	245
Cheesman v. Exall	201
Chicago Ry. Co. v. Ross	320
Childers v. Wooler	32
Chrysler v. Canaday	25
Churchill v. Siggers	71
Cibber v. Sloper	175
Cincinnati Gazette Co. v. Timberlake	100
Citizens' Bank v. First Nat. Bank	27
Clark v. Adie	225
v. Chambers	331, 338
v. Cleveland	138
v. Molyneux	108
v. Rideout	200
Clarke v. Dickson	40, 43
v. Midland Ry. Co.	309
Clement v. Maddick	235
Clendon v. Dinneford	210
Cleveland R. Co. v. Terry	336
Cliff v. Midland Railway Co.	309, 311
Clothier v. Webster	302
Clough v. North-western Ry. Co.	206
Clowes v. Staffordshire Waterworks Co.	260
Cluff v. Mutual Ben. Life Ins. Co.	124

LIST OF CASES CITED.

	PAGE
Coaks v. Boswell	21
Cobbett v. Woodward	232
Codrington v. Lloyd	147
Coffin v. Coffin	97
Coggs v. Bernard	286
Cole v. Maundy	192
v. Stewart	182
v. Turner	119
Coleman v. New York & N. H. R. Co.	337
Collen v. Wright	20, 35, 36
Collett v. Foster	147
Collins v. Evans	32, 34
Collis v. Selden	315, 333, 334
Commonwealth v. Carey	154, 156
v. McLaughlin	154
Connolly v. Boston	327
Cook v. Hartle	212
Coombs v. New Bedford Cordage Co.	317, 319
Cooper v. Booth	71
v. Greeley	92
v. Harding	145
v. Willomatt	206, 210
v. Wooley	262
Coote v. Lighworth	134
Corbett v. Brown	31, 32
Corby v. Hill	310
Cornish v. Stubbs	192
Cory v. Bath	327
Cotterell v. Jones	76
Cotton v. Wood	283
Coulter v. American Exp. Co.	329
Coward v. Baddeley	121, 122
Cox v. Burbridge	267
Crafter v. Metrop. Ry. Co.	283
Craig v. Hasell	71
Crawshay v. Thompson	50
Crepps v. Durden	149

	PAGE
Crump v. Lambert	262
Cundy v. Lindsay	207
Curtis v. Platt	225
Cutts v. Spring	177
Dabney v. Manning	188
D'Almaine v. Boosey	237, 239
Dalton v. Angus	242, 243, 250
Damon v. Moore	165
Daniels v. Fielding	71
Danville Turnp. Co. v. Stewart	337
Darley Coll. Co. v. Mitchell	240
Davey v. South-western Ry. Co.	307, 329
Davies v. Jenkins	147
v. Mann	325, 326, 328
Davis v. Reeves	107
v. Russell	153
v. Shepstone	111
Davison v. Duncan	101
Dawkins v. Paulet	108
v. Rokeby	97
v. Saxe Weimar	97
Dawson v. Chamney	284
Dean v. Keate	281, 290
v. Peel	162
De Crespigny v. Wellesley	109
Delegal v. Highley	60, 61
Denton v. Great Northern Ry. Co.	35
Dewey v. Osborn	187
Dews v. Riley	142
Deyo v. Van Valkenburgh	139, 140, 148, 149
Dickinson v. Grand Junction Canal Co.	255
Dicks v. Yates	232
Dinks v. South Yorkshire Ry. Co.	308

LIST OF CASES CITED.

	PAGE
Dixon v. Bell	282
Dobell v. Stevens	26
Dodd v. Holme	242
Dodwell v. Burford	119
Doe v. Challis	187
v. Harlow	187
Donald v. Suckling	209
Donaldson v. Haldane	294
Doorman v. Jenkins	287
Dougherty v. Stepp	189
Dowling v. Hemmings	246
Doyle v. Hort	37
v. Russell	139
Dublin & Wicklow Ry. Co. v. Slattery	283, 306, 307, 310, 329
Dudgeon v. Thomson	225
Duff v. Budd	288
Dunham v. Powers	95, 96
Dunston v. Paterson	135
Eager v. Grimwood	164
Eaglesfield v. Londonderry	29
Earle v. Holderness	212
Eaton v. Boston & L. R. Co.	336
Electric Tel. Co. v. Brett	225, 227
Elliott v. Pray	314
Ellis v. Loftus Iron Co.	269
Embrey v. Owen	251, 252, 253
Emerson v. Davies	238
Emmens v. Pottle	9, 92
Eno v. Del Vecchio	246
Evans v. Carrington	21
v. Edmonds	32, 33
v. Walton	161, 163, 164
Fairmount Railway Co. v. Stutler	334
Farnsworth v. Garrard	290
v. Storrs	99

	PAGE
Farrant v. Barnes	289, 333
v. Thompson	182, 199
Farrar v. Beswick	214
Farwell v. Boston & W. R. Co.	317, 319
Filbert v. Hoff	184
Firbank v. Humphreys	36
Fisher v. Bristow	54
v. Prince	212
v. Thirkell	309
Fitzjohn v. Mackinder	65
Fletcher v. Smith	272
Flint v. Pike	99
Folsom v. Marsh	236, 237
Forde v. Skinner	119
Forster v. Forster	165
Foster v. Charles	45
Fouldes v. Willoughby	204, 214
Foulkes v. Metropolitan Ry. Co.	335
Fowler v. Hollins	206
Fox v. Mackreth	21
Frearson v. Loe	221, 224
Freeman v. Cooke	44
v. Venner	46
Frierson v. Hewitt	69
Fritz v. Hobson	263
Frogley v. Lovelace	191
Fryer v. Kinnersley	108
Fuller v. Fenner	84
v. Wilson	26
Gainsford v. Blachford	27
Gallwey v. Marshall	88, 90
Gannon v. Hargadon	259
Garr v. Selden	96
Gentry v. Madden	210
George v. Johnson	42
v. Skivington	332, 333
Gibbons v. Alison	71

LIST OF CASES CITED.

Giblin v. McMullen . . 287, 288
Godefroy v. Dalton . . . 294
Goffin v. Donnelly . . . 97
Goldsmid v. Tunbridge Wells Com'rs 260
Gordon v. Harper . . . 199
Gott v. Pulsifer 110
Goubaud v. Wallace . . . 231
Graham v. Peat 177
Grainger v. Hill . . . 70, 132
Gray v. Durland 167
v. North-eastern Ry. Co. 307
v. Russell 234
Green v. Elgie 147
Greenland v. Chaplin . . 325
Gregory v. Brunswick . 74, 76
v. Hill 125
v. Piper 190
Griffiths v. Dudley . . . 322
v. Teetgen . . . 162
Grill v. General Colliery Co. 287
Grinnell v. Wells 163
Griswold v. Sedgwick . . 136

Hall v. Corcoran 327
v. Fearnley . . 120, 121
v. Hollander . . . 163
Halley v. Stanton . . . 87
Hallmark's Case 35
Halls v. Thompson . . . 38
Hamilton v. Boston . . . 328
Hammack v. White . . . 283
Hampton v. Brown . . 181, 204
Hankinson v. Bilby . . . 82
Hardcastle v. South Yorkshire Ry. Co. 308
Hare v. Miller 98
Harper v. Luffkin . . . 161

Harris v. Brisco 71
v. Saunders . . . 206
v. Smith 181
Harrison v. Bush . . . 109
v. North-eastern Ry. Co. . 305, 306
Hart v. Aldridge 158
v. Frame . . 292, 293
v. Swaine 33
Hartley v. Cummings . . 160
Harvey v. Epes 211
v. Watson . . 173, 174
Hastings v. Brown . . . 221
Hatch v. Lane 103
Hay v. Cohoes Co. . . . 275
Haycraft v. Creasy . . 33, 34
Hayes v. Porter . . . 302, 303
Heaven v. Pender . . 315, 331, 333
Heckert's Appeal 297
Hedges v. Tagg 162
Heermance v. James . . . 170
Henderson v. Broomhead 95, 96
Henley v. Lyme Regis 302, 303, 335
Henwood v. Harrison . . 110
Hewlett v. Cruchley . . . 65
Hibbard v. Thompson . . 295
Hilbery v. Hatton . . . 206
Hill v. Bateman 148
v. Yates 153
Hilton v. Granville . . . 241
Hinton v. Dibdin 287
Hiort v. Bott 213
Hobson v. Todd 189
Hodges v. Windham . . . 175
Hogan v. Cregan 165
Hogg v. Ward 152
Holcomb v. Rawlyns . . 187
Hole v. Barlow 257

LIST OF CASES CITED.   xxiii

	PAGE		PAGE
Holley v. Mix	136, 195	Jackson v. Adams	83
Hollins v. Fowler	204	v. Smithson	266
Holly v. Boston Gas Co.	338	James v. Campbell	121
Holmes v. Mather	120, 121, 122	Janson v. Brown	269
v. North-eastern Ry.		Jarmain v. Hooper	148
Co.	315	Jarrold v. Houlston	232, 233
Hooper v. Lane	137	Jefferies v. Great Western	
v. Truscott	94	Ry. Co.	201
Hoosac Tunnel Co. v.		Jefferys v. Boosey	231
O'Brien	304	Jekyll v. Moore	97
Hopkins v. Crowe	149	Jendwine v. Slade	25
v. Tanqueray	19	Jenings v. Florence	71
Hopper v. Reeve	119	Joannes v. Bennett	108
Hotten v. Arthur	232	Johnson v. Weedman	211
Houck v. Wachter	265	Johnston v. Ewing	228
Houlden v. Smith	144	Johnston's Estate	300
Howe v. Finch	320	Joliffe v. Baker	32, 33
Howland v. Vincent	307	Jones v. Festiniog Ry. Co.	274
Hughes v. Macfie	338	v. Read	246
Humphries v. Brogden	248	Jordan v. Money	27
Humphrys v. Stanfeild	91		
Hunting v. Russell	179	Kain v. Old	19
Hurdman v. North-eastern		Kelly v. Byles	232
Ry. Co.	259	Kelsey v. Murphy	46
Hutcheson v. Peck	170, 171, 172	Kennedy v. Green	322
Hutchins v. Hutchins	13, 73	Killard v. Rooke	320, 322
Hyde v. Graham	191	Knight v. Gibbs	107
v. Noble	200	v. Legh	181
Hyman v. Nye	285	Knights v. Quarles	294
Ihl v. Forty-second St. R.			
Co.	340	Lafayette R. Co. v. Huffman	338
Ilott v. Wilkes	269	Laidlaw v. Organ	21
Ilsley v. Nichols	195, 196	Lake v. King	98
Indiana R. Co. v. Tyng	20	Lamb v. Stone	46
Insurance Co. v. Tweed	332	Lamphier v. Phipos	292, 295
Ireson v. Pearman	293	Lancashire Wagon Co. v.	
Irwin v. Dearman	169	Fitzhugh	210
Isaack v. Clark	211	Lancaster Co. Bank v.	
Israel v. Brooks	64	Smith	288

LIST OF CASES CITED.

	PAGE
Langridge v. Levy	333
Laughton v. Bishop of Sodor	103
Lawrence v. Obee	190
Leader v. Purday	233
Leather Cloth Co. v. American Leather Cloth Co.	48
Lee v. Jones	20, 23
Lemaitre v. Davis	243
Leverick v. Meigs	296
Lewis v. Clement	100
v. Fullarton	233
v. Jones	29
v. Levy	100
Leyman v. Latimer	87
Liford's Case	187, 189
Lister v. Perryman	52, 59, 67, 153
Little v. Hackett	337
Lockhart v. Lichtenthaler	336
Longman v. Winchester	232
Longmeid v. Holliday	334
Loomis v. Terry	268, 269
Lord v. Price	199
Losee v. Buchanan	271, 275
Louisville Canal Co. v. Murphy	339
Lowther v. Radnor	144
Lumby v. Allday	88
Lumley v. Gye	5, 77, 78, 79, 159, 160, 169
Lynch v. Knight	85, 169
v. Nurdin	339
v. Smith	339, 340
Lysney v. Selby	26
McAvoy v. Medina	203
v. Wright	43
McCombie v. Davies	206
Macdougall v. Knight	100
Macfadzen v. Olivant	197

	PAGE
McGiffin v. Palmer's Shipbuilding Co.	320
Machin v. Geortner	183
McLeod v. Jones	192
Madras Railway Co. v. The Zemindar	274
Malachy v. Soper	12, 49
Mangan v. Atterton	338
Manley v. Field	162
Manvell v. Thomson	169
Manzoni v. Douglas	283
Maple v. Junior Army Stores	232
Marshall v. York and Newcastle Ry. Co.	335
Martin v. Payne	163
Marzetti v. Williams	283
Mason v. Hill	252
Mathews v. Hursell	181, 204
Matthewson v. Stockdale	232
Matts v. Hawkins	246
Maunder v. Venn	127
Maxwell v. Hogg	231
v. Palmerston	269
May v. Burdett	266
Maydew v. Forrester	298
Mayhew v. Herrick	214
Medbury v. Watson	25, 26
Mellish v. Motteux	42
Mellor v. Watkins	192
Mellors v. Shaw	318
Menvil's Case	188
Merivale v. Carson	95, 110, 111
Merrifield v. Worcester	260
Mersey Docks v. Gibbs	302, 323
Metropolitan Bank v. Pooley	54, 71
Metropolitan Ry. Co. v. Jackson	283
Milan, The	337
Millar v. Taylor	231

LIST OF CASES CITED.

	PAGE
Millen v. Fawdry	193
Miller v. Foley	135
v. Proctor	300
Millington v. Fox	50
Mills v. Armstrong	337
Milwaukee R. Co. v. Arms	287
Miner v. Gilmour	252, 253, 254
Mitchell v. Jenkins	67, 68
Mogul Shipping Co. v. McGregor	73
Mohney v. Cook	327
Moore v. Meagher	12, 85, 86
v. Mourgue	298
v. Robinson	181, 204
v. Westervelt	304
Morgan v. Marquis	214
v. Ravey	284
v. Vale of Neath Ry. Co.	319
v. Varick	187
Morison v. Salmon	50
Morris v. Ashbee	233
Mortin v. Shoppee	118
Munster v. Lamb	95, 96, 97
Murchie v. Black	242
Murgoo v. Cogswell	269
Murray v. Bogue	233
v. Hall	185
Neilson v. Harford	220
Nelson v. Liverpool Brewery Co.	309
Newall, In re	219, 220
Newcomb v. Boston Protective Dept.	327
New World, The	287
Nichols v. Marsland	272, 273
Nicholson v. Coghill	62, 63
Nitroglycerine Case	121
Nixon v. Jenkins	215

	PAGE
Norris v. Litchfield	326
North-eastern Ry. Co. v. Wanless	283, 306, 329
North Pen. R. Co. v. Mahoney	339
O'Donoghue v. Hussey	104
Olmstead v. Miller	85
Onslow v. Horne	90
Oppenheim v. White Lion Hotel Co.	284, 285
Ormrod v. Huth	32, 34
Osborne v. Gillett	129
v. North-western Ry. Co.	330
Outcalt v. Durling	200
Overend v. Gibb	301, 302
Oxley v. Holden	224, 225
Page v. Robinson	182
Palmer v. Dewitt	234
Panton v. Williams	59, 67
Pappa v. Rose	304
Park v. Hammond	298
Partridge v. Gilbert	246
v. Scott	242
Pasley v. Freeman	18, 26, 37, 44, 46
Pater v. Baker	49, 50
Paterson v. Wallace	318
Pattison v. Jones	106, 108
Peake v. Oldham	82
Peard v. Jones	89
Pearse v. Coker	187
Pease v. Chaytor	143, 144
Peek v. Derry	30, 32, 33, 34
v. Gurney	21, 31, 47
Penn v. Bibby	219, 220
v. Present	183
Penruddock's Case	194

LIST OF CASES CITED.

	PAGE		PAGE
Perham v. Coney	211	Reddie v. Scoolt	168
Peyton v. London	245	Redgrave v. Hurd	32, 39, 41
Phillips v. Homfray	129	Reese Mining Co. v. Smith	32, 33
Philp v. Squire	172	Regina v. Clarke	168
Philpott v. Kelley	210	v. Cotesworth	120
Pickard v. Sears	211	v. James	116
Pickering v. Dowson	42	v. Saddler's Co.	40
Pike v. Fay	28	v. St George	116
Pilkington v. Scott	160	v. Veley	104
Pippet v. Hearn	70	Revenga v. Mackintosh	65
Pitt v. Donovan	49, 50	Rex v. Abingdon	98
Pittsburgh R. Co. v. Devinney	320	v. Burdett	93
v. Vining	338	v. Creevy	98
Pixley v. Clark	275	Reynell v. Sprye	30, 39
Playford v. United Kingdom Tel. Co.	334	Reynolds v. Kennedy	62
		Rich v. Pierpont	295
Plimpton v. Malcolmson	219, 222, 223	Richards v. Jenkins	249
		v. Rose	244
Polhill v. Walter	45	Richardson v. Silvester	47
Polley v. Lenox Iron Works	212	Riley v. Baxendale	317
Powell v. Evans	300	v. Horne	288
Prideaux v. Bunnet	25	Rist v. Faux	164
Priestley v. Fowler	317, 319	Roberts v. Connelly	167
Proctor v. Webster	98	v. Smith	317
Purinton v. Chamberlain	34	v. Wyatt	201
Pursell v. Horn	120	Robinson v. May	102
Puterbaugh v. Reasor	336	Rodgers v. Nowill	50
Pym v. Great Northern Ry. Co.	129	Rogers v. Arnold	201
		v. Palmer	34
		Rohan v. Sawin	152, 153
Quartz Hill Mining Co. v. Eyre	53, 69	Roope v. D'Avigdor	130
		Rose v. Miles	263, 264
		Ross v. Fedden	273
		Rowbotham v. Wilson	240
Radley v. London and Northwestern Ry. Co.	329	Roworth v. Wilkes	237
		Rylands v. Fletcher	260, 271, 272, 275
Randall v. Trimen	20, 36		
Rawstron v. Taylor	254		
Reading v. Royston	178	St Helen's Smelting Co. v. Tipping	258, 259, 261
Reading's Case	184		

LIST OF CASES CITED. xxvii

	PAGE
Sampson v. Hoddinott	251, 252, 253
Sanborn v. Neilson	175
Sankey v. Alexander	30, 39
Sargent v. ——	167
v. Gile	208
Saunders v. Smith	234, 236
Savacool v. Boughton	141
Savil v. Roberts	68, 73
Sayles v. Briggs	57
Schneider v. Heath	42
Schuneman v. Palmer	172, 173
Scott v. Ely	136
v. Shepherd	332
v. Stansfield	95
Scribner v. Beach	123, 125
Seaman v. Bigg	89
v. Nethercliff	95, 96
Seton v. Lafone	20, 36
Severin v. Keppell	216
Seward v. the Vera Cruz	129
Sheckell v. Jackson	101
Shergold v. Holloway	140
Shipley v. Fifty Associates	271, 247
Shorland v. Govett	195
Simar v. Canaday	25
Simmons v. Lillystone	214
v. Mitchell	82
Simpson v. Holliday	221
Sinclair v. Eldred	62
Singer Machine Co. v. Wilson	50, 228
Singer Manuf. Co. v. Loog	228
Singleton v. Bolton	51
Six Carpenters' Case	195, 196, 197
Smith v. Ashley	92
v. Chadwick	23, 26
v. Higgins	102

	PAGE
Smith v. Hughes	21
v. Kay	30
v. Kenwick	272
v. Land Corp.	27, 31, 39, 40, 41
v. Midland Ry. Co.	262
v North-western Ry. Co.	225, 226
v. Smith	336
v. South-western Ry. Co.	332
v. Stewart	87
v. Sydney	145
v. Thackerah	243
v. Tett	187
Snow v. Allen	64
Solomon v. Vintner's Co.	245
South v. Denniston	167
Southcote v. Stanley	311
Speight v. Oliviera	163
Spiers v. Brown	233
Springfield v. Harris	254
Stanley v. McGauran	39, 40
Standard Bank v. Stokes	246
Starr v. Jackson	181
Stead v. Anderson	225
Stebbins v. Eddy	25
Stedman v. Smith	247
Steele v. Brannan	100
v. Southwick	92
Stephens v. Myers	118
v. Wilkins	140
Stevens v. Midland Ry. Co.	68
v. Sampson	99
Stockdale v. Hansard	98
Stockley v. Hornridge	75
Stoner v. Todd	219, 224
Story v. Walthew	298
Stowe v. Thomas	233
Stroyan v. Knowles	242

LIST OF CASES CITED.

	PAGE
Suggs v. Anderson	123
Sutton v. Huffman	164
v. Johnstone	62
v. Wauwatosa	327
Swain v. Stafford	60
Sweeny v. Old Colony Ry. Co.	306, 309, 310, 311, 329
Sweet v. Benning	234, 236
v. Sweet	236
Swift v. Winterbotham	47
Sykes v. Dixon	160
v. Sykes	50, 51
Tarlton v. Fisher	139, 141
Tebbut v. Bristol & E. Ry. Co.	315
Terry v. Hutchinson	163, 164
Terwilliger v. Wands	84, 85
Tharsis Sulphur Co. v. Loftus	304
Thomas v. Churton	96
v. Quartermaine	322, 330
v. Welch	221
v. Winchester	333
Thompson v. Rose	216
v. Ross	127, 163
v. Shackell	110
Thorley v. Kerry	91
Thorogood v. Bryan	336, 337
v. Robinson	214
Thrussell v. Handyside	315, 330
Thurston v. Hancock	241, 242
Tickell v. Read	126
Timothy v. Simpson	155
Todd v. Flight	309
Toole v. Young	233
Tolhausen v. Davies	306
Tootle v. Clifton	260
Trusler v. Murray	238
Tuberville v. Savage	117

	PAGE
Tuff v. Warman	328, 329, 330
Tullidge v. Wade	197
Turner v. Ambler	59, 67
v. Harvey	21
v. Robinson	231, 234
v. Sullivan	99
v. Winter	221
Ullee, In re	168
United Telephone Co. v. Harrison	224
Unwin v. Heath	226
Usill v. Hales	100
Van Brunt v. Schenck	187
Vanderbilt v. Mathis	63, 67
Van Wyck v. Aspinwall	103
Vaughan v. Taff Vale Ry. Co.	273, 274
Vernon v. Keys	25, 38, 39
Vincent v. Cornell	208
v. Stinehour	121
Wait v. Richardson	186
Waite v. N. E. Ry. Co.	338, 340
Wakefield v. Buccleuch	241
Wakelin v. South-western Ry. Co.	283
Wakeman v. Robinson	121
Walker v. British Guarantee Assoc.	299
v. Cronin	78, 79, 80, 127, 158
Walsh v. Whiteley	320
Walsham v. Stainton	75
Walter v. Howe	232
v. Sample	66
v. Selfe	261, 262
Ward v. Clark	83
v. Hobbs	22

LIST OF CASES CITED.

	PAGE
Wason, Ex parte	97
v. Walter	98, 99, 100, 101
Watkin v. Hall	109
Watling v. Oastler	319
Watson v. Gray	245
v. McCarthy	87
Weaver v. Ward	120
Webb v. Beavan	82, 86
v. Hill	62, 63
Weblin v. Ballard	322
Webster v. Bailey	42
v. Hudson River R. Co.	337
Weedon v. Timbrell	173, 174
Wegmann v. Corcoran	220
Welfare v. London & B. Ry. Co.	311
Wellock v. Constantine	130
Wells v. Abrahams	130
Wennhak v. Morgan	84
Wesson v. Washburn Iron Co.	264
West v. Nibbs	195
Western Bank v. Addie	34, 36, 40
West London Bank v. Kitson	29
Weston v. Arnold	245
Whalley v. Lanc. Ry. Co.	xvi
Wheatley v. Chrisman	252
Wheaton v. Peters	236
White v. Demary	216
v. Garden	207
Whitehead v. Greetham	294
Whitney v. Boardman	42
v. Peckham	63
Wilkins v. Aikin	237
Wilkinson v. Fairrie	315
v. Haygarth	185
v. Proud	248

	PAGE
Willans v. Taylor	63
Williams v. Clouch	318
v. Esling	189, 190
v. Great Western Ry. Co.	306
v. Hill	86
v. Smith	145, 147
Wilson v. Brett	287
v. Goit	84
v. New Bedford	275
v. Newberry	273
Wilton v. Webster	174, 175
Winsmore v. Greenbank	171, 172
Winter v. Henn	165
Winterbottom v. Derby	265
v. Wright	334
Wood v. Boosey	233
v. Cooper	297
v. Leadbitter	191
v. Waud	258
Woodley v. Metropolitan Ry. Co.	330
Wootton v. Dawkins	269
Wren v. Weild	50
Wright v. Court	137
v. Malden R. Co.	338
v. Ramscot	269
Wyatt v. Barnard	233
Wyndham v. Wycombe	175
Yarmouth v. France	330
Yeates v. Prior	24
York & North Midland Ry. Co. v. Hudson	301
York v. Pease	99
Young v. Spencer	182
Zoebisch v. Tarbell	314

INTRODUCTION.

INTRODUCTION.

FOR the purposes of one first approaching the subject, the term 'tort' cannot be defined in language not itself needing definition.

Indeed, no definition, helped out even by explanation, can convey a full conception of the meaning of such an expression as 'the law of torts'; nothing short of careful study of the specific torts of the law will suffice. The difficulty grows out of the fact that there is no such thing as a typical example, an actual tort, that is to say, which contains all the elements entering into every other. One is as perfect as another; and each of the torts of the law differs, not merely in point of fact from the rest, but in its legal constituents as well.

Still, it is important to get some helpful conception, if possible, of the meaning of the term before entering upon the study of the particular torts. And fortunately there are some things in common to all; which things too, if not at first sufficiently intelligible, may be explained in a way to make the matter instructive to the beginner, and prepare him the better for the more special study of the subject to follow.

Putting, then, common features together in the way of definition, a tort may be said to be a breach of duty, fixed by law, and redressible by a suit for damages[1]. Each of the parts of the definition, however, will need explanation.

Consider in the first place the phrase 'breach of duty.' What does that mean? The answer cannot be given directly and shortly. There is no constant factor in the 'duty'; what would constitute a breach of duty in the case of one tort would not constitute it in the case of another. Still, the various duties involved in the different torts are capable of being grouped into some three or four classes, upon a basis not wanting in instructiveness.

In one of these classes the breach of duty is stated in terms apparently significant of an actively guilty state of mind. This phase of the breach of duty may be manifested in either of two forms; in one, the breach consists in the doing an act fraudulently; in the other, in doing it maliciously. And without the facts upon which the conception of fraud or malice is predicated, there is no redress in damages; that is, there is no tort.

It should be said, however, and the fact should be well observed, that the legal way of stating a conclusion from facts is here and elsewhere often stronger than the facts in themselves seem to justify. The law looks to manifestations, and then, it may be, declares that they proceed from fraud, malice, or other motive, and will hear no denial while the external facts stand; in other words, the law has a dictionary of its own.

[1] The term 'tort,' or its adjective 'tortious,' is sometimes used for convenience of cases in which there could be no action for damages; as, e.g., to express wrongful conduct. But the common acceptation of the term, especially in the expression 'law of torts,' is that of a wrong for which a suit for damages can be maintained.

Subject to this observation, fraud or malice is, then, an element of the right of action in the first class of cases. But it may be observed that, while the law of torts presents a very clear conception of fraud and its consequences, it has not determined, with any great precision, what constitutes malice[1]; and the law still hardly knows how to deal with *admitted* malice in respect of civil liability, outside of a few cases. As yet it is only feeling its way, and that in no perfectly assured direction[2].

Fraud as a necessary element of liability in tort is confined almost entirely to cases of misrepresentation; malice is a necessary element in actions for malicious prosecution, slander of title, so-called[3], and for interfering with contracts[4]. Malice may also become a turning-point in actions for defamation, upon a defence that the occasion of the publication made it presumptively lawful; but its presence or absence is immaterial to the right of action itself[5].

Another step will bring the student to a class of cases in which, though there is often a manifest intention on the part of the defendant to do the very thing for which he has been sued, the law now takes no

[1] See Part I. ch. II. § 4. A wrongful motive or a wrongful act may, it seems, constitute malice.

[2] Comp. Bowen *v.* Hall, 6 Q. B. Div. 333, with Chasemore *v.* Richards, 7 H. L. Cas. 349, 388; L. C. Torts, 525.

[3] This subject, however, belongs on the whole to fraud, as will be seen in ch. I.

[4] The last-named wrong refers to cases like Bowen *v.* Hall, 6 Q. B. Div. 333, following and explaining Lumley *v.* Gye, 2 El. & B. 216, and L. C. Torts, 306. See ch. IV. of Part I.

[5] Actions for defamation (slander or libel) may thus be treated as marking a transition from the first to the second phase of tort.

account of the state of his mind, supposed or actual, so far as the right of action is concerned. The plaintiff's right of redress no longer depends upon his ability to shew, in any way, that the defendant did the act in question from wrongful motives or even intentionally; and hence the want of such motives, or of intention, is no defence. Nor indeed is negligence, or the want of negligence, any necessary part of the case.

Here, then, is a class of cases in which the tort consists in the breach of what may be called an absolute duty; the act itself (in some cases it must have caused damage) is unlawful and redressible as a tort. The cases in which this is true are, speaking generally, cases of violence apparently about to be committed upon one's person[1], or actually so committed[2], restraint of liberty[3], interfering with the relation of master and servant with notice thereof[4], interfering in one way or another with the possession[5], ownership[6], or enjoyment[7] of property, and failing to keep safely dangerous things.

One other phase of the breach of duty remains. From regarding, first, a positive mental attitude of the defendant; and secondly, disregarding the existence or non-existence of such an attitude; the law, thirdly, passes over to cases in which it regards, as an essential fact, what may be considered as a negative mental attitude. In the class of cases now reached the law

---

[1] Assault.   [2] Battery.   [3] False imprisonment.
[4] E.g. enticing away or seducing a servant.
[5] Trespass to lands or goods.
[6] Conversion, 'trover' in the old law, a wrong relating to goods.
[7] E.g. nuisance and interference with ancient rights. The latter wrong, however, is commonly treated as a case for injunction.

takes account of the fact that the defendant has not directed proper attention to danger attending some act or omission of his, or, if he has, that he has not conducted himself as he ought to have done in the situation. He has failed, e.g., to exercise due care; and the failure, assuming damage to have followed, constitutes a tort. This phase of the breach of duty is the domain of negligence[1].

The meaning of the first part of the definition is now, it is hoped, somewhat cleared up. The result may be shortly put thus: Looking to one class of cases, a tort is (so far) a breach of duty effected by fraud or by malice. Looking to a second class, a tort is a breach of duty, absolute, regardless of fraud, malice, intention, or negligence. Looking to a third class, a tort is a breach of duty effected by negligence[2]. These divisions of the breach of duty will be found to cover all cases of tort in the law as it now exists.

Further, it may be remarked that the breach of

[1] The law does not, in point of fact, stop to consider the actual state of mind of the defendant as a ground of liability in actions for negligence; and the text, it will be seen, only says that negligence 'may be considered as a negative mental attitude.' It is believed, however, that there is always in fact a negative or passive state of mind in cases of negligence; the defendant's mind has not been duly aroused to the danger, or if the defendant is sensible of the situation, he has not exerted his will to avoid harm. And it is believed that it is useful and instructive to call attention to this. But the actual standard of the law is external.

[2] It should be observed, however, that the result shews only the outward aspect of the breach of duty. For the deeper meaning, the student must await the examination to be made of the specific torts of the law. It could not be shewn here without making this introduction prolix, and going over ground to be examined, necessarily, later.

duty, in whatever form, may be committed by anyone having natural capacity. The law of torts affords a strong contrast, in this particular, both to the law of contract and to the criminal law. Liability in contract depends, indeed, upon capacity to contract; but want of such capacity may be either natural or artificial. One must be of sound mind and at least twenty-one years of age to bind oneself by contract[1]. Liability under the criminal law depends also, generally speaking, upon the existence of capacity to commit crime; but want of this too may be natural or artificial. A person must be of sound mind and at least seven years of age to be subject to punishment under the criminal law.

There may be difficulty sometimes in applying the rule of natural capacity; but the difficulty can hardly arise except in cases requiring proof of fraud, malice, or negligence, and then as a rule only in suits against infants. Where the doing of the act creates of itself liability, that is, where there is a breach of the absolute duty, a defence of incapacity would be contrary to the fact, and could not, it seems, be allowed. The fact that the defendant was a person of unsound mind[2], or a child of tender years, would not be material. It would be enough that the act done was of the will.

Cases requiring proof of fraud, malice, or negligence would perhaps create no difficulty where the defendant

[1] Infants' contracts for necessaries are an exception.

[2] Quære, in regard to civil liability committed by a madman in a frenzy, though the act was intended? In some cases necessity would excuse a tort by anyone, as where a person is chased upon another's close by a savage beast. But suppose A threatens to kill B unless B will trespass upon C's land, and B does the act; will it affect the case that B is an infant, insane, or idiotic?

was a person of unsound mind, not accountable to the criminal law; an action of tort could hardly be maintained. A madman may, indeed, be guilty of fraud or malice in some sense (cunning, it is well known, is a common trait of the insane), but not in the sense in which it would be necessary to create liability, as, e.g., in an action for deceit or for malicious prosecution[1]. And clearly a madman cannot exercise diligence.

It is only the case then of an infant defendant that can raise serious difficulty. An infant of sound mind, twenty years of age, or much less, is liable for any tort for which an adult might be sued; an infant of five years could not be liable for negligence probably, and of course would never be sued for torts requiring proof of fraud or malice. But within these extremes, and it may be also without them, there is a region of uncertainty, in which the courts, if called upon to act, must act according to the best lights they may have, in each particular case; the question of capacity being probably a question of fact[2].

Consider in the next place that the duty in question is 'fixed by law.' This will serve to distinguish tort from contract; for in contract the duty is commonly fixed by the parties, in the terms of the agreement.

[1] Compare Emmens v. Pottle, 16 Q. B. Div. 354, 356, Lord Esher.
[2] There is a difficulty of another kind touching the liability of infants, and that is where what would be a tort in other cases, e.g. a fraudulent representation, is the inducement to a contract. But the rule in regard to such cases is, that there can be no liability in tort if to enforce the action would virtually fix upon the infant liability for breach of contract. The case is or may be quite different where the tort follows the contract; there to enforce an action for the tort would not be to enforce the contract.

But this is not always the case; it happens not infrequently that the parties to a contract leave terms to be supplied by the evidence of custom or by the law itself. In such cases a violation of the term so to be supplied might even before the Judicature Act make a case of tort or of breach of contract, at the election of the injured party; the duty being fixed by law, or, what would come to much the same thing, by custom, the breach could be treated as a tort. Thus, if a common carrier at London were to contract with A to deliver at York certain goods put into the carrier's hands, and fail to do so, he would be presumptively liable to A, as for a tort, or for breach of contract, at A's election.

A breach of an implied term of a contract may then, it seems, be treated as constituting a tort whenever the term is supplied by law or by custom; but this is not now a matter of much importance in regard to the subject under consideration. Nor, indeed, was it so formerly, for the injured party had a clear right of action for breach of contract, at all events; and the question was only one of the preferable remedy. Still, it is to be remembered that theoretically the law of torts overlaps that of contract at the place indicated.

It is not to be inferred that there cannot be a tort in respect of the breach or the invalidity of a contract the terms of which are all fully expressed. If the contract contain a false warranty, it is broken in the breach of the warranty; and breach of an affirmative warranty[1], fraudulently made, may be treated as a tort. So too, what is of much importance, a contract founded

[1] A warranty affirming a fact, as distinguished from one promising something.

upon a false and fraudulent representation, though not amounting to a warranty, may be repudiated, and an action for tort maintained; or the contract may be treated by the injured party as binding, and an action for tort brought to recover damages for the loss caused by getting him into the contract. The explanation is, that the breach of duty sued upon is not in reality a term, express or implied, of the contract; the duty violated is fixed by law,—a duty not to defraud. In this view, then, the law of tort still further overlaps that of contract[1].

Consider, finally, the phrase in the definition 'redressible by a suit for damages.' Does this imply that the plaintiff must have sustained some loss or detriment? Not necessarily. There are many cases in which the defendant would not be allowed to shew that the plaintiff had not suffered a pennyworth. On the other hand, there are many cases in which the plaintiff cannot recover judgment without proving that the act or omission of the defendant caused a loss to him.

In regard to this, the law has laid down certain arbitrary rules; and that being the case, about all that could be said towards making clear the conception of tort in this particular would be to state the cases in which loss must, and those in which it need not, be proved. But at this stage of the student's work it

---

[1] In regard to the case of warranty, if what is said supra is not understood, it should be observed that warranty in itself, where it consists in the affirmation of a fact, is a contract only by courtesy of language; and in general it is only false warranties of that kind that are treated as torts. As a statement of fact a warranty is like a representation; and if fraudulent, the breach of duty is like that committed in a case of misrepresentation apart from the contract.

would be a questionable service to enumerate the torts which fall upon the one and the other side of the line of loss. The student can, however, satisfy himself, if he will, by referring to the 'Statement of Duty' at the head of the several chapters of the text; where the words 'prejudice,' 'detriment,' and 'damage' are used in their ordinary sense of 'loss,' or 'special damage.'

To constitute damage within the meaning of such a phrase as 'suit for damages,' whether loss is necessary or not, there must have been an infraction of some legal as distinguished from a moral right. But 'legal' right includes cases in which the right is in process of consummation at the time of the infraction, and cases in which a person is at the time receiving, actually or potentially, a gratuity[1].

Examples of the statement just made should be given here and now, or its meaning may not be seen. The following will, it is hoped, serve the purpose: A and B are negotiating for the sale by the former to the latter of a horse. By false and fraudulent representations concerning the animal, C induces B to break off the negotiations. A has, it seems, sustained damage, and can maintain an action against C[2].

If, however, the case is such that the plaintiff had only a hope or an expectation, though well founded, of obtaining something of value from another, in regard to which no contract had been made, no negotiations entered into, and no enjoyment begun, he will not be

---

[1] Post, Part I. ch. IV. § 3; Part II. ch. III. § 3; Moore v. Meagher, 1 Taunt. 39, 44, Ex. Ch.

[2] Malachy v. Soper, 3 Bing. N. C. 371; s. c. L. C. Torts, 54—59.

deemed to have suffered damage by the defendant's causing his hope or expectation to be frustrated. This too may need the aid of an example: A makes his will in favour of B; and C by false and fraudulent representations induces A to revoke the gift. B has sustained no damage, and cannot maintain an action against C[1].

A word more. The fact that a tort is redressible in damages serves to distinguish the offence from a crime; which is redressed by prosecution on behalf of the Crown, for the purpose of punishing the accused, by imprisonment, fine, or forfeiture. But most crimes which are attended with loss may also be treated as torts, at least after the Crown has prosecuted. Homicide is an exception, apart from cases falling within statute. It will be seen, then, that the law of torts, which we have found overlapping the law of contracts on one side, overlaps on the other the criminal law. But the greater part by far of the domain of tort lies between the two extremes.

In explanation of the examples given throughout the following pages it is to be observed, that when a particular act or omission under consideration is said to be a 'breach of duty,' or of 'legal duty,' or of the 'duty under consideration,' it is assumed that other elements of liability, if there be such, are present. Further, 'breach of duty' or the like implies a right of action in damages.

[1] Hutchins v. Hutchins, 7 Hill, 104; s. c. L. C. Torts, 207, an American example.

SPECIFIC TORTS.

PART I.
BREACH OF DUTY TO REFRAIN FROM FRAUD OR MALICE.

CHAPTER I.

DECEIT.

§ 1. Introductory.

Statement of the duty. A owes to B the duty to forbear to mislead him to his prejudice by false and artful representations, apt to mislead.

1. Deceit is a ground of defence to the enforcement of a contract, and is also ground for proceedings by the injured party to rescind a contract. In such cases the same facts, apart from the wrong-doer's knowledge of the actual state of things, are necessary for establishing the deceit as are necessary to an action of or for deceit. Hence, with the exception mentioned, authorities concerning the proof of deceit in cases of contract are authorities in regard to actions for damages by reason of deceit.

2. The action at law for damages by reason of deceit is called indifferently an action *of* deceit or an action *for* deceit.

3. When it is said that a particular representation is a breach of duty, or of legal duty, or of the duty under consideration, it is to be understood that the other elements necessary to constitute the complete breach of duty (where not referred to) are supposed to be present.

In order to establish a breach of the duty above stated, and to entitle B to civil redress therefor, B, unless he come within one of the qualifications to the rule, must make it appear to the court (1) that A has made a false representation of material facts; (2) that A made the same with knowledge of its falsity; (3) that B was ignorant of its falsity, and believed it to be true; (4) that it was made with intent that it should be acted upon; (5) that it was acted upon by B to his damage[1]. But each of these general elements of the rights of redress must be separately examined and explained, and the qualifications to the same presented. The designation of the parties as A and B may now be dropped, and B will be spoken of as the plaintiff, and A as the defendant.

§ 2. Of the Representation.

It is proper first to consider the meaning of the term 'representation,' and its nature, and thus to ascertain what is the foundation of the action under consideration. A representation then, in contemplation of law, may be defined, for the present purpose, to be any clear impression of fact, created upon the mind of the plaintiff, by act, not amounting to a warranty, of the defendant sufficient to govern the conduct of a man of ordinary intelligence.

The difference in aspect (and that is all that calls for remark here) between a representation and a warranty may be put as follows: While the latter as well as the former may be a statement of fact, it is always annexed to some contract and is part of that contract; the warranty is indeed a contract itself[2], though a subsidiary one, dependent upon the main agreement. A representation, however, is in no case more than inducement to a contract; it is never part of one. To carry it into a contract would be to make it a warranty. And again, there may be a representation,

[1] Pasley v. Freeman, 3 T. R. 51; s. c. L. C. Torts, 1.
[2] Brownlie v. Campbell, 5 App. Cas. 925, 953, Lord Blackburn.

such as the law will take cognizance of, though no contract was made or attempted between the one who made the representation and the one to whom it was made.

This would be sufficient to distinguish the two terms, if it were necessary to a warranty that it should be expressly annexed to the contract-in-chief; but it is not, and that fact sometimes creates difficulty. In written contracts there can seldom be difficulty in determining whether a particular statement is a warranty or a representation (when it is one or other), for the warranty must be part of the writing, since a warranty must be part of the contract-in-chief[1], and it will either be directly incorporated into the general writing or be so connected with it by apt language[2] that there can be no doubt of the intention of the parties.

The difficulty is with oral contracts, and then for the greater part only in regard to sales of personalty. Whether the statement in question is a representation or a warranty is, however, a question of intention; and an intention to create a warranty is shewn, it seems, by evidence of material statements of fact made as an inducement to the sale, at the time the bargain was effected, or during negotiations therefor which have been completed in proper reliance upon the statements[3]; provided nothing at variance with the inference of intention is shewn[4]. If the statement was not so made, it is a representation if it is anything. What difficulty remains is in the application of the rule; and that is a matter for works treating of contracts or torts in detail.

A warranty of fact, however, when broken may be

[1] Kain v. Old, 2 B. & C. 627.
[2] A warranty may indeed be implied, i.e. arise without language, but such cases are aside from the present purpose. The difficulty under consideration concerns the effect of language used.
[3] See Hopkins v. Tanqueray, 15 C. B. 130.
[4] Such appears to be the effect of the cases. See Benjamin, Sales, § 613.

treated, it seems, as a case of misrepresentation, giving rise to an action for deceit if the elements necessary to liability in a proper case of misrepresentation are present[1]; and this, it is believed, is true whether the warranty was express or implied. Indeed, in case of implied warranty the breach appears to be enough to make the case one of deceit[2]. This reduces the matter to a question of the form of action. But it is very doubtful whether an action based on deceit could be maintained where the evidence shewed nothing but a breach of warranty. That would be a variance; the action should be on the warranty as such.

The representation requires, as the definition indicates, an act. There are, it is true, cases in which legal consequences may attend absolute silence; but there are probably no cases in which an action for damages on account of silence alone can be maintained. There must be some additional element to make silence actionable[3]. If the silence consist in withholding part of the truth of a statement, it may be actionable, as will be seen later; but in such a case it is, properly speaking, only part of the representation. The silence amounts to saying that what has been stated is all. There is a duty to speak in such a case, and it is only when there is such a duty that silence has any legal significance.

Indeed, even passive concealment, that is, intentional withholding of information, when not attended with any active conduct tending to mislead, is insufficient to create a cause of action. For example: The defendant, knowing of

---

[1] See Indianapolis R. Co. v. Tyng, 63 N. Y. 653.

[2] Collen v. Wright, 8 El. & B. 647; Randell v. Trimen, 18 C. B. 786; Seton v. Lafone, 18 Q. B. D. 139; post, p. 36.

[3] The question of the effect of silence is perhaps more frequently seen in defences than as a ground of action. For a case of defence see Lee v. Jones, 17 C. B. N. S. 482; s. c. 14 C. B. N. S. 386.

the existence of facts tending to enhance the price of tobacco, of which facts the plaintiff is ignorant, to his knowledge, buys a quantity of tobacco of the plaintiff at current prices, withholding information of the facts referred to (no question being asked to bring them out). This is no breach of duty to the plaintiff[1]. Again: The defendant buys of the plaintiff land in which there is a mine, the defendant knowing the fact, and knowing that the plaintiff is ignorant of it. The defendant does not disclose the fact in the negotiations for the purchase. This is no breach of duty[2].

An act, however, attending what would otherwise be a case of perfect silence, in regard to the fact in question, may have the effect to create a representation, and lay the foundation so far for an action; but the act must be significant and misleading. For that purpose, however, it may be slight[3]; a nod of the head may no doubt be enough, so may a withdrawing of attention from some point to which it is being or about to be directed.

But as has just been said, the act attending the silence must be significant and misleading; if not, it will count for nothing. For example: The plaintiff sues the defendant for damages caused by the sale to him by the defendant of animals having a contagious disease. Statute prohibits the sending of such animals to market, and imposes a

[1] Laidlaw v. Organ, 2 Wheat. 178, Supreme Court U. S. See Smith v. Hughes, L. R. 6 Q. B. 597; Evans v. Carrington, 2 De G. F. & J. 481; Peek v. Gurney, L. R. 6 H. L. 377, Lord Cairns; Coaks v. Boswell, 11 App. Cas. 232, Lord Selborne. 'Whatever may be tho case in a court of morals, there is no legal obligation on the vendor to inform the purchaser that he is under a mistake, not induced by the act of the vendor.' Blackburn, J. in Smith v. Hughes, supra.

[2] Fox v. Mackreth, 2 Bro. C. C. 400, 420, a leading case in equity. See Turner v. Harvey, Jacob, 169, 178.

[3] Turner v. Harvey, Jacob, 178, Lord Eldon.

penalty for violating the prohibition. The animals in question have, however, been inspected by the public officer and passed before the sale. The seller has made a written statement that the animals must be taken 'with all faults,' and that no warranty is made and no compensation for defects will be given. These facts do not shew any representation by the defendant that the animals are not affected with disease, or create any right to damages in favour of the plaintiff[1]; though it is possible that the case might have been different had there been no such statement by the seller as that mentioned[2].

In a word, then, the supposed representation must be clear and certain; the plaintiff does not make out the alleged breach of duty if his evidence shew only a statement or act of vague or indefinite import. This rests upon the plain ground that the average man would not rely and act upon statements of an indefinite nature. The fact that they are of such a nature would put him upon inquiry before acting, if acting were seriously contemplated; and then if he should act, he would have acted upon the information so obtained and not upon the indefinite statements. Hence, whether he acted or did not act, the author of those statements would not be liable.

The representation need not, however, be created by language; there is no distinction between an impression created by words and one created by other acts. If the impression is capable of being stated as an existing or past fact, and is such as might govern the conduct of an average man in regard to some change of position in contemplation, it is enough. In a word, it may be entirely implied. Indeed, it appears to be unnecessary that the implication should

[1] Ward v. Hobbs, 4 App. Cas. 13, affirming 3 Q. B. Div. 150.
[2] See Badger v. Nichols, 28 L. T. N. S. 441, Blackburn, J. referred to by Lord Cairns in Ward v. Hobbs, but apparently with doubt.

be adverted to or consciously present to the mind at the time of the change of position; a fact to be brought out fully somewhat later.

It follows that, to constitute a false representation, it is not necessary that statements made should be made in terms expressly affirming the existence of some fact. If the alleged misrepresentation be made by the defendant in terms such as would naturally lead the plaintiff to suppose the existence of a particular state of facts, that is as much as if statements had so been made in exact terms[1].

It should be noticed that there is a difference in fact between vagueness and ambiguity. Vagueness, as we have seen, is fatal to the idea of a legal representation; but ambiguity in an impression may only mean that more than one fact has been impressed upon the mind, not that none at all has been left there. In such a case as this the only question that can arise in reason or in law is whether, assuming the facts impressed to be clear and definite, the plaintiff reasonably acted upon the one which was false. That he did this it devolves upon him to shew.

The point is illustrated by a case recently before the House of Lords[2]. That was an action for deceit, in which it appeared that the prospectus of a company in process of formation to take over certain iron-works contained the following statement: 'The present value of the turnover or output of the entire works is a million pounds sterling per annum.' This statement might mean either that the works had actually turned out more than a million's worth at present prices within a year or yearly, or only that the works were capable of turning out so much; in the former case it was false, in the latter it might be true. It was held that the plaintiff, who had been induced to buy shares

[1] Lee v. Jones, 17 C. B. N. S. 482; s. c. 14 C. B. N. S. 386.
[2] Smith v. Chadwick, 9 App. Cas. 187; s. c. 20 Ch. Div. 27.

in the undertaking, must shew that he had acted upon the statement in the sense in which it was false.

Where a term of art, having a technical and also a popular meaning, has been used, the case may be affected by presumption. Between parties engaged in the same vocation, the presumption (probably) would be, that the representation was to be taken in the technical sense; if they were not, there would perhaps be no presumption either way. In either case it would be necessary, judging from the decision in the House of Lords just stated, for the plaintiff to shew that he had acted upon the representation in the sense in which it was false; and even then there could not be a cause of action if the defendant made the statement with reasonable ground to suppose that it would be acted upon in the sense in which it was true. And in that presumption might help him. The presumption, however, in any case, would only be prima facie, and so conclusive only in the absence of evidence opposed to it.

Another case may be mentioned. A statement of fact may have one meaning in one place and another in another; in such a case it would seem that the statement should be understood as intended in the sense in which it is commonly used where it was made [1], unless, indeed, it was made there by one residing where it is used in a different sense. In this latter case the courts would (probably) consider the party bound only by that meaning which he would have reason to suppose was conveyed.

Upon the principle that there can be no breach of the legal duty in question unless the supposed representation be definite enough to justify a prudent man, i.e. the average man, in relying upon it, there must be something more than

---

[1] See Yeates *v.* Prior, 6 Eng. 58, an American case stated in Bigelow, Fraud, 500.

the expression of a mere opinion. It would not be enough for a vendor, not warranting his statement, to say that a certain valve would consume smoke and save fuel[1], or that certain pictures were the works of old masters[2], or that his property was worth a certain sum[3]. Whatever weight such statements might have, and in point of fact they might come with much weight in particular cases, they still would, if not warranted or affected by very special facts, fall without the notice of the law.

Representations in regard to the value of property about to be sold often give rise, however, to difficult questions. The general rule, as already indicated, is plain enough; 'simplex commendatio non obligat.' But what is 'simplex commendatio'? A simple statement of value by a vendor is a clear case on the one hand; a plain statement of fact going to make up value, as the age of a horse, is an equally clear case on the other. But what of statements falling between the two extremes? The question cannot be definitely answered; most of the cases that arise have to be determined upon the special facts attending them. That is to say, particular rules can seldom be framed to reach them, and general rules have only a remote bearing upon them[4].

One or two rules, however, of a limited nature, have been laid down touching the subject. There are well-considered cases in America in which a distinction is drawn

[1] Prideaux v. Bunnett, 1 C. B. N. S. 613.
[2] Jendwine v. Slade, 2 Esp. 572.
[3] Vernon v. Keys, 12 East, 632; s. c. 4 Taunt. 488, Ex. Ch.
[4] The American courts have had to deal much with so-called representations of value. The following are important cases: Simar v. Canaday, 53 N. Y. 298; Chrysler v. Canaday, 90 N. Y. 272; Medbury v. Watson, 6 Met. 246 (Mass.); Stebbins v. Eddy, 4 Mason, 414, Story, J.

between statements of value made by a vendor and statements of the same kind made by a stranger to the title. While the former are without the law in ordinary cases, the latter, if false, may constitute actionable misrepresentation. For example: The defendant, not being the seller of the property, falsely states that a tannery has on a previous sale brought a certain price. This is a misrepresentation within the law[1].

Again, it is settled law that statements of the income of property, or of the rental receipts of a leasehold estate to be sold, would constitute representations of fact. For example: The defendant, seller of a public-house, falsely tells the buyer, the plaintiff, that the receipts of the house have been £160 per month, and that the tap is let for £82 per annum, and two rooms for £27 per annum. This is a false representation, and not a mere statement of value[2]. And this would be equally true if the statement were that the present 'value' of the property is a certain sum per year; for that would mean its annual return[3].

Statements concerning the pecuniary condition of an individual are not necessarily statements of opinion, and when distinctly and specifically made may be breaches of the duty under consideration. For example: The defendant says to the plaintiff, 'F is pecuniarily responsible. You can safely trust him for goods to the amount of £3,000.' This is a representation of fact[4].

Slight expressions, however, are sufficient to put statements of this character on the footing of statements of

[1] Medbury v. Watson, 6 Met. 246 (Mass.).
[2] Dobell v. Stevens, 3 B. & C. 623. See Fuller v. Wilson, 3 Q. B. 58; Lysney v. Selby, 2 Ld. Raym. 1118, leading case.
[3] See Smith v. Chadwick, 9 App. Cas. 187, ante, p. 23.
[4] Pasley v. Freeman, 3 T. R. 51; s. c. L. C. Torts, 1. Such representations must now be proved by writing signed by the party to be charged. 9 Geo. 4, c. 14.

opinion. For example: The defendant, in answer to inquiries as to the circumstances and credit of a third person, says to the plaintiff, 'I should be willing to give him credit for anything he wanted.' This statement cannot safely be acted upon by the plaintiff. The mere fact that the *defendant* may be willing to give him credit does not necessarily justify the plaintiff in doing so[1].

The rule of certainty further requires that the representation should relate to present or past facts; if it relate to matters in the future, it cannot justify a prudent man in acting upon it, unless it comes to a contract, and then it will not be a legal representation[2].

In most cases of uncertain statements, consisting of opinion or prediction as distinguished from the uncertainty of vagueness, there will be implied a plain representation of fact, to wit, that the party knows of nothing making his expressed statement false. And there is strong reason to believe that the courts would take cognizance, not indeed of the opinion or prediction, but of this implied though none the less real representation, if it should be false.

This observation is founded upon the language of Lord Justice Bowen in a recent case[3]. It was there said in substance that if facts were not equally known to both parties, a statement of opinion by the one who knew the truth very often involves a statement of fact, 'for he impliedly states that he knows facts which justify his opinion.'

The statement in question was that a certain person was a 'most desirable tenant,' and the court took cognizance of it. But there may be some doubt whether such a

[1] Gainsford *v.* Blachford, 7 Price, 544.
[2] See Jorden *v.* Money, 5 H. L. Cas. 185; Citizens' Bank *v.* First National Bank, L. R. 6 H. L. 352, 360.
[3] Smith *v.* Land Corp., 28 Ch. Div. 7.

statement amounts to opinion in contemplation of law; it was not directly decided to be such. An American case, however, may be stated, which speaks to the very case of an opinion: The defendant, a cattle-dealer, desiring to sell cattle to the plaintiff, makes a statement in the way of opinion that the cattle will weigh 900 lbs. and upwards per head. He has already weighed them, and knows that their average weight is considerably below 900 lbs. This is a breach of duty[1].

A similar observation to that above made should be made in regard to representations looking to the future, whether in the way of prediction or of promise. As prediction the case would fall without the notice of the law; and so it would as promise, unless the promise came to a contract. But either as prediction or as promise there would ordinarily be an implied representation that the party making it knew of nothing which made his statement a sham. Thus, if a person were to say that a certain vessel would arrive on the morrow, that would amount to a representation that he knew nothing to the contrary; if he knew that she was at the bottom of the sea, there would, or there might be, a case for the courts. Again, if a person were to promise to pay for goods bought by him on credit, intending at the time not to pay for them, there would be a case for the courts on the footing of misrepresentation[2]; for the party's promise is a plain representation of present intention to fulfil his undertaking. Such cases are, however, more commonly treated as cases for rescission of the contract.

It is evident that the party wronged may not in any of these cases of implied representation have adverted to the representation behind the actual language; indeed, it would

---

[1] Birdsey v. Butterfield, 34 Wis. 52. See also Pike v. Fay, 101 Mass. 134.

[2] Bristol v. Wilsmore, 1 B. & C. 514.

seldom happen that he had adverted to the fact. But that would not affect the case; the implied statement has, or may have, influenced the party's conduct, notwithstanding the fact that he may have been unconscious of the precise nature of the influence. Had attention been directed to the matter he would certainly have said that the language implied the representation behind it, to wit, that nothing was known to the defendant falsifying his expressed opinion, prediction, or promise.

Again, to come within the notice of the law, the representation, if not made by a lawyer to a layman, or by a man professing familiarity with the law to one not familiar with it, must, it seems, be more than a mere representation of what the law is. The reason of this has sometimes been said to be that all men are presumed to know the law; 'ignorantia legis neminem excusat.' But it may be doubted whether that is the true ground of the rule; if it were, misrepresentation of the law by one's legal counsel could hardly be made the foundation of any liability. A better reason appears to be that the law is understood by all men to be a special branch of learning; and hence what one layman may say to another will seldom have the effect to alter conduct. But whatever the ground, the rule appears to be treated as settled[1], though it probably has not been actually decided that evidence of reliance upon a representation of law is not admissible where the parties stood on equal footing[2].

When further it is said that the representation must be of a character to affect the conduct of a prudent man, i.e.

[1] See Lewis v. Jones, 4 B. & C. 506; Beattie v. Ebury, L. R. 7 Ch. 777, 804; Englesfield v. Londonderry, 4 Ch. Div. 693, Jessel, M. R., explaining the nature of a representation of law. And see West London Bank v. Kitson, 13 Q. B. Div. 360, 363, Bowen, L. J.

[2] See Pollock, Torts, 243.

when it is said that the representation must, in the language of the books, be material, it is not to be implied that the law will not take notice of the case if influences from other sources may have operated upon the plaintiff. The only question upon this point is whether the representation made by the defendant was adequate to influence, and did influence, the plaintiff, not whether it was the sole inducement to the action taken; if it was sufficient to influence him, and did influence him to some real extent, that is enough. The courts will not be astute to find that one of several inducements present was not adequate to the damage[1]. Indeed, if the defendant has accomplished his purpose by his misrepresentation, he will not be permitted to say that the act was immaterial[2].

Finally, it is for the plaintiff to shew that the representation was false. But a representation is false in contemplation of law as well as of morals if it is false in a plain, practical sense; if, that is to say, it would be apt to create a false impression upon the mind of the average man. For example: The prospectus of a company about to construct a railway describes the contract for the work as entered into at 'a price considered within the available capital of the company.' The fact is, that there is a merely nominal capital of £500,000, and from this the sum of £50,000 is to be deducted for the purchase of the concession for making the railway, and the contract price for making it is £420,000. The representation is false; the term 'available capital' not being a true description of capital to be raised by borrowing[3]. Again: Particulars of the sale of a hotel by auction, August 4, 1882, state that the premises are let to A, 'a

[1] Peek v. Derry, 37 Ch. Div. 541; Reynell v. Sprye, 1 De G. M. & G. 660; Sankey v. Alexander, Ir. R. 9 Eq. 259.
[2] Smith v. Kay, 7 H. L. Cas. 750.
[3] Central Ry. Co. v. Kisch, L. R. 2 H. L. 99.

most desirable tenant,' at a certain rental, for a long term. On May 1, 1882, Lady Day quarter's rent was wholly unpaid, and a distress was then threatened. On May 6, A pays part of the sum due; on June 13, another part, and shortly before the auction the rest. No part of the Midsummer rent has been paid. The representation is false[1].

An example in contrast with the foregoing may be stated. A prospectus of a company formed for buying a certain business declares that the price of purchase is a stated sum, and that no 'promotion money' is to be paid to the directors of the company for making the purchase. In fact, the sum paid for the business is somewhat less than the sum stated in the prospectus, and shares of the stock representing the difference are now transferred, part to the directors of the company who effected the purchase, which part is afterwards transferred to the company on complaint, and part to the solicitors in the transaction. This is not misrepresentation[2].

The defendant cannot, then, escape liability by shewing that the representation was, if literally taken, true, or true if taken in some forced or unnatural sense. So too the defendant cannot rely upon the truth of the actual language used, when that is but part of the whole state of facts, and what was suppressed would, had it been stated, have given to the language used a contrary effect. If the part suppressed would have made the part stated false, there is a false representation[3]. For example: The plaintiff, being

[1] Smith v. Land Corp., 28 Ch. Div. 7.

[2] Arkwright v. Newbold, 17 Ch. Div. 301. 'Nobody was ever lucky enough to sell a property without having some considerable deduction made out of the gross price, there being such persons as auctioneers and solicitors to be paid.' James, L. J.

[3] Peek v. Gurney, L. R. 6 H. L. 377, 403, Lord Cairns; Central Ry. Co. v. Kisch, L. R. 2 H. L. 99, 113; Corbett v. Brown, 8 Bing. 33.

about to supply the defendant's son with goods on credit, asks the defendant if the son has property of the value of £300, as the son has asserted. The defendant answers in the affirmative, stating that he has advanced the sum to his son, but failing to state that his son has given his promissory note for the amount. This is a false representation, though true in a literal sense[1].

§ 3. OF DEFENDANT'S KNOWLEDGE OF FALSITY.

In order to entitle a plaintiff to recover damages for misrepresentation, it is necessary for him to prove that the defendant made the false representation fraudulently. In a proceeding, indeed, in what would formerly have been called a court of equity, a contract may be rescinded, or its enforcement successfully resisted, for an innocent misrepresentation, that is to say, for a false representation justly believed to be true at the outset by the party who made it; but if damages are sought, fraud must be proved, as well in such a proceeding as in one which under the old system would have been called legal[2].

Fraud, within the meaning of this rule, may be proved in one of three ways, according to the nature of the case. It may be proved by shewing (1) that the defendant made the representation with knowledge of its falsity, or (2) that he made it without reasonable ground to believe it true[3],

---

[1] Corbett v. Brown, supra.

[2] Joliffe v. Baker, 11 Q. B. D. 255; Arkwright v. Newbold, 17 Ch. Div. 301, 320; Redgrave v. Hurd, 20 Ch. Div. 1; Reese Mining Co. v. Smith, L. R. 4 H. L. 64; Collins v. Evans, 5 Q. B. 820, Ex. Ch.; Ormrod v. Huth, 14 M. & W. 650, Ex. Ch.; Childers v. Wooler, 2 El. & E. 287; Evans v. Edmonds, 13 C. B. 777, 786.

[3] See the cases last cited; Peek v. Derry, 37 Ch. Div. 541. This, the latest case, contains the most specific declaration in regard to proof of fraud, though it does not touch (3) of the text. Lopes, L. J. makes an elaborate division of (2). 37 Ch. D. at p. 585.

or (3) that he made it under circumstances in which he was so related to the facts that it was his duty to know whether the representation was true or not. Proving the allegation in any of these ways is often, especially in common law pleading, called proving the 'scienter'[1]; and the burden of proof is upon the plaintiff.

The first and second of these phases of fraud bear, upon examination, a close resemblance to each other; and for ordinary purposes they may be considered as equivalents. The second is really a case of false representation made with knowledge, if regard be had to what it implies. If a man make a positive statement, he impliedly affirms that he is in possession of facts which justify the same; and if he is not, he has told what he knows to be false[2], or, more accurately, what the average or standard man would know to be false. It is, however, the *implied* representation which he knows to be false.

Accordingly, for ordinary purposes, it will be enough to establish knowledge of falsity to shew that the representation was made without reasonable ground to believe it true. In other words, an allegation of fraud of the first form mentioned may be proved by facts shewing the second; and the converse would no doubt be true also. And then it is no answer to the case that the defendant in fact believed the representation to be true; belief, i.e. rational belief,

[1] From the term used in the early Latin precedents of declaration.
[2] Haycraft v. Creasy, 2 East, 92, 103, Lord Kenyon; Evans v. Edmonds, 13 C. B. 777, 786, Maule, J.; Hart v. Swaine, 7 Ch. D. 42, 46, Fry, J.; Joliffe v. Baker, 11 Q. B. D. 255, 259, Williams, J.; Brownlie v. Campbell, 5 App. Cas. 925, 953, Lord Blackburn. Further, see Reese Mining Co. v. Smith, L. R. 4 H. L. 64, 79, Lord Cairns: 'If persons take upon themselves to make assertions as to which they are ignorant whether they are true or not, they must in a civil point of view be held as responsible as if they had asserted that which they knew to be untrue.' See also Peek v. Derry, 37 Ch. Div. 541, 581.

requires sufficient grounds. It is equally obvious that the plaintiff fails if his evidence is met by credible evidence that the defendant reasonably believed his representation to be true; for that means that he had reasonable ground to believe the same[1].

Thus far of ordinary cases. For the purposes, however, of a strict application of law, the first and second phases of fraud appear not to be equivalents. It does not, in strictness, prove that a man knew that a statement made by him was false, to shew that he knew nothing about the facts affirmed; it only shews, as has been seen, that the *implied* representation of the possession of grounds of belief was false, scienter. And there may be cases under criminal statutes, or statutes relating to bankruptcy, in which the distinction is important, thus making it necessary to prove knowledge of falsity strictly[2]; and questions of tort might arise out of such cases.

The third phase of fraud is quite different. There the defendant, being under a duty to know the facts[3], cannot shew that he made the representation in the belief that it

[1] Haycraft v. Creasy, 2 East, 92; Collins v. Evans, 5 Q. B. 820, Ex. Ch.; Ormrod v. Huth, 14 M. & W. 650, Ex. Ch.; Barley v. Walford, 9 Q. B. 197. There was till very lately some doubt whether the court would weigh the grounds of the defendant's belief where he shewed some grounds. See the difference of opinion between the Lord Chancellor and Lord Cranworth in Western Bank v. Addie, L. R. 1 H. L. Sc. 145. But the Court of Appeal has just decided that the grounds must be reasonable. Peek v. Derry, 37 Ch. Div. 541. Contra in America. Carroll v. Hayward, 124 Mass. 120.

Collins v. Evans, supra, finally settled the rule that it is necessary to prove fraud in an action for damages on account of misrepresentation.

[2] Comp. Rogers v. Palmer, 102 U.S. 263. Conversely, if statute make reasonable belief a test, actual belief is not enough. Purinton v. Chamberlain, 131 Mass. 589.

[3] Knowledge of facts ought not to be implied, contrary to the

was true. It may not then be strictly true that the plaintiff must prove the scienter in any ordinary way. Still the defendant was aware that it was his duty to know the true state of things, and if he did not perform that duty he must have known the fact, whereas his representation is an implied assertion that he has performed that duty. Thus then, even in this phase of the subject, the plaintiff may be considered as shewing fraud on the part of the defendant.

But there is another and perhaps more satisfactory view to be taken. The defendant stands in a peculiar situation in regard to the facts; the facts are specially within his reach; they are not facts that others may, even by inquiry, know as well. The result is, that any representation made by him touching them is likely to carry great weight, greater, all else being equal, than representations made in other cases. This fact may well be held enough to govern his conduct, and to require him to know the truth of the representation; in a word, he may well be held to warrant the representation to be true, and warranting it, he cannot require the party with whom he has dealt to prove that he knew it to be false when he made it[1].

This third phase of fraud may then be treated as a case either of implied warranty or of deceit; the injured party has his election in the matter. It is believed that cases of implied warranty generally are capable of being treated as falling under the head of deceit as thus explained. A typical illustration will serve to make the application of

---

truth, except where there is some duty to know them. Hallmark's Case, 9 Ch. Div. 329, Bramwell, L. J.

[1] See Collen v. Wright, 8 El. & B. 647, Ex. Ch., Willes, J. for the majority. Cockburn, C. J. dissented as to the form of action. See Denton v. Great Northern Railway Co. 5 El. & B. 860, in regard to representations by railway time tables.

these remarks clear: If a person assume to act for another in respect of a matter over which he has no authority, he renders himself liable for misrepresentation to the person whom he may thus have misled, though he may have honestly believed that he had the authority assumed[1]. The matter of his authority was a fact peculiarly within his own means of knowledge, and it was therefore his duty to acquaint himself with the situation.

Cases falling under this phase of the subject appear, however, to stand upon narrow ground, and the principle of liability is not to be extended to cases not clearly within it. Thus, the fact that a person allows his name to be used as director or trustee of a corporation or other company, in prospectuses containing false representations, does not impose upon him in law the duty to know the truth of the statements and so subject him to liability. To prove such fact is not to prove fraud[2].

What creates the duty to know the facts is a difficult question to answer; perhaps it is incapable of being answered in the way of any very perspicuous proposition. The following rule, laid down by an Irish judge, is wanting somewhat in definiteness, but it is doubtful whether the nature of the case permits anything better: What a man must know, it was in substance declared, must have regard to his particular means of knowledge and to the nature of the representation; and this must be subject to the test of the knowledge which a man, paying that attention which everyone owes to his neighbour in making a representation

---

[1] Collen v. Wright, 8 El. & B. 647, 658, Cockburn, C. J. See also Randell v. Trimen, 18 C. B. 786; Firbank v. Humphreys, 18 Q. B. D. 54; Seton v. Lafone, id. 139, Denman, J. The majority in Collen v. Wright would no doubt have agreed that an action for deceit could have been maintained.

[2] Western Bank v. Addie, L. R. 1 H. L. Sc. 145.

to be acted upon, would have acquired in the particular case by the use of such means[1].

§ 4. On Plaintiff's Ignorance of Falsity.

The next element of the breach of duty is that requiring the plaintiff to have been ignorant of the truth of the matter concerning which the representation was made, and to have believed that it was true.

Both of these situations must, in general, be true of the plaintiff; he must have been ignorant of the true state of things, and have trusted the representation of them as made by the defendant. He must have been deceived; and to render the defendant liable the plaintiff must have been deceived by the defendant. If the plaintiff had knowledge of the facts in question, or if without having knowledge thereof he acted upon independent information, and not upon a belief of the truth of the defendant's representation, he is in the one case not deceived at all, and in the other is not deceived by the person of whom he complains. And the burden of proving such facts rests upon the plaintiff[2].

Should a purchaser of property therefore make investigation of his own in regard to the truth of representations made by the vendor, he will be barred from alleging that the latter made false representations. More than this, if in such a case there was no warranty, the purchaser cannot say that the vendor concealed facts of importance from him; provided nothing was done or said to prevent the purchaser from making as ample investigation as he chose. For example: The defendant, vendor of a large tract of land, represents the estate to contain only fifty or sixty acres of

[1] Doyle v. Hort, 4 L. R. Ir. 661, 670, Palles, C. B.
[2] Pasley v. Freeman, 3 T. R. 51; s. c. L. C. Torts, 1.

untillable soil, and the plaintiff, the purchaser, before the sale, examines all the land more than once. The defendant is not guilty of a breach of duty to the plaintiff, though it turns out that the estate contains three hundred acres unfit for cultivation[1].

Aside from such cases, there are few cases in which the plaintiff, if he was actually ignorant of the true state of facts and supposed the representation to be true, is considered by the law as fixed with knowledge of the facts; the duty resting upon him being only a general duty of diligence, rather than a duty, like that in the preceding section, towards the opposite party. The imputation of knowledge is then of much lessened force; it is generally, indeed, reduced to a case of presumptive evidence, if it arises at all.

Authorities there have been in which it is laid down that if the means of knowledge be equally open to both parties, the plaintiff, as a prudent man, must be deemed to have availed himself of such means (or is not to be excused if he has not done so), and hence that, in contemplation of law, he has not been deceived by the defendant; the result being that, unless there was a warranty, no action can be maintained.

Thus, Lord Ellenborough has said that a seller is liable to an action for deceit if he fraudulently misrepresent the quality of the property in some particular 'which the buyer has not equal means with himself of knowing[2].' And statements to the same effect have been made by other judges[3].

In the light, however, of recent authorities this doctrine could hardly be sustained at the present time. Indeed,

[1] Halls v. Thompson, 1 Smedes & M. 443, an American example.
[2] Vernon v. Keys, 12 East, 632.
[3] Statements to that effect have been very common in America. See Bigelow, Fraud, 522.

CHAP. I.] DECEIT. 39

Lord Ellenborough himself appears to have limited his proposition; for immediately after the foregoing quotation he adds the alternative statement, in regard to the seller's liability for the fraudulent misrepresentation, 'or if he do so in such a manner as to induce the buyer to forbear making the inquiries' which he would otherwise have made. It may be hard to believe that a plaintiff did not avail himself of means of knowledge if directly at hand; but there is in principle, and by authority, only a probability of fact to be overcome even in such a case. There is no conclusion of law either that the plaintiff availed himself of the means, or that it was his duty to do so; the plaintiff may still shew that he was misled by the defendant's representation [1]. For example: A prospectus of a company in process of formation falsely states that the capital stock is a certain sum, and the plaintiff is induced by this statement to subscribe for shares of stock in the company. The plaintiff might have learned the true state of things by examining the records of the company which were open to his inspection, but does not make the examination. He is not barred of redress [2].

The case is not varied in law by the circumstance that the plaintiff may have made some partial examination on his own behalf; if still he was misled, and prevented from making such examination as otherwise he would have made, he will be entitled, so far, to recover [3]. For example: Representations concerning a hotel about to be sold at auction are made by the seller in printed particulars of sale.

[1] Central Ry. Co. v. Kisch, L. R. 2 H. L. 99, 120; Smith v. Land Corp., 28 Ch. Div. 7; Redgrave v. Hurd, 20 Ch. Div. 1, 13, Jessel, M. R.; Reynell v. Sprye, 1 De G. M. & G. 668, 709; Stanley v. McGauran, 11 L. R. Ir. 314; Sankey v. Alexander, Ir. R. 9 Ex. 259, 316.

[2] Central Ry. v. Kisch, supra.

[3] Smith v. Land Corp., 28 Ch. Div. 7; Vernon v. Keys, 12 East, 632, supra.

The buyer, having seen the statements, sends his agent to look over the premises to see whether it will be advisable to buy. The agent goes accordingly, and having made some examination, advises the purchase, which is made. The buyer may shew that he was induced by the representations of the seller to buy[1].

The subject may be further illustrated by a quite different sort of case. Every man is presumed to know the contents of a written contract signed by him; but no presumption of knowledge will stand in the way of a charge of fraud made in regard to the contents of the writing. No doubt it would be imprudent not to read or to require the reading of an instrument before signing or accepting it; indeed, the courts would turn a deaf ear to a man who sought to get rid of a contract solely on the ground that its terms were not what he supposed them to be. But the case would be different where a plaintiff charged fraud upon the defendant in reading the contract to him, or in stating its terms, or in secretly inserting terms not agreed upon[2].

The usual course of proceeding in regard to cases of the kind now under consideration is to rescind the contract; but such a course may have become impossible[3]. And whether it be possible or not, it is a well-established rule of law that one who has been induced by fraud to enter into a contract, whether executory or wholly (as by sale and payment) executed, may treat the contract as binding, retain its fruits, and sue for the fraud by which it was effected[4].

---

[1] Smith v. Land Corp., supra.

[2] Stanley v. Mc Gauran, 11 L. R. Ir. 314; Albany Sav. Inst. v. Burdick, 87 N. Y. 40.

[3] See Clarke v. Dickson, El. B. & E. 148.

[4] Clarke v. Dickson, El. B. & E. 148; Regina v. Saddlers' Co., 10 H. L. Cas. 404, 421, Blackburn, J.; Western Bank v. Addie, L. R. 1 H. L. Sc. 167.

Hence in the case of a written contract knowingly misread, misstated, or miswritten the party wronged may (probably) maintain an action of deceit for the damage he may have incurred, while at the same time treating the contract as in itself valid.

But the defendant must have been guilty of fraud, as by purposely misreading or misstating the instrument. Should he profess to state no more than the effect of a long writing, he could not, it seems, be liable in damages for a mistake; though equity would reform the instrument at the instance of the party injured.

The explanation of all this is not far to seek. It is not for one who admits that he has been guilty of endeavouring to mislead another to say to him, when called to account, 'You ought not to have trusted me; you were negligent; you ought to have made inquiry[1].' The law requires, indeed, the exercise of prudence by both parties; but that is all. If prudence on the one side has been disarmed by misconduct on the other, the law cannot justly refuse relief. Besides, the case of a plaintiff so situated is quite different from that of a defendant so related to the facts as to be bound to know the truth. In this latter case no one has misled the defendant; in the case under consideration, on the other hand, the misrepresentation has, upon the hypothesis, misled the plaintiff.

The case will of course be different if the defendant's representation was not of a nature to mislead, as where it is a statement of mere opinion, or where it did not in fact mislead. And where the facts are open to the plaintiff equally with the defendant, there is a presumption, it seems, that the plaintiff availed himself of the means of inquiry; which presumption must be overcome before he can recover.

[1] Smith v. Land Corp., supra, Bowen, L. J.; Redgrave v. Hurd, supra. So too in Albany Sav. Inst. v. Burdick, 87 N. Y. 40.

When the defendant induces the plaintiff to abstain from seeking information, mere concealment of material facts may become a breach of duty; and redress will not be refused in such a case merely because a sharp business man might not have been deceived. Nor is the rule of law different when the defendant suggests examination to the plaintiff, but in such a way as to indicate that such a step would be quite unnecessary. So it is held in America. For example: The defendant, in selling to the plaintiff property at a distance, suggests to the plaintiff that he go and look at the property 'as their judgment might not agree, and, if not satisfied, he would pay the plaintiff's expenses; but if satisfied the plaintiff should pay them himself.' This is deemed to justify the plaintiff in acting upon the defendant's representations without examining the property[1].

Even though a party sell at the risk of the purchaser, 'with all faults,' as he may, he will have no right to practise fraud; and if he should do so he will be liable as for a breach of his legal duty to the purchaser. For example: The defendant sells to the plaintiff a vessel, 'hull, masts, yards, standing and running rigging, with all faults, as they now lie.' He, however, makes a false statement, that the 'hull is nearly as good as when launched', and takes means to conceal defects which he knew to exist. This is a breach of duty to the plaintiff[2]. But the case would be different if the seller, though aware of the defects, do nothing to conceal them .

When the parties, by reason of physical or mental

---

[1] Webster v. Bailey, 31 Mich. 36.

[2] Schneider v. Heath, 3 Campb. 506. See Whitney v. Boardman, 118 Mass. 242, 247; George v. Johnson, 6 Humph. 36 (Tenn.).

[3] Baglehole v. Walters, 3 Campb. 154 (overruling Mellish v. Motteux, Peake, 156); Pickering v. Dowson, 4 Taunt. 779; Bywater v. Richardson, 1 Ad. & E. 508.

infirmity on the one side, or of the fact that the one party is in the occupation or management of the other's business, or has the general custody of his body, do not stand upon an equal footing, the objection to a suit for false representations, that the party to whom they were made was negligent in not making inquiry or examination, has still less force. Examples of this class of cases may be readily found in the case of transactions with aged persons, or with cestuis que trust by trustees, or with wards by guardians.

Not even the subsequent acts of accepting and paying for goods upon delivery will bar the purchaser of redress, though the goods were open to his inspection at the time, if the fraud was not then discovered, and especially if such acceptance and payment were procured by fraudulent artifices on the part of the vendor[1]. For example: The defendant, a manufacturer and vendor of tobacco, knowingly uses damaged tobacco in the manufacture, and intentionally uses boxes of green lumber; and while the tobacco is being made up he exhibits to the plaintiff from time to time, in order to mislead him, specimens of tobacco as of the kind he (the defendant) is supplying the plaintiff, when in fact the defendant is supplying him with a different and inferior kind. Notwithstanding acceptance of the goods and payment for them, the plaintiff is entitled to damages against the defendant[2].

§ 5. OF THE INTENTION THAT THE REPRESENTATION SHOULD BE ACTED UPON.

In regard to that element of the breach of duty under consideration which requires the plaintiff to prove that the

[1] See Clarke v. Dickson, El. B. & E. 148.
[2] Mc Aroy v. Wright, 25 Ind. 22. An act does not amount to the waiver of a wrong unless it be done with knowledge of the wrong.

defendant intended his representation to be acted upon, it is to be observed that, while the rule is probably inflexible, its force appears chiefly in those cases in which the deception was practised with reference to a negotiation with a third person, and not with the defendant. In cases of that kind, an instance of which is found in false representations to the plaintiff of the solvency of a third person[1], it is plain that the transaction with such third person, though shewn to have been caused by the defendant's false representation, affords no evidence of an intention in the defendant that the representation should be acted upon by the plaintiff. It would be perfectly consistent with mere evidence that the plaintiff acted upon the defendant's misrepresentation in a transaction with a third person, that the defendant, though he knew the falsity of his representation, did not know, and had no reason to suppose, that the plaintiff would act upon it. The representation might, for all this, have been a mere idle falsehood, such as would not justify anyone in acting upon it.

It follows that where a party complains of false representations, whereby he was caused to suffer damage in a transaction with some third person, it devolves upon him to give express evidence either that the defendant intended that he should act upon the representation, or that the plaintiff was justified in inferring such intention,—it matters not which[2]; and that it is not enough to prove that the misrepresentation was made with knowledge of its falsity[3].

When, however, the effect of the false representation was to bring the plaintiff into a business transaction with

[1] Pasley v. Freeman, 3 T. R. 51, ante, p. 26.
[2] See Freeman v. Cooke, 2 Ex. 654; Cornish v. Abington, 4 H. & N. 549.
[3] See Pasley v. Freeman, 3 T. R. 51; s. c. L. C. Torts, 1.

the defendant, the case is quite different. Proof of such a fact shews at once the intent of the defendant to induce the plaintiff to act upon the representation; and it follows that no evidence need be offered of an intention to this effect, or of reasonable ground to suppose an intention. The principle appears most frequently in cases of sales; the rule of law being, that if the plaintiff, the purchaser, establish the fact that the defendant, the vendor, knew that his representation was false, it is not necessary for the plaintiff to give other evidence to shew that the defendant intended to mislead the plaintiff. That is already proved[1]. For example: The defendant sells a horse as sound, knowing that he is not sound. Further evidence to shew the existence of an intent to defraud the plaintiff is not necessary[2].

Indeed, it is probably not necessary in any case, if the cause of action is carefully stated, that it should appear that the defendant intended to *injure* the plaintiff. It has already been stated that a person honestly professing to have authority to act for another is liable as for fraud for the damages sustained, if he has not the authority[3]. In such cases it is obvious that the representation may have been made for the benefit of the plaintiff[4]. So too in cases in which the defendant has made the misrepresentation with knowledge of its falsity, it is plain that he may really have desired and expected that the plaintiff would derive a benefit from the transaction.

§ 6. OF ACTING UPON THE REPRESENTATION.

It is fundamental that the defendant's representation should have been acted upon by the plaintiff, and acted upon to his injury, to enable him to maintain an action for

[1] Foster *v.* Charles, 6 Bing. 396; s. c. 7 Bing. 105; Polhill *v.* Walter, 3 B. & Ad. 114. [2] Id.
[3] Ante, p. 36. [4] See Polhill *v.* Walter, 3 B. & Ad. 114.

the alleged breach of duty[1]. Indeed, fraudulent conduct or dishonesty of purpose, however explicit, will not afford a cause of action unless shewn to be the very ground upon which the plaintiff acted to his damage. The *defendant must have caused the damage.*

So strong is the rule upon this subject that it is deemed necessary to this action that the damage as well as the acting upon the representation must already have been suffered before the bringing of the suit, and that it is not sufficient that it may occur. For example: The defendant induces the plaintiff to indorse a promissory note before its maturity by means of false and fraudulent representations. An action therefor cannot, according to American law, be maintained before the plaintiff has been compelled to pay the note[2].

A person who has been prevented from effecting an attachment upon property by the fraudulent representations of the owner or of his agent is deemed in America, and the same view would probably be entertained in England, to have suffered no legal damage thereby, though subsequently another creditor should attach the whole property of the debtor and sell it upon execution to satisfy his own debt[3]. The person thus deceived, having acquired no lien upon or right in the property, cannot lose any by reason of the deceit. The most that can be said of such a case, it has been observed, is that the party intended to attach the property, and that this intention has been frustrated[4]; and it could not be certainly known that that

[1] Pasley v. Freeman, 3 T. R. 51; Smith v. Chadwick, 9 App. Cas. 187; Freeman v. Venner, 120 Mass. 424.

[2] Freeman v. Venner, supra.

[3] Bradley v. Fuller, 118 Mass. 239. But see Kelsey v. Murphy, 26 Penn. St. 78.

[4] Id.; Lamb v. Stone, 11 Pick. 527.

intention would have been carried out¹. If the attachment had been already levied and was then lost through the deceit, the rule would of course be different².

It must appear, moreover, that the *plaintiff* was entitled to act upon the representation; and this will depend upon the intention of the defendant. The representation may have been intended for (1) one particular individual only (in which case he alone is entitled to act upon it), or (2) it may have been intended for any one of a class, or (3) for any one of the public, or (4) it may have been made to one person to be communicated by him to another. Anyone so intended, who has acted upon the misrepresentation to his damage, will be entitled to redress for any damage sustained by acting upon the representation³. For example: The defendants put forth a prospectus to the public, containing false representations for the purpose of selling shares of stock in their company. The plaintiff, as one of the public, may act upon the representations, and, having bought stock of the *company*, recover damages for the loss sustained thereby⁴.

§ 7. OF SLANDER OF TITLE AND TRADE MARKS.

The foregoing presentation of the law supposes that the representation was made to or for the plaintiff. But there is another class of cases, with several branches, in which the situation is different. A representation may be made *of* a man or *of* his property to his injury, as well as to

¹ Bradley *v.* Fuller, supra.
² Id.
³ Richardson *v.* Silvester, L. R. 9 Q. B. 34; Swift *v.* Winterbotham, L. R. 8 Q. B. 244; Peek *v.* Gurney, L. R. 6 H. L. 377.
⁴ Id. Contra, if the shares are bought on the market. Peek *v.* Gurney, supra.

him; still this class of cases (probably) stands upon the same footing as the cases which have been under consideration[1].

False representations *of* a person may consist, either (1) in disparaging his credit, or the title to his property, or his property itself, or (2) in infringements of his trade mark or sign or badge of business. The subject of misrepresentations made to the plaintiff of the credit of a third person has been considered[2]; and (in principle) there is no difference between such a case and that of misrepresentations to a third person of the plaintiff's pecuniary standing. The representation having been acted upon to the plaintiff's damage by the person to whom the defendant made it, the latter is liable for the former's loss.

If the representation relate to the plaintiff's title to property or to the quality of the property itself, the wrong done is termed slander of title; if it be an attempt to palm off the defendant's goods in trade as the goods of the plaintiff, it will commonly be the case of an infringement of his trade mark[3].

In the action for slander of title, it devolves upon the plaintiff to prove that the statement of the defendant was

[1] See L. C. Torts, 54—59, 69—72.
[2] Ante, pp. 26, 27.
[3] An infringement of a patent, it should be observed, is not so much an attempt to obtain the benefit of another's reputation in business as to make and vend the very same article, to do which an exclusive right has been given to another. There is no necessary attempt to deceive anyone in the infringement of a patent; and the same is measurably true of infringements of copyrights. These subjects, therefore, do not belong to the law of deceit. An invasion of a patent or a copyright is simply an invasion of a right of property, like a trespass upon real estate. Indeed, the same is now become, to some extent, true of trade marks. Leather Cloth Co. *v.* American Leather Cloth Co., 4 De G. J. & S. 137; post, p. 228.

false, was made with actual malice[1], and that it has been accompanied with some actual, specific damage[2].

The interpretation put upon the elements of the action by the authorities shews that they are substantially equivalent to the corresponding elements of the ordinary action of deceit[3]. The false representation (which clearly must have been material, and otherwise of the nature of the representation above considered) must, it seems, have been made with knowledge of its falsity and with intent to deceive; this appears to be the meaning of the 'actual malice' above mentioned[4]. For example: The defendant states to a third person with whom the plaintiff has made a contract for the sale of certain lands, that the plaintiff's 'title to those estates will hereafter sooner or later be contested. At the time they were sold by Mr Y [the plaintiff's vendor], he was not in a state of soundness and competency to do so.' The defendant makes this statement as trustee of the particular lands, in good faith, believing it to be true. This is no breach of duty to the plaintiff[4]. The same case would afford an example of the necessity of proof of actual damage by supposing that the plaintiff had not been negotiating for the sale of the lands at the time of the statement[5].

And the question of the defendant's liability must turn, further, upon the evidence whether the third person, to

---

[1] Pater v. Baker, 3 C. B. 831, 868; Pitt v. Donovan, 1 Maule & S. 639.

[2] Malachy v. Soper, 3 Bing. N. C. 371. See L. C. Torts, 54—59.

[3] The form of declaring has been on the model of the action for slander or libel. See Bigelow, Fraud, 557, 558. But the significant facts are that the plaintiff must prove the falsity of the statement, actual malice, and damage. Such facts are no necessary part of the plaintiff's case in an action for defamation, as will be seen.

[4] Pitt v. Donovan, supra.   [5] Malachy v. Soper, supra.

whom the defendant made the false statement, was deceived by and acted upon that *particular* statement. If such person knew the truth of the matter, or acted upon other information regardless of the defendant's statement, the latter could not be deemed in any proper sense to have caused the damage of which the plaintiff complains[1].

With regard to the law of trade marks (using this as a generic term to cover all kinds of signs and badges of business), similar observations are to be made. In order to sustain an action of *deceit* for a breach of duty by the defendant to the plaintiff in the use of a trade mark, it must appear (1) that the defendant knew of the existence of the plaintiff's mark when he committed the alleged wrong, (2) that he intended to palm off the goods as the goods of the plaintiff, or to represent that the business which he was carrying on was the plaintiff's business, or business of which the plaintiff had a special patronage, and (3) that the public were deceived thereby[2]. For example: The defendant sells a medicine labelled 'Dr Johnson's ointment,'—the label being one which the plaintiff had previously used, and was still using when the defendant began to make use of the same. The plaintiff cannot recover

---

[1] See Pitt v. Donovan, 1 Maule & S. 639; Pater v. Baker, 3 C. B. 831, 868; Wren v. Weild, L. R. 4 Q. B. 730; L. C. Torts, ut supra.

[2] Sykes v. Sykes, 3 Barn. & C. 541; s. c. L. C. Torts, 66; Rodgers v. Nowill, 5 C. B. 109; Morison v. Salmon, 2 Man. & G. 385; Crawshay v. Thompson, 4 Man. & G. 357, 379, 383. See Bigelow, Fraud, 560, 565. In a proceeding for *injunction* it is not necessary, in ordinary cases, to prove the defendant's knowledge or intent to deceive. Simple priority of use of the mark is enough. See Millington v. Fox, 3 Mylne & C. 338; Singer Machine Co. v. Wilson, 3 App. Cas. 376. The subject of trade-marks is being gradually assimilated to the law of property, and actions for deceit are apparently becoming infrequent under the influence of a better right.

without shewing that the defendant has used the label for the purpose of indicating that the medicine has been prepared by the plaintiff[1]. Again: The plaintiff Sykes is a maker of powder-flasks and shot belts, upon which he has placed the words 'Sykes Patent.' There is no valid patent upon them, in fact, as has been decided by the courts; but the maker has continued to use the words upon the goods to designate them as of his own making. The defendant, whose name is also Sykes, makes similar goods, and puts upon them the same words, with a stamp closely resembling that of the plaintiff, so as to sell the goods 'as and for' the plaintiff's goods. This is a breach of duty[2].

[1] Singleton v. Bolton, 3 Doug. 293. This supposes, of course, that the medicine was not patented.
[2] Sykes v. Sykes, supra.

CHAPTER II.

MALICIOUS PROSECUTION.

§ 1. Introductory.

Statement of the duty. A owes to B the duty to forbear to institute against him a prosecution, with malice and without reasonable and probable cause, for an offence falsely charged to have been committed by B.

1. When a termination of prosecution is referred to without further explanation, such a termination is meant as will, in connexion with the other elements of the action, permit an action for malicious prosecution.
2. The word 'prosecution' includes such civil actions as may be the subject of a suit for malicious prosecution.
3. The term 'probable cause' is used for brevity in this chapter for 'reasonable and probable cause[1].'

In order to maintain an action for a malicious prosecution, three things are necessary, and possibly four, to wit, (1) the prosecution complained of must have terminated before the action for redress on account of it is commenced; (2) it must have been instituted without probable cause; (3) it must have been instituted maliciously; (4) actual damage must be proved in cases in which the charge in itself would not be actionable, assuming that an action for

[1] There may be some slight difference in meaning between 'reasonable' and 'probable' cause. See the language of Tindal, C. J. in Broad *v.* Ham, 5 Bing. N. C. 722, 725, quoted in Lister *v.* Perryman, L. R. 4 H. L. 521, 530, 540.

CHAP. II.] MALICIOUS PROSECUTION. 53

malicious prosecution is maintainable in such a case. And it devolves upon the plaintiff to prove all these facts.

Actions for malicious prosecution are brought, for the greater part, only for wrongful criminal prosecutions. For a civil suit instituted of malice and without probable cause there is no redress[1], except in peculiar cases; and these appear, at least in the main, to be cases of actions involving charges of 'scandal to reputation or the possible loss of liberty[2]', such as 'proceedings in bankruptcy against a trader, or the analogous process of a petition to wind up a company[3]'. Whether there are other cases for the action is doubtful.

§ 2. OF THE TERMINATION OF THE PROSECUTION.

The action for a malicious prosecution is given for the preferring in court of a *false* charge, maliciously and without proper grounds. And, as it cannot be known by satisfactory evidence whether the charge is true or false before the verdict and judgment of the court trying the cause, it is deemed necessary for the defendant to await the termination of the proceeding before instituting an action for malicious prosecution. Or, as the reason has more commonly been stated, if the suit for the alleged malicious prosecution should be permitted before the prosecution itself is terminated, inconsistent judgments might be rendered,—a judgment

---

[1] 'In the present day, and according to our present law, the bringing of an ordinary action, however maliciously, and however great the want of reasonable and probable cause, will not support a subsequent action for malicious prosecution.' Quartz Hill Mining Co. v. Eyre, 11 Q. B. Div. 674, 690, Bowen, L. J. Actions for malicious civil suits are common in the United States.

[2] Id. at p. 691, Bowen, L. J.; Pollock, Torts, 265, 266.

[3] Pollock, 266; 11 Q. B. Div. 691.

in favour of the plaintiff in the action for the prosecution and a judgment against him in that prosecution[1]; and it is often said that judgment against the party prosecuted would shew, and that conclusively, that there was probable cause for the prosecution[2].

It will be seen in the next section (relating to probable cause) that this is an erroneous view of the effect of the judgment. But since conviction would shew that the charge was not false, it would be fatal to any action for malicious prosecution. This is true even though the prosecution take place in a proceeding from which there is no appeal. Conviction in such a case is equally fatal with a conviction in a tribunal from the judgment of which the defendant has a right of appeal; since to allow the action for malicious prosecution would be (so it is deemed) virtually to grant an appeal; a thing contrary to law in the particular case. For example: The defendant procures the plaintiff to be arrested (falsely, maliciously, and without probable cause, as the latter alleges) and tried before a justice of the peace on a criminal complaint of assault and battery. The plaintiff (then defendant) is convicted, and no appeal is allowed by law. The defendant is not liable for malicious prosecution[3].

It is often said that the plaintiff must have been acquitted of the charge preferred, to enable him to sue for malicious prosecution. But this, though a clear rule of law to a certain extent, is by no means universally true. An

[1] Fisher v. Bristow, 1 Doug. 215.
[2] Castrique v. Behrens, 3 El. & E. 709. See Besébé v. Matthews, L. R. 2 C. P. 684; 1 Smith's Leading Cases, 258, 6th ed. But an action for malicious prosecution against the present plaintiff, by proceedings against him in bankruptcy, may be maintained notwithstanding an adjudication against him, if this has been set aside. Metropolitan Bank v. Pooley, 10 App. Cas. 210.
[3] Besébé v. Matthews, L. R. 2 C. P. 684.

CHAP. II.]   MALICIOUS PROSECUTION.   55

acquittal would, indeed, be a bar to another prosecution for the same cause; while anything short of an acquittal in fact or in law would leave the accused still liable to trial. Nevertheless, there are several classes of cases in regard to which it is not necessary that the proceedings in the prosecution in question should have gone the length of an acquittal. These will now be shewn.

It is not necessary it seems to the termination of a civil suit, such as will permit an action for malicious prosecution, that the suit should have gone to actual judgment, or even to a verdict by the jury. A civil suit is entirely within the control of the plaintiff, and he may withdraw and terminate it at any stage; and, should he take such a step, the suit is terminated. For example: The defendant (in the suit for malicious prosecution) writes in the docket book, opposite the entry of the case against the plaintiff, 'Suit withdrawn.' This is a sufficient termination of the cause for the purposes of the now plaintiff [1].

It is not necessary, indeed, according to American law that the party should make a formal entry of the withdrawal or dismissal of the suit, in order (without a judgment or verdict) to terminate it sufficiently for the purposes of an action by the opposite party. Any act, or omission to act, which is tantamount to a discontinuance of the proceeding has the same effect. For example: The defendant, having procured the arrest of the plaintiff in a civil cause, fails to enter and prosecute his suit. This is a termination of the proceeding [2].

If, however, the (civil) prosecution went to judgment, the judgment must have been rendered in favour of the defendant therein, in order to enable him to sue for mali-

[1] Arundell v. White, 14 East 216.
[2] Cardival v. Smith, 109 Mass. 158.

cious prosecution. Judgment against the defendant would conclusively establish the plaintiff's right of action; it could not, therefore, be treated as a false prosecution[1], though it might have been attended with malice;—unless, indeed, it was concocted in fraud.

In a criminal trial the situation is, indeed, different. Such a proceeding is instituted by the Crown, and, when by indictment, is under the control of the attorney-general, or other prosecuting officer; it is never under the control of the prosecutor. He has no authority over it; and, this being the case, he cannot, in principle, be bound by the action of the prosecuting officer. Should such officer, therefore, enter a dismissal of the suit before the defendant, having been duly indicted, has been put in jeopardy, this act, it seems, gives no right to the prisoner against the prosecutor. The course of proceeding was not arrested by the prosecutor, and he has a right to insist that the law shall take its regular course, and place the prisoner in jeopardy, before he shall have the power to seek redress. For example: The defendant procures the plaintiff to be indicted for arson. The prosecuting officer, failing in obtaining evidence, enters a 'nolle prosequi' before the jury is sworn. The prosecution is not terminated in favour of the prisoner[2].

If, however, the prosecution was arrested by the grand jury's finding no indictment upon the evidence, and the consequent discharge of the prisoner, this is, it seems, an end of the prosecution, such as will enable him (other elements present) to bring the action under consideration[3]. And the same is true when the prosecution is begun by

---

[1] Or, as the case is sometimes put, judgment for the plaintiff would shew that he had probable cause for the prosecution, a point to be considered hereafter.

[2] Bacon v. Towne, 4 Cush. 217 (Mass., Shaw, C. J.).

[3] See Byne v. Moore, 5 Taunt. 187; L. C. Torts, 181.

complaint before a magistrate who has jurisdiction only to bind over or discharge the prisoner. The magistrate's entry that the prisoner is discharged entitles him, other elements being present, to bring an action. And this is true, though the prosecutor withdraw his prosecution. For example: The defendant prefers against the plaintiff a charge of forgery before a justice of the peace, who has authority only to bind over or discharge the prisoner. The justice's minutes contain the following entry: 'After full hearing in the case, the complainant withdrew his prosecution, and it was thereupon ordered' that the plaintiff be discharged. An action for malicious prosecution is now proper[1].

In none of the foregoing classes of cases has there been an acquittal of the party prosecuted, or anything tantamount in law to an acquittal. To be acquitted in a prosecution for crime (the only case calling for remark), the accused must have been put in jeopardy; but a state of jeopardy is not reached until the swearing of the petit jury. Hence if acquittal were necessary, an action for malicious prosecution could not be instituted upon the failure of the grand jury to find an indictment, or upon the discharge of a magistrate who has no power to convict. In neither case has the prisoner been in jeopardy. The fact appears to be that, notwithstanding the language of some of the judges, a termination of the proceedings with an acquittal, actual or virtual, is necessary only in case of an indictment or information against the prisoner. In other cases, it is only necessary that the prosecution should be dismissed[2].

[1] Sayles v. Briggs, 4 Met. 421 (Mass.).

[2] The rule requiring an acquittal of the party prosecuted is founded upon an early English statute entitled 'Malicious Appeals'. Westm. 2, c. 12 (13 Edw. I). By this statute it was ordained that when any

By way of summary, the various rules of law may be thus stated: A civil suit is terminated (1) when the plaintiff has withdrawn, or otherwise discontinued, his action; or (2) when judgment has been rendered in favour of the defendant. A criminal suit is terminated (1) when the prosecution, if brought before a magistrate, has been dismissed, or (2) when, if preferred before the grand jury, that body has found no indictment; or (3) when, an indictment having been found, and the prisoner having been put in jeopardy, a verdict acquitting the prisoner has been rendered. Perhaps the prisoner should also have been discharged; but he is entitled to a discharge in all these cases.

§ 3. OF THE WANT OF PROBABLE CAUSE.

Supposing the plaintiff to have begun his action after the termination of the prosecution, it then devolves upon

person maliciously 'appealed [that is, accused and prosecuted] of felony surmised upon him, doth *acquit* himself in the King's Court in due manner,' &c., the appellor shall be imprisoned and be liable in damages to the injured party.'' A few years later statutes were passed against conspiracies to indict persons maliciously. L. C. Torts, 190. Between these statutes and the statute first mentioned, and taking its shape from them, the action for malicious prosecution arose. Had the statute always been referred to in the modern authorities, the explanation of the subject would have been more satisfactory than it has sometimes been. The statutes applied to cases of prosecutions for felony alone; and in such cases only, it seems, is an acquittal necessary. All other cases stand, so far as the statutes affect the law, as at common law. Prosecutions for misdemeanours, prosecutions before inferior courts, and civil prosecutions, are left to the wisdom of the judges (except those falling within the statute of Malicious Distresses in Courts Baron, which required proof only of malice and a false complaint. L. C. Torts, 192).

him further to establish the defendant's breach of duty by shewing that he instituted the prosecution without probable cause[1]. And this appears to mean that he ought to shew that no such state of facts or circumstances was known as would induce one of ordinary intelligence and caution to believe the charge preferred to be true. Or, conversely, probable cause for preferring a charge of crime is shewn by 'facts which would create a reasonable suspicion in the mind of a reasonable man[2].'

To act, therefore, on very slight circumstances of suspicion, such as a man of caution would deem of little weight, is to act without probable cause. For example: The defendant procures the arrest of the plaintiff upon a charge of being implicated in the commission of a robbery, which in fact has been committed by a third person alone, who absconds. The plaintiff, who has been a fellow-workman with the criminal, has been heard to say that he (the plaintiff) had been told, a few hours before the robbery, that the robber had absconded, and that he had told the plaintiff that he intended to go to Australia. The robber has also been seen, early in the morning after the robbery, coming from a public entry leading to the back door of the plaintiff's house. The defendant has no probable cause for the arrest[3].

But though the prosecutor be in a situation to shew that he had probable cause, so far as regards the strength of his information, still if he did not believe the facts and rely upon them in procuring the arrest, he has committed a breach of duty towards the person arrested. For

[1] Turner v. Ambler, 10 Q. B. 252.
[2] Broughton v. Jackson, 18 Q. B. 378; Panton v. Williams, 2 Q. B. 169, Ex. Ch.
[3] Busst v. Gibbons, 30 Law J. Ex. 75. Comp. Lister v. Perryman, L. R. 4 H. L. 521, as to hearsay.

example: The defendant goes before a magistrate and prefers against the plaintiff the charge of larceny, for which there was reasonable ground in the facts within the defendant's cognizance. The defendant, however, does not believe the plaintiff guilty, but prefers the charge in order to coerce the plaintiff to pay a debt which he owes to the defendant. The defendant has acted without probable cause[1].

The question of probable cause is to be decided by the circumstances existing at the time of the arrest, and not by the turn of subsequent events[2]. If the defendant had then such grounds for supposing the plaintiff guilty of the crime charged as would satisfy a cautious man, he violates no duty to the plaintiff in procuring his arrest, though such grounds be immediately and satisfactorily explained away, or the truth discovered by the prosecutor himself. For example: The defendant procures the plaintiff to be arrested for the larceny of certain ribbons, on reasonable grounds of suspicion. He afterwards finds the ribbons in his own possession. He is not liable[3].

On the other hand, in accordance with the same principle, if the prosecutor was not possessed of facts justifying a belief that the accused was guilty of the charge, it matters not that subsequent events (short of a judgment of conviction, as to which presently) shew that there existed, in fact, though not to the prosecutor's knowledge, circumstances sufficient to have justified an arrest by any one cognizant of them. He has violated his duty in procuring the arrest. For example: The defendant to an action for malicious prosecution shews facts sufficient to

---

[1] Broad v. Ham, 5 Bing. N. C. 722. Had the defendant believed the charge, it could not have been material that he procured the arrest mainly for the purpose of getting his pay.
[2] Delegal v. Highley, 3 Bing. N. C. 950.
[3] Swain v. Stafford, 4 Ired. 392, 398 (North Carolina).

CHAP. II.]   MALICIOUS PROSECUTION.   61

constitute probable cause, but does not shew that he was cognizant of such facts when he procured the plaintiff's arrest. The defence is not good[1].

It has, however, been frequently declared that a judgment of conviction is conclusive evidence of the existence of probable cause[2]. But this, it will be seen, is inconsistent with the rule that the question of probable cause is to be determined by the state of facts within the prosecutor's knowledge (supposing him to have acted bona fide upon such facts) at the time of the arrest. Judgment of conviction does not, in point of fact, prove that the prosecutor at the time had reasonable grounds to suspect the guilt of the prisoner, such grounds, that is, as would have induced a cautious man to arrest the suspected person. It would be more accurate to say that the Statute of Malicious Appeals, which in reality lies at the foundation of the law concerning criminal prosecutions, by plain implication exempted the prosecutor (of felony) from liability in case of the conviction of the prisoner[3].

[1] Delegal *v.* Highley, 3 Bing. N. C. 950.
[2] See ante, p. 54. Contra, Burt *v.* Place, 4 Wend. 591 (N. Y).
[3] Ante, p. 58, n. If the statute be followed, this will be true only in cases of conviction of what was felony at common law. In other cases the conviction could not, by the statute, bar an action; nor could it bar an action for malicious prosecution on grounds of estoppel, because the parties to the two actions are different; the criminal suit being between the Crown and the prisoner. The judgment could not, properly taken, be more than prima facie evidence of probable cause, even if, of itself alone, it could be considered as amounting to any evidence on that point. The question before the petit jury, as has elsewhere been observed (post, p. 63), is, not whether there was probable cause for the arrest, within the knowledge of the prosecutor, but whether the prisoner is guilty. However, the language of the decisions is that the conviction is conclusive of probable cause; and the author at one time considered this to be correct. L. C. Torts, 196, 197.

There are other seeming anomalies relating to this phase of probable cause; one of them is found in the effect accorded to the action of the grand jury, or to that of a magistrate who has power only to bind over the accused for trial. That action is said to furnish prima facie (i.e. sufficient) evidence in regard to probable cause, in a suit for malicious prosecution. For example: The now defendant prosecutes the now plaintiff before the grand jury, on a charge of larceny, and the grand jury throws out the bill. This is deemed prima facie evidence of want of probable cause in the present suit[1]. Again: A magistrate binds over a person accused of crime, who is afterwards tried and acquitted. This is deemed prima facie evidence of probable cause in an action against the prosecutor for malicious prosecution[2].

Further, it has been seen[3] that in certain peculiar cases an action for a malicious civil suit may be brought. Now while it is held that the mere omission to appear and prosecute an action, whereby the defendant obtains a judgment of nonsuit, is no evidence of want of probable cause[4], it is deemed that a voluntary discontinuance, being a positive act[5], may shew prima facie evidence of the same. For example, taking a case from the old law which permitted an arrest in an ordinary civil suit: The now defendant procures the now plaintiff to be arrested and held to bail in an action on contract. The case comes on for trial very shortly afterwards, and the plaintiff discontinues his

---

[1] See Nicholson v. Coghill, 6 Dowl. & R. 12, 14, Holroyd, J.; Broad v. Ham, 5 Bing. N. C. 722, 727, Coltman, J.

[2] See Reynolds v. Kennedy, 1 Wils. 232; Sutton v. Johnstone, 1 T. R. 493, 505, 506.

[3] Ante, p. 53.

[4] Sinclair v. Eldred, 4 Taunt. 9; Webb v. Hill, 3 Car. & P. 485.

[5] Sed qu. of the relevancy of such fact.

suit. This is deemed prima facie evidence of want of probable cause[1].

Again, the mere abandonment of the prosecution by the prosecutor, and the acquittal of the prisoner, are no evidence of a want of probable cause[2]. Such facts in themselves shew nothing except that the prosecution has failed. It may still have been undertaken upon reasonable grounds of suspicion[3]. But it is held that the circumstances of the abandonment may be such as to indicate prima facie a want of probable cause. For example: The defendant presents two bills for perjury against the plaintiff, but does not himself appear before the grand jury, and the bills are ignored. He presents a third bill, and, on his own testimony, the grand jury return a true bill. The defendant now keeps the prosecution suspended for three years, when the plaintiff, taking down the record for trial, is acquitted; the defendant declining to appear as a witness, though in court at the time and called upon to testify. These facts indicate the absence of probable cause[4].

The American courts have had difficulty with several of these same questions. While it has been both held[5] and denied[6] that a judgment of guilty by a trial magistrate is conclusive of probable cause, it has been held by some courts, as in England, that the finding of a committing magistrate is prima facie evidence in the suit for malicious

[1] Nicholson v. Coghill, 6 Dowl. & R. 12; Webb v. Hill, 3 Car. & P. 485.
[2] Willans v. Taylor, 6 Bing. 183; Vanderbilt v. Mathis, 5 Duer, 304; s. c. L. C. Torts, 178.
[3] The magistrate or grand jury decides whether there is reasonable ground for putting the prisoner upon trial; the petit jury decides whether the prisoner is guilty.
[4] Willans v. Taylor, 6 Bing. 183.
[5] Whitney v. Peckham, 15 Mass. 243.
[6] Burt v. Place, 4 Wend. 591, 598 (N. Y.).

prosecution[1]; a discharge being treated as prima facie evidence of want of probable cause[2], and a commitment as prima facie evidence of the contrary[3].

Other American courts have taken a different view of the matter, denying that the magistrate's action is sufficient evidence in the action for malicious prosecution. How can it be, they say in effect, that what is no evidence at all before the grand jury in the same case can be prima facie evidence before a petit jury in a different case[4]? To this reasoning it might be added that the magistrate (and the same would be true of the grand jury) does not consider what prompted the prosecutor, but whether there is now sufficient evidence to justify holding the accused further for trial. But the contrary doctrine, after all, is only a doubtful application of the rule of the relevancy of a later fact to prove an earlier.

If the prosecutor take the advice of a practising lawyer upon the question whether the facts within his knowledge are such as to justify a complaint, and act bona fide upon the advice given, he will be protected even though the counsel gave erroneous advice. That is, he will be protected, though in fact he might not have been in possession of facts such as would have justified a prosecution without the advice. For example: The defendant states to his attorney the facts in his possession concerning a crime supposed to have been committed by the plaintiff. The attorney advises the defendant that he can safely procure the plaintiff's arrest. The defendant is not liable, though the facts presented did not in law constitute probable cause[5].

---

[1] Burt v. Place, 4 Wend. 591, 598 (N. Y.); Bacon v. Towne, 4 Cush. 217 (Mass.).

[2] Bostick v. Rutherford, 4 Hawks, 83 (North Carolina).

[3] Burt v. Place and Bacon v. Towne, supra.

[4] Israel v. Brooks, 23 Ill. 575. [5] Snow v. Allen, 1 Stark. 502.

CHAP. II.]   MALICIOUS PROSECUTION.   65

The prosecutor must, however, as the proposition itself states, act bona fide upon the advice given, if he rest his defence upon such a ground alone[1]. For example: The defendant procures the arrest of the plaintiff, having first taken the advice of legal counsel upon the facts. This advice is erroneous, and it is not acted upon in good faith, believing it to be correct; the arrest being procured for the indirect and sinister motive of compelling the plaintiff to sanction certain illegal bonds. The defendant is liable[2].

If, after taking legal advice and before the arrest, new facts come to the knowledge of the prosecutor, he cannot justify the arrest as made on advice, unless such new facts furnish further evidence of the guilt of the suspected party. If they should be of a contrary nature, casting new doubt upon the party's guilt, the prosecutor cannot safely proceed to procure an arrest except upon new advice; unless indeed the entire chain of facts in his possession shall satisfy the court that there existed a reasonable ground for his action. To make use of the advice given, when the new facts indicate that the accused is not guilty, is not to act upon the advice in good faith[3].

Again, if the only defence be that the prosecutor acted upon legal advice, a breach of duty may still be made out if it appear that the prosecutor untruly stated to the attorney the facts within his knowledge. The plaintiff's case, so far

[1] The prosecutor might plead both the advice of counsel and also the facts themselves within his knowledge; and if then it should appear that he did not act upon the advice in good faith, or that he did not state all the facts to the attorney, he would still be protected, probably, if the facts should shew a reasonable ground for the arrest.

[2] Revenga v. Mackintosh, 2 Barn. & C. 693. See Hewlett v. Cruchley, 5 Taunt. 277, 283.

[3] See Fitzjohn v. Mackinder, 9 C. B., N. S. 505, 531, Ex. Ch. Cockburn, C. J.

B. T.   5

as it rested on the proof of want of probable cause, would be established by shewing that the actual facts known to the prosecutor (differing from those on which the advice was obtained) shewed that he had no reasonable ground for instituting the prosecution.

The result is, that the defence of advice of legal counsel, to establish probable cause, must not be resorted to as a mere cover for the prosecution, but must be the result of an honest and fair purpose; and the statement made at the time by the prosecutor to his counsel must be full and true, and consistent with that purpose[1].

This defence of having acted upon legal advice is, it seems, a strict one, confined to the case of advice obtained from lawyers admitted to practise in the courts. Such persons are certified to be competent to give legal advice, and their advice when properly obtained and acted upon is conclusive of the existence of probable cause. But if the prosecutor act upon the advice of a person not a lawyer, and therefore not declared competent to give legal advice, the facts must (probably) be shewn upon which the advice was obtained, however honestly and properly it was sought and acted upon. It is not enough in America that the advice was given by an officer of the law, professing familiarity with its principles, if such a person were not a lawyer. For example: The defendant procures the arrest of the plaintiff upon advice of a justice of the peace, with whom he has been in the habit of advising on legal matters; but the justice is not a lawyer. This is not evidence of probable cause[2].

The want of probable cause cannot be inferred from mere evidence of malice, since a person may maliciously prosecute another whom he has the strongest evidence against; whom,

---

[1] Walter v. Sample, 25 Penn. St. 275.
[2] Beal v. Robeson, 8 Ired. 276 (North Carolina).

indeed, he may have caught in the commission of the crime[1]. There must be some evidence, apart from the proof of malice, indicating that the prosecutor instituted the suit under circumstances which would not have induced a cautious man to act.

It should be observed, finally, that it is necessary for the plaintiff, even in a jury case, to convince the *judge* of the want of probable cause upon the facts proved. The facts material to the question of probable cause must be found by the jury; but the judge decides whether the facts so found establish probable cause or want of it[2].

§ 4. OF MALICE.

The plaintiff, to make out a breach of duty by the defendant, must also produce evidence such as will indicate that the prosecution was instituted with malice towards the accused. Malice cannot be inferred from the mere proof of a want of probable cause[3], any more than want of probable cause can be inferred from mere proof of malice. A man may institute a prosecution against another without the least motive of malice towards him, though he had not adequate grounds for doing so.

The jury must be allowed, and it is their duty, to pass upon the question of malice as a distinct matter. There is, therefore, no such thing in the law of malicious prosecution as the implied malice or malice in law of slander and libel[4]. For example: Evidence having been introduced in an action for a malicious prosecution, which shewed that the defendant had instituted the prosecution without probable cause,

[1] Turner *v.* Ambler, 10 Q. B. 252, 257.
[2] Panton *v.* Williams, 2 Q. B. 169, Ex. Ch.; Lister *v.* Perryman, L. R. 4 H. L. 521.
[3] Vanderbilt *v.* Mathis, 5 Duer, 304; L. C. Torts, 178.
[4] Mitchell *v.* Jenkins, 5 B. & Ad. 588.

the judge instructs the jury that there are two kinds of malice, malice in law and malice in fact, and that in the present case there was malice in law because the prosecution was wrongful, being without probable cause. This is erroneous; the existence of malice is a question for the jury[1].

The evidence offered to establish the facts which go to shew the want of probable cause may, however, indicate the existence of malice; and in such a case the jury may find the existence of a malicious motive without further proof. But there must be some evidence indicating actual malice[2].

It is not necessary, however, notwithstanding the language of some of the old decisions[3], to prove the existence of an intense hostility and rancour: evidence of slight hostility, or of the existence of any sinister motive, or indirect motive of wrong, is sufficient. For example: The defendant is shewn to have displayed unnecessary zeal in a prosecution of the plaintiff, by publishing the proceedings against him. This is evidence of malice[4].

§ 5. Of Damage.

If the charge upon which the prosecution was instituted was of the commission of a charge such as (being untrue) would have constituted actionable slander had it not been preferred in court, the plaintiff, upon proof of the termina-

[1] Mitchell v. Jenkins, 5 B. & Ad. 588.
[2] Id.
[3] Savil v. Roberts, 1 Salk. 13.
[4] Chambers v. Robinson, 2 Strange, 691. See Stevens v. Midland Ry. Co. 10 Ex. 356, that by the term malice is meant any indirect motive of wrong. 'Any motive other than that of simply instituting a prosecution for the purpose of bringing a person to justice is a malicious motive.' And see Abrath v. North Eastern Ry. Co. 11 Q. B. Div. 440, 450, where Bowen, L. J. spoke of proceedings 'initiated in a malicious spirit, that is, from an indirect and improper motive, and not in furtherance of justice.'

tion of the prosecution, the want of probable cause, and malice, has made out a case, and is entitled to judgment. It is not necessary for him to prove that he has sustained any pecuniary damage. For example: The defendant causes the plaintiff to be indicted for the stealing of a cow, falsely, without probable cause, and of malice. The plaintiff is entitled to recover without producing evidence that he has sustained any actual damage[1].

But it has been decided that it is only for the prosecution of a charge the verbal imputation of which in pais would constitute actionable slander that the mere institution of the prosecution can be actionable without specific damage[2]. For example: The defendant falsely prefers against the plaintiff a simple charge of assault and battery, without cause and with malice. The plaintiff cannot recover for a malicious prosecution without proof of actual pecuniary damage[3].

It follows that this action for a malicious prosecution cannot be maintained without proof of damage when the prosecutor has procured the indictment of the plaintiff for the commission of that which is not a criminal offence. For example: The defendant procures the plaintiff to be indicted for the killing of the former's cattle. The plaintiff must prove special damage; the offence, though charged as a crime, being only a trespass[4].

§ 6. OF ANALOGOUS WRONGS.

If the prosecution fail by reason of the circumstance that

[1] See Byne *v.* Moore, 5 Taunt. 187, Mansfield, C. J.; s. c. L. C. Torts, 181; Frierson *v.* Hewitt, 2 Hill, 499 (South Carolina).
[2] Byne *v.* Moore, supra. See Quartz Hill Mining Co. *v.* Eyre, 21 Q. B. Div. 674, 692.
[3] Byne *v.* Moore, supra.
[4] Frierson *v.* Hewitt, supra.

the court in issuing its warrant exceeded its jurisdiction, or that the warrant or indictment was defective, it might not be clear in principle whether the accused should sue for malicious prosecution or for slander; supposing the charge to have been defamatory. It would give him an obvious advantage to sue for slander since then he would not be compelled to prove a want of probable cause or the existence of malice; and the proper remedy is deemed to be an action for malicious prosecution[1].

In this connection attention should be directed to actions for abuse of the process of the courts. An action is given by law for such an act without requiring the plaintiff to prove either the termination of the proceeding in which the abuse of process has taken place, or the want of probable cause for instituting that proceeding. For example: The defendant under process of the court in an action for a debt not due, procures the plaintiff through duress to deliver valuable property (a ship's register) to him. The defendant is liable in damages, without evidence of the termination of the suit or of the want of probable cause[2]. Nor (probably) need malice be proved[3].

To maintain such an action, however, the plaintiff's case must be something other than a proceeding for a malicious prosecution. The ground of action must be, not a false prosecution (that is, a prosecution upon an accusation which has been tried and not sustained), but an unlawful use of legal process; and such an act may be committed as well in the course of a well-founded prosecution as in a false one.

[1] Pippet v. Hearn, 5 B. & Ald. 634.
[2] Grainger v. Hill, 4 Bing. N. C. 212; s. c. L. C. Torts, 184.
[3] No question was raised on this point in Grainger v. Hill, supra; but there can be no doubt of the correctness of the statement of the text, if the action was not in reality for a malicious prosecution.

CHAP. II.]   MALICIOUS PROSECUTION.   71

If the wrong suffered consist in an unlawful arrest, the action will be for a false imprisonment, of which hereafter, or for a malicious arrest[1]; if it consist in an unlawful extortion of a contract or of property, the action will in substance be for duress, an example of which has already been given[2]. Other instances may be found in actions for malicious issuance of a warrant[3], the levying of an execution for more than is due[4], and the malicious causing an extent to issue against one on behalf of the Crown[5]. These are cases of the wrongful resort to, rather than of abuse of process.

Recent decisions have also brought to light the existence of a right of action for maintenance[6]. This is a tort founded upon early statutes making maintenance a criminal offence[7]; an action for damages being permitted only where the defendant has aided the prosecution of some suit in which he had no interest, or, it seems, motive other than that of stirring up or keeping alive strife. It has lately been decided that if the defendant's action was based on charity, reasonable or not, the action will fail[8].

[1] Jenings v. Florence, 2 C. B., N. S. 467. See 32 & 33 Vict. c. 62, § 18; Daniels v. Fielding, 16 M. & W. 200; Gibbons v Alison, 3 C. B. 181.

[2] In case a contract were thus obtained, the injured party could elect to affirm the validity of the contract, and sue for the duress, or he could deny the validity of the agreement, and plead the duress in an action upon it.

[3] Cooper v. Booth, 3 Esp. 135; Phillips v. Naylor, 4 H. & N. 565.

[4] Churchill v. Siggers, 3 El. & B. 938; Jenings v. Florence, supra.

[5] Craig v. Hasell, 4 Q. B. 481.

[6] Bradlaugh v. Newdegate, 11 Q. B. D. 1; Harris v. Brisco, 17 Q. B. Div. 504; Metropolitan Bank v. Pooley, 10 App. Cas. 210.

[7] It is doubtful if a corporation can be liable for the offence. 10 App. Cas. at p. 218, Lord Selborne.

[8] Harris v. Brisco, supra.

CHAPTER III.

CONSPIRACY.

§ 1. INTRODUCTORY.

Statement of the duty. A owes to B the duty to forbear to carry out, wholly or partly, against him, to his damage, any unlawful conspiracy entered into with C.

The law of conspiracy, in its civil aspect, has been treated as a branch of the law of malicious prosecution; and with that subject it has, indeed, in one of its features, a close connexion. Civil actions for conspiracy were formerly instituted, in most cases, for redress on account of unlawful combinations for instituting criminal prosecutions of the grade of felony. Combinations for other unlawful purposes were redressed in other forms of actions; generally, it appears, in an action of deceit, sometimes, however, in an action of trespass.

Distinct and peculiar rules of law prevailed in former times concerning conspiracies of the first-named class. A writ of conspiracy could be sustained only by proof of an actual combination to indict the plaintiff of felony, with the other elements of an action for malicious prosecution. Failure to prove the combination was fatal, even though enough were proved to establish a right of action for a simple false prosecution. The action for the latter offence was a distinct proceeding. In later times the writ of conspiracy was employed for the redress of prosecutions below the grade of felony; and then it came to be considered unnecessary, in such an action, to establish an actual combination, notwithstanding the allegation of conspiracy. The law, however, relating to prosecutions for *felony* remained as before, and the plaintiff failed if the evidence shewed that the prosecution was instituted or procured by but one person[1].

This distinction, however, has in modern times become obsolete. An action for an alleged conspiracy can now be maintained in any case otherwise proper, though the plaintiff be unable to prove that the unlawful act complained of was undertaken by more than one person[2]. The result is, that conspiracy as a ground of civil liability has nearly disappeared from the English law[3], leaving little else than a phase of agency. The existence, then, of an actual conspiracy being unnecessary to the plaintiff's action, nothing remains, if he prove against but one person, except that which would be the ground of action against that person had he been alone sued. The case would then be nothing more than an action for deceit, malicious prosecution, false imprisonment, or other like tort, according to the nature of the wrong actually provable.

But it would hardly be satisfactory to leave the subject here. If it be said of conspiracy, as it may be, that it is no longer the ground of civil redress even when damage has followed, it may be answered that the same is true of malice

[1] See upon this subject the historical notes on malicious prosecution and conspiracy, in the author's Leading Cases on Torts, pp. 190—196, 210—214.

[2] Savill *v.* Roberts, 1 Lord Raym. 374, 379; 1 Saund. 230, note; Mogul Shipping Co. *v.* McGregor, coram Lord Coleridge, Aug. 1888; Hutchins *v.* Hutchins, L. C. Torts, 207.

[3] The case is different with criminal liability; that remains a great branch of the law.

generally; nor is fraud alone a ground of liability. And though conspiracy may not be an element of liability in the same sense that either of these may be, still there are cases where the defendant's liability turns wholly upon the question of the existence of a conspiracy and his participation therein. It may become important then to know whether in a particular case there has been a conspiracy.

There are, indeed, three phases of the subject which make it important to consider conspiracy in a book on torts. First, the plaintiff may have so stated his case against a defendant, who did not in fact participate in the doing of the harm complained of, as to be unable to recover with evidence of anything, such as an ordinary agency, short of conspiracy[1]; the existence of a conspiracy has then become an element of *his* case. Secondly, the case may be such that no damage could be inflicted, in rerum natura, without an unlawful combination[2]. Thirdly, it may be that in a case turning on malice, e.g. a case of malicious prosecution, the only means of proving the malice is to prove a conspiracy.

§ 2. Of Malice and the Combination.

In the sense of the existing law, a conspiracy is simply a confederacy or combination of two or more persons to commit an unlawful act, or to do a lawful act in an unlawful manner. The wrong is a phase of malice; the conspiracy itself constituting, or at least forming evidence of, the malice alleged by the plaintiff[3].

To make a party liable with others for a conspiracy resulting in damage, he must either have originally colluded with the rest, or afterwards joined them as an associate, or

---

[1] See Gregory v. Brunswick, 6 Man. & G. 953, 959.
[2] Id.
[3] Id. 205, 953.

actually participated in the execution of the scheme, or afterwards adopted it. A defendant cannot be found guilty by evidence of mere silent observation, even with approval, of the conspiracy. For example: The defendant is shewn to have been cognizant of, and to have (silently) approved, the unlawful enticing away of the plaintiff's daughter. This is not sufficient to establish a conspiracy and breach of duty; the defendant not having thereby become a party to the plot[1].

Nor is it material, where the object of the unlawful combination is plunder and gain to the conspirators, that some of them derive no benefit from the execution of the scheme. They are equally liable, though the overt acts were committed by others who refused to divide, or failed to obtain, the spoil. For example: Several agents, of whom the defendant is one, conspire to injure their common principal, and succeed; the defendant is liable though he derives no benefit from the success[2].

It is equally well settled that though there was no intention of making a profit out of the scheme, but only a desire to harass and inflict loss upon the plaintiff, the action is maintainable. For example: The defendant, an attorney, knowing that his client has no just claim against the plaintiff, maliciously and without probable cause, procures, in concert with his client, an arrest and civil prosecution of the plaintiff. The defendant is liable for the damage sustained by the plaintiff[3].

Again, as has already been suggested, there may be cases in which the wrong could not be done without an unlawful combination; in such a case proof of conspiracy must, it seems, be made. Thus, one man alone could hardly

[1] Brannock v. Bouldin, 4 Ired. 61 (North Carolina).
[2] Walsham v. Stainton, 1 De G. J. & S. 678.
[3] Stockley v. Hornidge, 8 Car. & P. 11.

succeed in hissing an actor off the stage; and though others might join him, there would probably be no redress, however unjust the act. But preconcert would make a different case. For example: The defendant and others conspire to prevent the plaintiff, an actor, from performing at a theatre, and, in pursuance of the conspiracy, employ others to go to the theatre and interrupt the plaintiff in his part, and the plan is carried out, to the damage of the plaintiff. The defendant is liable[1].

§ 3. OF DAMAGE.

It is of the essence of liability for conspiracy, when conspiracy is made a ground of civil action, that it cause damage. For example: The defendants are alleged to have conspired together, maliciously and without probable cause, to institute, and to have instituted, an action against the present plaintiff in the name of a third person, for their benefit. No damage is alleged. The plaintiff cannot recover[2].

[1] Gregory v. Brunswick, 6 Man. & G. 205, 953.
[2] Cotterell v. Jones, 11 C. B. 713.

CHAPTER IV.

MALICIOUS INTERFERENCE WITH CONTRACT.

§ 1. INTRODUCTORY.

Statement of the duty. A owes to B the duty to forbear to induce, maliciously, C to break a contract between B and C (to B's special damage?).

§ 2. OF MALICE.

The subject of malicious interference with the contracts of others, causing a breach of them, is a tort of but recent distinct and settled recognition. To entice away a servant from his master has been wrongful from early times[1]; but that is a statutory doctrine[2], peculiar, it seems, to the case of servants who labour with their hands[3]. In such cases it is not necessary that the act of the defendant should have been malicious.

Since the year 1853 it has been held that for a third person maliciously to induce a party to a contract to break his undertaking is actionable, at least if damage ensue. For example: W is under an engagement with the plaintiff

[1] See Lumley v. Gye, 2 El. & B. 216; s. c. L. C. Torts, 306. This case is an epitome of the history of the whole subject. See especially the dissenting opinion of Mr Justice Coleridge.

[2] Statute of Labourers, 23 Edw. 3.

[3] Wightman, J. in Lumley v. Gye; Bowen v. Hall, 6 Q. B. Div. 333.

to sing exclusively at his theatre for a certain season. The defendant 'maliciously intending to injure the plaintiff' induces W to break her contract and refuse to sing for the plaintiff during the time agreed upon. This is a breach of duty[1].

What the term 'malice' means in such a case was not left quite clear by the case cited. An expression of Mr Justice Crompton in that case might indicate that to cause the breach with notice of the existence of the contract would be sufficient to constitute malice[2]; but that would be to put a dangerous check upon common and generally deemed lawful acts of competition, and something more than this has accordingly been deemed necessary[3]. In a late reconsideration of the subject in a similar case of contract for exclusive services, not manual, the Court of Appeal treated malice as a necessary part of the plaintiff's case, and considered the term as meaning that the defendant must have sought to induce the party to break his contract 'for the indirect purpose of injuring the plaintiff, or of benefiting the defendant at the expense of the plaintiff[4].' A malicious act of that kind was held to be a wrongful act[5]. This appears to mean that the act is shewn to be wrongful if the plaintiff shews that it was done without any just motive, or without the existence of any right[6].

[1] Lumley v. Gye, supra.

[2] 'It must now be considered clear law that a person who wrongfully and maliciously, or, which is the *same thing*, with notice, interrupts the relation subsisting between master and servant,' &c.

[3] See Pollock, Torts, 452, where the point is strongly urged.

[4] Bowen v. Hall, 6 Q. B. Div. 333, 338, Lord Esher; Lord Coleridge dissenting. The argument that the damage was caused, not by the defendant, but by the party who broke his contract, was answered by Lord Esher's saying that the result was both intended and brought about by the defendant.   [5] Id.

[6] See Walker v. Cronin, 107 Mass. 555, 562, 564. Welles, J. for

§ 3. OF DAMAGE.

Whether other damage than that of the breach of the contract is necessary has not been clearly determined; though there is intimation that it is[1]. It is enough to constitute damage, however, at least in America, that a service for no fixed time, and therefore at will, has been interrupted. For example: The defendant maliciously induces journeymen shoemakers to leave the plaintiff's employment. This is a breach of duty, for the plaintiff was entitled to the fruits and advantages to arise from a continuance of the employment[2].

It will be seen that in the example given there is not so much as a breach of contract, for the shoemakers, being journeymen, had a right to leave at any time. There was, however, legal damage because the plaintiff had a right to receive their services, without interference by others, so long as they were disposed to give them; he would have a right against others to the enjoyment of their services even as a gratuity[3]. It is doubtful, however, whether interference with such a right, or with that in the example, could, in itself, be considered special damage. There may be ground then for considering the question as

the court: 'Every one has a right to enjoy the fruits and advantages of his own enterprise, skill, and credit. He has no right to be protected against competition; but he has a right to be free from malicious and wanton interference, disturbance, or annoyance. If disturbance or loss comes...from the merely wanton or malicious acts of others, without the justification of competition or the service of any interest or lawful purpose, it then' is unlawful.

[1] See Bowen v. Hall, 6 Q. B. Div. 333, 337; Pollock, Torts, 451, 452. Special damage was alleged in Lumley v. Gye, and shewn in Bowen v. Hall.
[2] Walker v. Cronin, 107 Mass. 555.
[3] See post, Part II. ch. III. § 3; ante, p. 12, in Introduction.

still an open one, whether for the purposes of this action special damage must be proved[1].

§ 4. Conclusion: Contract not Property.

What has been said in exposition of the statement of the duty in question will, regardless of the question of special damage, serve to shew, when read in contrast with cases of wrongs to property in the ordinary sense, that contract is not treated as property, though the first impression from the subject might be that it was. The distinction between rights of property and rights of contract is not impugned. The former are absolute, and breach of them is a breach therefore of an absolute duty; that is to say, it is not necessary to consider the motive with which an interference with a right of property takes place. Nor indeed is special damage necessary to constitute the tort.

[1] Walker v. Cronin, however, is within the Statute of Labourers, and the courts may think it best in other cases to require proof of special damage.

CHAPTER V.

SLANDER AND LIBEL.

§ 1. INTRODUCTORY.

Statement of the duty. A owes to B the duty to forbear to publish of B (1) defamation in its nature actionable per se, (2) defamation in its nature not actionable per se to the damage of B.

1. Defamation is any language or representation, oral or written, tending to bring the person of whom it is published into hatred, ridicule, or disgrace, or to injure him in respect of his vocation.

2. The term 'representation' is here used to denote painting, picture, sign, or effigy.

3. Slander is oral defamation.

4. Libel is defamation by writing, printing, or representation.

5. Publication is the making defamation known to a third person.

6. Whenever language is spoken of as defamatory it is understood to be false.

7. What the phrase 'defamation in its nature actionable per se' means will be made known by the proposition of law following, and the consideration of its parts.

The general proposition of law is, that the first of the two above-stated duties is violated by A by the publication of words, language, or representations of a false and defama-

tory character concerning B, in either of the following ways:
(1) where A imputes to B the commission of a criminal
offence punishable by imprisonment, or other corporal
penalty, in the first instance[1]; (2) where he imputes to
B the having a contagious or infectious disease of a disgraceful kind; (3) where he makes an imputation concerning
B in respect of his office, business, or occupation; (4) where
he makes an imputation concerning B tending to disinherit
him; (5) where the defamation is a libel. Each of these
classes of defamation must be examined.

§ 2. OF THE INTERPRETATION OF LANGUAGE.

Before proceeding to the consideration of any of these
classes of breaches of duty, it should be observed that, subject perhaps to one exception, the language or representation
complained of is to be understood presumptively in its
natural and usual sense, i.e. in the sense in which the persons
who heard or read or saw it, as men of ordinary intelligence,
would understand it[2]. It is not to be construed in a milder
sense (mitiori sensu) merely because it is capable, by a forced
construction, of being interpreted in an innocent sense.
For example: The defendant publishes of the plaintiff the
following words: "You are guilty of the death of D." This
is an imputation of the commission of murder, and is not
to be construed mitiori sensu[3].

[1] Pollock, Torts, 209. It is not enough that the offence is punishable by 'fine in the first instance, with possible imprisonment in default of payment'. Id., referring to Webb v. Beavan, 11 Q. B. D. 609. The offence charged need not be indictable. Webb v. Beavan.

[2] Hankinson v. Bilby, 16 M. & W. 442; Simmons v. Mitchell, 6 App. Cas. 156. Whether the words are legally defamatory or not is, commonly at least, a question of law. Capital Bank v. Henty, 7 App. Cas. 741.

[3] Peake v. Oldham, 1 Cowp. 275; s. c. L. C. Torts, 73.

CHAP. V.]   SLANDER AND LIBEL.   83

It should, however, be clear, in order to make language actionable without proof of damage, that the imputation was slanderous or libellous (according to its nature) within the meaning of some one of the above-stated five classes. If this be not the case it will not be deemed a breach of the duty; and this too whether the question of interpretation come before the court or before the jury. In one case, at least, the interpretation adopted has been apparently contrary to the understanding of men of ordinary intelligence; and that is where an imputation is made of what would ordinarily be understood as a crime, but the language of which does not necessarily import a crime in the legal sense. Such at least is the case in America. For example: The defendant publishes of the plaintiff the following words: 'He has taken a false oath against me in Squire Jamison's court.' This is deemed not to be an imputation of the commission of perjury[1]; the term 'perjury' signifying the taking of a false oath knowingly, before a court of justice, with reference to a cause pending.

Apart from this particular exception in regard to the legal sense of a crime, it follows from what has been said that it is immaterial whether the defamatory charge be affirmative and direct, or indirect so as to be matter of inference merely, or that it is ironical, or that it is made in allegory or other artful disguise. It is enough that the charge would naturally be understood to be defamatory by men of average intelligence.

[1] Ward v. Clark, 2 Johns. 10; s. c. L. C. Torts, 81. 'The offence need not be specified...at all if the words impute felony generally. But if particulars are given, they must be legally consistent with the offence imputed.' Pollock, Torts, 210, referring to Jackson v. Adams, 2 Bing. N. C. 402.

84   LAW OF TORTS.   [PART I.

§ 3. OF THE PUBLICATION OF DEFAMATION AND SPECIAL DAMAGE.

In accordance with observation 5, supra, it should be noticed that defamation is not published when addressed only to the plaintiff[1]. That is, the language or representation cannot in such a case be actionable. And this is true, though the alleged wrong be directly followed by great dejection of mind on the part of the plaintiff, and consequent sickness and inability to carry on his usual vocation, and expense attending upon his restoration to health or upon the employment of help to carry on his business. For example: The defendant says to the plaintiff, 'You stole my horse.' The plaintiff, a farmer, suffers immediate distress of mind and body, becomes sick and unable to attend to his work, his crops suffer, and he is compelled to employ extra help to carry on necessary work. The defendant has not violated any legal duty to the plaintiff[2].

Indeed, if the language or representation complained of be not actionable per se (that is, if it be not actionable without the proof of some special damage), the fact that the publication of the defamation occurred in the presence of a third person who (by authority) reported it to the plaintiff with such a result as that stated in the foregoing example, would not make the defamer liable[3].

This, however, proceeds upon the ground that the effect of distress merely is not such damage as the law regards when the defamation is not actionable per se. The rule of

[1] Communication of defamation by the defendant to his wife is not publication. Wennhak v. Morgan, 20 Q. B. D. 635.
[2] Compare Terwilliger v. Wands, 17 N. Y. 54, 63, and Wilson v. Goit, Id. 442, which, taken together, justify the example.
[3] Terwilliger v. Wands, 17 N. Y. 54, 63, reaffirmed in Wilson v. Goit, Id. 442, and overruling Bradt v. Towsley, 13 Wend. 253, and Fuller v. Fenner, 16 Barb. 333.

law upon this subject is, that defamation not actionable per se (that is, defamation not included under any of the five heads) may be a breach of duty if it be attended with special damage. But special damage (and damage of a general nature as well) must be the natural and usual result of the wrong complained of, just as effect follows a true cause; and, in relation to defamation, it is deemed that nothing else than damage resulting from injury to *character* comes within the principle. Damage resulting from *fear* of injury to character, or from wounded feelings, is not alone damage to character, since character can only be injured when it has been defamed before a third person, except in that it may have been injured in the eyes of the defendant himself; but for this the defendant is not legally liable.

The damage complained of must then in all cases, whether general or special, have been sustained through the action of a third person. Special damage may so result in several ways, so as to make the publication of defamation actionable when it would not be actionable per se; as by the loss of a marriage. For example: The defendant charges the plaintiff, an unmarried female, with unchastity in the presence and hearing of C, to whom the plaintiff is engaged to be married. C, in consequence of the charge, immediately terminates the engagement. The defendant is liable to the plaintiff[1].

The same would be true of the loss of the consortium of a husband[2]. The same would also be true of the refusal to the plaintiff of civil entertainment at a public-house[3]. So of the fact that the plaintiff has been turned away from the house of her uncle, and charged not to return until she

[1] See Terwilliger *v.* Wands, 17 N. Y. 54, 60.
[2] Lynch *v.* Knight, 9 H. L. Cas. 577.
[3] Olmsted *v.* Miller, 1 Wend. 506 (N. Y.). See Moore *v.* Meagher, 1 Taunt. 39.

shall have cleared up her character¹; and so in general of the loss by the plaintiff even of gratuitious hospitable entertainment².

The peculiarity of the law of slander and libel arises, however, in the case of defamation actionable per se; and the consideration of the special phases of such defamation will now follow. But let it be again observed, that in defamation arising under any of the heads now to be separately examined, the plaintiff establishes the breach of duty, and consequently his right to recover, without proof of damage³.

§ 4. OF THE IMPUTATION OF HAVING COMMITTED A CRIME.

The authorities are not altogether in harmony in regard to the question whether it is necessary that the charge, if true, would subject the object of it to punishment, or whether the test in this particular is the degradation involved; but the weight of authority favours the latter as the test, assuming that the offence charged is in law a crime. Although, then, the charge shew that the punishment has already been suffered, and do not render the plaintiff liable to indictment, the degradation involved in the (false) accusation renders the defendant liable. For example: The defendant says of the plaintiff, 'Robert Carpenter [the plaintiff] was in Winchester jail, and tried for his life, and would have been hanged had it not been for L, for breaking open the granary of farmer A, and stealing his bacon.' The defendant is liable⁴. Again: The defendant says of the plaintiff, 'He was arraigned at Warwick for stealing of twelve hogs, and, if he had not made good friends, it

[1] Williams v. Hill, 19 Wend. 305 (N. Y.).
[2] Id.; Moore v. Meagher, 1 Taunt. 39.
[3] Webb v. Beavan, 11 Q. B. D. 609.
[4] Carpenter v. Tarrant, Cas. Temp. Hardw. 339. The words were false.

had gone hard with him.' The defendant is liable[1]. Again: The defendant says of the plaintiff, 'He is a convict, and has been in the Ohio penitentiary.' The plaintiff is entitled to maintain an action, the words being false[2].

§ 5. OF THE IMPUTATION OF HAVING A CONTAGIOUS OR INFECTIOUS DISEASE OF A DISGRACEFUL KIND.

By the early common law a charge to come under this head must have been of the having the leprosy, or the plague, or the syphilis. At the present time the duty has come to be so far enlarged as to require the forbearance from publishing false accusations concerning another of the having any disease of a contagious or infectious nature involving disgrace. For example: The defendant falsely charges the plaintiff with having the gonorrhœa. This is actionable per se[3].

This doctrine of law proceeds upon the ground that charges of such a kind tend to exclude a person from society; and the rule requires the charge to be made in the present tense. To accuse another of the having had a disgraceful disease is not actionable without proof of special damage. For example: The defendant says of the plaintiff, 'She has *had* the pox.' The defendant is not liable though the charge be false, unless the plaintiff prove some specific damage[4].

[1] Halley *v.* Stanton, Croke Car. 268. The words were false.
[2] Smith *v.* Stewart, 5 Barr, 372 (Penn.). It would be otherwise if the words were true. Baum *v.* Clause, 5 Hill, 199 (N. Y.). A person is no longer a felon after suffering the punishment of felony; so that the fact that he was once a felon would not sustain a plea of the truth of a charge of felony. Leyman *v.* Latimer, 3 Ex. Div. 352.
[3] Watson *v.* McCarthy, 2 Kelly, 57, an American authority. See Bloodworth *v.* Gray, 7 Man. & G. 334.
[4] See Carslake *v.* Mapledoram, 2 T. R. 473; s. c. L. C. Torts, 84.

§ 6. OF AN IMPUTATION AFFECTING THE PLAINTIFF IN HIS OFFICE, BUSINESS, OR OCCUPATION.

In order that defamation arising under this head alone should be actionable per se, it should have a natural tendency to injure the party complaining, in his occupation. It is not enough that it may possibly so injure him. If it has not a natural tendency to injure him in this respect, that is, if it would not be the usual effect of the charge to injure the plaintiff in his occupation, as by causing removal, the plaintiff cannot recover without proving a special damage. For example: The defendant publishes of the plaintiff, a clerk to a gas-light company, the words, 'You are a disgrace to the town, unfit to hold your situation for your conduct with harlots. You are a disgrace to the situation you hold.' The plaintiff cannot recover without proof of actual damage, the language not having a natural tendency to cause the plaintiff's discharge from his employment[1].

Defamation has a natural tendency to injure the plaintiff in his office, business, or occupation, within the meaning of the rule, when it strikes at his qualification for the performance of the duties of his situation, or when it alleges some misconduct or negligence in the course of transacting these duties[2]. For example: The defendant charges the plaintiff, a clergyman, holding the office of pastor of a church, with incontinence. This may be ground of an action[3]. Again: The defendant says of the plaintiff, a lawyer, the words having relation to the plaintiff's professional qualifications, 'He is a dunce.' This

---

[1] Lumby v. Allday, 1 Tyrwh. 217; s. c. L. C. Torts, 87.
[2] Id.
[3] Gallwey v. Marshall, 9 Ex. 294.

may perhaps be treated as a breach of the defendant's legal duty to the plaintiff[1].

When the defamation complained of does not shew on its face that it was published of the plaintiff in relation to his occupation, this must be made to appear[2]; though even then, as has been stated, the defamation will not be actionable unless it had a natural tendency to injure the plaintiff in his occupation, in the sense already explained. In cases, however, in which the imputation is alleged to have been made of the plaintiff in his occupation, when the same does not have the natural tendency mentioned, it may be shewn by the plaintiff that the defamation *was* published under circumstances which bring the case within the rule of liability. But without such evidence, the plaintiff must fail. For example: The defendant charges the plaintiff, as a physician, with incontinence. This does not imply disqualification, or necessarily professional misconduct; and, without evidence connecting the imputation with the plaintiff's professional conduct, he cannot recover[3].

If the imputation in itself come within the rule of liability under this head, it matters not that it was published of a servant, even one acting in a menial capacity. For example: The defendant utters the following of the plaintiff, a menial servant, before the latter's master, 'Thou art a cozening knave, and hast cozened thy master of a bushel of barley.' The defendant is liable to the plaintiff, the imputation being false[4].

It is probably actionable to impute disqualification of a

[1] Peard *v.* Jones, Croke Car. 382. It is doubtful whether a court would now treat such a statement as actionable.
[2] Ayre *v.* Craven, 2 Ad. & E. 2.
[3] Id.
[4] Seaman *v.* Bigg, Croke Car. 480.

person holding a merely honorary or confidential office, not of emolument[1]. It certainly is so to impute to such a person misconduct in the office[2]. For example: The defendant says of the plaintiff, who holds a public office of mere honour, 'You are a rascal, a villain, and a liar.' This is a breach of the duty under consideration[3].

In all cases included under the present section, it is necessary that the plaintiff should have been in the exercise of the duties of the particular vocation at the time of the alleged publication of the defamation[4]. For example: The defendant says of the plaintiff, who had been a lessee of tolls at the time referred to by the defendant, 'He was wanted at T; he was a defaulter there.' The words are not actionable per se[5].

§ 7. OF AN IMPUTATION TENDING TO DISINHERIT THE PLAINTIFF.

If the words tend to impeach a present title of the plaintiff, the action, though commonly called an action for *slander* of title, is not properly speaking an action of slander: as has already been stated, such a case is simply an action for deceit, to be governed by the rules of law prevailing upon that subject[6].

Cases of actions for defamation tending to defeat an expected title are rare, and appear to have been confined to charges impeaching the legitimacy of birth of an heir

---

[1] Onslow v. Horne, 3 Wils. 186.
[2] Id.
[3] Aston v. Blagrave, Strange, 617.
[4] Bellamy v. Burch, 16 M. & W. 590; Gallwey v. Marshall, 9 Ex. 294.
[5] Bellamy v. Burch, supra. Some of the old cases are contra, but they were overruled.
[6] See ante, p. 47.

apparent. Such an imputation has been deemed actionable, as being likely to cause the plaintiff's disherison. For example: The defendant publishes of the plaintiff, an heir apparent to estates, the words, 'Thou art a bastard.' The defendant is liable without proof of special damage[1].

§ 8. OF AN IMPUTATION CONVEYED BY WRITING, PRINTING, OR REPRESENTATION; THAT IS, OF LIBEL.

The four preceding sections exhaust the possible heads of oral defamation, actionable per se; that is, of slander. Libellous defamation may also be conveyed in any of the four ways above considered; but it may also be conveyed in other ways. A libel is a writing, print, picture or effigy, calculated to bring one into hatred, ridicule, or disgrace.

The definition shews that the law of libel is of wider extent than that of slander. Many words when written or printed become actionable per se which, if they had been orally published, would not have been actionable without proof of actual damage. And, besides these, there is the whole class of defamatory representations, such as picture and effigy, which in their nature are incapable of oral publication. Whether the distinction is well founded or not, the manner of the publication, as libel, makes it actionable[2]. For example: The defendant writes and publishes of the plaintiff the following: 'I sincerely pity the man that can so far forget what is due not only to himself, but to others, who, under the cloak of religious and spiritual reform, hypocritically, and with the grossest impurity, deals out his malice, uncharitableness, and falsehoods.' The plaintiff can maintain an action for libel[3]. Again: The defendant prints the following of the plaintiff: 'Our army swore

[1] Humphrys v. Stanfeild, Croke Car. 469.
[2] Thorley v. Kerry, 4 Taunt. 355; s. c. L. C. Torts, 90.
[3] Thorley v. Kerry, supra.

terribly in Flanders, said Uncle Toby; and if Toby was here now, he might say the same of some modern swearers. The man at the sign of the Bible [the plaintiff] is no slouch at swearing to an old story.' The imputation is libellous, though not importing perjury[1]. Again: The defendant prints the following of the plaintiff: 'Mr. Cooper [the plaintiff] will have to bring his action to trial somewhere. He will not like to bring it in New York, for we are known here, nor in Otsego, for he is known there.' The publication of this language is deemed libellous[2].

At common law, no immunity is conferred upon the proprietors, publishers, or editors of books, newspapers, or other prints, for the publication of defamation. They are liable for the publication of libellous matter in their prints, though the publication may have been made without their knowledge or against their orders[3]. This is not true of newsvendors[4]. And it is held in America that if the alleged libel were of such a nature that a man of common intelligence could not know that it was intended for a libel, and it was not in fact known that it was, neither the editor nor the proprietor of the printing establishment, or of the print, would be liable[5].

§ 9. OF THE TRUTH OF THE CHARGE.

The truth of the charge, whether it was made orally or by printed or written language, is in English law a good defence to an action for the publication of alleged defamation, though malicious and not reasonably believed to be true, at least if oral. Evidence of such a fact shews,

[1] Steele v. Southwick, 9 Johns. 214 (N. Y.).
[2] Cooper v. Greeley, 1 Denio, 347 (N. Y.).
[3] A Libel Law Amendment Bill touching newspapers is pending now.
[4] Emmens v. Pottle, 16 Q. B. Div. 354.
[5] Smith v. Ashley, 11 Met. 367 (Mass.).

indeed, that the charge is not defamatory. A person has no right to a false character; and his real character suffers no damage, such at least as the law recognizes, from speaking the truth.

This rule appears to go to the extent of justifying a party in publishing of another the fact that he has suffered the penalty of the law for the commission of crime, even though he may have been pardoned therefor and have since become a good and respectable citizen. For example: The defendant publishes of the plaintiff the statement that the latter had several years ago stolen an axe. That is true, though, after conviction thereof, the plaintiff was pardoned, and has since become a trusted citizen and an office-holder. The accusation is deemed justifiable in law[1].

Belief in the truth of the accusation, however, is not a defence[2], though it is provable in mitigation of damages[3]. And this is equally true of the editors and publishers of books, newspapers, or periodicals, as of other persons[4].

The truth of effigy, picture, or sign, so far as such may relate to the physical person of the party intended, and not to his character, is (probably) no justification of a malicious publication. A man is not responsible for his physical peculiarities, and may well invoke the protection of the courts against one who will parade them before the public.

§ 10. OF MALICE AND PRIVILEGED COMMUNICATIONS.

To constitute slander or libel, it used to be said that malice was necessary; but malice in this connexion was, and still is sometimes, spoken of as of two kinds, malice in

[1] Baum v. Clause, 5 Hill, 199 (N. Y.). See Rex v. Burdett, 4 B. & Ald. 314, 325.
[2] Campbell v. Spottiswoode, 3 Best & S. 769.
[3] Odgers, Slander, 302, 589.
[4] Campbell v. Spottiswoode, supra.

law and malice in fact. The first is presumptive; the second is actual[1]. Actual malice is not necessary to the plaintiff's case; and if it is still important for any purpose to retain the old form of statement, it may be said that malice is presumed in all cases of legal slander or libel; but the effect of the presumption may sometimes be avoided in law, and then the plaintiff can recover only upon proof of actual malice. The effect of the presumption may be thus stated: The publication of defamation is presumed to have been done of malice, and justifies a verdict for the person defamed without further proof. For example: The defendant goes to the plaintiff's relatives and falsely charges him with theft. This is sufficient to justify a verdict for the plaintiff: he need not offer evidence to establish malice. Further, the defendant would not be permitted to *deny* that the charge was made maliciously, whatever the fact[2].

If this were all, the result would be that, unless the defendant could prove the truth of the charge, he would be liable. But this would be to lay an embargo upon the freedom of speech hardly to be tolerated. There are circumstances under which men must, humanly speaking, speak without danger their convictions, however erroneous; the law could not but permit it, and does permit. In permitting, there is no denial of malice; there is no malice, as has just been said, to deny. The plaintiff's case has merely been avoided by matter of justification; the facts are admitted, but ground is shewn why the plaintiff should not avail himself of them.

There are, in a word, occasions in which certain per-

---

[1] Actual malice appears to be treated as a subjective conception; that is, as a motive. See Abrath *v.* North-Eastern Ry. Co. 11 App. Cas. 247, 251, Lord Bramwell; ante, chapter 2, § 4. But see Holmes, Common Law, chapter 4. Malice in law is a pure fiction.

[2] Hooper *v.* Truscott, 2 Bing. N. C. 457; s. c. 2 Scott, 672.

sons[1] are excused for publishing what would otherwise be actionable defamation. The publication of the charge or representation in such cases is in legal language said to be privileged; the charge or representation itself being termed a privileged communication.

Privileged communications are of two kinds; absolutely privileged and prima facie privileged communications. A communication is absolutely privileged when the fact that it was published with actual, provable malice, that is, malice in fact, is immaterial, not affecting the excuse. In other words, a communication is absolutely privileged when evidence that it was published with actual malice is not admissible. A communication is prima facie privileged when evidence on the part of the plaintiff *is* admissible to shew that the communication was published with actual malice. In the former case, the defence is a perfect one and cannot be disturbed; in the latter, it is perfect, provided evidence of malice be not offered by the plaintiff.

Under the head of absolutely privileged communications, there are several classes of cases. First of these in importance come statements made in the course of judicial proceedings. Whatever is said orally, or stated in writing, in the course of such proceedings by those concerned therein, is absolutely privileged; this in the interest of freedom and independence in the administration of justice. It matters not, so that the language was used in the course of judicial proceedings, whether it was material or relevant; it is deemed to be against public policy to permit any inquiry in regard to that[2]. It is enough if it relates to the cause

[1] Merivale *v.* Carson, 20 Q. B. Div. 275, 280, Lord Esher.
[2] Munster *v.* Lamb, 11 Q. B. Div. 588 (counsel); Scott *v.* Stansfield, L. R. 3 Ex. 220 (judge); Seaman *v.* Netherclift, 2 C. P. Div. 53 (witness); Henderson *v.* Broomhead, 4 H. & N. 569 (statements in pleadings); Dunham *v.* Powers, 42 Vermont, 1 (jury men).

before the court. For example: Counsel for the defendant, in the course of arguing a criminal cause, makes base insinuations against the prosecutor in relation to the evidence given, which insinuations would be actionable if not privileged. No action can be maintained for making them; no inquiry into their bearing upon the case will be allowed[1]. Again: A witness on the stand, after examination, volunteers a statement in vindication of himself, which contains a charge of crime against a stranger to the trial. This is not actionable[2]. Again: The defendant, during the deliberations of a jury of which he is a member, held in the jury room, concerning their verdict in a suit brought by the present plaintiff, says he would not believe the plaintiff under oath, and accuses him of having obtained an insurance of property by fraud, and afterwards of committing perjury in a suit for the insurance money. That trial has no connexion with the case before the jury, but the defendant acts honestly, believing himself to be in the discharge of his duty. This is no breach of duty to the plaintiff[3].

This protection extends to the allegations contained in the written pleadings of causes[4]. So, likewise, to those of affidavits made in the course of a trial[5], even though the persons making them be not parties to the cause[6]; and to statements of a coroner holding an inquest[7]. In a word, it applies apparently to all statements made in the discharge of duty at court.

The law upon this subject has been thus (in substance)

[1] Munster v. Lamb, supra.
[2] Seaman v. Netherclift, supra.
[3] Dunham v. Powers, supra.
[4] Henderson v. Broomhead, 4 H. & N. 569, 577.
[5] Garr v. Selden, 4 Comst. 91 (N. Y.).
[6] Henderson v. Broomhead, supra.
[7] Thomas v. Churton, 2 Best & S. 475.

generalized: No action either for slander or libel can be maintained against a judge, magistrate, or person sitting in a judicial capacity over any court, judicial, military[1], or (probably) naval, recognized by and constituted according to law; nor against suitors, prosecutors, witnesses, counsel, or jurors, for anything said or done relative to the matter in hand, in the ordinary course of a judicial proceeding, investigation, or inquiry, civil or criminal, by or before any such tribunal, however false, malicious, or irrelevant, it may be[2].

A like rule of law to that by which defamatory statements made in the course of judicial proceedings are privileged governs all statements and publications made in the course of the proceedings of Parliament[3]. The occasion is deemed to afford an absolute justification for the use of language otherwise actionable, so long as it relates to the proceedings under consideration. No member of Parliament is liable in a court of justice for anything said by him in the House to which he belongs, or in which he has duties to perform, however offensive the same may be to the feelings or injurious to the reputation of another[4].

This privilege, however, is absolute only within the walls of the House, or of such other places as committees of Parliament are authorized to occupy[5]. It is not personal, but local. A member who publishes slander or libel generally, outside of such locality, stands, it seems, on the same footing with a private individual. For example: A

---

[1] Jekyll v. Moore, 2 Bos. & P. N. R. 341; Dawkins v. Rokeby, L. R. 8 Q. B. 255; s. c. 7 H. L. 744, 752 (witness); Dawkins v. Saxe Weimar, 1 Q. B. D. 499.

[2] Starkie, Slander and Libel, 184 (4th ed. by Folkard); Munster v. Lamb, 11 Q. B. Div. 588, and cases cited.

[3] 3 & 4 Vict. c. 9; Odgers, Slander, 187.

[4] See Ex parte Wason, L. R. 4 Q. B. 573; Coffin v. Coffin, 4 Mass. 1.

[5] Goffin v. Donnelly, 6 Q. B. D. 307.

member of Parliament prints and circulates generally a speech delivered by him in the House, containing language defamatory of the plaintiff. This is a breach of duty[1].

The same protection is extended to persons presenting petitions to Parliament and with the same restriction. The printing and exhibiting a false and defamatory petition to a committee of Parliament, and the delivery of copies thereof to each member of the committee, is justifiable, unless perhaps the petition is a mere sham, fraudulently put forth for the purpose of defaming an individual. But a publication to any others than the members of the committee, or at any rate to others than members of Parliament, removes the protection, and renders the author liable[2].

The occasions above presented are the only ones in which the publication of defamation is absolutely justified. The occasions which afford a prima facie protection to defamatory publications must now be considered. The defendant here shews privilege as before; but now, it should be noticed, the plaintiff may in turn shew (actual) malice.

The class of cases of defamatory communications which fall under this head is both extensive and often complicated. It will be useful to divide it into two branches; to wit, communications pertaining to matters before the public, and communications pertaining to matters kept private.

Proceedings before church organizations for the discipline of members thereof are, in America at least, quasi-judicial, and afford protection, prima facie in kind, for the

---

[1] Rex v. Abingdon, 1 Esp. 226; Rex v. Creevey, 1 Maule & S. 273; Stockdale v. Hansard, 9 Ad. & E. 1. As to private circulation of speeches among constituents, see Wason v. Walter, L. R. 4 Q. B. 73, 95.

[2] Lake v. King, 1 Saund. 131 b, where this is conceded; Hare v. Miller, 3 Leon. 138, 163. See Proctor v. Webster, 16 Q. B. D. 112, as to communications to the Privy Council.

utterance of defamatory language, if it have any pertinency to the matter under consideration. For example: The defendant, while on trial before a church committee for alleged falsehood and dishonesty in business, says of the plaintiff, 'I discharged him for being dishonest, — for stealing. That is the cause of this trouble.' The defendant is not liable in the absence of evidence that he was actuated by express malice[1].

Accounts of trials before the judicial tribunals, if sufficiently full to give a correct and adequate impression of the proceedings, and if not attended with defamatory comments, are prima facie privileged[2]. If, however, the same should be malicious, partial, or followed by comments containing defamatory matter, the privilege would fail, and the publisher, editor, and author would be liable for any defamation thereby spread. For example: The defendant prints a short summary of the facts of a certain case in which the plaintiff has acted as attorney. The account of the trial states that the then defendant's counsel was extremely severe and amusing at the expense of the present plaintiff. It then sets out parts of the speech of the defendant's counsel which contain some severe reflections on the conduct of the plaintiff as attorney in that action. The defendant is liable[3].

An abridged report of a trial in one of the superior courts may, however, be privileged if it be fair and accurate in substance, so as to convey a just impression of what took place, and be free from objectionable comments[4]. And the

[1] York v. Pease, 2 Gray, 282; Farnsworth v. Storrs, 5 Cush. 412 (Mass. cases).

[2] See Stevens v. Sampson, 5 Ex. Div. 53, as to reports furnished by one not connected with the newspaper.

[3] Flint v. Pike, 4 B. & C. 473.

[4] Turner v. Sullivan, 6 Law T. N. s. 130; Wason v. Walter, L. R. 4 Q. B. 73, 87.

same is true of like reports of proceedings in Parliament[1]. The report of a judgment alone may be printed[2].

The objection to defamatory comments applies equally well when they are put into the form of a heading to the report. For example: The defendant prints an account of a trial in which the plaintiff was involved, heading the same 'Shameful conduct of an attorney,' the attorney referred to being the present plaintiff. The publication is not privileged[3].

The editor or writer may, however, use a heading properly indicative of the nature of the trial, if it do not amount to comment. That is, the subject of the trial may be stated. For example: The defendant prints a report of a trial under the heading 'Wilful and corrupt perjury.' But this is only a statement of the charge made against the plaintiff at the trial. There is no breach of duty[4].

The privilege appears to extend to the publication of ex parte judicial proceedings[5], and it protects the publication of preliminary and final proceedings alike; and this though the tribunal declines to proceed, for want of jurisdiction[6].

But no privilege is conferred upon the proprietors, editors, or publishers of the public prints for the publication of defamatory matter uttered in the course of public meetings though held under authority of law for public purposes. For example: The defendant prints an account of a public meeting of commissioners of a town, the body

[1] Wason v. Walter, supra. Secus of matter unfit for publication. Steele v. Brannan, L. R. 7 C. P. 261.

[2] Macdougall v. Knight, 17 Q. B. Div. 636.

[3] Lewis v. Clement, 3 Barn. & Ald. 702.

[4] Lewis v. Levy, El. B. & E. 537.

[5] Usill v. Hales, 3 C. P. D. 319. Contra in America. Cincinnati Gazette Co. v. Timberlake, 10 Ohio St. 548.

[6] Usill v. Hales, supra; Lewis v. Levy, El. B. & E. 537.

acting under powers granted by statute; and the report is a fair and truthful statement of what occurred at the meeting. It, however, contains defamatory language uttered concerning the plaintiff at the meeting. The defendant is liable[1]. But see R.S.C 1897, c.68, sec 8

It does not, indeed, make a case of privilege that a defamatory statement relates to a matter of great interest to the public, even though the public be at a point of unusual anxiety on the subject. For example: The defendant charges the plaintiff in a newspaper with treachery and bad faith in regard to money received by him to obtain the manumission of a fugitive slave in whom there was great interest in the community. The publication is not privileged[2].

The right to publish the proceedings of the courts of justice is based upon a supposed general utility to the public. It is more obviously to the advantage of the public that true accounts of the proceedings of Parliament should be placed before the people. Upon this principle, therefore, the publication of such proceedings is privileged, though they contain defamatory matter; though the privilege, as in the other cases mentioned, will not cover malicious publications. Without evidence of malice, the protection is complete. For example: The defendant publishes a true report of a debate in Parliament, upon a petition presented by the plaintiff for the impeachment of a judge. Defamatory statements against the plaintiff are made in the course of the debate, and these are published with the report. The defendant is not liable in the absence of malice[3].

[1] Davison v. Duncan, 7 El. & B. 229. See 44 & 45 Vict. c. 60, § 2. A Libel Law Amendment Bill touching newspapers is now (August, 1888) pending, and likely to pass.

[2] Sheckell v. Jackson, 10 Cush. 25 (Mass.).

[3] Wason v. Walter, L. R. 4 Q. B. 73. The protection in this case was extended also to comments made in an honest and fair spirit.

Communications made to the proper public authorities, upon occasions of seeking redress for wrongs suffered or threatened, in which the public are concerned, or in which the party making or receiving the communication is alone concerned, are privileged, prima facie, if believed to be true by the party seeking redress, unless the form of the communication itself shew malice. For example: The defendant honestly[1] charges the plaintiff with being a thief, the charge being made before a constable acting as such, after the defendant had sent for him to take the plaintiff into custody. The defendant is not liable in the absence of evidence of actual malice[2].

Upon the same principle, honest statements at public meetings, as by a taxpayer and voter at a town meeting, held to consider an application from the tax assessors of the town for the use of money for a particular purpose, may (probably) be privileged so far as they bear upon the matter before the meeting, though they be defamatory. For example: The defendant, at a town meeting held on application of the tax assessors to consider the reimbursing the assessors for expenses incurred in defending a suit for acts done in their official capacity, honestly but falsely charges the assessors with perjury in the suit. Being a taxpayer and voter, he is not liable to any of the persons defamed, unless shewn to have been actuated by malice[3].

A similar protection is, it seems, to be extended to persons acting under the management of bodies instituted by law, and having a special function of care over the interests of the public. While honestly acting within the limits of their function, they are prima facie exempt from liability for defamatory publications made. For example: The de-

[1] Honestly = believing the imputation true.
[2] Robinson v. May, 2 Smith, 3.
[3] Smith v. Higgins, 16 Gray, 251 (Mass.).

fendants, trustees of a College of Pharmacy,—an institution incorporated for the purpose, among other things, of cultivating and improving pharmacy, and of making known the best methods of preparing medicines, with a view to the public welfare,—make a report to the proper officer concerning the importation of impure and adulterated drugs, falsely but honestly charging the plaintiff with having made such importations; the report being made after investigation caused by complaints made to the defendants of the importation of such drugs. The defendants are not liable unless they acted with express malice towards the plaintiff[1].

The use of the public prints is sometimes justifiable to protect a person against the frauds or depredations of a private citizen; and when this is the only effectual mode of protection, persons are (probably) prima facie protected in adopting it even against innocent men. For example: The defendant, a baker, employing servants in delivering bread in various towns, inserts in a newspaper published in one of the towns a card, stating that the plaintiff 'having left my employ, and taken upon himself the privilege of collecting my bills, this is to give notice that he has nothing further to do with my business.' The communication is honest. It is privileged in the absence of evidence of actual malice[2].

Statements made to the public in vindication of character publicly attacked are privileged, prima facie, if they are honest, at least if made through proper channels[3]. For example: The defendant publishes a newspaper article containing reflections upon the plaintiff's character, in reply to an article by the plaintiff assailing the defendant's

---

[1] Van Wyck v. Aspinwall, 17 N. Y. 190.
[2] Hatch v. Lane, 105 Mass. 394.
[3] Laughton v. Bishop of Sodor, L. R. 4 P. C. 495.

character. The defendant acts honestly, in defence of himself. The communication is prima facie privileged[1].

Indeed, it may not affect the case that the names of other men are drawn into the controversy and tarnished. The party attacked may in reply falsely criminate others if the charges against them are honestly made, are not malicious, and are reasonably deemed necessary for self-vindication. And such reply may be made by the party's agent as well as by himself. For example: The defendant, an attorney, writes and publishes a letter in vindication of the character of one of his clients, in reply to certain charges of conspiracy preferred and published against the latter. The defendant's letter contains defamatory charges against a third person, among them one of perjury. The defendant is not liable if he wrote the letter in honest vindication of his client's character, and without actual malice, using terms reasonably warranted under the circumstances in which he wrote[2].

It remains to consider the case of prima facie privileged communications concerning matters kept entirely private. And here at the outset a general distinction must be observed, which separates the class of cases now to be noticed from those above considered, or at least from all except the cases relating to communications in vindication of character. With the exception of this last class of cases, all the foregoing have been cases, it will be noticed, in which the privileged communication in question was made voluntarily, that is, without request from another having an interest therein. Indeed, communications in defence of character are made, or may be made, without actual request; but the first attack, especially when publicly made, may properly be considered a challenge to reply. It

---

[1] O'Donoghue v. Hussey, Ir. R. 5 C. L. 124, Ex. Ch.
[2] Regina v. Veley, 4 Fost. & F. 1117.

is therefore equivalent to a request, and the reply cannot be considered as voluntarily made. In regard to the other cases above presented, the communication is necessarily voluntary in most cases; and the fact, therefore, that the communication has been voluntarily made can, it seems, have nothing to do with the question of liability.

When, however, the communication relates to a matter treated as private, the case may assume a different aspect. Here it may or may not be necessary to volunteer a reflection upon another's character; and when it is not, it will be dangerous to do it, for it may indicate malice and thus overturn the protection of privilege. Dangerous it will be, not necessarily fatal; fatal as matter of law it cannot in any case be.

Two classes of cases there, indeed, appear to be, in one of which to volunteer the communication will endanger the privilege, in the other it will not.

One of these arises from the circumstance that the situation of the party publishing the defamation towards the party of whom it is published is such as to render it highly improbable that the former was actuated by malicious motives towards the latter, when the communication was made to a party having an interest in it; the other from the circumstance that the parties between whom the communication passes sustain a relation of close confidence to each other, either of very near relationship (by blood or marriage) or of pecuniary connexion.

Under the first of the two classes is to be mentioned the case of communications made by a master (or late master) concerning the conduct of his servant, made to a neighbour or friend about to take the servant into his employ. The master violates no duty of law to his servant in such a case by making honest statements to his neighbour derogatory of the servant's character; but if his action was volunteered, the privilege will be endangered. For example: The defendant, having discharged his servant the plaintiff for supposed misconduct, and hearing that he was about to be engaged by a neighbour, writes a letter to his neighbour, informing him that he has discharged the plaintiff for dishonesty, and that he cannot recommend him; the charge of dishonesty being false, but believed by the defendant to be true. The defendant has a prima facie right to make the statement; but the fact that he volunteered it may be considered on the question of malice[1].

It is, then, clear that in cases arising under the first class (such as cases between master and servant), the fact that the communication has been voluntarily made does not necessarily prevent the charge from being prima facie privileged. Its effect at most is only to require the defendant to give strong evidence that he acted honestly in what was done[2]. But of course the plaintiff is at liberty to overturn this evidence if he can, by shewing that the defendant was in fact actuated by malice in making the charge.

Under the second of the two classes, where there exists a very near relationship, or a pecuniary connexion of confidence, between the parties, may be mentioned the case of a parent admonishing his daughter against the attentions of a particular person, who is falsely charged with the commission of a crime; or of a partner advising his copartner to have no partnership dealing with another on the false ground, e.g. that he is a swindler or thief. It is certainly safe to volunteer the statement of a false accusation in such cases; that is, it can have no bearing upon a question of malice that the statement was volunteered.

A confidential relation by pecuniary connexion is, however, for the purposes of this protection, much wider than

[1] See Pattison v. Jones, 8 B. & C. 578, 584, Bayley, J.
[2] Id. Littledale, J.

might be supposed from the case of partners last mentioned. A confidential relation, within the scope of the protection to voluntary communications, (probably) arises wherever a continuous or temporary trust is reposed in the skill or integrity of another, or the property or pecuniary interest, in whole or in part, or the bodily custody, of one person, is placed in charge of another[1]. Besides the cases above stated, this definition will cover communications made by an attorney to his client concerning third persons with whom the client is, or is about to be, engaged in business transactions[2]; communications made to an auctioneer of property concerning the sale by persons interested in the property[3]; communications of landlords to their tenants imputing immoral conduct to some of the inmates of the premises[4]; and many other cases of a like nature.

Voluntary communications in all of these cases are justifiable on the ground that the party receiving them has a right to expect them: and it may be laid down as a broad rule, that, wherever a right to expect the communication may reasonably be supposed to exist, the communication will be protected, whether it was voluntary or not. Indeed, the case in hand is still stronger; the matter is generally one of protection to the person making the communication as well as of protection to the one to whom it is made.

On the other hand, it is a general rule of law that communications honestly made, in answer to needful inquiries, are privileged. But a communication is not necessarily privileged because of being made upon request. If it should be unnecessarily defamatory under the circumstances, the privilege would be lost. Such fact would, indeed, shew

[1] Bigelow, Fraud, 262.
[2] See Davis v. Reeves, 5 Ir. C. L. 79.
[3] Blackham v. Pugh, 2 C. B. 611.
[4] Knight v. Gibbs, 3 Nev. & M. 467.

that the writer or speaker was actuated by malice, and would thus destroy the protection which may have been available to the party, and restore to the plaintiff his right of redress[1].

Again, a communication made upon request is not protected unless the request come from a proper person, or at least from one whom the defendant has reason to suppose a proper person. If the defendant know, or have good reason to know, that the party making the inquiry has no interest in the matter in question other than that of curiosity, the defendant manifestly is not justified in making the communication. Even the near relatives of a person interested in the subject of the communication cannot by request afford protection to every one to publish defamation of another. For example: The defendant, formerly but not at present pastor of a lady, writes a letter to the lady, on request of her parents, warning her against receiving attention from a certain person, the letter containing false and defamatory accusations against him. The communication is not privileged[2].

It should be noticed that it devolves upon the defendant to shew, not only the existence (at the time or before) of the relation between the parties, but also that he acted in good faith, believing that his communication was true[3]. And this statement applies throughout the law of prima facie

[1] Fryer v. Kinnersley, 15 C. B. N. s. 422.
[2] Joannes v. Bennet, 5 Allen, 169 (Mass.). Perhaps the communication would have been privileged had it come from the lady's present pastor; and it clearly would have been protected had it been written on request of the lady herself.
[3] Pattison v. Jones, 8 B. & C. 578; Dawkins v. Paulet, L. R. 5 Q. B. 94, 102; Clark v. Molyneux, 3 Q. B. Div. 237; Odgers, Slander, 199. It is not necessary for the defendant to shew reasonable grounds of belief. Clark v. Molyneux, supra, at pp. 244, 248, 249. Comp. the rule in deceit, ante, p. 34, note 1.

privilege. It has already been observed that the defendant's belief in the truth of the charge is no defence in cases not of privileged communications[1].

This subject of privileged communications may be summarized by the following proposition, subject, however, to such explanation as the foregoing remarks suggest: A communication believed to be true, and made bona fide upon any subject-matter in which the party communicating has an interest, or in reference to which he has a duty to perform, is privileged, if made to a person having a corresponding interest or duty, although it contains defamatory matter, which, without such privilege, would be actionable[2].

It follows from this, that no privilege is afforded the mere repetition of defamation; and this is true by the weight of authority, though the party repeating it give the name of the person from whom he received it. The repetition of the language is generally deemed actionable to the same extent, and doubtless with the same qualifications, as is the original publication[3]. For example: The defendant says to a third person concerning the plaintiff, 'You have heard of the rumour of his failure,'—merely repeating a current rumour that had come to his ears that the plaintiff had failed. The defendant is liable, if there was no such relation between him and the party to whom he made the communication as would cause the latter to expect a communication on such matters[4].

Criticism cannot be defamation, unless it strikes at personal character. It is protected therefore, not because it is privileged, for it is not, but because it is not defa-

[1] Ante, p. 93.
[2] Harrison v. Bush, 5 El. & B. 344.
[3] De Crespigny v. Wellesley, 5 Bing. 392; s. c. L. C. Torts, 151.
[4] Watkin v. Hall, L. R. 3 Q. B. 396.

mation[1]. However severe it may be, however unjust in the opinion of men capable of judging, so long as the critic confines himself to 'fair' criticism of another's works, the act cannot be treated as a breach of duty. But if the critic turn aside from the proper purpose of criticism, and hold up one's person or character to ridicule, he becomes liable[2].

The criticism of works of art, whether painting, sculpture, monument, or architecture, falls within the rule. For example: The defendant says of a picture of the plaintiff, placed on exhibition, 'It is a mere daub.' The defendant, if fair in his criticism[3], cannot be held liable to an action for defamation, however unjust the criticism[4].

The conduct too of public men amenable to the public only, and of candidates for public office, is a matter proper for public discussion. It may be made the subject of hostile criticism and animadversion, so long as the writer keeps within the bounds of an honest intention to discharge a duty to the public, and does not make the occasion a mere cover for promulgating malicious and false allegations. The question in such cases therefore is, whether the author of the statements complained of has transgressed the bounds within which comments upon the character or conduct of a public man should be confined;—whether, instead of fair comment, the occasion was made an opportunity for grati-

---

[1] Merivale v. Carson, 20 Q. B. Div. 275; Campbell v. Spottiswoode, 3 Best & S. 769, 780. What all men may do is no privilege, but only what *some* men may. Id.

[2] Id.; Carr v. Hood, 1 Campb. 355, note; Odgers, Slander, 39.

[3] See Henwood v. Harrison, L. R. 7 C. P. 606, 626, Willes, J. But see Pollock, Torts, 221; Merivale v. Carson, 20 Q. B. Div. 275, 283, as to 'fair criticism.'

[4] Thompson v. Shackell, Moody & M. 187. See Merivale v. Carson, supra; Gott v. Pulsifer, 122 Mass. 235.

fying personal vindictiveness and hostility[1], as by making false charges of disgraceful acts[2]. In a word, fair criticism or comment upon the real acts of a public man is one thing; it is 'quite another to assert that he has been guilty of particular acts of misconduct[3]'.

If, however, an officer, or an office sought, be not subject to direct control by the public,—if the same be subordinate to the authority of someone having a power of removal over the incumbent,—then (probably) there exists no right to animadvert upon the conduct of such subordinate officer or candidate through public channels; for in such a case the question appears to be one of capacity or fitness for a particular vocation. Though engaged in business of the public, the officer is not a 'public man' but a servant. The proper course to pursue in case of supposed incapacity or unfitness of the party for the position would be to state the case to the superior officer alone, and call upon him to act accordingly[4].

It must be understood that the law of slander and libel applies only to defamation in pais; that is, to defamatory charges not prosecuted in a court of justice. If the defamation consist of an accusation prosecuted in court, the accused must seek his redress by an action for a malicious prosecution, in regard to which the right to recover depends, as has been seen, upon quite different rules of law[5].

[1] Campbell v. Spottiswoode, 3 Best & S. 769, 776; Merivale v. Carson, 20 Q. B. Div. 275, 283.
[2] Davis v. Shepstone, 11 App. Cas. 187.
[3] Id. at p. 190.
[4] Comp. Odgers, 223, 224.   [5] See Chapter II.

PART II.

BREACH OF ABSOLUTE DUTY.

CHAPTER I.

ASSAULT AND BATTERY.

§ 1. INTRODUCTORY.

Statement of the duty. A owes to B the duty to forbear (1) to offer with force to do hurt to his person, within reach; or (2) to hit or touch him in anger, rudeness, or negligence, or in the commission of any unlawful act.

There is so much in common in the law of the two wrongs of assault and battery, and the two are so often coincident, that the terms are not always used with discrimination. 'Assault' is constantly used in the books to include 'battery[1].' But they are, or may be, separate and distinct wrongs, and it is therefore necessary to draw the distinction between them clearly.

§ 2. OF ASSAULTS.

An assault is an attempt, real or apparent, to do hurt to another's person, within reaching distance. It is an *attempt* to do harm, stopping short of actual execution[2]. If the attempt be carried out by physical contact, the act

---

[1] See the proposed definition in the draft Criminal Code of 1879; Pollock, Torts, 183.

[2] Words are no assault; but they may be a menace and so actionable, with proof of actual damage. L. C. Torts, 225—227.

becomes a battery; but the act is equally unlawful and actionable when it stops with a mere attempt to inflict hurt. It is not alone a blow that, because of unpermitted contact with the person, is unlawful. The sensibility of danger may be rudely excited; and feelings of that kind are within the protection of the law quite as much as the feeling produced by blows. It is actionable for A to shake his fist in the face of B[1].

In ordinary cases of assault, the question whether the defendant actually intended to do harm cannot, as the definition implies, enter into the case. If reasonable fear of present bodily harm has been caused by the threatening attitude, the effect of an assault has been produced; and not even a disclaimer by the wrong-doer coincident with his act could, it seems, prevent liability. One may well complain of a man who points a pistol at him, though the man truly declare that he does not intend to shoot[2]; for the effect of an assault, the putting one in fear, is produced.

But it may appear in a particular case that an expressed purpose, or want of purpose, is a determining fact in solving a doubt; that is, it may be such a part of the act in question as to turn the scales in deciding whether an assault has been committed. A denial of present purpose to do harm, or any language indicating a want of such purpose, may serve, under the circumstances, to prevent the excitement of any reasonable fear of present bodily harm. If then it appear that the supposed wrong was committed in such a manner that the plaintiff must have

---

[1] Bacon's Abr. 'Assault and Battery,' A.
[2] See Reg. v. St George, 9 Car. & P. 483, 493, Parke, B; Bacon's Abr. 'Assault and Battery,' A; 1 Hawkins, P. C. 110; Pollock, Torts, 184, doubting Blake v. Barnard, 9 Car. & P. 626, 628, and Reg. v. James, 1 C. & K. 530. Mr Pollock says that Reg. v. St George, ut supra, 'would almost certainly be followed at this day.'

CHAP. I.] ASSAULT AND BATTERY. 117

known that no present violence was intended, the act is not an assault. For example: The defendant, on drill as a soldier, putting his hand upon his sword, says to the plaintiff, 'If it was not drill-time, I would not take such language from you.' This is not an assault, since the language used, under the circumstances, shews that there was no present attempt, real or apparent, to commit bodily violence[1].

If, however, the plaintiff have reason to believe that harm was intended, there is an assault, whether the defendant did or did not intend harm. So at least it is held in America for the purpose of civil redress. For example: The defendant in an angry manner points an unloaded gun at the plaintiff, and snaps it, with the apparent purpose of shooting. The gun is known by the defendant to be unloaded; but the plaintiff does not know the fact, and has no reason to suppose that it is not loaded. The defendant is liable for an assault, though he could not have intended any harm to the plaintiff[2]. .

The parties must generally have been within reach of each other, not necessarily within arm's reach, for an assault may be committed (as already appears) by means of a weapon or missile; and in such a case it is only necessary that the plaintiff should have been within reach of the projectile. And even when the alleged assault is committed with the fist, it is not necessary that the plaintiff should have been within arm's reach of the defendant, provided the defendant was advancing to strike the plaintiff, and was restrained by others from carrying out his purpose when almost within reach of the plaintiff. For example: The defendant advances towards the plaintiff in an angry manner, with clenched fist, saying that he will

[1] See Tuberville v. Savage, 1 Mod. 3.
[2] Beach v. Hancock, 27 N. H. 223.

pull the plaintiff out of his chair, but is arrested by a person sitting next to the plaintiff between him and the defendant. The act is an assault, though the defendant was not near enough to strike the plaintiff[1].

In like manner, if the defendant should cause the plaintiff to flee in order to escape violence, he may be guilty of an assault, though he was at no time within reach of the plaintiff: it is enough that flight or concealment becomes necessary to escape the threatened evil. For example: The defendant on horseback rides at a quick pace after the plaintiff, then walking along a foot-path. The plaintiff runs away, and escapes into his garden; at the gate of which the defendant stops on his horse, shaking his whip at the plaintiff, now beyond danger. This is an assault[2].

It will be observed, from the statement of the duty which governs this branch of the law, that a mere assault is a civil offence; and hence the person assaulted has a right of action, though he may not have suffered any loss or detriment from the offence. In such a case, however, unless the assault were outrageous, he could (probably) recover only nominal damages[3].

§ 3. OF BATTERIES.

A battery consists in the unpermitted application of force by one man to the person of another. A battery, therefore, is mainly distinguishable from an assault in the fact that physical contact is necessary to accomplish it. But, as the definition indicates, this contact need not be effected by a blow: any forcible contact may be sufficient. For example: The defendant, an overseer of the poor, cuts

[1] Stephens v. Myers, 4 Car. & P. 349; s. c. L. C. Torts, 217.
[2] Mortin v. Shoppee, 3 Car. & P. 373.
[3] The damages recovered in Stephens v. Myers, supra, were one shilling.

off the hair of the plaintiff, an inmate in the poor-house, contrary to the plaintiff's will, and without authority of law. This is a battery, and the defendant is liable in damages[1]. Again: The defendant, in passing through a crowded hall, pushes his way in a rude manner against the plaintiff. This is also a battery[2].

It is not necessary that the defendant should come in contact with the plaintiff's body. It is sufficient if the blow or touch come upon the plaintiff's clothing. For example: The defendant, in anger or rudeness, knocks off the plaintiff's hat. This is enough to constitute a battery[3].

Indeed, it is not necessary that the plaintiff's body or clothing be touched. To knock a thing out of the plaintiff's hands, such as a staff or cane, would clearly be a battery; and the same would be true of the striking a thing upon which he is resting for support, if the effect be to cause a fall or concussion to the plaintiff. For example: The defendant strikes a horse upon which the plaintiff is riding, causing the animal to plunge and throw the plaintiff. This is a battery[4]. Again: The defendant drives a vehicle against the plaintiff's carriage, throwing the plaintiff from his seat. This also is a battery[5]. Again: The defendant runs against and overturns a chair in which the plaintiff is sitting. This too is a battery[6].

It appears from the foregoing examples that it is not necessary to constitute a battery that the touch or blow or

[1] Forde v. Skinner, 4 Car. & P. 239.
[2] Cole v. Turner, 6 Mod. 149; s. c. L. C. Torts, 218.
[3] Mr Addison gives this as an example of a battery, without citing authority; but there can be no doubt of its correctness. Addison, Torts, 571 (4th ed.).
[4] See Dodwell v. Burford, 1 Mod. 24.
[5] Hopper v. Reeve, 7 Taunt. 698.
[6] Id. It was held immaterial in this case whether the chair or carriage belonged to the plaintiff or not.

other contact should come directly from the defendant's person. Indeed, a battery may be committed at any distance between the parties if only some violence be done to the plaintiff's person. The hitting one with a stone, or an arrow, or other missile, is no less a battery than the striking one with the fist. It is not necessary even that the object cast should do physical harm; the battery consists in the unpermitted contact, and not in the damage. For example: The defendant spits or throws water upon the plaintiff. This is a battery, though no harm be done[1].

A battery may be committed without the least intention to do the plaintiff harm; it may be the result simply of negligence. For example: The defendant, a soldier, handles his arms so carelessly in drilling as to hit the plaintiff with them. This is a battery, though the act was not intended[2]. The above-mentioned case of the defendant running into the plaintiff's carriage is another example[3].

Indeed, a person may be guilty of a battery where his act is directly caused by another person, provided the de-

---

[1] See Regina v. Cotesworth, 6 Mod. 172; Pursell v. Horn, 8 Ad. & E. 602. A word of explanation is necessary as to the latter case. The plaintiff had sued for a battery by throwing of water on him, and had failed to prove it, though he proved certain consequential injuries, and had a verdict for below forty shillings. The damages not reaching forty shillings, and a battery not having been proved, the plaintiff was not entitled (under the statute) to the costs given him. He now attempted to shew that he had not sued for a battery at all, or, if he had, that a battery had been admitted by the defendant's plea; which, if true, would save him his costs as given by the jury. But the court decided against him, and cut down the costs allowed; thus holding that to throw water upon a person is a battery.

[2] Weaver v. Ward, Hob. 134. Quære, whether many of the actions for bodily injuries, sued for as torts by negligence, could not be redressed by suing for assault and battery? It would obviously be to the plaintiff's advantage so to sue. See Holmes v. Mather, L. R. 10 Ex. 261. [3] See also Hall v. Fearnley, 3 Q. B. 919.

CHAP. I.] ASSAULT AND BATTERY. 121

fendant was engaged at the time in an unlawful proceeding. For example: The defendant, when about to discharge a gun unlawfully at a third person, is jostled just as the gun is fired, and the direction of the shot is changed so as to cause the plaintiff to be hit. This is a battery[1].

But while a battery may be committed without intention, it is not to be supposed that every unintentional physical violence done to another will constitute a battery. There is no battery, according to the just tendency of modern authority, unless the action of the defendant was voluntary, or the result of negligence, or of the doing of something forbidden by law[2]. No man when doing that which is lawful should be held liable for consequences which he could not prevent by prudence or care, though another suffer bodily injury thereby. For example: The defendant's horse, upon which the defendant is lawfully riding in the highway, takes a sudden fright, runs away with his rider, and against all the efforts of the defendant to restrain him, runs against and hurts the plaintiff. This is not a battery or other breach of duty[3].

And even though the action of the defendant was voluntary (that is, intentional), it will not necessarily constitute a battery. For example: The defendant, walking near the plaintiff, suddenly turns round, and in so doing hits the plaintiff with his elbow. This is not a battery[4].

[1] See James *v.* Campbell, 5 Car. & P. 372, where the defendant, in fighting with another, hit the plaintiff with his fist.

[2] Coward *v.* Baddeley, 4 H. & N. 478, Martin, B. infra; Holmes *v.* Mather, L. R. 10 Ex. 261;.Wakeman *v.* Robinson, 1 Bing. 213; Hall *v.* Fearnley, 3 Q. B. 919; Brown *v.* Kendall, 6 Cush. 292 (Mass.) Vincent *v.* Stinehour, 7 Vermont, 62; Nitroglycerine Case, 15 Wall. 524, Sup. Court U. S.

[3] See Vincent *v.* Stinehour, 7 Vt. 62, and example cited by Williams, C. J.; and see Holmes *v.* Mather, supra, a still stronger case.

[4] A case put by Martin, B. on the argument in Coward *v.* Bad-

Nor is there necessarily a battery though (not merely the general action of the defendant, as in the last example, but) the specific act of contact be intentional, for it may have been done in sport; though sport could doubtless be carried to such an extreme as to constitute the act a battery. It is not even a decisive test, always, to inquire whether the act was done against the plaintiff's will. The plaintiff may be engaged in criminal conduct at the time; or he may be lying unconsciously in an exposed condition; or with the best of intentions he may be doing that which the defendant rightly thinks dangerous to life or property. In the first of these cases, an arrest of the plaintiff by laying on of hands will be justifiable; in the second case, an arousing or removal of him will be proper; and, in the third, the laying on of hands to attract his attention is lawful[1]. In none of these cases is there a battery, though the contact be against the will of the plaintiff.

If, however, the act were done in a *hostile* manner the case would be different[2]; and the question whether the act was hostile (probably) furnishes the criterion, when the same was voluntary, and not the result of negligence or other unlawful conduct. In the two latter cases, it matters not, as has already been seen, whether the act was hostile or not.

A battery may also be committed in an endeavour to take one's own property from the wrongful possession of another. If the party in possession should refuse to surrender the property, the owner should resort to the courts to obtain it, or await an opportunity to get possession of it in a peaceful manner. He has no right to take it out of the hands of the possessor by force. For example: The defendant, finding the plaintiff in wrongful possession of the

deley, 4 H. & N. 478. See Brown *v.* Kendall, 6 Cush. 292; Holmes *v.* Mather, supra. See further, Holmes, Common Law, 105, 106.

[1] As to the last case, see Coward *v.* Baddeley, supra. [2] Id.

CHAP. I.] ASSAULT AND BATTERY. 123

former's horse, beats the plaintiff, after a demand and refusal to give up the animal, and wrests the horse from the plaintiff's possession. This is a battery[1].

§ 4. OF JUSTIFIABLE ASSAULT: SELF-DEFENCE:
SON ASSAULT DEMESNE.

There are a few cases in which a man is entitled to take the law into his own hands and inflict corporal injury upon another. Among these are to be noticed the right of a parent to give moderate correction to his minor child; the (probable) right of a guardian to do the like to a minor ward; the right of a schoolmaster (when not prohibited by law or school ordinance) to do the like to his scholars; the (possible) right of a master to do the like to young servants; and the right of officers of reform, discipline, or correction, to do the like towards the refractory who have been committed to their charge.

Aside from cases of one of these classes, the right to do that which would otherwise amount to an assault or a battery is confined to two or three cases, all of which are justified on grounds either of self-defence or generally that the plaintiff really caused the act of which he complains[2]. In the language of the old law the wrong complained of by the plaintiff was 'son assault demesne'. A person cannot be liable for an act which he himself has not committed or caused, either personally or by another authorized to act for him. Hence if the plaintiff himself caused the act complained of, the defendant cannot be liable to him for it.

[1] Andre v. Johnson, 6 Blackf. 375, an American authority. See Suggs v. Anderson, 12 Ga. 461. But the defendant could keep his horse. Scribner v. Beach, 4 Denio, 448, 451 (N. Y.).

[2] The statute 24 & 25 Vict. c. 100, §§ 42—45, in regard to summary proceedings, may be noticed in this connexion.

The first case to be noticed in which the justification of son assault demesne is allowed, is where the plaintiff himself began an attack upon the defendant. The right of self-defence is sanctioned as well by the municipal law as by the law of nature. And the right extends to the use of physical force in the protection of property as well as of the person of the defendant, provided the property be at the time in the defendant's possession. No one has a right, except under authority of law, to seize upon the property of which the owner is in possession, and he does so at the risk of sustaining bodily violence in the act. For example: The plaintiff, a creditor of the defendant, seizes the defendant's horses (which the latter is using) for the purpose of obtaining satisfaction of his debt. The defendant resists and strikes the plaintiff. He is not liable if he did not exceed the bounds of defence[1].

If the owner or person entitled to possession was out of possession at the time of committing the alleged assault or battery, he will not be permitted to say, by way of defence, that the plaintiff caused the assault by having previously taken wrongful possession, or by having wrongfully detained the defendant's property. Such is not a case of son assault demesne, as the example already given of the horse taken from the plaintiff's possession by violence shews[2].

And though a trespasser should make an assault upon the owner of property, and seek to take it out of the owner's possession, the owner is allowed to use no greater force in resisting the unlawful act than may be necessary for the defence of his possession[3]. If he should reply to the tres-

[1] See Cluff v. Mutual Ben. Life Ins. Co., 13 Allen, 308; s. c. 90 Mass. 317.   [2] Ante, pp. 122, 123.

[3] The allowable force in such a case is expressed by the words of the old pleading, 'molliter manus imposuit',—the defendant gently laid his hands upon the plaintiff.

CHAP. I.]   ASSAULT AND BATTERY.   125

passer's attempt with a force disproportionate to the provocation, the act will then be his own battery, and not the plaintiff's; or again in the technical language of the old pleading, the plaintiff can then reply to the defendant's plea of son assault demesne, that the tort was 'de injuria propria sua',—the defendant's own wrong. For example: The defendant, owner of a rake which is in his own hands, knocks the plaintiff down with his fist, upon the plaintiff's taking hold of the rake to get possession of it. The defendant is liable[1]. Again: The defendant strikes the plaintiff repeated blows, knocking her down several times, upon her refusal to quit the defendant's house. The plaintiff is entitled to recover[2].

Nor is it lawful for the owner of property, in defence of his possession, to make an attack upon the trespasser without first calling upon him to desist from his unlawful purpose, unless the trespasser is at the time exercising violence. In the example last given, the defendant would have been liable for a mere hostile touch had he not first requested the plaintiff to leave his premises; unless she had entered his premises with force[3].

In the next place, it is to be observed that a person may not only make reasonable defence of his own person, and of the possession of his own property, but he may do the same towards the members of his own family when attacked[4]; and perhaps also towards the inmates of a house at which he is then receiving hospitality. Certain it is, that a servant may justify a battery as committed in defence of his master[5]; that is, he may do anything in his master's defence which his master himself might do. And, on the other

[1] Scribner v. Beach, 4 Denio, 448 (N. Y.).
[2] Gregory v. Hill, 8 T. R. 299.   [3] See Scribner v. Beach, supra.
[4] 1 Black. Com. 429.
[5] Reeve, Domestic Rel. 538 (3rd ed.).

hand, notwithstanding some doubts in the books, a master may justify a battery as committed in defence of his servant. For example: The plaintiff attacks the defendant's servant, whereupon the defendant assists his servant to the extent of repelling the attack, and no further. The defendant is not liable[1].

A person may also justify the use of a proper amount of physical force as rendered in quelling a riot or an affray at the instance of a constable or other officer of the peace[2], or perhaps of his own motion, when no officer is present.

§ 5. OF VIOLENCE TO OR TOWARDS ONE'S SERVANTS.

It will have been observed that a double breach of duty may be committed by the same assault or battery; one to the immediate person to whom the violence is done, and, where such person is a servant or a child or wife of the plaintiff, another breach to the person whom he or she was serving or assisting. It follows that each has a right of action against the wrong-doer in respect of the breach of his own individual right; the servant or other for the violence (that is, for the assault or battery), and its proper consequences, and the master, parent, or husband, for the loss of service or assistance.

There will be this difference, however, between the rights of action of the master and the servant (using these terms generically), that the latter will be entitled to recover judgment for the mere assault and battery, though no damage were actually inflicted; while the former will be entitled to judgment only in case he can prove either (1) that the violence committed was such as to disable the person who sustained it from rendering the amount of aid which he or she

---

[1] Tickell v. Read, Lofft, 215.
[2] Year-Book, 19 Hen. 6, pp. 43, 56; L. C. Torts, 270.

was able to render before the act complained of; or (2) that such person was, by reason of the violence, caused to depart from or abandon the service or abode of the plaintiff[1]. That is, the master must have sustained an actual damage[2]; but, if he has thus been injured, he is entitled to recover therefor, even though the defendant's act consisted only in violent demonstrations. For example: The defendants, by menaces and angry demonstrations against the plaintiff's servants, cause them to leave and abandon the plaintiff's service. The defendants are liable; though no bodily violence was committed upon the servants[3].

In regard to the master's right of action, it matters not how slight the services may be which the servant could render: if he could render any, and has been disabled or driven away, the master's rights have been violated, and the wrong-doer is liable to him. For example: The defendant commits an assault and battery upon the plaintiff's daughter, and disables her from serving at the head of his table, as she has been accustomed to do. The plaintiff is entitled to recover for the loss of service[4].

The plaintiff must, however, either have been entitled to require the services of the party assaulted or beaten, or he must have been in the actual enjoyment of them, if they

[1] The authorities upon this subject are mostly ancient, but they are still law. See L. C. Torts, 226, 227.

[2] In the case of an assault or battery upon one's wife, the husband at common law joined in the action; but the real *right* of action lay in the wife. And, in times of servitude, the master could perhaps sue for an assault or battery committed upon his villein, even though the former sustained no damage. L. C. Torts, 227.

[3] Year-Book, 20 Hen. 7, p. 5; L. C. Torts, 226; and compare Walker *v.* Cronin, 107 Mass. 555.

[4] The following cases, though actions for seduction, will justify this example: Bennett *v.* Allcott, 2 T. R. 166; Maunder *v.* Venn, Moody & M. 323; Thompson *v.* Ross, 5 H. & N. 16.

were gratuitous. A parent cannot maintain an action for an assault or a battery committed upon his child after the child's majority, unless he or she was then actually in the parent's service; nor could the parent maintain an action for such an injury committed upon his child during the child's minority, if the parent had in any way divested himself of the right to require his child's services[1].

It is laid down that only the parties to a contract (and their successors in right) can maintain an action for a breach thereof; and hence that if, in the course of performing a contract between the defendant and the plaintiff's servant, the defendant commit a battery upon the servant, which battery works a breach of the terms of the contract, the plaintiff has no right of action for the loss of service following. For example: The defendants, common carriers of passengers, are paid by the plaintiff's servant for safe passage from A to B. On the way, the servant is severely bruised, wounded, and injured by reason of the failure of the defendants to carry him safely according to their agreement; and the plaintiff thereby loses the injured person's service for a period of nineteen weeks. The plaintiff is deemed not entitled to recover; the injury being deemed the result of a breach of contract with the servant[2].

Whether the case would have been different had the carrier had notice of the relation between the plaintiff and the passenger is not clear; probably it would not. It is clear that without notice there would be no ground for liability. But the doctrine of the case itself has been much and, it seems, justly criticised[3].

[1] Questions of this sort have generally arisen in actions for seduction; and, since the subject must be elsewhere fully examined, it need not be further pursued at present. See Chapter III.

[2] Alton v. Midland Ry. 19 C. B. N. S. 213; s. c. 15 Jur. N. S. 672.

[3] See the same case again, post, Part III. § 9.

CHAP. I.] ASSAULT AND BATTERY. 129

By the common law, rights of civil action for injuries done to the person (and indeed all rights of action ex delicto, excepting for the wrongful taking or detention of property and like acts[1]), cease with the death of the party injured or of the wrong-doer. 'Actio personalis moritur cum persona.' And this rule, though not without the gravest doubts, has been held to apply to actions by masters for the killing of their servants[2]. The rule that the action dies with the death of either party permits, however, an action by the master for damages between the time of the injury of the servant and his death, where death was not immediate[3].

§ 6. OF FELONY.

There is an old formula of the law that 'trespass is merged in felony'; and assault or battery is a trespass. But the meaning of this maxim is somewhat uncertain. The better view, however, so interprets it as materially to modify if not destroy its force in the natural sense of the language; for it has been considered to mean this, that where the wrongful act amounts to felony, the injured party ought first, in duty to the public, to see that the cause is prosecuted criminally to conviction (or at least wait until

[1] See Phillips v. Homfray, 24 Ch. Div. 439; also the early statutes, 4 Edw. III. c. 7, 25 Edw. III. st. 5, c. 5, and the modern one, 3 & 4 Wm. IV. c. 42; Pollock, Torts, 56, 57. And Lord Campbell's Act, 9 & 10 Vict. c. 93, gives a right of action to the personal representative 'for the benefit of the wife, husband, parent and child of the person' killed. See Seward v. The Vera Cruz, 10 App. Cas. 59 (overruling The Franconia, 2 P. D. 163); Pym v. Great Northern Ry. Co., 4 Best & S. 396, Ex. Ch.; Bulmer v. Bulmer, 25 Ch. D. 409.

[2] Osborne v. Gillett, L. R. 8 Ex. 88, Bramwell, B. dissenting strongly. Mr Pollock doubts whether the decision would be followed by the Court of Appeal. Torts, 55, 56.

[3] Baker v. Bolton, 1 Camp. 493; Osborn v. Gillett, L. R. 8 Ex. 88, 90, 98.

B. T. 9

that is done by some one) unless the failure can be excused. That condition performed, he may sue the offender; otherwise not[1]. But it is admittedly difficult to apply the rule, at least if it is considered to be the duty of the injured party to prosecute; for how could such a duty be enforced[2]?

[1] Pollock, Torts, 172—174. See Ex parte Ball, 10 Ch. Div. 667, 673; Roope v. D'Avigdor, 10 Q. B. D. 412; Wells v. Abrahams, L. R. 7 Q. B. 554 (casting doubt upon Wellock v. Constantine, 2 H. & C. 146).

[2] See Wells v. Abrahams, supra, at p. 563.

CHAPTER II.

FALSE IMPRISONMENT.

§ 1. INTRODUCTORY.

Statement of the duty. A owes to B the duty to forbear to impose without authority of law, and without B's consent, a total restraint upon B's freedom of locomotion.

1. The terms 'writ,' 'warrant,' 'precept,' and 'process,' are, in this chapter, used synonymously.

2. The term 'irregular,' as applied to a writ, refers to some improper practice on the part of the person who obtains the writ. A writ is sometimes absolutely void for irregularity[1], and sometimes only voidable.

3. Since 1869 arrests in civil suits have been prohibited, except in a few special cases[2], so that the particular facts of many of the older authorities no longer occur; but the principles upon which they rested have not been changed.

§ 2. OF THE NATURE OF THE RESTRAINT.

A false imprisonment consists in the total, or substantially total, restraint of a man's freedom of locomotion, without authority of law, and against his will. Such an act may be committed not only by placing a man within

---

[1] As a writ in execution of a judgment which has been discharged to the knowledge of the person suing out the same.
[2] 32 & 33 Vict. c. 62, § 4.

prison walls, but also by restraint imposed upon him in his own house or room, or in the highway, or even in an open field[1].

Any general restraint is sufficient to constitute an imprisonment; and though this be effected without actual contact of the person, it will be actionable if unlawful. Any demonstration of physical violence which, to all appearance, can be avoided only by submission, operates as effectually to constitute an imprisonment, if submitted to, as if contact and force had been exercised. For example: The defendant, an officer, says to the plaintiff, 'I want you to go along with me,' with a show of authority or of determination to compel the plaintiff to go. This is an imprisonment, though the defendant do not touch the plaintiff[2].

A person may also be imprisoned, though he had not the full power of locomotion before the restraint was imposed. It appears to be sufficient if his will has been so overcome that he would not attempt to escape the restraint if he had the physical ability of locomotion. For example: The defendant, a creditor of the plaintiff, goes with an officer to the plaintiff's house, to compel him to give security for or make payment of his debt, which is not due. The plaintiff is found sick in bed; whereupon the officer tells him that they have not come to take him, but to get a certain article of property belonging to the plaintiff, though, if he will not deliver that or give security, they must take him or leave some one in charge of him. The plaintiff, much alarmed, gives up the article. This is an imprisonment[3].

[1] Lib. Ass. (22 Edw. III.), p. 104, pl. 85, a very old case, but good law.
[2] Brushaber v. Stegemann, 22 Mich. 266, 268.
[3] Grainger v. Hill, 4 Bing. N. C. 212; s. c. L. C. Torts, 184.

The submission, therefore, to the threatened and reasonably apprehended use of force is not to be considered as a consent to the restraint, within a maxim which has frequent application in the law of torts: 'volenti non fit injuria.' And the imprisonment continues until the party is allowed to depart, and is involuntary until all general restraint ceases, and the means of effecting it are removed.

It is not enough that restraint is imposed upon one's freedom of proceeding in a particular desired direction. The detention must be such as to cause escape in any direction to amount to a breach of the restraint; the restraint should be circumscribing, except, perhaps, where the only place of escape is an almost impassable one. For example: The defendant, an officer, stationed at a particular point to prevent persons from passing in a certain direction, restrains the plaintiff from passing that way, but leaves another way open to him, of which, however, he does not wish to avail himself; and, thus detained, the plaintiff stands there for some time. This is not an imprisonment[1].

It follows from the last proposition, and from what had been stated before, that a person detained within walls is none the less imprisoned by reason of the fact that he may make an escape through an unfastened window or door; since such an act would be a breach of the restraint. If it would not be, there is no imprisonment; supposing that

[1] Bird v. Jones, 7 Q. B. 742. 'A prison may have its boundary large or narrow, invisible or tangible, actual or real, or indeed in conception only; it may in itself be moveable or fixed; but a boundary it must have, and from that boundary the party imprisoned must be prevented from escaping; he must be prevented from leaving that place within the limit of which the party imprisoned could be confined.' Id. Coleridge, J.

the unfastened door or window affords a ready means of escape.

§ 3. OF ARRESTS WITH WARRANT.

Supposing the restraint imposed to amount to an imprisonment, it is to be noticed that the imprisonment must be a false one, that is, it must be an illegal restraint of freedom, in order to constitute it a breach of duty. Under what circumstances, then, is an imprisonment illegal? It would be impracticable to answer this in the way of any general rule, and quite as much so to enumerate all the cases. The most common and important case of justification, rendering lawful, that is to say, what otherwise would be unlawful, is where an officer has made an arrest under a lawful warrant of a court of justice[1]. This case will be taken for consideration.

It is to be observed at the outset that (supposing the writ to have been properly issued) the officer, in executing his precept, must arrest the person named in it. If he do not, though the arrest of the wrong person was made through mere mistake, it may be a case of false imprisonment. And this appears to be true, though the party arrested bear the same name as the party against whom the writ is directed. For example: The defendant, a constable, asks the plaintiff if his name is J. D., to which the plaintiff replies in the affirmative; whereupon the defendant takes the plaintiff into custody, the plaintiff not being the person intended by the writ. This is a case of false imprisonment[2].

If, however, the plaintiff, though not the person intended by the writ, should intentionally do anything to mislead

---

[1] See observation 3, p. 131, of arrests in civil suits.

[2] Coote v. Lighworth, F. Moore, 457. It is to be noticed that the plaintiff in this case did nothing to induce the officer to arrest him as the person intended.

the officer, and cause the latter to believe that the former was the person meant by the precept, the officer commits no breach of duty in making the arrest. The plaintiff's action is a consent, and something more. For example: The defendant, a sheriff, arrests the plaintiff under process of court, upon a representation made by her that she was E. M. D., and the person against whom the writ had issued; with the intention of procuring the defendant to arrest her under his writ. The defendant, believing the representation to be true, makes the arrest. This is not a breach of duty[1].

The officer's writ, however, should so describe the person to be arrested that he may know whom to arrest; or, rather, that a person whom he proposes to arrest may know whether to resist or submit. If the warrant be defective in this particular, the officer acts at his peril in serving it; and he will be liable to anyone whom he may arrest under it. For example: The defendant, a constable, arrests the plaintiff under a writ reciting the commission of a felony by John R. M., and then commanding the officer to arrest the said *William* M. The defendant is (probably) liable for false imprisonment, though the plaintiff is the person intended[2].

It follows that the officer may be liable if there be a misnomer in the warrant of the person intended, though the person actually meant was arrested, and that, too (in other respects), on legal grounds. For example: The defendants cause the plaintiff, whose name is Eveline, to be arrested under the name of Emeline in the warrant. This is a breach of duty, though the plaintiff, in her proper

[1] Dunston *v.* Paterson, 2 C. B. N. s. 495. The sheriff, however, had detained the plaintiff improperly after discovering his mistake, and for this he was held liable.
[2] Miller *v.* Foley, 28 Barb. 630 (N. Y.).

name, was legally liable to such an arrest[1]. But the case would have been different had the plaintiff been known alike by either name[2].

The officer also loses the protection of his precept if he fail to act in accordance with the duty enjoined by it. He must follow the tenor of his writ, and not surpass his authority. For example: The defendant arrests the plaintiff beyond the precincts named in the writ. This is a false imprisonment[3].

It is further to be noticed that, though the writ and arrest be valid, the protection of the officer may be lost by oppressive or cruel conduct. For example: The defendant, charged with a writ simply to take the body of the plaintiff, unites with the person at whose instance the arrest is made in illegally extorting money from the plaintiff by working upon his fears. The defendant is liable for a false imprisonment[4].

The officer's protection may also be lost by a detention after the warrant has expired. The warrant, however valid at first, will not justify such an act. If the officer has reason for holding the prisoner after the expiration of the warrant, he must procure a new writ. He can hold the prisoner only for a reasonable time before his examination: after that time, the warrant (that is, the original warrant of arrest) loses its vitality. For example: The defendant arrests the plaintiff, and takes him before a magistrate on a charge of larceny, detaining him for a period of three days, in order that the party whose goods had been stolen might have an opportunity to collect his

---

[1] Scott v. Ely, 4 Wend. 555 (N. Y.).
[2] Griswold v. Sedgwick, 1 Wend. 126 (N. Y.).
[3] This is too fundamental to have been much agitated in the courts. No authority is needed for the example.
[4] Holley v. Mix, 3 Wend. 350 (N. Y.).

witnesses and prove the crime. This is a false imprisonment, the detention being unreasonable[1].

When an arrest has been made upon a valid writ, the officer may detain the prisoner on any number of other valid writs which he has at the time, or which may afterwards, during the detention, reach him. But if the officer make the arrest on a void writ, or in an otherwise illegal manner, he has no right to detain the party on any valid writ which may be in his hands; for the officer, upon a principle elsewhere stated, cannot avail himself of a custody effected by illegal means to execute valid process[2]. The prisoner should first be permitted to go at large, and then arrested under the valid writ. For example: The defendant improperly arrests the plaintiff without a warrant, and while holding him in custody delivers him to an officer. The defendant afterwards receives a valid writ for the plaintiff's arrest from an officer who held it at the time of the arrest. The plaintiff has a right of action for a false imprisonment[3].

The principle to be derived from the cases (to restate this important doctrine in the language of the courts[4]) is, then, that where the officer legally arrests the party in one action, the arrest operates virtually as an arrest in all the actions in which the officer holds writs against him at the time; for it would be an idle and useless ceremony to arrest the party in the other cases. And this detainer will hold good, though the court may, upon collateral grounds, unconnected with the act of the officer, order the party to be discharged from the first arrest. But where the officer has

[1] Wright v. Court, 4 B. & C. 596. The prisoner should have been taken before a magistrate at once.
[2] Hooper v. Lane, 6 H. L. Cas. 443. [3] Barratt v. Price, 9 Bing. 566.
[4] Tindall, C. J. in Barratt v. Price, and Williams, J. in Hooper v. Lane, supra.

illegally arrested the party, he is not in custody under the first writ, but is suffering a false imprisonment; and such false imprisonment, being no arrest in the original action, cannot operate as an arrest under the other writs in the officer's hands.

It is important, in the next place, to inquire into the right of an officer to retake a prisoner under the original warrant, after an escape. It is clear that if the escape was made without the consent of the officer, while the writ was still in force, the prisoner may be retaken on the old precept, without rendering the officer liable to an action for false imprisonment. In case of an escape permitted by the officer, his right of retaking on the old writ will depend on the nature of the case. In civil cases, an officer who has arrested a man may, it seems, retake him before the return of the writ, though he voluntarily permitted him to escape immediately after the arrest. So at all events it was held under the old law. For example: The defendant arrests the plaintiff in civil process, and on the following day releases him upon the latter's request. Two days afterwards, the defendant rearrests the plaintiff on the old writ and commits him to gaol, where he remains until he gives bail; the old process not being yet returnable (that is, being still in force). This is not a breach of duty on the part of the officer[1].

In regard to criminal cases, there has been some conflict of authority in America in regard to the right to take the prisoner without new process. It has sometimes been decided that the prisoner may be so retaken[2]. In later

[1] Atkinson *v.* Matteson, 2 T. R. 172. See 32 & 33 Vict. c. 62, § 4.
[2] Clark *v.* Cleveland, 6 Hill, 344 (N. Y.). In this case, the prisoner had been let to bail in the wrong county, and then released from custody; and, in an action by him for malicious prosecution, it was held that the plaintiff was still liable to arrest under the original warrant, and that, therefore, the proceedings not being terminated, the action could not be maintained.

decisions, this doctrine has been denied to be law, except in so far as it may apply to the case of a prisoner who, after escape, has returned and given himself into custody of the officer: in this case the prisoner can be detained under the old writ[1]. And this appears to be the true rule and distinction. For example: The defendant, an officer of the peace, clothed with a warrant to arrest the plaintiff upon a charge of larceny, executes the writ upon her, and takes her before a justice of the peace, who receives her recognizance to appear for trial at another court upon a certain day. She is then discharged from arrest. No court is held at the place and time stated. Afterwards the defendant rearrests her upon the old warrant, and takes her before another magistrate. This is a false imprisonment[2].

An arrest made under a void writ will generally render the officer, as has already been stated, liable to an action for false imprisonment. But in order to subject him to such liability, the writ must have been actually void; that is, of no more validity than waste-paper. If it be voidable merely, or if, though void, the fact do not appear on the face of the writ, the precept affords a protection to the person who serves it[3].

Now a writ will be void (1) if it be materially defective in language; an example of which may be seen in the case above stated, where the writ failed to shew who was intended by the precept.

A writ will be void (2) if the whole proceeding in which it was issued was beyond the jurisdiction of the court granting it. For example: The defendant executes a warrant against the plaintiff for the collection of road taxes;

[1] Doyle v. Russell, 30 Barb. 300 (N. Y.).
[2] Id.
[3] Tarlton v. Fisher, 2 Doug. 671; Deyo v. Van Valkenburgh, 5 Hill, 242 (N. Y.).

the warrant being issued by a justice of the peace who has no authority over such taxes. The writ is void, and the defendant is liable for false imprisonment[1].

A writ will be void (3) where the court, though having jurisdiction over the subject-matter of a proceeding, has no authority to institute it by a warrant. For example: The defendant, an officer, executes a warrant for the arrest of the plaintiff in a complaint for the non-payment of wages. The court issuing the writ has jurisdiction over such cases, but has no power to issue a warrant; a summons being the only process allowed. The writ is void, and the defendant is liable[2].

In all of these cases, the writ is said to shew its invalidity upon its face, and when this is the case the officer is not bound to serve it. The effect of the second and third of these rules is to require the officer to know the general extent of the jurisdiction of the court which he is serving. Further than this the law does not go; and in other cases the officer will be protected, though his writ were voidable, and liable to be set aside for error, or even though it were actually void[3]. Cases of this kind are always within the limits of the court's general jurisdiction; and the officer is not liable, since, though bound to know the extent of the court's jurisdiction, he is not presumed to know the nature and propriety of all the proceedings in a cause. If his writ do not indicate its invalidity on its face, the officer is safe, though the writ ought not to have issued.

To put the case in the form of a more general proposition, as laid down upon great consideration in an American authority, a ministerial officer is protected in the execution of process, whether the same issue from a court of limited or

[1] Stephens v. Wilkins, 6 Barr, 260 (Penn.).
[2] Shergold v. Holloway, 2 Strange, 1002.
[3] See Deyo v. Van Valkenburgh, 5 Hill, 242 (N. Y.).

of general jurisdiction, though such court have not in fact authority in the particular instance, provided that on the face of the process it appears that the court has jurisdiction of the subject-matter, and nothing appears therein to apprise the officer that the court has not authority to arrest the body of the party named in the process. For example: The defendant, a constable, arrests the plaintiff under a warrant from a justice of the peace issued upon a judgment against the plaintiff in an action within the jurisdiction of the court. The court has authority in such cases to issue a warrant, but in this particular instance the suit has not been instituted by the issuance of the necessary process for the appearance of the then defendant, now plaintiff. The defendant has violated no duty to the plaintiff, and is not liable, though the court had no authority to issue the warrant under such circumstances, the writ not indicating the fact[1]. Again: The defendant, an officer, arrests the plaintiff, a member of Parliament, privileged at the time from arrest, the writ not indicating the fact. This is not a false imprisonment[2].

The clerk of the court (probably) will also, like the officer who serves the precept, be liable in case he made out the writ in a defective form. He has done that which he has no right to do, and is impliedly forbidden to do; and he must therefore stand upon the same footing with the officer.

The clerk may also be liable when the officer who serves the writ is not liable. And this will be the case whenever the writ, though regular on its face (and hence a justification to the officer), was issued without orders of the court, under circumstances in which such issuance is not by law allowed. For example: The defendant, clerk of an inferior court,

[1] Savacool v. Boughton, 5 Wend. 170 (N. Y.); s. c. L. C. Torts, 241.
[2] Tarlton v. Fisher, 2 Doug. 671.

issues a writ of capias on which the plaintiff is arrested, without the presence or intervention of the court, upon a default of the plaintiff, as to the granting of which the law requires that the judge should exercise certain judicial functions. The defendant is guilty of a breach of duty, and is liable to the plaintiff; and this too though he only conformed to the usual practice of the court in such cases, since a court cannot delegate to another its judicial functions[1].

The clerk will also (probably) be liable, like both the officer and the judge, when the writ, issued by order of the court, shews upon its face that the whole cause was without the jurisdiction of the judge. It will be different, however, if, while the proceeding was within the jurisdiction of the court, the particular act merely, commanded by the court, was in excess of its jurisdiction, without the clerk's knowledge. The clerk is a merely ministerial officer, like the sheriff or constable, and is no more bound than such officer to know of the legality of orders of the court within its jurisdiction. For example: The defendant, clerk of a county court, by order of the judge signs and seals a writ for the arrest and imprisonment of the plaintiff for a period of thirty days, after a certain date, upon failure to conform to an order of court; when the order of commitment should have required an earlier arrest. The defendant is not liable, though the judge (as will be seen) would be[2].

The judge of an inferior court, if he authorizes the arrest, is liable whenever the officer, acting in strict accordance with his precept, is liable; provided the precept be not void for defective language. As the judge does not make out the writ, he cannot be liable for such defect; and the clerk is not his agent or servant[3]. In other cases, that

[1] Andrews v. Marris, 1 Q. B. 3.
[2] Dews v. Riley, 11 C. B. 434.
[3] Carratt v. Morley, 1 Q. B. 18.

is, when the court has not jurisdiction of the cause, the proceeding is coram non judice : the court loses its judicial function, and the judge becomes a mere private citizen[1].

But more than this, the judge may be liable when the officer is not. This will be true whenever the judge has plainly exceeded his jurisdiction, though in a matter not affecting the officer. For example : The defendant, a justice of the peace, fines the plaintiff under the game laws, as he may do, and then sends him to gaol without any attempt to levy the penalty upon his goods, which he has no right to do. He is liable for false imprisonment; though the officer who executes the writ is not[2].

When the question of the court's jurisdiction turns on matter of fact, it is laid down as well settled that a judge of a court of record with limited jurisdiction, or a justice of the peace acting judicially, with special and limited authority, is not liable to an action of trespass (of which the action for false imprisonment is an example) for acting without jurisdiction, unless he had the knowledge or means of knowledge, of which he ought to have availed himself, of that which constitutes the defect of jurisdiction[3]. And it lies upon the plaintiff in every case to prove the fact[4].

[1] The Marshalsea, 10 Coke, 68 b ; s. c. L. C. Torts, 278, note.

[2] Hill v. Bateman, 2 Strange, 710. The arrest was justifiable, so far as the sheriff was concerned, because, though in the particular instance unauthorized, it was still within the powers of the justice to grant such a writ in a proper case; that is, after an ineffectual attempt to levy the penalty upon the party's goods. The officer was not bound to know whether such an attempt had been made. Probably he would have been liable had he known that no such attempt had been made; and this knowledge might perhaps have been easily proved. But, until it was proved, the officer could not be liable.

[3] Calder v. Halket, 3 Moore, P. C. 28, Parke, B.; Pease v. Chaytor, 32 L. J. Mag. Cas. 121, Blackburn, J.

[4] Calder v. Halket and Pease v. Chaytor, supra, in which Carratt v. Morley, 1 Q. B. 18, apparently contra, is doubted.

For example : The defendant, a justice of the peace, having jurisdiction to grant a capias in certain classes of civil offences, committed within his district, orders the arrest of the plaintiff, on suit brought against him by a third person, for an offence committed without his district. The defendant, however, has no knowledge that the act was committed beyond his district, nor is he put upon notice of the fact by anything arising before the arrest. He is not liable for a false imprisonment[1], unless he acted maliciously and without probable cause[2].

When, however, the question of jurisdiction does not depend upon the proof of certain facts, but upon a question of law, the judge acts at his peril; and, if he order the arrest of an individual when he has no jurisdiction, not determinable on facts, he will be liable for false imprisonment. For example: The defendant, judge of a court of record of limited jurisdiction, directs the arrest of the plaintiff for contempt of the process of the court, and commits him to gaol. The commitment is unauthorized, and is made under a mistake of law about the powers of the defendant, and not under mistake as to the facts: the statute requiring that the process (under the circumstances) should have been issued by the court of another county. The defendant is liable[3].

From the statement of the foregoing principles and

[1] See Pease *v.* Chaytor, supra, opinion of Blackburn, J. at pp. 125, 126, from which this example is framed. Another example may be seen in Lowther *v.* Radnor, 8 East, 113, 119. A distinction must, however, be noticed (which was pointed out in Pease *v.* Chaytor) between a proceeding to prevent the enforcement of a judgment in such a case—*that* would be proper—and an action against the judge of the court, as in the example.

[2] Id. But the case could then be an action for malicious prosecution.

[3] Houlden *v.* Smith, 14 Q. B. 841.

examples, it will be seen (1) that the officer alone may be liable for false imprisonment; as where he executes his writ upon the wrong person, without the latter's fault : (2) that the clerk alone may be liable; as where, without direction from the judge, he issues a precept regular in form, and within the jurisdiction of the court, but which he had no right at all to issue : (3) that the judge alone may be liable; as where, having jurisdiction over the cause, he orders the issuance of the warrant under circumstances in which the act was improper : (4) that the officer and the clerk may alone be liable; as where the writ contains substantially defective language : (5) that all three may be liable ; as where the whole cause, in the course of which the writ is issued (at the command of the judge), is without the jurisdiction of the court.

This is not all. The liability for a false imprisonment may extend to the attorney at whose instance the proceeding was begun, and, further still, to his client who authorized him to begin it. Indeed, this will always be the case wherever it can be properly said that the wrongful imprisonment was ordered or participated in by the client.

When the judge assumes the power of ordering the warrant, upon a statement of the grounds, the act (with the exception to be stated presently) is his own, and not the attorney's or his client's[1]; and this, too, though counsel were urgent for the issuance of the writ[2]; the attorney or client has not set a ministerial but a judicial officer in motion[3]. If this be the extent of the connexion of the

[1] Carratt *v.* Morley, 1 Q. B. 18; Williams *v.* Smith, 14 C. B. N. s. 596; Smith *v.* Sydney, L. R. 5 Q. B. 203.

[2] Cooper *v.* Harding, 7 Q. B. 928.

[3] In this appears one chief distinction between an action for false imprisonment and one for malicious prosecution. 'The party making the charge [before a magistrate] is not liable to an action for

attorney and client with the arrest, neither can be liable, whether the writ was granted upon a mistaken view of the law by the judge in regard as to his jurisdiction (in which case *he* would be liable), or was issued in a materially defective form (in which case the clerk and the officer would be liable): the act is that of another. Illustrations may be seen in the examples above given. Hence the attorney and client may not be liable, though the process was void on its face[1].

The attorney, and his client with him, may, however, become liable in a case in which the arrest has been thus ordered by the judge. Such a result will come about whenever the attorney participates in any manner in effecting the arrest after the issuance of the improper warrant. For example: The defendants, attorney and client in a former litigation against the present plaintiff, having obtained an erroneous warrant against the latter from the judge, the attorney personally puts the precept into the officer's hands, and directs him to serve it. The defendants are both liable; the attorney because of his personal interference, the client because bound by the act of his attorney in the ordinary course of the litigation[2]. Again: The defendant, an at-

---

false imprisonment because he does not set a ministerial officer in motion, but a judicial officer. The opinion and the judgment of a judicial officer are interposed between the charge and the imprisonment.' Austin *v.* Dowling L. R. 5 C. P. 534, 540, Willes, J.

[1] Carratt *v.* Morley, 1 Q. B. 18. The author withdraws his criticism on this case, made in his Leading Cases on Torts, p. 280. The client had done nothing but to ask for a writ; and the court, acting judicially, granted it. The act was, therefore, the act of the judge, and not of the party. The latter, to be liable, must either have directed the execution of the writ after its issuance, or have obtained it from the court in an irregular manner, or have participated in the execution of it.

[2] Barker *v.* Braham, 2 W. Black. 866; s. c. L. C. Torts, 235.

CHAP. II.]   FALSE IMPRISONMENT.   147

torney, indorses with his name and residence an invalid warrant, issued against the plaintiff. This makes him a participant in the false imprisonment which follows[1]; and his client also.

When the writ of arrest is issued through misconduct of the attorney, or material misrepresentations (even though not fraudulent), or even through his mistake, the act is not the act of the judge, unless he had no jurisdiction to grant the writ, but of the attorney, and of his client whom he represents[2]. The consequence is, that the last named are both liable for false imprisonment upon the execution of the precept; even though they take no further steps in the matter than those involved in obtaining the writ[3]. For example: The defendants, attorney and client in a former suit against the present plaintiff, obtain a warrant therein for the latter's arrest upon material misrepresentations made in an affidavit upon which the warrant is awarded, on account of which misrepresentations the warrant is, after the plaintiff's arrest, set aside. They are both liable[4]. Again: The defendant, by his attorney, in a former suit against the now plaintiff, procures the arrest therein of the last named under a writ issued by mistake against a person not bearing the name of the present plaintiff. This is a false imprisonment, and the defendant is liable, although

[1] Green v. Elgie, 5 Q. B. 99.

[2] Williams v. Smith, 14 C. B. N. s. 596; Codrington v. Lloyd, 8 Ad. & E. 449; Collett v. Foster, 2 Hurl. & N. 356. See Davies v. Jenkins, 11 M. & W. 745.

[3] This is what is meant when it is said that the attorney and his client are liable in case of irregularity in obtaining the writ. Irregularity (in this sense) is the act of the party and not of the court. See Codrington v. Lloyd, 8 Ad. & E. 449.

[4] Williams v. Smith, 14 C. B. N. s. 596. The action was not sustained in this second suit because the misrepresentations were not material.

10—2

the person intended was arrested[1]. Again : The defendants, attorney and client in a former civil action against the now plaintiff, in which they obtained judgment against him, obtain a warrant for the arrest of the plaintiff by virtue of the judgment, after a discharge therefrom of the plaintiff by proceedings in insolvency, of which the defendants had notice. They are liable for false imprisonment; unless it can be shewn that the discharge was obtained by fraud[2].

It will thus be seen that there may be cases in which all the parties named will be jointly liable, client, attorney, officer, clerk, and judge. Such will be the result where the attorney personally directs the officer to serve a writ upon the plaintiff, issued by the judge's order, in a civil cause, wholly beyond the jurisdiction of his court.

There is a structural distinction between civil and criminal cases; the parties are different. A civil suit is a litigation between individuals: a criminal suit is a litigation between the Crown and an individual. The prosecutor in a criminal action does not represent the plaintiff in a civil suit. A civil proceeding is instituted in the interest and for the benefit of the plaintiff, and is under his control throughout: the plaintiff is 'dominus litis.' False steps and misconduct on his behalf in the course of the litigation will therefore bind him, as has already been seen. The prosecutor of crime, however, is not a party to the litigation instituted by him. The proceeding is not carried on pri-

[1] See Jarmain v. Hooper, 6 Man. & G. 827.

[2] Deyo v. Van Valkenburgh, 5 Hill, 242 (N. Y.). This is the exception alluded to above, by which the attorney and client are liable, though the judge has been merely asked to grant the warrant. But it was misconduct to ask for the warrant when it was known that the judgment had been discharged, unless proof could be brought that the discharge was fraudulent. The judge, having no jurisdiction to grant the warrant in such a case, would also be liable.

marily in his interest; and he has no control over its course. The consequence is, he cannot be bound by the action of the attorney-general or other prosecuting officer. He may, however, bind himself, and become liable for a false imprisonment by acts of his own, or of counsel whom he may employ to assist the Crown. If the prosecutor or his attorney should personally direct the service of an invalid writ, whether void or only voidable, he would be liable to the party arrested[1]. *Ch.*

Before an action for false imprisonment under process of court can be maintained, it is necessary that the writ should be set aside, unless it appear to be absolutely void. For if the process be merely voidable, it is valid until quashed; and hence the arrest must, till then, be legal. If, however, the process be absolutely void, and the action be brought against the proper party or parties, it is not necessary (probably), either in cases of civil or in criminal arrests, to have it set aside before suing for false imprisonment. For example: The defendant procures the arrest of the plaintiff on a warrant issued upon a judgment which the former knows to have been discharged; and the plaintiff sues for false imprisonment without first having the writ set aside. The action is maintainable; the writ being absolutely void[2]. Again: The defendant, a justice of the peace, procures the arrest of the plaintiff upon four convictions before him of baking bread on one and the same Sunday; the law permitting but one conviction in such a case. The defendant is liable for false imprisonment, though the wrongful convictions be not first quashed[3].

[1] Hopkins *v.* Crowe, 4 Ad. & E. 774.
[2] Deyo *v.* Van Valkenburgh, 5 Hill, 242 (N. Y.).
[3] Crepps *v.* Durden, 2 Cowp. 640. In this case there was no arrest, but merely a levy on the plaintiff's goods for the amount of the penalty; but the principle would be the same.

In both civil and criminal cases, however, the action is to be distinguished from a suit for malicious prosecution. The writ in an action for a false imprisonment, made under process of court, may have been, as regards the party or parties sued for the tort, either void or voidable[1]; and, in such a case, the action is maintainable without proof of malice, or of want of probable cause, or of the termination of the prosecution. In an action for malicious prosecution, however, it matters not whether the writ was void, voidable, or valid; but the plaintiff, as has been seen, has the burden of proving all the facts just stated.

§ 4. OF ARRESTS WITHOUT WARRANT.

It is not necessary, however, in all cases that an arrest for an infraction of the law should be made under authority and by command of a warrant. There are occasions on which the utmost promptness of action is required for the attainment of the ends of justice in the apprehension of law-breakers; and the necessities of society have in such cases furnished a justification for the arrest of offenders without a formal warrant of a court of justice. But the law does not encourage the making of arrests in this manner: on the contrary, in the interest of liberty, it prefers a slower and more deliberate proceeding by warrant, issued upon solemn oath concerning the facts, in all cases in which the administration of justice can thus be efficiently carried out.

The occasions on which arrests without warrant are considered justifiable upon the above stated ground are

---

[1] It will be noticed that to sustain an action against the officer who served the writ, or against the clerk, the writ must have been void on its face; while it is enough in *this* respect, to sustain an action against the judge or attorney and client, that the writ was only voidable.

well defined. In the first place, it must be well understood that the right to make such arrests is confined altogether to infractions of the criminal law. In no case can an officer make an arrest in a civil cause without the protection of a warrant. It may be true, as has already been stated, that, in cases of the release of a prisoner arrested on process in a civil action, the officer may retake the party without obtaining a special warrant for this particular purpose; but that is because he has already a warrant, which is still in force. Hence, the officer does make the arrest under a writ; and he must justify his act under that writ.

The first case to be mentioned in which an arrest can be made without a warrant, is when the arrest is made upon the spot, at the time of the breach of the peace. Such a case comes directly within the reason above mentioned, namely, the necessities of society; nor could there be any use of requiring an affidavit and warrant in such a case, even if the delay might not be fatal. The right thus to arrest on the spot applies equally to all breaches of the peace, whether the act be a crime or a misdemeanour.

An arrest without warrant may also be made by an officer of the law, qualified for the making of arrests, upon 'suspicion of felony,' to use a common expression of the books. The meaning of this is, that if in an action for false imprisonment, without warrant (that is, *because* without warrant), the officer can shew that, though no felony was in fact committed, he had probable cause to suppose that the prisoner had committed such a crime, he has violated no duty to the plaintiff in thus making the arrest. For example: The defendant, a constable, having probable cause to believe that the plaintiff is guilty of the felony of receiving or aiding in the concealment of stolen goods, arrests him without a warrant, and conveys him to gaol, where he detains the prisoner until he can make application to a magistrate for a warrant against him as a receiver of stolen goods. The warrant is refused, and the prisoner at once discharged. The defendant is not liable[1].

The officer's suspicion must, however, as above intimated, be a reasonable ground to suppose the prisoner guilty of a felony; that is, it must be such a strong suspicion as would justify a man of caution in entertaining a belief in the party's guilt. If the circumstances do not warrant such a belief, even though in fact a felony has been committed, the officer violates his duty to the plaintiff by arresting him without process of court[2]. For example: The defendant, a constable, arrests and imprisons the plaintiff, without process, under the following circumstances: The cart of the plaintiff, a butcher, is passing along the highway, when a person, in the habit of attending fairs, stops the cart and says to the officer (defendant), 'These are my traces, which were stolen at the peace-rejoicing last year.' The defendant asks the plaintiff how he came by the traces. The plaintiff replies that he saw a stranger pick them up in the road, and bought them of him for a shilling; whereupon he is taken into custody, and, on examination before a magistrate, discharged. This does not shew probable cause for the arrest, and the defendant is liable[3].

In the authority from which this example is taken, the whole case was given to the judges, with power to act as a jury so far as might be necessary for the decision of the

---

[1] Rohan v. Sawin, 5 Cush. 281 (Mass.).

[2] The process would justify the officer in such a case, since the granting of it would be a declaration of the judge that there exists probable cause to believe the party guilty. The term 'probable cause' here, as in the chapter on Malicious Prosecution, is used for 'reasonable and probable cause.'

[3] Hogg v. Ward, 3 H. & N. 417; s. c. L. C. Torts, 252.

question before them. It therefore does not appear from the decision, whether the question of probable cause is to be considered as a question for the judge or for the jury; and the point was expressly left undecided by the judges.

The question has, indeed, been one of some difficulty. In some of the cases, it has been tacitly assumed that the jury must determine whether the officer had probable cause for taking the plaintiff into custody[1]; in others, that it is for the court to say whether the facts proved shew proper cause[2]. The point has, however, been decided in accordance with this latter view, though not without expressions of regret[3]; making the rule to conform to that of actions for malicious prosecution.

If the analogy furnished by the law of actions for malicious prosecution is to be fully carried out, and it appears reasonable that it should be, it will also be necessary for the officer to shew that this reasonable ground for making the arrest consisted of facts within his own possession at the time of the arrest, and that he cannot justify on facts which afterwards came to his notice. Nor, on the other hand, if his justification lie in the facts before him at the time of taking the party into custody, will his defence be overturned by evidence of facts indicating innocence, that came to his notice after the imprisonment[4].

At common law, no valid arrest without a warrant can be made for a misdemeanour, except on the spot[5]. To arrest

[1] Beckwith *v.* Philby, 6 B. & C. 635; Rohan *v.* Sawin, 5 Cush. 281 (Mass.).
[2] Hill *v.* Yates, 8 Taunt. 182; Davis *v.* Russell, 5 Bing. 354.
[3] Lister *v.* Perryman, L. R. 4 H. L. 521, 531, 538, 539.
[4] See ante, pp. 60, et seq.
[5] Whether and how far this may have been changed in regard to the duties of policemen in large cities cannot here be considered. See 1 Stephen's, History of Criminal Law, 197, 199, 200; Pollock, Torts, 190.

a man, without process, on suspicion that he has committed a misdemeanour, although upon probable cause for his arrest, is a breach of duty. For example: The defendant, a constable, arrests the plaintiff without a writ on the statement of J. M., that the plaintiff has committed the offence of perjury, by wilfully and corruptly making a false affidavit in a judicial proceeding before the Honourable W. W., judge of a court, and he takes the plaintiff into custody upon this charge, at the direction of J. M. He is liable to the plaintiff for a false imprisonment[1]; though he would not have been, had the offence charged been a felony.

And the arrest must not only have been made upon the spot: it must also have been made, in the case of an actual breach of the peace, before the breach has entirely ceased. For example: The defendant, a constable, takes the plaintiff into custody without a warrant under the following circumstances: The plaintiff had been making a disturbance about certain premises in the night-time, and had refused, on request of the defendant, to desist. Perceiving that the defendant intends to arrest him, the plaintiff flees and is pursued, overtaken, and arrested; the disturbance having previously ceased. The defendant is liable[2].

In the case of affrays, however, an arrest may be made without a warrant not only during the actual breach of the peace, but so long as the offender's conduct shews that the public peace is likely to be endangered by his acts. Indeed,

[1] Bowditch v. Balchin, 5 Ex. 378. See Commonwealth v. Carey, 12 Cush. 246, 252 (Mass.); Commonwealth v. McLaughlin, Id. 615, 618.

[2] Compare Baynes v. Brewster, 2 Q. B. 375, where the defendant, on such facts, was a private citizen; but the rule would have been the same had he been an officer, as the language of Mr Justice Williams in that case shews.

while those are assembled together who have been committing acts of violence, and the danger of renewal continues, the affray may be said to continue; and during the affray, thus understood, the officer may arrest the offender not only on his own view, but even on the information or complaint of another. This is true even of an arrest by a private citizen[1]. For example: The defendant arrests the plaintiff without process under the following circumstances: The plaintiff had entered the defendant's shop to make a purchase, when a dispute arose between the plaintiff and a servant of the defendant, resulting in an affray between them. The defendant, coming into the shop during the affray, orders the plaintiff to leave, which he refuses to do; the violence having then ceased, though there is still danger of a renewal of the affray. The defendant now gives the plaintiff into the custody of an officer. This is no breach of duty to the plaintiff[2].

The example given leads to the consideration of the nature of the right of a private citizen to arrest offenders without process of court; for it is (probably) lawful for such a person to make an arrest upon a warrant under the same circumstances in which an officer could do so.

The rule of law in regard to arrests for misdemeanours by private citizens is the same as prevails concerning officers; they are entitled to make the arrest without process while the breach of the peace is going on or (in accordance with the explanation given) still continues. But a private citizen has no right to make an arrest, without a writ, for a misdemeanour after its termination, though the breach of peace was committed about his own premises[3].

[1] Timothy v. Simpson, 1 Cromp. M. & R. 757; s. c. L. C. Torts, 257; Baynes v. Brewster, 2 Q. B. 375, 386.
[2] Timothy v. Simpson, supra.
[3] Baynes v. Brewster, supra.

In regard to felonies, the rights of officers and private citizens are different. While an officer can arrest without a warrant upon probable cause, though no felony has been committed, a private citizen can safely make an arrest without a warrant only (1) when the felony charged has actually been committed, and (2) when there was probable cause for supposing the party arrested to be guilty[1].

[1] Allen v. Wright, 8 Car. & P. 522; s. c. L. C. Torts, 265. In Commonwealth v. Carey, 12 Cush. 246, 251, Chief Justice Shaw, in a dictum, states the rule thus: 'A private citizen, who arrests another on a charge of felony, does it at the peril of being able to prove a felony actually committed by the person arrested.' But that appears to be a mistake.

CHAPTER III.

ENTICEMENT AND SEDUCTION.

§ 1. INTRODUCTORY.

Statement of the duty. A owes to B the duty to forbear to procure or cause C to deprive B of C's service or consortium.

The law of enticement and seduction gives a right of redress (1) for wrongfully interrupting the relation of master and servant, or of husband and wife, and (2) for wrongfully preventing the renewal of such relation, or in the language of the books for 'harbouring' the servant or wife. 'Enticement' here means enticing away from service.

The relation of master and servant is sustained not only between persons one of whom has contracted to perform services for the other, but also between persons one of whom gives his services to the other gratuitously, and possibly between persons one of whom is under the custody or guardianship of the other. The relation thus expressed therefore includes (1) that of master and servant ex contractu, (2) of master and servant ex gratia, (3) of parent and child, and (4) of guardian and ward.

The law of enticement differs so slightly from the law of seduction, that these subjects can be conveniently treated as one in nearly all their legal features. Unless, then, the contrary be indicated, it will be understood that what is said under either designation will apply, where the facts permit, to the other subject[1].

The whole subject will now be examined in the order indicated in the paragraph explaining the use of the term master and servant; the subject of husband and wife following the various divisions relating to service.

§ 2. OF MASTER AND SERVANT EX CONTRACTU.

Any person who, with notice of the existence of the relation of master and servant, interrupts that relation, without the consent of the master, by procuring the servant to depart from his master's service, violates a duty which he owes to the latter, and becomes liable in damages to him. For example: The defendant entices away from the service of the plaintiff his journeymen shoemakers, with notice of their relation to the plaintiff, persuading them to enter into his, the defendant's, service. This is a breach of duty[2].

It matters not in cases of a binding engagement to service that the servant had not yet entered upon the performance of the service at the time of the enticement or seduction. If by the terms of the contract or the apprenticeship (for there is no difference between an ordinary contract of hiring and an apprenticeship, so far as the present subject is concerned) the master has a right to

[1] The terms 'seduction' and 'enticement' are often indifferently used in the old, and sometimes in the later, books. A journeyman, for example, is said to have been seduced, when he has been enticed away from his master's service. See the marginal note to Hart v. Aldridge, 1 Cowp. 54.

[2] Hart v. Aldridge, supra; Walker v. Cronin, 107 Mass. 555.

require performance of the services at the time of the enticement, he has a right of redress for a wrongful interference with that right. For example: The defendant induces the plaintiff's gardener to refuse altogether to carry out his engagement to make the plaintiff's gardens, though the gardener, owing to dissatisfaction with his engagement, has already absented himself for a considerable time from his duties under the contract of hiring. The defendant is liable[1].

In the foregoing examples, the defendant had notice of the existence of the relation of master and servant when he procured the servant to leave his master. Now, notice of the existence of this relation is necessary in all cases of actual service: in the absence of notice, the party enticing away or seducing the servant violates no duty to the master. But it matters not that such party had no notice at first of the existence of the relation, if he afterwards acquire notice and then persist in keeping the servant away from his master. For example: The defendant employs the plaintiff's servant, upon application by the latter; the servant having left the plaintiff during the existence of his contract of service, of which, however, the defendant is ignorant. Afterwards the plaintiff informs the defendant that the person employed by him is his (the plaintiff's) servant. The plaintiff requests the servant to return to him, and the servant refuses; and the defendant then continues to keep him in his employ. The defendant is liable for so continuing to keep the servant, though not for taking him into his service[2].

In order, however, to maintain an action for preventing a renewal of the service (for harbouring a servant), and

[1] Compare Lumley v. Gye, 2 El. & B. 216; s. c. L. C. Torts, 306.
[2] Blake v. Lanyon, 6 T. R. 221.

not for interrupting it, it is necessary that there should be a binding contract of service. If there be no such engagement, the defendant cannot be liable to the plaintiff for persuading the servant to stay where he is rather than return to the plaintiff, since the plaintiff neither has any right to require the service in such a case, nor is he at the time in the enjoyment of it as a gratuity. For example: The defendant receives, without notice, a person who has been acting in the service of the plaintiff under a contract void by the Statute of Frauds, and afterwards, on notice of the plaintiff's claim to the service, during the term of service agreed upon, refuses to send the person away. This is no breach of duty to the plaintiff[1].

Some question has been made, whether this doctrine concerning the liability of one who wrongfully entices away, seduces, or harbours another's servant is an exception to established rules of law, and must therefore be confined strictly to cases of enticing servants in the ordinary sense of persons performing manual labour for an employer, or whether such cases are not, on the contrary, merely special instances of a wider rule of law[2]. But it appears to have become established that this subject is a special one, and not an example. For inducing one to break a contract generally, there is no liability, unless the act was malicious, as has been seen in a previous chapter[3]. That is a different thing from the present subject.

§ 3. OF MASTER AND SERVANT EX GRATIA.

It was formerly a matter of some doubt if an action could be maintained for interrupting, with notice, the

[1] Sykes v. Dixon, 9 Ad. & E. 693. See also Hartley v. Cummings, 5 C. B. 247; Pilkington v. Scott, 15 M. & W. 657.

[2] Lumley v. Gye, 2 El. & B. 216. See Bowen v. Hall, 6 Q. B. Div. 333.

[3] Ante, chap. IV. Part I.

gratuitous relation of master and servant. It was sometimes supposed that inasmuch as the master in such a case could not require the services, he had no right to them which could be infringed. But this view does not now obtain. Though a person may not be able to require the bestowment of a gratuity, he has a right to it when it is bestowed, and in the course of receiving it, and no one may interrupt his actual enjoyment of the gratuity[1]. Hence if a person be actually engaged in giving his services to another, anyone who, with notice, voluntarily interrupts the service violates a legal duty to the recipient of the gratuity, and becomes liable in damages. For example: The defendant, with notice, entices away a young woman while she is in the gratuitous service of the plaintiff, and thereby deprives the plaintiff of the benefit of her help. The plaintiff is entitled to recover damages therefor[2].

Indeed, it matters not in such cases that the person enticed was actually under obligation to another; if the latter do not insist upon his rights, no third person can set up those rights to escape liability for a wrongful act. For example: The defendant, with notice, seduces a married woman while she is rendering gratuitous service to the plaintiff, her father. The defendant is liable, and cannot set up in defence the paramount right of the woman's husband to her help[3].

As was observed, however, in the preceding section, and as follows from what has been said in the present, no action can be maintained for mere harbouring a servant ex gratia, though with notice: the action lies solely for enticing the person away or otherwise interrupting the performance of

[1] See ante, p. 12.
[2] Evans v. Walton, L. R. 2 C. P. 615. The young woman in this case was the plaintiff's daughter, but she was of age.
[3] Harper v. Luffkin, 7 B. & C. 387.

the service while the servant is disposed to, and engaged in, the performance of it. When the servant has put an end to the relation, the rights of the master at once terminate.

§ 4. OF PARENT AND CHILD.

A parent's right of action against one who has seduced or enticed away his child is the right of action of a master sub modo. That is to say, it requires the existence of the relation of master and servant between the parent and the child, but the right of action, as will presently be seen, is not co-extensive with the right to require the child's service. The action in question does not turn upon parental authority or upon the kinship of parent and child.

The law gives a right of action for the child's seduction so long at least as the child remains at home, and renders any part of her service to the parent; and this is true, even though the child has attained majority, as would follow from what has been said in the preceding section, and as will further appear in the present.

But the relation may be severed (for the present purpose) by the child alone; the right of action is gone when the child leaves her parent's house, and has no intention of returning[1], or while she is away in the service of an-

---

[1] Dean v. Peel, 5 East, 45. See Griffiths v. Teetgen, 15 C. B. 344; Manley v. Field, 7 C. B. N. S. 96; Hedges v. Tagg, L. R. 7 Ex. 283. In America, however, the *father's* right of action is considered to depend, not upon the will of the child, but upon the will of the parent; and hence, notwithstanding the absence of the child from her father's house at the time of the seduction, the father has a right of action if he has not divested himself of his right to require her services, even though she were at the time of the wrong in the service of another with her father's permission. For example: The defendant seduces the plaintiff's daughter under the following circumstances: The daughter, at the age of nineteen, with the consent of her father, the plaintiff, goes to live with a relative, for whom she works when she

other. It is considered, however, that, if the parent's control over his child was divested by fraud, he may treat it, on discovering the fraud, as never having been abandoned, and maintain an action against the seducer. For example: The defendant hires the plaintiff's daughter from his service with intent to seduce her, and by this means obtains possession of her person, and seduces her. The plaintiff is entitled to recover as if the daughter had been seduced while in his own service[1].

It seems not necessary that the child should have performed specific *acts* of service. But the performance of the slightest acts, such as pouring tea at the table[2], is enough to shew the ability to render service; and such ability is laid down to be the gist of the action[3]. Where, however, parent and child are living together, that fact shews, it seems, a presumptive right of action[4]; where the child is away for a time, but not out on service, an

pleases, receiving pay for her labour. While thus at her relative's house, she is seduced and got with child by the defendant, and at once returns to her father's, and is there cared for. She, however, had no intention, but for the seduction, to return to her father. The defendant has violated a duty to the plaintiff, since the plaintiff had a right to require his daughter's services at the time of the seduction. Martin *v.* Payne, 9 Johns. 387 (N. Y.); s. c. L. C. Torts, 286.

This, however, is the extent of the American rule. If the power of the parent over his daughter be gone at the time of the seduction, whether by his own consent in emancipating her or binding her out to service, or by the act of the law in taking her away from him, the seducer has violated no legal duty to him; though there has been some doubt as to the application of this doctrine in the case of the return of the daughter to the parent after the seduction. See p. 167.

[1] Speight *v.* Oliviera, 2 Stark. 493. See Evans *v.* Walton, L. R. 2 C. P. 615, 624.
[2] See note to Grinnell *v.* Wells, 7 Man. & G. 1044; ante, p. 127.
[3] Hall *v.* Hollander, 4 B. & C. 660; ante, p. 127.
[4] Thompson *v.* Ross, 5 H. & N. 16; Terry *v.* Hutchinson, L. R. 3 Q. B. 599, 602.

intention on her part to return is presumptively sufficient, for that shews that she has not severed (de facto) the relation[1].

The father's right of action continues, as has already been observed, after the daughter has come of age, if the relation of master and servant is still in operation between them. If the parent continue to exercise authority over the daughter after her majority, and she continue to submit, she is still his servant, though not under an actual engagement to serve him; and seduction under such circumstances is a breach of legal duty to the parent. For example: The defendant seduces the plaintiff's daughter, aged twenty-two years. Prior to and at the time of the seduction, the daughter has been living part of the time with her brother, who resides about a mile from her father's house, and part of the time with her father. She has not received wages from her brother, and when at home has worked for her mother, the plaintiff buying her clothing. The daughter is the plaintiff's servant, and the defendant is liable[2].

It has been held that the seduction should be followed by pregnancy or disease to entitle the plaintiff to recover[3], but there is some doubt of the soundness of this[4]. The American rule is, that where the proper effect of the connection is an incapacity to labour, by reason of which the plaintiff loses the services of his daughter and servant, the loss of such services entitles the plaintiff to recover against the seducer. The same principle which gives a master an action where the connection causes pregnancy

[1] Terry v. Hutchinson, supra.
[2] Sutton v. Huffman, 3 Vroom, 58 (N. J.); Rist v. Faux, 4 Best & S. 409, Ex. Ch.
[3] Eager v. Grimwood, 1 Ex. 61.
[4] Evans v. Walton, L. R. 2 C. P. 615, 617; Abrahams v. Kidney, 104 Mass. 222.

applies to the case of sexual disease, and, indeed, to all cases where the proper consequence of the act of the defendant is a loss of health resulting in an incapacity for such service as could have been rendered before. For example: The defendant seduces the plaintiff's minor daughter, by reason of which, without becoming pregnant (or being affected with sexual disease), she suffers general injury in health, so that it becomes necessary for the plaintiff to send her away for her recovery; whereby he incurs expense and loses his daughter's services. The defendant is liable[1].

If, however, the loss of health be caused by mental suffering not the consequence of the seduction, but produced by subsequent intervening causes, the loss of service is not the proper consequence in contemplation of law of the defendant's act; and hence the action cannot be maintained. For example: The defendant seduces the plaintiff's minor daughter, and subsequently abandons her, in consequence of which she suffers such distress of mind as to bring illness upon her, and incapacitate her for performing services for the plaintiff; no pregnancy or disease resulting by direct consequence of the seduction. The defendant is not liable, it seems, to the plaintiff[2].

If a loss of service follow as the proper effect of the defendant's act, it is held in America to be immaterial that he accomplished his purpose without resorting to seductive arts. The willingness of the daughter cannot affect the parent's rights[3]; though the ready consent of the young woman might be ground for mitigation of damages[4].

[1] Abrahams v. Kidney, supra; Boyle v. Brandon, 13 M. & W. 738.
[2] Boyle v. Brandon, supra; Abrahams v. Kidney, supra.
[3] Damon v. Moore, 5 Lans. 454 (N. Y.)
[4] Hogan v. Cregan, 6 Rob. 138 (N. Y.), criticised in Damon v. Moore, supra. Comp. Winter v. Henn, 4 Car. & P. 494 and Forster v.

What has been said in the preceding paragraphs concerning the parent's right of action for loss of service must be understood of the father's claim to damages. During his guardianship of the daughter, the right of action belongs to him alone. Should he be removed by the law from his natural position of authority, or should he die during the child's minority, the question arises of the mother's right of action against the seducer. It is clear if the guardianship of the child has been given to her, she has a right of action for the loss of service ; though it may be doubted if at the present time the mere relation of guardian, apart from that of parent, would, in all cases, afford a right of action for the child's seduction,—a point to be further adverted to in the next section.

A difficulty arises where the mother, upon the death of the father, or his removal from the guardianship, simply continues to exercise authority over her daughter, and to receive her (voluntary) obedience, without having received an appointment as guardian. The mother's right of action has sometimes been supposed to turn upon the question of her right to require the child's support in such a case,— a doubtful point of law. It is now well settled in America, however, that so long as the daughter continues to give obedience and service to her mother, the latter has a right

Forster, 33 L. J. Prob. & M. 150, n., as to criminal conversation : post, p. 175. Perhaps this would be true if the daughter were a notoriously loose character, and had already brought her family to mortification. In general, the damages in an action by a parent for seduction are not confined to the loss of service. While the loss of service is of the gist of the action, still when the loss is established, and shewn to have been caused by the defendant's acts, the court permits the jury to give damages for the disgrace that has been inflicted upon the plaintiff's family. L. C. Torts, 294. But, if the sense of disgrace had already befallen his family by the daughter's conduct, the defendant could hardly be liable for anything beyond the loss of service.

of action for a wrongful interruption of the daughter's position of servant[1]. For example: The defendant seduces the minor daughter of the plaintiff, a widow. The daughter, having previously been in the service of the defendant, and then in the service of D, returns from the latter person to her mother to aid her during sickness in the family. While thus with her mother for a day or two, she is got with child by the defendant. The defendant has violated a legal duty to the plaintiff, and is liable in damages[2].

The authority from which this example has been given went one step further, and decided that the mother's right of action was not affected by the fact that the daughter, when seduced, was actually in the service of another, so long as she indicated a willingness to consider her mother as still entitled to her assistance. The case would of course be different in England if the daughter had no intention to return to her mother.

There is also conflict of American authority concerning the mother's right of action in such cases where the daughter in her illness returns to her mother, and is supported and cared for during her sickness. The daughter's return, however, under such circumstances does not indicate that she had any intention of returning before the seduction; and, unless the mother is considered to have the legal right to require her daughter's service, it is difficult to see how she could be entitled, even under the American rule, to sue for the seduction in a case of that kind[3].

[1] This also follows from what has been said in § 2, supra.
[2] Gray v. Durland, 51 N. Y. 424.
[3] The mother's right of action in such cases is denied in South v. Denniston, 2 Watts, 474 (Penn.); Roberts v. Connelly, 14 Ala. 235. It is supported in Sargent v.——, 5 Cowen, 106 (N. Y.). It is obvious that the rules of law as to cases like those stated must remain in uncertainty and conflict until the nature of the mother's authority is definitely settled. It is still more doubtful whether the mother of a

The child is not entitled to sue for her own seduction, since she has consented to the act; though if the seduction was effected under a promise of marriage, which is afterwards broken, the young woman has a right of action. But the action is then for the breach of promise of marriage, and not for the seduction. For like reason the parent is barred if he consented to the act, or perhaps if he facilitated it by his own misconduct in respect of the morals of his daughter. For example: The defendant is permitted by the plaintiff to visit his daughter as a suitor, after notice that he is a married man and a libertine; the defendant, on inquiry by the plaintiff as to this matter, representing that his wife is an abandoned character, and that he will soon obtain a divorce from her, and then marry the plaintiff's daughter. The defendant afterwards, while continuing his visits at the plaintiff's house, seduces the young woman. The plaintiff is not entitled to recover for the seduction[1].

§ 5. OF GUARDIAN AND WARD.

Not only the parent, but anyone standing 'in loco parentis,' and receiving, to his own benefit, the services of a child, is entitled to maintain an action for loss of services against anyone who wrongfully interrupts the rendering of them, or makes the full rendering of them impossible. For example: The defendant seduces the plaintiff's niece, the parents of the young woman being dead, and the plaintiff standing 'in loco parentis.' The defendant is liable, though the young woman has pro-

daughter not born in lawful wedlock could maintain an action in a case like that of the text. The mother would not be even guardian for nurture. See Regina v. Clarke, 7 El. & B. 186; In re Ullce, 53 L. T. N. s. 711, af'd. 54 L. T. N. s. 286, Ch. Div.

[1] Reddie v. Scoolt, Peake, 240. Comp. cases of criminal conversation, p. 175.

CHAP. III.] ENTICEMENT AND SEDUCTION. 169

perty left her by her parents, and performs but slight services[1].

The right of action in all such cases, and in cases strictly of guardian and ward, depends (probably) upon the fact that the guardian or person standing 'in loco parentis' is receiving the services (however slight) to his own benefit. If the guardian have merely the supervision of the ward and her income, while she lives elsewhere, or performs service for herself, the guardian simply receiving her wages and acting as her trustee, it is improbable that he can sue for her seduction[2].

On the whole, the only difference between the case of master and servant ex gratia on the one hand, and parent and child and guardian and ward on the other hand, appears to be that in the former case the services must be substantial, and the damages would (probably) be confined to actual loss suffered; whilst in the other two cases the services may be nominal, such as might be presumed where persons so related live together[3].

§ 6. OF HUSBAND AND WIFE.

To entice away one's wife is a civil wrong for which the offender is liable to the injured husband[4]. The gist of the action, however, is not, it seems, the loss of assistance, but the loss of the consortium of the wife, which term implies an exclusive right, against an invader, to her affection,

[1] Manvell v. Thomson, 2 Car. & P. 303. And, as in the case of an action by the father, damages may be given beyond the value of the services. Irwin v. Dearman, 11 East, 23.

[2] In early times the ward was the guardian's chattel. Lumley v. Gye, 2 El. & B. 216, 250, 257.

[3] For this paragraph the author is indebted to his learned friend, Mr R. T. Wright.

[4] In regard to the converse case, enticing away the husband, see Lynch v. Knight, 9 H. L. Cas. 577; Cooley, Torts, 267, 2nd ed.

companionship, and aid[1]. But in America it is held not necessary that there should be any separation or pecuniary injury; in which respect the action resembles that of a parent for the seduction of his daughter. For example: The defendant, by false insinuations against the plaintiff, and other insidious wiles, so prejudices and poisons the mind of the plaintiff's wife against him, and so alienates her affections from him, as to induce her to desire and seek to obtain, without just cause, a divorce; and by his false insinuations and wiles succeeds in persuading the wife to refuse to recognize the plaintiff as her husband. The defendant is liable; though no actual absence of the wife is caused[2].

This example, it will be observed, does not go to the extent of declaring a person liable for enticing away or corrupting the affections of the wife by reason of charges against the husband which are *true;* but there can be little doubt that such an act would be a breach of duty to the husband[3]. The constancy and affection of a wife are all the more valuable to him if his conduct is bad, since they may save him from ruin.

A difference is deemed to exist, however, between the act of a parent and that of other persons with regard to persuading a wife to leave her husband. In the case of one not a parent, it is not necessary that bad motives should have inspired the act[4]. Such a person has no right to entice or persuade a wife to leave her husband. It does not follow, however, that mere advice to a married woman

[1] See 3 Black. Com. 139, 140; Bigaouette *v.* Paulet, 134 Mass. 123.
[2] Heermance *v.* James, 47 Barb. 120 (N. Y.).
[3] See Bromley *v.* Wallace, 4 Esp. 237. The conduct of the husband could be shewn only in mitigation of damages. Id.
[4] See Hutcheson *v.* Peck, 5 Johns. 196 (N. Y., Kent, C. J.); Bennett *v.* Smith, 21 Barb. 439 (N. Y.).

by a stranger to leave her husband, upon representations by the wife, would be unlawful; advice in such a case is one thing, and enticement is another.

In regard to a parent, however, it is considered that it is no breach of duty to the husband for such a person, upon information that his daughter is treated with cruelty by her husband or is subjected to other gross indignities such as would justify a separation, to go so far as to persuade her to depart from her husband; though it subsequently appear that the parent's persuasion was based on wrong information[1]. It is held that bad motives must have actuated the parent in order to make him liable[2]. This seems to mean that the parent must either have enticed his daughter to leave or to stay away out of ill-will towards her husband, and not by reason of any good ground for their separation; or that he must have some end to gain of personal benefit to himself. In the absence of facts of this character, the parent is not liable, according to American authority, for persuading his daughter to absent herself from her husband on information justifying (if true) a divorce or even a departure of her own motion; though a stranger in blood would be liable.

Any person who receives a married woman into his house, or suffers her to stay there after receiving notice from the husband not to harbour her, is deemed, presumptively, to violate a duty which he owes to the husband[3]. But anyone may, notwithstanding such notice, harbour the wife out of humanity, on her representations of cruel treatment. For example: The defendant receives the plaintiff's wife into his house upon representations of ill-

[1] Bennett v. Smith, 21 Barb. 439, 443 (N. Y.).
[2] Hutcheson v. Peck, supra.
[3] Winsmore v. Greenbank, Willes, 577; s. c. L. C. Torts, 328. See Addison, Torts, 905 (4th ed.).

treatment by her husband; and he continues to permit her to remain there after notice from the plaintiff not to do so. The defendant is not guilty of a breach of duty to the plaintiff[1].

Liability for harbouring must (probably) be limited to cases in which the defendant has clear notice that the wife's act in coming to him, or in staying with him, is intended as a separation by her from her husband, and a repudiation of his claims as such. A man cannot at the present day be liable in damages for allowing a married woman to remain in his house a few days after notice not to do so, if she deny that she has abandoned her husband and claim that she is merely visiting, or that she is away from home for some other temporary and reasonable purpose. The defendant's liability, when it exists, rests upon the ground that he is a party to the unlawful purpose of depriving the plaintiff of the benefit of some advantage embraced under the designation of the consortium of his wife[2]. If the wife were disposed to stay an unreasonable length of time after notice from the husband, that fact would perhaps be sufficient to cause him to suspect her true purpose, and to render him liable in case he continued to permit her to remain.

It is settled law in America that the mere fact of receiving another's wife is not unlawful, even though no explanation whatever be offered[3]. There must be an enticing or harbouring with reference to a wrongful separation. It is not enough even that the defendant take the plaintiff's wife to the defendant's house, upon request by her, unless

[1] Philp v. Squire, Peake, 82.
[2] Winsmore v. Greenbank, Willes, 577; Hutcheson v. Peck, 5 Johns. 196 (N. Y.); Schuneman v. Palmer, 4 Barb. 225 (N. Y.).
[3] Barnes v. Allen, 1 Keyes, 390 (N. Y.); Schuneman v. Palmer, 4 Barb. 225 (N. Y.). See also Winsmore v. Greenbank, supra.

he has notice that she is abandoning her husband; though he has been required by the plaintiff not to harbour her. For example: The defendant and the plaintiff are farmers and neighbours, residing about two miles apart. Their wives are relatives, and the plaintiff's wife often visits the defendant's; the defendant taking her to his house in his wagon. The plaintiff's wife on one occasion being so at the defendant's house, the plaintiff gives the defendant written notice not to harbour her, but to return her to his residence from which he (the defendant) has taken her. The defendant having stopped with the lady near her husband's house, she goes to enter it, but finds the door locked, and returns to the defendant, requesting him to take her to his house. The defendant shews her the notice, and advises her not to go, but she makes light of the matter, and is taken to the defendant's house. The next day the defendant carries her home; and the plaintiff brings suit for the harbouring. The action is not maintainable; the defendant not having attempted to influence the wife to leave her husband[1].

So much for enticing away a man's wife. In regard to cases of criminal conversation with one's wife, an action was formerly given by the common law for this wrong[2], and still is given in America. This action was abolished by act of Parliament in the year 1857, and the redress turned over to the Divorce Court[3]. The act permits the husband on a petition for dissolution of the marriage, or for judicial separation, or on a petition limited to such object only, to claim damages from anyone for committing adultery with his wife; and the claim is to be tried in the

[1] Schuneman v. Palmer, supra.
[2] Weedon v. Timbrell, 5 T. R. 357; Harvey v. Watson, 7 Man. & G. 644.
[3] 20 & 21 Vict. c. 85, §§ 33, 59.

same way and subject to the same rules as actions for criminal conversation formerly[1]. It is necessary then to consider the old law to understand the new.

The right of action for criminal conversation rested upon the same ground as that for enticing the wife away from her husband, to wit, the loss of consortium[2]; and it arose accordingly without regard to the infliction of pecuniary damage[3].

It follows that upon separation, by articles of agreement, the husband, having voluntarily parted with his wife's consortium, could not maintain an action for criminal conversation with his wife[4]. But if the separation was without any relinquishment by the husband of his right to the society of his wife, the action was maintainable. For example: The defendant, having entered into a contract for the support of the plaintiff's wife at his (the defendant's) house, the wife goes there under the agreement, and the defendant seduces her. The act is a breach of duty to the plaintiff, for which the defendant is liable[5].

The mere fact of the husband's infidelity to his wife does not change the nature of the defendant's act in seducing and debauching her; though it may possibly, in contemplation of law, affect its enormity. For example: The defendant seduces and has criminal intercourse with the plaintiff's wife. Proof is offered by the defendant that the plaintiff had shewn the greatest indifference and want of affection towards his wife; that while she lay dangerously ill at Y, the plaintiff (a navy surgeon), though his vessel was at Y, and he landed almost daily, was often at

[1] § 33. [2] Weedon v. Timbrell, 5 T. R. 357.
[3] Wilton v. Webster, 7 Car. & P. 198.
[4] Harvey v. Watson, 7 Man. & G. 644.
[5] See Chambers v. Caulfield, 6 East, 244. Weedon v. Timbrell has been limited to this extent.

the door of the house where his wife lay sick, without visiting her, or shewing any anxiety or concern for her; and at the same time that he had been guilty of adultery and had contracted a venereal disease. This is no defence to the action[1]; though it might be considered in mitigation of damages[2].

If, however, the husband was accessory to his own dishonour, the case is different: he could not complain of an injury to which he had consented[3]. For example: The plaintiff allows his wife to live as a prostitute, and the defendant then has intercourse with her. This is no breach of duty to the plaintiff[4].

Mere negligence as to the wife's behaviour, inattention, or dulness of apprehension, or even permission of indecent familiarity in the husband's presence, are, however, deemed insufficient to bar a recovery for criminal conversation with the wife; though such facts might be proved in reduction of damages. Unless the conduct of the husband amount to consent to the defendant's act of intercourse, the defendant is liable[5].

It follows from what has been said that condonation of the wife's offence does not excuse the man who debauched her: the sole consequence of the condonation is to preclude the husband from obtaining a divorce. For example: The defendant has criminal intercourse with the plaintiff's wife, and, when fatally sick, she discloses the fact to her husband. The plaintiff continues to care for her kindly until her death. The defendant is liable[6].

[1] Bromley v. Wallace, 4 Esp. 237, overruling Wyndham v. Wycombe, Id. 16.
[2] Id.   [3] 'Volenti non fit injuria.'
[4] See Cibber v. Sloper, cited 4 T. R. 655; Hodges v. Windham, Peake, 39; Sanborn v. Neilson, 4 N. H. 501.
[5] 2 Greenleaf, Evidence, §§ 51, 56; L. C. Torts, 338. But comp. p. 168, ante.
[6] Wilton v. Webster, 7 Car. & P. 198.

CHAPTER IV.

TRESPASSES UPON PROPERTY.

§ 1. Introductory.

Statement of the duty. A owes to B the duty (1) to forbear to enter B's close without permission; (2) to forbear to take or interfere with possession of B's chattels, without permission; unless, in either case, A has a better right than B to the possession of the property.

1. The term 'close' signifies a tract of land, whether physically enclosed or not.
2. 'Breaking and entering the close' is an ancient term of the law, now nearly gone out of use, indicating an unlawful entry upon land. The term 'entry' or 'unlawful entry' will be used in the present chapter as synonymous with 'breaking and entering', unless the contrary be indicated.
3. A trespass to land is an unlawful entry upon land; a trespass to goods is an unlawful taking or interfering with the possession of goods. All other wrongful acts connected with the trespass are aggravation of the trespass.

§ 2. Of Possession.

In order to maintain an action solely for damages for a trespass to land, and not merely for the recovery of the land, it is necessary for the plaintiff to have had possession of the premises entered at the time of the entry. A person who enters the land of another without the latter's permission, the latter having been previously unlawfully deprived of possession or the land having never been in his possession, *may*, indeed, violate a duty to the person entitled to the possession; but the law requires the latter to get possession of the land before giving him damages for the wrong committed.

If, however, the party had possession at the time of the entry, and the trespasser ejected him, it would not be necessary for him to recover possession before he could sue for damages for the wrongful entry and expulsion; he had possession at the time of the trespass and disseisin, and that is sufficient for the purposes of such an action. He could not, however, recover damages for the loss sustained by reason of the disseisor's *occupancy*, until after a re-entry, —a point to be further considered hereafter.

On the other hand, possession at the time of the entry, if held under a claim of right, is prima facie sufficient in all cases to enable a person to maintain an action for an entry upon the land without permission; and possession alone is not only prima facie but absolutely sufficient against all persons who have not a better right than the possessor. It follows that one who is in possession of land under a claim of title, though without right, may recover for an entry by a wrong-doer; that is, by one who enters without a right to do so. For example: The defendant enters without permission upon land in the possession of the plaintiff, whose possession is under a void lease. The defendant is liable[1].

---

[1] Graham *v.* Peat, 1 East, 244. 'Any possession is a legal possession against a wrong-doer.' Lord Kenyon. See Cutts *v.* Spring, 15 Mass. 135; s. c. L. C. Torts, 341.

But as above implied, the defendant is not necessarily guilty of breach of duty to such a possessor because he (defendant) does not own the land. He may still have a legal or an equitable interest in the premises; he may be a lessee of the land, or he may be a trustee of the same or the latter's cestui que trust. In any of these cases, he would be entitled to enter upon the premises, if he could do so without breaking the peace. Indeed, a licensee may have a right to make a peaceable entry, though he has no interest whatever in the soil, and could have no right of entry against a person entitled to the possession. For example: The defendant enters without permission premises of which the plaintiff is wrongfully in possession; the act being done by direction of the owner of the land, who is entitled to possession. The defendant violates no duty to the plaintiff[1]; though the case would have been different had he entered without authority of the owner[2].

If there be two persons in a close, each asserting that the premises are his, and each doing some act in the assertion of the right of possession, he who has the better title or right is considered as being in possession; and the other is a trespasser[3]. The former is therefore (probably) in a position to demand damages of the latter for his wrongful entry. For example: The defendant is in possession of land without right, and so continues after the plaintiff, who is the owner, enters to take possession, ploughing the land. The defendant is guilty of trespass to the plaintiff[4]. Again: The defendant is in occupancy of land jointly with

[1] Chambers v. Donaldson, 11 East, 65.
[2] The subject of rights of entry in general will be considered hereafter, § 3. It is introduced here merely to shew the consequences of possession.
[3] See Reading v. Royston, 2 Salk. 423.
[4] Butcher v. Butcher, 7 B. & C. 399.

the plaintiff, claiming to be a tenant in common of the premises with the plaintiff. His claim, however, is unfounded, and the plaintiff is owner of the close. The defendant may be treated by the plaintiff as a trespasser[1].

If neither of the parties in occupancy has a right to the close, the question whether either of them has violated a duty to the other, supposing each to claim possession, will turn upon the 'exclusive priority of possession'. The one who first entered, if he took exclusive possession, will be entitled to damages against the other; if he did not so take, neither can recover against the other. For example: The defendants claim a right to take cranberries in an unoccupied field under a license from one H. The plaintiffs have previously entered into possession of the land, and forbidden all persons by public notice to take cranberries therefrom, except on certain conditions with which the defendants do not comply. H, under whom the defendants claim, had entered before the entry of the plaintiffs; but neither H, nor the defendants, nor the plaintiffs, have any right to the soil or the berries; and neither ever had exclusive possession. The defendants have (probably) violated no duty to the plaintiffs[2]; and so e converso[3].

There is this important distinction between the law relating to possession of real property and that relating to possession of personalty: to enable a plaintiff to recover for trespass to realty, he must have had a possession in fact; while a plaintiff may recover for trespass to personalty if he had a *right* to possession. To assimilate the two cases, it is often said that the right to possession of personalty draws possession in law. Whoever then has a right of possession of a chattel, whether it be towards all the world or only towards the defendant, is in a position to sue for an

[1] Hunting *v.* Russell, 2 Cush. 145 (Mass.).
[2] Barnstable *v.* Thacher, 3 Met. 239 (Mass.).   [3] Id.

interruption of his enjoyment thereof. For example: The defendant, without permission, takes goods out of the possession of A, after A has sold them to the plaintiff, but before they have been delivered to him. This is a breach of duty to the plaintiff[1].

It may be remarked in this connection that by the common-law rules of pleading, the plaintiff in an action either of trespass or trover, always alleged that the property was his. But this allegation was deemed to be fulfilled by evidence that he came into possession of the goods in a lawful manner. Evidence that the plaintiff had got hold of the property by theft, violence, or other wrongful act, without title or right, would not support the allegation of property; and it follows that such a person could not claim that interfering with his supposed possession would be a breach of duty[2]. The same is of course true still.

What constitutes possession in fact, however, as distinguished from a right of possession, is one of the difficult questions of the law, especially when it comes to the application of definition to particular cases. Contact certainly is not necessary; it is enough so far as that is concerned, that no one is opposing possession and that the power to take the property into hand exists. That conception of the term which on the whole most nearly harmonizes with the authorities on specific situations appears to be this: (1) a power of control over property, and (2) a purpose to exercise the same for the benefit, at the time, of the holder, or facts from which such a purpose could be assumed if the mind were directed to the object of possession. It is clear that without these two facts there is no true possession in the eye of the law; but to say that there *is* possession in all cases with them would be to say that

[1] Bacons's Abr. Trespass C. 2; L. C. Torts, 370.
[2] Buckley *v.* Gross, 3 Best & S. 566. See post. pp. 202.

the authorities are in harmony. A mere servant may have 'detention' or custody, but as servant can have no possession, according to current views, because a servant does not hold in his own right[1]; but what of an agent[2], or a bailee for hire, or a tenant at will? The authorities are not agreed. It is often said that none of them has possession. Thus, some say of tenants at will that both tenant and landlord cannot be in possession at the same time, and the landlord certainly is possessed. Others treat both as having the *rights* of possessors; and this appears to be the more just view[3].

A reversioner or remainder-man can maintain an action for injuries done to his interest, notwithstanding the fact that the land is in the possession of a tenant. Injuries done to such interests are not, however, in strictness of common-law ideas, trespasses. The trespass consists in the wrongful entry upon the land, and this is a tort to the tenant, and not to the landlord or remainder-man; since it is an interference with the possession, which belongs to the tenant. For example: The defendant enters upon the plaintiff's land, held by a tenant, in the assertion of a right of way, driving thereon his horses and cart, and continuing so to do after notice from the plaintiff to quit. The defendant has violated no duty to the plaintiff[4].

[1] Year Book, 13 Edw. IV, 9, 10, pl. 5; 21 Hen. VII, 14, pl. 21; Harris *v.* Smith, 3 Serg. & R. 20 (Penn.); Hampton *v.* Brown, 13 Ired. 18 (North Carolina). These are all common-law authorities; but the point is not free from doubt. See Holmes, Common Law, 226—228; Moore *v.* Robinson, 2 B. & Ad. 817; Mathews *v.* Hursell, 1 E. D. Smith, 393 (N. Y.).

[2] See Knight *v.* Legh, 4 Bing. 589, Best, C. J. holding that an agent might bring trover, as having possession.

[3] See Starr *v.* Jackson, 11 Mass. 519, where the cases are reviewed; and see Markby, Elements of Law, § 388, 3rd ed.

[4] Baxter *v.* Taylor, 4 B. & Ad. 72. The action was 'case'.

Damage done to the inheritance in the case of leasehold or mortgaged land is waste if committed by the tenant or mortgagor, and a tort which may be deemed to be in the nature of a trespass, if committed by a stranger. But whatever term may be applied to the act, it is a breach of duty to the landlord or mortgagee, for which he is entitled to recover damages. For example: The defendant, a tenant, or a mortgagor, or a licensee, or a stranger, cuts down trees on land owned by the plaintiff, or of which he is mortgagee or remainder-man, without the plaintiff's consent. This is a breach of duty to the plaintiff, and the defendant is liable to him in damages; though the plaintiff is not in possession[1].

A similar rule of law prevails in regard to injuries done to personal property, held on lease or on pledge, or by a mortgagor in possession. For an injury done to the possessor's interest merely, that is, for a simple unlawful taking of the goods, the remedy belongs to the possessor alone; but for an injury done to the reversion, or to the mortgagee if the goods be mortgaged, the landlord or the mortgagee is entitled to treat the act as a breach of duty to him and call for redress[2]. For example: The defendant levies on and sells goods in the possession of S, whose right to the possession rests upon an agreement by the plaintiff to convey the same to him upon the payment of notes given therefor. The defendant has not been led by the plaintiff to suppose that the goods belong to S; on the contrary, the defendant has notice at the time of the levy

---

[1] See Young v. Spencer, 10 B. & C. 145; Page v. Robinson, 10 Cush. 99 (Mass.); Cole v. Stewart, 10 Cush. 181. None of these are cases of actions by remainder-men, but they cover such cases in principle. The form of action at common law is 'case' and not trespass.

[2] In 'case', or trover, at common law. See Farrant v. Thompson, 5 B. & Ald. 826, where trover was brought.

of the plaintiff's title. The defendant's act in disposing of the goods is a breach of duty to the plaintiff, and he is liable in damages; though the right of possession is in S[1].

A man's close includes, at least according to American law, not only his actually enclosed land, but also all adjoining unenclosed lands held by him; and, if he be in possession of any part of his premises, he is in possession of the whole, unless other parts be occupied by tenants or by persons who claim adversely to him. The owner has the 'power of control' and the 'purpose to exercise the same' for himself; he is therefore in a proper position to recover damages for trespasses committed in any part of his premises, the unenclosed as well as the enclosed[2]. For example: The defendant, without permission, enters and cuts timber in an open woodland of the plaintiff, adjoining a farm upon which the plaintiff resides. The plaintiff is in possession of the woodland, and is entitled to recover[3].

The foregoing proposition in regard to possession of adjoining unenclosed land supposes that the party injured has a right to the possession of the enclosed premises actually occupied by him. One, however, who is in possession of land without title or right can (probably) have no such extended possession; the rights of a bare possessor are limited by the bounds of his immediate occupation and

[1] Ayer v. Bartlett, 9 Pick. 156 (Mass.).
[2] Such possession is often called 'constructive', but that term, like the term 'symbolical' possession, is apt to darken counsel. Possession is surely real when one's control can be extended over the property at any time. See Markby, Elements of Law, §§ 353, 359, 360, 3rd ed.
[3] Machin v. Geortner, 14 Wend. 239 (N. Y.); Penn v. Preston, 2 Rawle, 14 (Penn.). 'I hold that there is no usage of the country, nor rule of the common law, nor any reason requiring a man to enclose his timber land, and that for any possible purpose that can be named the woods belonging to a farm are as well protected by the law without a fence as with one.' Tod, J. in Penn v. Preston.

control. For example: The defendant, having wrongful possession of the south end of a lot, cuts timber upon the north end thereof, lying without the limits of his actual occupation; which timber has been purchased and duly marked by the plaintiff. The land on which the timber stood is not in the possession of the defendant, and the plaintiff is entitled to damages for the violation of his right of property; though he has no right to the land[1]. Again: The defendant, without right or authority, enters upon an open woodland adjoining enclosed land in the wrongful possession of the plaintiff. The act is no breach of duty to the plaintiff[2].

One of several co-tenants, whether of real or of personal property, cannot maintain an action for acts relating to the common property, not amounting to an ouster; because all the co-tenants have equal rights of possession and property. For example: The defendant, co-tenant of land with the plaintiff, cuts and carries away therefrom timber, at the same time denying to the plaintiff any right in the premises, but not withholding possession from him. The defendant has violated no duty to the plaintiff[3].

If, in the case of real estate, the act of the defendant, however, amount to an ouster of the plaintiff from the possession of the common property, the act is a trespass, and the defendant is liable; provided, at least, an action of ejectment would at common law be maintainable. For example: The defendant, being co-tenant with the plaintiff of a certain room in a coffee-house, expels therefrom the

[1] Buck v. Aiken, 1 Wend. 460 (N. Y.). The plaintiff became possessed of the trees as soon as they were cut down by the defendant.

[2] It is difficult to find judicial authority for this example, because, perhaps, of its simplicity. Its correctness is clear.

[3] Filbert v. Hoff, 42 Penn. St. 97, following Reading's Case, 1 Salk. 392.

plaintiff's servant, in derogation of the plaintiff's right of occupation. The defendant is liable to the plaintiff in damages; since an action of ejectment for restoration to possession would lie[1].

Whatever amounts to, or if persisted in might amount to, an effectual privation of the associate tenant of participation in the possession of the common property amounts to an ouster, even though there be no actual expulsion or withholding of possession from him. For example: The defendant, co-tenant with the plaintiff of a certain close, digs up the turf and carries it away, without the plaintiff's consent. This is an ouster, for which the defendant is liable to the plaintiff in damages; since, if the cotenant were permitted to take the turf, he would be entitled to dig away the soil below the turf, and might thus effectually deprive his fellow of his right to the possession[2].

If the criterion of this remedy between co-tenants for an ouster be the question whether an ejectment would be maintainable, it follows that an action for trespass in respect of *goods* held in common cannot be maintained by one cotenant against another; for an action of ejectment lies for the recovery of land only. Nor, indeed, is there any authority in opposition to this deduction; the question of the right of action having, so far as the reported authorities go, always arisen in regard to common rights in

[1] Murray v. Hall, 7 C. B. 441; s. c. L. C. Torts, 343. Ejectment was originally an action of trespass, and was always deemed to include trespass. Hence, if that form of remedy may be used, trespass lies. This is the reasoning; but it is difficult to see how ejectment could be allowed a co-tenant.

[2] Wilkinson v. Haygarth, 12 Q. B. 837. The defendant would not have been liable to an action for *trespass* for taking and carrying away the growing grass or crops. Id. Accounting between co-tenants was provided for by 4 Anne, c. 16, § 27, where one co-tenant has taken more than his share of the profits.

realty[1]. Some decisions in America have denied the remedy even when resorted to in cases of real property[2].

In respect of personal property, however, it will be seen in the next chapter that an action for the conversion of the common chattel can be maintained in certain cases. The difficulty thus relates more to the form of action than to the substance of things. It may therefore be laid down, that for one tenant in common of personal property to withhold possession of the chattel from his associate, or to expel him from participation in the possession, or to appropriate to himself more than his share of the profits arising from the property, is a breach of legal duty to the latter, for which the law gives redress[3].

It has been observed that, in order to maintain an action for trespass to land, possession of the land at the time of the wrongful entry is necessary. But the law does not allow a person who has wrongfully entered, to take and enjoy the profits of the close, or to commit depredations upon the premises during his occupancy, without a reckoning. If the owner or person entitled to the possession subsequently obtain possession of the close, the law treats him, by the fiction of relation, as having been in possession during all the time that has elapsed since he was ejected from the premises.

The consequence is, that upon his re-entry he becomes entitled to sue for the damage which he has sustained at

[1] See the cases cited in L. C. Torts, pp. 358—360.

[2] Wait v. Richardson, 33 Vermont, 190. See also Bennet v. Bullock, 35 Penn. St. 364, 367.

[3] The difficulty in the way of an action for trespass is that the defendant, tenant in common, had a right of possession, and that is inconsistent with that action. But in an action for the conversion of a chattel, it matters not that the defendant had a right of possession. The gist of such an action is not (as it is in trespass) the wrongful taking possession, but the conversion of the plaintiff's right.

CHAP. IV.] TRESPASSES UPON PROPERTY. 187

the hands of the party who has usurped the possession. The remedy thus allowed is called an action for mesne profits; that is, for the value of the premises during the period in which the plaintiff has been kept out of possession by the defendant. The plaintiff is also entitled to recover for all wrongful entries upon and damages done to his property in the mean time[1]. For example: The defendant enters upon premises of the plaintiff, of which the plaintiff has been disseised, and removes buildings therefrom. The plaintiff subsequently re-enters, and then brings suit for damages done to his property. He is entitled to recover[2].

There is conflict of authority in regard to the existence in the disseisee of a right of action for mesne profits against one who, before the plaintiff's entry, had succeeded the disseisor by descent or purchase; that is, in the language of the law, against a stranger. On the one hand, it is said that to take a supposed title from another cannot be a trespass, and therefore mesne profits arising during the latter's occupation cannot be recovered of him[3]. On the other hand, the apparent injustice of this doctrine, towards the owner, has been urged, and the contrary conclusion reached[4]. Between the extremes of these rulings, however,

---

[1] Liford's Case, 11 Coke, 46, 51. As to cases between landlord and tenant see 15 & 16 Vict. c. 76, § 214; Smith v. Tett, 9 Ex. 307; Doe v. Harlow, 12 Ad. & E. 40; Doe v. Challis, 17 Q. B. 166; Pearse v. Coker, L. R. 4 Ex. 92. Mesne profits may now be had in a suit to recover the land.

[2] Dewey v. Osborn, 4 Cowen, 329 (N. Y.). This case shews also that the party on re-entry is in a position to sue for every entry upon his lands made without authority.

[3] Liford's Case, 11 Coke, 46, 51; Barnett v. Guildford, 11 Ex. 19, 30; Case v. De Goes, 3 Caines 261, 263 (N. Y.); Van Brunt v. Schenck, 10 Johns. 377, 385 (N. Y.); Dewey v. Osborn, 4 Cowen, 329, 338.

[4] Holcomb v. Rawlyns, 2 Cro. Eliz. 540 (decided before Liford's Case); s. c. L. C. Torts, 363; Morgan v. Varick, 8 Wend. 587 (N. Y.).

there is an important class of cases in America, in regard to which there is little conflict. These are cases in which the defendant claims under one who has been let into possession under legal process. In cases of this kind, it has been held that the defendant is not liable for mesne profits; and it seems just, as well as conformable to the doctrine of trespass upon lands, that one who has obtained possession under the disseisor by process of law should be presumed by third persons to be rightfully possessed while the process (and the possession by virtue of it) continues in force. For example: The defendant enters and occupies land of the plaintiff under a writ of possession, executed against one who had wrongfully disseised the plaintiff. The writ is afterwards set aside, and the plaintiff resumes possession. The defendant is not liable for the profits consumed during his occupancy[1]. Again: The defendant enters and takes possession of the plaintiff's land under a license from one who has been put into possession against a wrong-doer under a writ of restitution, which writ is afterwards quashed. The defendant is not liable for the mesne profits[2].

It would seem also that purchasers, third persons, under judicial sales, should stand in a like situation; for, though they do not acquire title from parties let into possession under legal process, they take through the sheriff, who may reasonably be presumed to have authority to sell. And there is judicial authority for this view[3]. It would (probably) be otherwise if the purchaser should be the person who had instituted the invalid proceedings under which he was let into possession[4].

[1] Bacon v. Sheppard, 6 Halst. 197 (N. J.), following Menvil's Case, 13 Coke, 19, 21.
[2] Case v. De Goes, 3 Caines, 261 (N. Y.), following Menvil's Case.
[3] Dabney v. Manning, 3 Ohio, 321.
[4] See further L. C. Torts, 362–366.

CHAP. IV.] TRESPASSES UPON PROPERTY. 189

The non-liability of the purchaser or heir extends, however, only to profits consumed by him. If such person sow the land, or cut down trees, or grass, or crops, and sever and carry them away, or sell them to another, the disseisee, after regress, may take the things severed wherever he can find them, or, if he cannot find them, recover their value of the person lately in possession. The regress of the disseisee has relation to the beginning of the last occupation, and the title to the things severed is therefore in him, which title the carrying away and disposing of do not divest[1].

§ 3. OF WHAT CONSTITUTES A TRESPASS TO 'PROPERTY.

The gist of an action for trespass to land consists in the wrongful entry upon it. And any entry upon land in the rightful possession of another, without license or permission, is a breach of duty to the possessor; and this too though the land be unenclosed. It follows that an action is maintainable for such an entry, though it be attended with no damage to the possessor. For example: The defendant without permission enters upon unenclosed land in the lawful possession of the plaintiff, with a surveyor and chain carriers, and actually surveys part of it, but without doing any damage. The act is a breach of duty to the plaintiff, and the defendant is liable at least to nominal damages[2].

The act is a breach of duty (though not in strict technical sense a trespass) even if the close entered be a private way, if only the plaintiff has a right of passage

[1] See Liford's Case, supra. But of course if the owner take away the things severed, the defendant can recoup their value in trespass for the mesne profits. Id.

[2] Dougherty v. Stepp, 1 Dev. & B. 371 (North Carolina); Hobson v. Todd, 4 T. R. 71, 74. Buller, J.: 'The right has been injured.' Should the defendant repeat the offence, he may be made to smart for it in damages. Williams v. Esling, 4 Barr, 486 (Penn.).

along or across it; it matters not that the plaintiff has no right to the soil[1]. For example: The defendant deposits articles at various times in a passage-way to the use of which he has no right, and the plaintiff has a right, though the ownership of the soil is in another. The defendant is liable; though he removes the articles in every instance before the plaintiff desires to pass out, and never in fact hinders the plaintiff in entering or in going out of the passage[2].

A close is deemed to have been broken and entered even though the act was not in fact committed within it, but only against its bounds. To bring anything against such bounds without permission is a trespass. For example: The defendant, without permission, drives nails into the outer wall of the plaintiff's building, which stands upon the line of the plaintiff's premises. This is a breach of duty, for which the defendant is liable in damages[3]. Again: The defendant heaps up dirt close to the plaintiff's boundary wall, and the dirt, of itself, falls against the wall. This is a trespass[4].

An entry upon land, or a taking of goods, is justifiable when effected either (1) by license or consent of the party or (2) by license of the law, a license being a mere permission to do what otherwise would be unlawful. It does not create a property right. The term 'license or consent of the party', as here used, has reference to an express consent, either in answer to a request for permission, or by specific or general invitation by the possessor[5]. Cases of this kind sufficiently explain themselves, and need not be dwelt upon. The term

[1] The action under the old system was 'case', not trespass. See p. 197, (3).
[2] Williams v. Esling, 4 Barr, 486 (Penn.); s. c. L. C. Torts, 371.
[3] Lawrence v. Obee, 1 Stark. 22.
[4] Gregory v. Piper, 9 B. & C. 591.   [5] E.g. a shopkeeper.

'license of the law', as here used, includes all other cases in which the entry or taking possession was lawful. In cases of the first kind the license is revocable in respect of future acts, though it be made by contract, unless it is 'coupled with an interest'; the licensor may be liable for breach of contract, and yet revoke the license, so as to take away the licensee's permission[1]. A license is 'coupled with an interest' when it comprises or is connected with a grant[2].

The second kind needs some special explanation. The law licenses an entry upon the land of another, or the taking possession of another's goods, in many cases; and in these the license cannot be revoked by the party affected. The first in importance of these cases is where the law has commanded the entry or the taking possession; the entry and levy of a sheriff by virtue of a valid precept being a good example.

A second case is where an entry is made into an inn, or into the coach of a common carrier of passengers. Such an entry is lawful if the party be in a fit condition to be received, paying in advance when required.

A third case is where the party in possession of land has bound himself by debt to another, without any stipulation in regard to the place of payment. In such a case, the creditor is allowed by law to enter his premises for the purpose of demanding payment[3].

A fourth of these cases is where the party in possession holds as tenant a piece of real property of another. In such a case, the law allows the latter to make an entry upon the land for the purpose of ascertaining whether his

[1] Wood v. Leadbitter, 13 M. & W. 838; Hyde v. Graham, 1 H. & C. 593. But the licensee may sometimes be entitled to an injunction against the revocation. Frogley v. Lovelace, Johns. 333.
[2] Wood v. Leadbitter, supra, at p. 844.
[3] 3 Black. Com. 212.

interests are properly regarded by the possessor. For example: The defendant leases land to the plaintiff, and subsequently enters to see if the latter has committed waste. This is no breach of duty to the plaintiff[1].

A fifth case is where goods have been placed upon a man's land under a tenancy at will, or, it seems, where goods have been sold which lie upon the premises of the vendor. In the absence of any special agreement or general custom concerning the delivery of the goods, the owner may go upon the premises and take them[2]. For example: The plaintiff lets premises to the defendant at will, on the terms that the defendant shall have reasonable time to remove his goods, after notice to quit. The defendant enters accordingly after termination of the lease, to get his goods, against the plaintiff's refusal to allow him. This is no breach of duty[3].

A sixth case is where the owner of land has wrongfully burdened another with the possession of his (the former's) goods. In such a case, the goods may be taken and put upon the owner's premises; and neither the taking of the goods nor the entry upon the owner's premises is unlawful. For example: The defendant takes an iron bar and sledge belonging to the plaintiff, and puts them upon the plaintiff's land; the plaintiff having first brought them upon the defendant's premises, and then, without permission, having left them there. The entry is lawful[4].

A seventh case is where a man's goods, without his act, have got upon the land of another. In such a case,

---

[1] 3 Black. Com. 212.
[2] Cornish v. Stubbs, L. R. 5 C. P. 334; Mellor v. Watkins, L. R. 9 Q. B. 400; McLeod v. Jones, 105 Mass. 403 (sale of goods on vendor's land).
[3] Cornish v. Stubbs, supra.
[4] Cole v. Maundy, Viner's Abr. Trespass, 516.

CHAP. IV.] TRESPASSES UPON PROPERTY. 193

the owner of the goods may enter and take them. For example: The defendant enters upon the plaintiff's land to get apples, which, by the action of the wind, have fallen from the defendant's trees into the plaintiff's close. The defendant is not liable[1]. Again: The defendant enters upon the plaintiff's land to get his own goods which the plaintiff has wrongfully taken and put there. This is lawful[2]; though it would have been otherwise had the plaintiff come properly into possession of the goods[3].

An eighth case is where a person enters the premises of another to save life or to succour a beast in danger. Such an act is not a trespass; but it is said that the case would be different if the entry was made to prevent a person from stealing the owner's beast, or to prevent cattle from consuming his corn[4]. The distinction made between the cases is that in the former case the loss of the animal would be irremediable, that is, that particular animal (which might be very valuable) could not be replaced; while in the latter case, the animal might be recovered from the thief, or the corn replaced by purchase or by a new crop; all corn being substantially alike. The distinction, however, sounds mediæval.

A ninth case is where the plaintiff brings or suffers a nuisance upon his premises, to the peculiar injury of his neighbour. In a case like this, the latter may enter and abate the nuisance. For example: The defendant enters upon the plaintiff's premises, and removes the eaves of a shed, which overhang the defendant's land and in rainy

[1] Millen v. Fawdry, Latch, 119, 120. It would be otherwise if the defendant should shake the trees. Bacon's Abr. Trespass, F.
[2] Viner's Abr. Trespass, 1 (A); L. C. Torts, 382.
[3] L. C. Torts, 381.
[4] Bacon, ut supra.

weather drip upon his premises. This is no breach of duty to the plaintiff[1].

A tenth case is where an entry has been made upon land of another by reason of necessity, without the fault of the person entering. Such an entry is justifiable. For example: The defendant runs into the plaintiff's premises to escape a savage animal, or the assault of a man in pursuit of him. The defendant is not liable[2]. Again: The defendant enters upon the plaintiff's premises to pass by a portion of the highway which at this point is wholly flooded, but without the act of the defendant. The entry is justifiable[3].

In all the foregoing cases, and others might be added to them, the entry must have been peaceably made, and without doing unnecessary damage, and any damage done should (probably) be paid for or repaired[4].

It has already been seen that a trespass to property consists in an unlawful entry of land or taking of goods, and a trespass by imprisonment in an unlawful arrest. There is one case, however, in which, by reason of subsequent acts, a person may be treated as a trespasser notwithstanding the lawfulness of the entry or taking possession, or of the arrest; the result thus being to deprive the party of the justification of the lawfulness of the original act, and, by a fiction of law, to make him a trespasser ab initio. According to this fiction, one who has taken possession of goods, or entered upon land by virtue of a license of the law, becomes a trespasser ab initio (notwithstanding the lawfulness of the levy or entry), if he afterwards, while

---

[1] Penruddock's Case, 5 Coke, 100 b; L. C. Torts, 388, where various distinctions as to such cases are mentioned.
[2] Year Book, 37 Hen. VI, p. 37, pl. 26.
[3] Absor v. French, 2 Show. 28.
[4] See Chambers v. Bedell, 2 Watts & S. 225 (Penn.).

acting under the license, commit an act which in itself amounts to a trespass[1]. For example: The defendant, a sheriff, remains an unreasonable length of time in the plaintiff's house in possession of goods taken by him in execution. He is a trespasser ab initio[2].

But, in order to become a trespasser ab initio, the subsequent act must, it has been held, be a technical trespass: if it be not, the party is not to be treated as a trespasser from the beginning, though the act committed be wrongful and subject him to liability. For example: The defendant, an officer, enters upon the plaintiff's premises by virtue of a lawful writ, to make a levy for debt. While there, in the course of his business as an officer, he wrongfully extorts money from the plaintiff. He is not a trespasser from the beginning of his entry, though the extortion was a breach of duty for which he would be liable in damages; extortion not being a trespass[3]. Again: The defendant refuses to deliver up a distress on the plaintiff's goods upon due tender by the plaintiff of the rent due. The defendant is not a trespasser[4].

These examples, on examination, will shew the importance of the doctrine of trespass ab initio. If the person's conduct make him obnoxious to this doctrine, it follows (probably) that all acts done, such as, in the case of an officer, levies made, intermediate the entry and the trespass, are void; since, his entry being a trespass, he could not, according to general principles of law, thereafter do an act against the will of the occupant which would be legal[5]. Besides, he would be liable for the entry as well as

[1] Six Carpenters' Case, 8 Coke, 146; L. C. Torts, 386.
[2] Ash v. Dawnay, 8 Ex. 237.
[3] Shorland v. Govett, 5 B. & C. 485. See Six Carpenters' Case, supra. But compare Holley v. Mix, 3 Wend. 350 (N. Y.).
[4] West v. Nibbs, 4 C. B. 172.
[5] Compare Ilsley v. Nichols, 12 Pick. 270 (Mass.), denying certain

the after-acts. The doctrine does not, therefore, concern the form of remedy alone.

This doctrine of trespass ab initio applies, however, only against persons who have entered or taken goods by license of law. A person cannot treat as a trespasser from the beginning one to whom he has himself given permission to enter or take his goods, whatever be the nature of his subsequent acts[1]. For example: The defendant, by permission of the plaintiff's wife, enters the plaintiff's house in his absence, and while there wrongfully gets possession of papers, and carries them away. This does not make him a trespasser ab initio[2].

As the subsequent act must, it seems, amount to a trespass, it becomes necessary to ascertain somewhat precisely the technical signification of the term. It is difficult to define a trespass, but the following will serve to indicate the proper meaning of the term: (1) Any wrongful contact with the plaintiff's person is a trespass. (2) Any wrongful entry upon the plaintiff's land or interference with the plaintiff's possession of personalty is a trespass. (3) Any wrongful act committed directly with force is a trespass, though no physical contact with the person of the plaintiff or with his property be produced; as in the case of an imprisonment without contact, or the firing a gun

early dicta. Ilsley v. Nichols decides that a levy made by breaking open the outer door of an occupied dwelling-house (a house is a man's castle) is invalid, and the officer is liable for the value of the goods taken as well as for the unlawful entry. The same result should in principle follow if, by an act subsequent to the entry, he become a trespasser from the beginning. The doctrine of trespass ab initio is put upon the ground that the subsequent act indicates a prior purpose to commit a trespass. Six Carpenters' Case, supra. But this is a fiction and not very satisfactory.

[1] Six Carpenters' Case, supra.
[2] Allen v. Crofoot, 5 Wend. 506 (N. Y.).

CHAP. IV.] TRESPASSES UPON PROPERTY. 197

under the plaintiff's window, to alarm the inmates of his house. In cases like these, force is said to be implied. Upon the same ground, the seduction of the plaintiff's wife, daughter, or servant might be considered as a trespass, and the act has sometimes been so treated by the courts[1]: the consent given was not the plaintiff's consent. But the later view is different[2].

On the other hand, (1) a mere non-feasance (that is, a pure omission) cannot be a trespass[3]; (2) nor can there be a trespass where the matter affected was not tangible, and hence could not be immediately injured by force, as in the case of an injury to reputation or health; (3) nor can there be a proper trespass where the right affected is incorporeal, as a right of common or way; (4) nor where the interest injured exists in reversion or remainder, and is not in possession; (5) nor where there is no right of action immediate upon the act in question[4].

Lastly, to constitute a trespass to property, the thing affected must, though tangible, be capable of ownership as property. Wild animals, untamed, are deemed property only while in the actual or constructive possession of the keeper: upon effectual and final escape, they cease to be property, and may be killed, or taken and retained by any one, at least if he is not aware of the prior ownership. And a wild, savage animal straying at large may be killed, though the owner be known to be in pursuit[5].

[1] Tullidge v. Wade, 3 Wils. 18; 1 Chitty, Pleading, 126, 133.
[2] Macfadzen v. Olivant, 6 East, 387. Chitty, however, prefers the old doctrine. 1 Pleading, 133.
[3] Six Carpenters' Case, 8 Coke, 146.
[4] See 1 Chitty, Pleading, 166. But quaere whether the effect of the rule of trespass ab initio might not be had in some of these cases, as in the third and fourth.
[5] 2 Kent, Com. 348, 349. See post, p. 269, note 1.

CHAPTER V.

CONVERSION.

§ 1. INTRODUCTORY.

Statement of the duty. A owes B the duty to forbear to exercise dominion (1) over B's general property in personal chattels; and (2) over B's special property in the like things.

1. By 'general property' is commonly meant the ownership of property, subject, it may be, to a right of possession for a time in another.
2. By 'special property' is meant a right of possession only.
3. By 'bare possession' merely is commonly meant a mere custody ('detention'), or a possession unlawfully obtained.
4. The action for converting property was formerly and is sometimes still called 'trover', a term meaning 'to find', which was used in the old precedents of declaration; the plaintiff, by a fiction, alleging that he had lost and the defendant had *found* and converted to his own use the chattel in question[1].
5. The action of 'trover' is an action to recover (not

[1] The allegation was at first probably real, arising perhaps from the common action for strays. See L. C. Torts, 422.

CHAP. V.] CONVERSION. 199

specific articles, but) damages for the conversion of chattels personal, or movable goods, to the value of the interest converted.

6. By an 'act of dominion' is meant an act tantamount to an exercise of ownership.

7. The action of detinue is not much used in modern times. Its object is to recover chattels in specie, or damages for their non-return if they cannot be had. It has been superseded largely by trover.

8. As in trespass, so in trover and in detinue, the thing alleged to have been converted must be capable of ownership as property[1].

§ 2. OF POSSESSION.

The possession of a chattel personal, that is, of a movable article, or the right of possession thereof, is necessary to support an action for conversion, just as it is to support an action for trespass. The plaintiff fails in trover if it appear that he has never acquired a right of possession, or if he has, that he has parted with it, and has not before suit become reinvested with the same. For example: The plaintiff is the purchaser of goods, which, however, remain in the seller's possession subject to a lien for the purchase price. The defendant, without authority, removes the goods from the seller's possession, doing no permanent injury to them. This is no breach of duty to the plaintiff[2]. Again: The defendant, a sheriff, wrongfully levies upon goods of the plaintiff in the hands of a lessee of the property, and carries the goods away. The plaintiff cannot treat the act as a conversion, though the tenant could, since the plaintiff was not entitled to the possession of the property[3].

[1] See ante, p. 197. [2] Lord v. Price, L. R. 9 Ex. 54.
[3] Gordon v. Harper, 7 T. R. 9. See Farrant v. Thompson, 5 B. & Ald. 826; ante, p. 182.

On the other hand, the right of possession of the chattels is sufficient to enable the general owner to sue for a conversion thereof, though he may not have the actual possession at the time of the wrongful act; because, as was stated in the preceding chapter, the right of possession of goods draws the possession, in contemplation of law. For example: The defendant buys a chattel belonging to the plaintiff from A, who had no right to sell it. The plaintiff, being the owner, is deemed to have been in possession of the chattel at the time of the conversion by the defendant[1].

A person having the special property of goods in his rightful possession can maintain an action for conversion against all persons who may wrongfully exercise dominion over them, though the act be done by command of the owner of the goods. For example: The defendant takes a horse out of the possession of the plaintiff, the plaintiff having a lien upon the animal. The defendant acts by direction of the owner, but without other authority. He is liable for conversion of the horse[2].

It follows that a person in the rightful possession (actual or legal) of goods, in which he has a special property, may maintain an action against the owner himself for any unpermitted disturbance or refusal of his possession; since, if the owner cannot give an authority to another to take the goods, he cannot take them himself. For example: The defendant, owner of a title-deed, in the possession of the plaintiff under a temporary right to hold it, takes it by permission of the plaintiff for a particular purpose, and then, during the continuance of the plaintiff's right to hold

[1] Hyde v. Noble, 13 N. H. 494; Clark v. Rideout, 39 N. H. 238; Carter v. Kingman, 103 Mass. 517.

[2] See Outcalt v. Durling, 1 Dutch. 443 (N. J.). The form of action in this case was trespass, but it might as well have been trover. The injured party could sue in either form in such cases.

it, refuses to redeliver it. The defendant has violated his duty to the plaintiff, and is liable for conversion[1].

One who has but a possession of chattels, though without a right to hold them against the owner, is also protected against all persons having neither a right of property nor of possession. The mere fact that the possessor of goods has no right to hold them, as against persons having a general or higher special property in the goods, gives no privilege to a stranger to interfere with the party's possession. So to interfere would be a breach of duty to the possessor which would render the person interfering liable for the value of the goods. For example: The defendant, a stranger, refuses to return to the plaintiff a jewel, which the latter has found and shewn to the defendant. The defendant's act is a breach of duty to the plaintiff, and he is liable for the value of the jewel[2].

It would be different, however, if the defendant acted under express authority of the owner, or of one entitled to the possession of the property. But, according to the prevailing doctrine, the defendant could not set up the rights of a third person (called the 'jus tertii') without authority from the latter[3]. That is, the defendant can deny the plaintiff's right only by shewing a better right in himself. And the same rule prevails in an action to recover the specific goods[4].

In order, however, that possession should confer the right to sue for conversion, the possession must, as in an action for trespass, be rightful for the time; (and such it

[1] Roberts v. Wyatt, 2 Taunt. 268.
[2] Armory v. Delamirie, 1 Strange, 505; s. c. L. C. Torts, 388.
[3] Jefferies v. Great Western Ry. Co., 5 El. & B. 802; Cheesman v. Exall, 6 Ex. 341; L. C. Torts, 426.
[4] Rogers v. Arnold, 12 Wend. 30 (N. Y.), reviewing the common-law authorities.

may be though subject to be defeated by the claim of one who has a superior right of property). In other words, a person who has acquired possession of goods unwarrantably, whether by theft or by fraud, force, or violence, or otherwise, *without title or right,* cannot maintain an action for conversion of the goods even against one who has taken them away from him in a like or any other manner[1].

In order to confer a right upon the finder of goods, he must therefore have taken possession in good faith, and not feloniously or by a trespass,—with a purpose of returning the property to the owner upon his appearance and proof of property.

The finding of a chattel does not, however, in all cases give a right to hold the article against all persons having no right of property in it; though the finding and taking possession were not unlawful as against the loser. The chattel may be found upon the premises of another, in such a situation as to indicate that it was voluntarily placed in possession of the owner of the premises. When this is the case, the possession of the article is deemed to be in the occupant of the premises, and not in the finder. The former can therefore maintain an action for conversion against the latter, should he refuse to surrender to him the chattel. For example: The defendant, a barber, receives from the plaintiff, a customer in his shop, a pocket-book containing money, which the plaintiff has discovered lying upon a table in the defendant's shop. The plaintiff, in handing the pocket-book to the defendant, tells him to keep it until he can discover the owner, and then return it to the loser. No one having called for the article, the plaintiff claims it, and the defendant refuses to give it to him. This is not a breach of duty to the plaintiff, since the fact that the pocket-book was left upon the defendant's

---

[1] See ante, p. 180; Buckley *v.* Gross, 3 Best & S. 566.

table indicates that the owner put it there by a voluntary act, and so put it into the defendant's keeping or possession[1].

If, however, the chattel be found in a position which indicates that it could not have been voluntarily placed there, but must have been unintentionally parted with, and so truly lost the moment it escaped the owner, it does not fall into the keeping or possession of the occupant of the premises unless he (or his servant) first discover it there. If another first find it, the possession, as between himself and the occupant, is in him, the finder. For example: The defendant, a shop-keeper, receives from the plaintiff a parcel, containing bank-notes, which the latter has picked up from the *floor* of the defendant's shop; the plaintiff, on handing the parcel to the defendant, telling him to keep the same till the owner claims it. The defendant advertises the parcel, but no one claims it, and three years having elapsed, the plaintiff requests the defendant to return to him the bills, at the same time tendering the cost of advertising, and even offering an indemnity. The defendant refuses. This is a breach of duty to the plaintiff, and the defendant is liable to him for conversion of the parcel[2].

The term 'possession' has the same meaning here and, indeed, everywhere that it has in cases of trespass[3]. Thus, a servant can, it seems, only hold; the possession is the master's. For example: The defendant takes goods out of possession of the plaintiff, a sheriff's deputy, without authority. The act is deemed not a breach of duty to the plaintiff, since he is but a servant, and so holds not in his

[1] McAvoy *v.* Medina, 11 Allen, 548 (Mass.).
[2] Bridges *v.* Hawkesworth, 21 L. J. Q. B. 75.
[3] Ante, p. 180. The meaning there ascribed to the term is intended to be of the widest application, where the possession is real and not merely de jure.

own right[1]; though it would be otherwise in regard to the sheriff.

§ 3. OF WHAT CONSTITUTES CONVERSION.

It has been seen that conversion consists in the exercise of an act of dominion over the movables of another; that is, it is a usurpation of ownership. And it matters not whether this was done with or without knowledge of the true state of the title, as will be seen: every man acts at his peril in exercising acts of dominion over property[2]. The distinction between trespass and conversion consists in this, that trespass is an unlawful taking, as for the mere sake of removing the property, while conversion is an unlawful taking or keeping in the exercise of the right of ownership[3].

There are two kinds of acts of dominion; first, where the wrong-doer appropriates to himself the goods of another; secondly, where, without appropriating them to himself, he deprives the owner, or person having the superior right, of their use.

The most common illustration of an act of dominion of the first kind is the case of a sale and delivery of goods, made without authority of the owner. Every sale without restriction by a person having no right to sell is a conversion, if followed by delivery, and renders the vendor

[1] Hampton v. Brown, 13 Ired. 18; ante, p. 181. But there is some doubt about this. See Moore v. Robinson, 2 B. & Ad. 817; Mathews v. Harsell, 1 E. D. Smith, 393 (N. Y.). For a consideration of the subject in detail see Holmes, Common Law, 226—228. And see Ashwell's Case, 16 Q. B. D. 190.

[2] See a qualification stated in Hollins v. Fowler, L. R. 7 H. L. 757, 768, Lord Blackburn, in regard to dealing with goods at the request of one having actual custody of them, in the bona fide belief that he is owner or has the owner's authority.

[3] See Bushel v. Miller, 1 Strange, 129; Fouldes v. Willoughby, 8 M. & W. 540, 551, Rolfe, B.

CHAP. V.] CONVERSION. 205

liable in an action of trover[1]. For example: The defendant, an officer, levies upon goods as the property of a third person, some of which belong to the plaintiff, takes them away, after being informed of the plaintiff's claim, and sells the whole. This is a conversion of the plaintiff's goods; though it would have been otherwise had the goods been mixed by the plaintiff with those of the third person, and a separation not offered by the plaintiff[2].

The same consequence follows where, having authority to make a sale, the party selling transgresses his right; since to do so is to assert that he may sell according to his own will, and that is to exclude the rights of all others. For example: The defendant, an officer, makes, unnecessarily, an excessive levy upon the plaintiff's goods, under a valid writ, and sells them. This is a conversion, since it is done in disregard of the defendant's authority, and according to the party's own will[3].

This principle that the sale of property with delivery is an act of dominion so as to render the seller liable for conversion if he had no right to sell as he did, applies equally whether the vendor knew or did not know the true state of the title, or the actual limit of his authority. Liability for converting the goods of another to one's own use does not depend upon the intent of the party exercising the act of dominion. For example: The defendant sells and delivers a horse of the plaintiff to a third person, the defendant having bought the animal from one who had no title to it, though the defendant supposed the contrary, and

[1] Quaere, whether a demand would be necessary? It seems not in principle, for the delivery of the goods would complete the conversion. There is, however, considerable conflict of authority upon this point in America. See the Am. ed. of this book, pp. 202, 213.
[2] See 2 Kent Com. 365.
[3] Aldred v. Constable, 6 Q. B. 370, 381. So to pledge the goods of another without authority. Carpenter v. Hale, 8 Gray, 157 (Mass.).

supposed himself to be owner of the horse at the time of the sale in question. The sale by the defendant is a conversion[1].

The purchaser too, in such a case, though he bought without notice, would acquire no right to hold the property, unless he bought in 'market overt'[2]. This supposes, however, that the vendor had no such title as would justify him in making an absolute sale. If for the time he has the *ownership* of the goods, even though his title was defeasible, a purchaser for value, without notice that the title is liable to defeat, acquires the property by his purchase, and cannot therefore be guilty of a conversion by refusing to restore the goods to the person who had the right to defeat his vendor's title.

Such would be the case where the purchaser's vendor had acquired his title from the plaintiff by means of a sale effected by false, and even by fraudulent, representations. Fraud of this character renders the sale voidable merely, and not void; and the consequence is, that the defrauded party has a right to rescind the sale so long as the property remains in the hands of the buyer from himself, or of any one claiming under him who is not a bona fide purchaser for value[3]. But inasmuch as the buyer, notwithstanding his fraud, acquired the title to the goods, he can convey that title; and more, he can convey a better right than he had himself, provided he sell to a bona fide purchaser for value.

Hence, not only would such purchaser be free from liability in refusing to return the goods to the defrauded

[1] Harris v. Saunders, 2 Strobh. Eq. 370, note (South Carolina). See McCombie v. Davies, 6 East, 538, Lord Ellenborough; Hilbery v. Hatton, 33 L. J. Ex. 190; Fowler v. Hollins, L. R. 7 Q. B. 616; s. c. 7 H. L. 757.

[2] Cooper v. Willomatt, 1 C. B. 672.

[3] Clough v. North-western Ry. Co. L. R. 7 Ex. 26.

party, but should that party obtain possession of them and refuse to deliver them to the purchaser from the intermediate seller, he (the defrauded party) would himself be liable in trover. For example: The defendants, having previously been owners of a quantity of iron, sell the same to P, who gives them a fraudulent draft (supposed by the defendants to be good) for the amount due for the property. P then sells the iron to the plaintiff, who buys for value, and without notice of the fraud. Subsequently, the defendants discover the fraud, and send their servant to take away the iron, now lying in port in a lighter alongside the plaintiff's wharf. The servant takes away the lighter and brings the iron therein to the defendants. The plaintiff has acquired a good title to the iron, and the defendants are guilty of a conversion[1].

There are other cases in which a person may by purchase for value and without notice acquire a better title than his vendor had. A purchaser of goods from one who has by the terms of sale reserved the right to buy back the property within a certain time, acquires (or may by such a transaction acquire) the title to the property, and having a good title, he may convey the same to one who purchases for value and without notice so as to cut off the original owner's right to repurchase. The consequence is, that the last purchaser is not guilty of a conversion by refusing to let the original owner have the goods upon a tender by him of the amount he was to pay for them, though made within the time agreed upon between him and his buyer. The case would be different, however, in regard to the buyer from the original owner. His act in making the sale would be lawful against the seller, if the seller should never offer to repurchase; but if the seller should offer to repurchase,

[1] White *v.* Garden, 10 C. B. 919. See, e converso, Cundy *v.* Lindsay, 3 App. Cas. 459.

and tender the price, his purchaser would be bound to return to him the goods, and, in case of failure, would be liable according to the terms of the contract.

If, however, the sale were upon condition that the title should not pass until the performance of some condition, the party, not having acquired the title, could not convey it; and an attempt to do so by a sale and delivery would, it seems, subject the buyer to liability for conversion. For example: The defendants purchase furniture from W, who had taken possession of the same upon an agreement that he should keep it six months, and if within that time he should pay a certain sum for it, it should be his; otherwise, he was to pay twenty-five per cent. of the price for the use. The sale to the defendants is made shortly after W takes possession of the furniture and before payment for it. A refusal by the defendants to restore the property to the plaintiff is a breach of duty to him, and makes them liable for the value of the furniture[1].

According to recent authorities, the holder of a pledge or pawn has such an interest in the chattel that he can dispose thereof by sale or repledge without subjecting the purchaser or repledgee to liability, and without subjecting himself thereto, except in either case upon a failure to produce the pledge or pawn upon tender of the debt to secure which the chattel was given. For example: The defendant has taken in pledge from S certain bonds, which the plaintiff had pledged to S for the security of a debt smaller than the amount of the debt of S to the defendant; the repledge being made before the maturity of the original debt[2], and before payment or tender thereof. The refusal

---

[1] Sargent *v.* Gile, 8 N. H. 325, denying Vincent *v.* Cornell, 13 Pick. 294 (Mass.).

[2] That is, while the bonds were still subject to redemption by the plaintiff.

of the defendant to return the bonds to the plaintiff except on tender to the defendant of the amount due to S is not a violation of duty to the plaintiff; nor would the act of S amount to a conversion, unless upon tender of the debt due to him he should fail to return the bonds[1].

One who has a special property in goods may or may not be able to dispose of his interest therein, according to the nature of his interest. Not every special property is alienable. In many cases of bailment, the special objects to be effected forbid that the bailee should have an assignable interest. Such is the case (1) where the bailment is made upon a trust in the personal skill, knowledge, or efficiency of the bailee. Such is the case (2) where the bailee has a mere lien upon the goods entrusted to him. And such is the case (3) where the bailment is at will. In either of these cases, any attempt by the bailee to assign his interest in the property, followed by delivery of possession, puts an end at once to the bailment. The consequence is, that the assignee acquires no title or right, and becomes liable on refusing to surrender the goods to the owner, even if not by merely taking them.

There is, however, a large class of bailments where the trust is accompanied with other incidents than those pertaining to a simple bailment, and where there is no element of personal trust, and none of the characteristics of an estate at will; and in this class it is clear that the bailee has an assignable interest. There can be no conversion, therefore, in the act of transferring such an interest merely, provided the assignee claims only the rights of the assignor; because the latter, having exercised no act of dominion over the property, but having dealt simply with his own interest, did not reinvest the owner with a right of possession. An

---

[1] Donald *v.* Suckling, L. R. 1 Q. B. 585; s. c. L. C. Torts, 394.

attempt by the bailee to dispose of the goods absolutely, however, would be different, if followed by a delivery of them. For though a bailee could not, without fault on the part of the owner (by holding him out as having a right to sell absolutely), dispose of anything beyond his own interest, the attempt to do so, followed by the overt act, would be to exercise dominion over the goods[1].

It is not always necessary that there should be an appropriation of the entire property held in order to effect a conversion of the whole. If the part appropriated be necessary to the use of the rest, as by rendering a sale of it impracticable, the part appropriation, if wrongful, will, it seems, be a conversion of the whole. For example: The defendant, a bailee by the plaintiff of wine in casks for sale by the cask, consumes part of the wine in one cask. This is (probably) a conversion of all the wine in that cask[2].

It appears to be immaterial to the plaintiff's right of recovery for the whole, that what remains is still in itself as good as if there had been no severance; the plaintiff has the right to the benefit to be obtained from it in its entirety, where that is a special benefit. This principle would apply to cases where separate articles are delivered under one entire contract of bailment or lease, even though the articles be separately enumerated and valued. The bailment or lease is still indivisible in contemplation of law, and conversion of part may be conversion of the whole[3].

[1] See ante, p. 205; Lancashire Wagon Co. *v.* Fitzhugh, 6 H. & N. 502; Cooper *v.* Willomatt, 1 C. B. 672.

[2] Philpott *v.* Kelley, 3 Ad. & E. 106, semble. The case was not so strong as the facts put in the example. See Clendon *v.* Dinneford, 5 Car. & P. 13; Gentry *v.* Madden, 3 Pike, 127 (Arkansas), stated in the Am. ed. of this book, p. 196.

[3] See Clendon *v.* Dinneford, supra.

If, however, separate articles be severally bailed or leased, by distinct contracts, though all be delivered and bargained for at the same time, the rule of law is (probably) different; a conversion of one of the articles or parts would not in such a case operate as a conversion of the whole.

If the owner of goods stand by and permit them, without objection, to be sold as the property of another, the purchaser acquires a good title, and is not liable to the owner for a refusal to deliver them to him. For example: The defendant purchases machinery of M, the legal title to which at the time of the sale is in the plaintiffs. The machinery is sold under a levy of execution against M, and the plaintiffs, though having notice of the levy, and having repeatedly conversed about it, before the sale, with the attorney of the party who made the levy, never lay any claim to the property until after the sale. The defendant's refusal to surrender the machinery to the plaintiff is not a breach of duty[1].

Appropriating an article held in bailment to a use not contemplated at the time of the contract of bailment may also constitute conversion. For example: The defendant hires of the plaintiff a horse to ride to York, and rides it beyond York to Carlisle. This is a conversion of the animal, entitling the plaintiff, on return of the property, at least to nominal damages, and to actual damages if any loss be in fact sustained by reason of the act[2].

It has sometimes been supposed that there can be no right of action for conversion in such cases, unless the chattel was injured in the misappropriation[3]. But there is

[1] Pickard v. Sears, 6 Ad. & E. 469, leading case.
[2] Isaack v. Clark, 2 Bulst. 306 ; Perham v. Coney, 117 Mass. 102.
[3] Johnson v. Weedman, 4 Scam. 495 (Ill.); Harvey v. Epes, 12 Gratt. 153 (Va). In the first of these cases a horse which the defendant had converted, died on his hands, directly after but not in consequence of

ground for doubting the correctness of this doctrine. The foundation of the action is the usurpation of the owner's right of property. It is true, the plaintiff in trover seeks to recover the value of the thing converted, but if he has received it back, or if it has been tendered back in proper condition, he will be allowed to recover no more (beyond nominal damages) than the amount of his loss[1]. But conversion itself is a cause of action; it is not necessary to prove special damage.

In all the foregoing cases, it will be observed that there is something more than an assertion, by word of mouth, of dominion over the chattel. An assertion alone, not followed by any act in pursuance of it, such as a refusal to surrender the chattel to the person entitled to possession, would not amount to a conversion. There must be some unauthorized interference with the plaintiff's right of possession. Even an attempted exercise of dominion, without right, appears to be insufficient to constitute a conversion, if the owner's right was not in fact interrupted. For example: The defendant, by an officer, makes a declaration of attachment of goods which he knows is already duly levied upon by the plaintiff, has a keeper appointed and then *suffers* the owner of the attached property to take it away and sell it, and receives part of the avails. This is deemed not a conversion[2].

---

the conversion. It was held that the owner had no cause of action. The plaintiff was not entitled to recover the value of the horse, but he had a cause of action, it should seem.

[1] Fisher *v.* Prince, 3 Burr. 1363; Earle *v.* Holderness, 4 Bing. 462; Cook *v.* Hartle, 8 Car. & P. 568. Judgment for the plaintiff in trover does not vest the property in the defendant. Brinsmead *v.* Harrison, L. R. 6 C. P. 584.

[2] Polley *v.* Lenox Iron Works, 2 Allen, 182 (Mass.), adopting the language of Heath, J. in Bromley *v.* Coxwell, 2 B. & P. 438, that 'to

In the foregoing kind of cases, the defendant has appropriated the goods in question to his own use. But, as has been stated, a wrongful act of dominion may be committed without so appropriating the goods. It is enough that the defendant has wrongfully deprived the plaintiff of the possession of his goods or usurped his rights over them, though for the benefit of a third person.

In cases of this kind it was formerly supposed that an intention to deprive the plaintiff of his goods was necessary; but this has been decided to be incorrect. The question still is whether there has been a wrongful exercise of dominion by the defendant; if there has been an unauthorized act which deprived the plaintiff of his property permanently or for an indefinite time, there has been a conversion[1]. If not, the contrary is true. For example: The defendant, manager of a ferry, receives on board his boat the plaintiff, with two horses. Before starting, the plaintiff is reported to the defendant as behaving improperly, and though he has paid his fare for transportation, and the defendant tells him that he will not carry the horses, and that they must be taken ashore, the plaintiff refuses to take them off the boat, whereupon the defendant puts them ashore, and has them taken to a livery for keeping. The plaintiff goes with the boat, and the next day sends to the livery stable for his horses. In reply, the plaintiff is told that he can have his horses by coming and paying the charges for keeping, otherwise they would be sold to pay expenses. They are sold accordingly, and damages as for a conversion are sought of the defendant. The action is not maintainable,

support an action of trover there must be a positive tortious act.' Here the defendant was merely 'suffered' to take and sell the property.
[1] Hiort v. Bott, L. R. 9 Ex. 86, 89, Bramwell, B.

since there is nothing to shew that the defendant wrongfully deprived the plaintiff, even for a moment, of his property[1].

Any asportation of a chattel, however, *for the use* of a third person amounts to a conversion, for the reason that the act is inconsistent with the right of dominion which the owner (or person entitled to possession) has in it[2]. And the same is true of an intentional, or possibly negligent, destruction of the chattel[3].

In the case of acts of co-owners (co-tenants) nothing short of a substantial destruction of the common property by the wrongful act of one of them can make him liable to the other or others for conversion[4]. This is on the ground that each of the common owners has a right to the entire possession and use of the property. A sale and delivery would not be enough; for the purchaser would only become a co-owner with the others[5]. But it is not necessary that there should be a physical destruction of the property, as by breaking it in pieces; it is enough that the common interest, or rather the plaintiff's interest, is practically destroyed, as by the defendant's selling the property in market overt[6].

Demand of the goods, followed by a refusal to deliver them, is always necessary unless the plaintiff can establish some other act of conversion. But if any act of conversion, apart from demand and refusal, has been committed, the injured party is entitled to bring suit without first de-

---

[1] Fouldes v. Willoughby, 8 M. & W. 540. For other examples, see Simmons v. Lillystone, 8 Ex. 431; Thorogood v. Robinson, 6 Q. B. 769.

[2] Fouldes v. Willoughby, supra.   [3] Ib.

[4] Farrar v. Beswick, 1 M. & W. 682, 688, Parke, B.; Morgan v. Marquis, 9 Ex. 145; Mayhew v. Herrick, 7 C. B. 229. Comp. the case of trespass, ante, pp. 184—186.

[5] Morgan v. Marquis, supra, Parke, B.

[6] Farrar v. Beswick, supra.

manding his property. In other cases, a demand and wrongful refusal will be necessary, since without them there has been no wrongful exercise of dominion[1]. For example: The defendant collusively purchases goods from a trader on the eve of the trader's bankruptcy, and takes the property into his own possession. The assignee of the trader brings trover without a demand. The action is not maintainable, since the defendant had been guilty of no conversion; the trader being competent to contract, though his contract of sale was liable to impeachment[2].

Of the last example, it should be observed that (in accordance with a principle already stated) the fraud of the trader and the defendant did not make the sale void; its only effect was to render it voidable. The contract was therefore binding until disaffirmed; and a disaffirmance could be made only by a demand of the goods, or by some act tantamount thereto. And the demand and refusal, that is, the conversion, must be apart from the bringing of suit, when such acts are necessary; for the cause of action must have arisen before suit was begun. In the example given, if the defendant had sold the goods, or improperly detained them after a disaffirmance of the sale, the action would have been maintainable[3].

A very common instance of the necessity of demand and refusal is where goods have been put into the hands of another for a special purpose, upon agreement to return them when the purpose is accomplished; in regard to which the rule is, that a breach of the contract by the mere failure so to return the goods does not amount to a conversion. Before the bailee can be liable in trover in such a case, supposing there had been no misappropriation

[1] Chitty, Pleading, 157; Nixon v. Jenkins, 2 H. Black. 135.
[2] Nixon v. Jenkins, supra.
[3] Bloxam v. Hubbard, 5 East, 407.

or other act of dominion, there must be a demand for the goods and a refusal to restore them[1]. An unqualified refusal will itself, in almost all cases, constitute a conversion[2].

A qualified refusal to deliver goods on lawful demand may, however, be only prima facie evidence of a conversion[3]. The defendant may have found the goods, and refused to surrender them to the plaintiff until he shall have proved his right to them. It follows from what has already been said that such a refusal is justifiable, since, if the plaintiff is not entitled to the goods by right, the defendant as finder has the better claim; and he cannot or may not know that the plaintiff may not be a pretender until he has furnished evidence that he is not. And other cases of the kind might be stated[4]; the only question, where the refusal to return is qualified, is whether it is reasonable[5].

If the demand be not made upon the defendant himself, but merely left at his house in his absence, it seems that a reasonable time and opportunity to restore the goods should be suffered to elapse before the defendant's non-compliance with the demand can be treated as a refusal amounting to a conversion. Non-compliance with the demand after a reasonable opportunity has been afforded to obey it is, however, clearly tantamount to a refusal, and is presumptive evidence of a conversion, casting upon the defendant the burden of explaining that the omission to deliver the goods was justifiable[6].

[1] Severin v. Keppell, 4 Esp. 156.
[2] Alexander v. Southey, 5 B. & Ald. 247, 250.
[3] Burroughes v. Bayne, 5 H. & N. 296; Alexander v. Southey, supra.
[4] See Pollock, Torts, 290, 291.
[5] Alexander v. Southey, supra, at p. 250.
[6] 1 Chitty, Pleading, 160; Thompson v. Rose, 16 Conn. 71; White v. Demary, 2 N. H. 546.

CHAPTER VI.

INFRINGEMENT OF PATENTS AND COPYRIGHTS.

§ 1. INTRODUCTORY.

Statement of the duty. A owes to B the duty (1) to forbear 'working or making', without B's license, anything patented by B; (2) to forbear to print for sale or exportation, or to import for sale or hire, any book of which B owns the copyright, without B's written consent, or knowing the same to have been so printed or imported, to sell, publish or expose or keep for sale or hire, without such consent, any such book[1].

The word 'book' (or its equivalent) is to be taken to include every volume, part or division of a volume, pamphlet, sheet of letter-press, sheet of music, map, chart, or plan, separately published[2].

Whether a particular act is an infringement of letters patent, or of a copyright, will depend upon the answer to two questions; what is the nature and extent of the right alleged to be infringed? and what is the nature of the act complained of? It has not been necessary heretofore to deal much with the nature of the plaintiff's right, since it has generally been obvious enough what it was; and attention has accordingly been drawn mainly to the con-

[1] The statutes are too prolix for further statement here.
[2] As in 5 & 6 Vict. c. 45, the general copyright act.

duct of the defendant. Now, however, the plaintiff's right, whether in a matter of patent or of copyright, is peculiar, and some attention must be given to that side of the subject; though matters of detail, both in regard to the nature of the right and of the defendant's conduct, must be left for special treatises upon the respective subjects.

§ 2. OF PATENTS FOR INVENTION.

A statute of the reign of James the First, aimed at monopolies and declaring them illegal, contains a saving clause in regard to letters patent, which forms the basis of the present law of patents for invention, and has never been essentially changed. The statute saves from the general condemnation and makes lawful 'letters patent and grants of privilege for the term of fourteen years or under, hereafter to be made, of the sole working or making of any manner of new manufactures within this realm, to the first and true inventor or inventors of such manufactures, which others at the time of the making of such letters patent and grants shall not use, so as they be not contrary to the law or mischievous to the state[1].'

This and subsequent statutes contain many provisions more or less minute concerning the steps to be taken to secure the benefit of such letters patent; and there are statutes of amendment in regard to matters which cannot be set out here; there are also statutes extending, in certain cases, the term of the letters for seven and in exceptional cases for fourteen years[2]; and finally there is a recent general revision of all the statutes on the subject[3].

[1] 21 Jac. I, c. 3.
[2] 46 & 47 Vict. c. 57, § 25.
[3] The statutes in order are 5 & 6 Wm. IV, c. 83 (in regard to disclaimers or memorandum of alterations, and providing a penalty for unauthorized use of patentee's name, or counterfeit of his stamp inter alia); 2 & 3 Vict. c. 67 (extending period in certain cases for

CHAP. VI.] INFRINGEMENT OF PATENTS, ETC. 219

Among the matters of chief importance in the steps necessary to acquire the right is the making out and sending to the Patent Office, with the application for the patent, a specification of the invention, with a short statement of the claim of the inventor at the end. The law provides for two specifications, a provisional and a complete one; though the former need not be made. It is important to understand the purposes of the two, and the distinctions between them.

The provisional specification is supposed to be drawn up before the inventor has fully perfected the details of his invention. It should describe generally and fairly the nature of the invention, with drawings if required, so that the invention may be understood; it need not enter into all the details in regard to the manner of carrying out the same[1]. Its purpose is only to protect the inventor until the description can be perfected in the complete specification; it is not made public, unless with that specification[2]. Indeed, if allowed by the law officer of the Crown, the earlier description cannot be impeached as too general[3].

The test of the sufficiency of any specification is laid down to lie in this, whether it would enable an ordinary workman, exercising the knowledge common to the trade, to make the machine. 'It need not give every detail, but it must not tax invention[4].' That is, if a workman of ordinary skill would not be able to construct a machine

seven years); 7 & 8 Vict. c. 69 (same for fourteen years); 15 & 16 Vict. c. 83 (Patent Law Amendment Act of 1852); 16 & 17 Vict. c. 115 (amending Act last named); 46 & 47 Vict. c. 57 (general revision of the statutes).

[1] In re Newall, 4 C. B. N. S. 269, 293, Byles, J.; Stoner v. Todd, 4 Ch. D. 58, Jessel, M. R.
[2] Stoner v. Todd, supra.
[3] Penn v. Bibby, L. R. 2 Ch. 127.
[4] Plimpton v. Malcolmson, 3 Ch. D. 531, Jessel, M. R.

from the description, without a series of experiments, the specification is insufficient[1].

The complete specification is of course a different thing from the provisional one. Unlike that, it must particularly describe and ascertain the nature of the invention and the manner in which it is to operate; and, as in the case of a provisional specification, it must also be accompanied by drawings if required[2]. The omission in either specification to mention anything which may be necessary for the beneficial enjoyment of the invention would be fatal; though this would not be the case if the thing omitted go only to the degree of such enjoyment[3].

The complete specification should not claim anything differing in substance from that contained in the earlier one; but on the other hand it need not extend to everything described there. Part of the earlier may, as has been said, be omitted altogether; or where the facts have been sufficiently described in the provisional specification for the purpose of a final one, the prior description may be referred to, without repeating it[4].

The rule concerning the final specification is, however, rigid. It must be free from all untrue statement, even such as may appear only upon a literal reading. If it contain an untrue statement such as, if literally acted upon, would mislead a competent workman, it is bad: and this though a competent workman would correct the error in practice[5]. For example: The plaintiff's specification, grammatically construed, claims to effect a particular result by two processes, one of which will not effect it. A skilled

[1] Wegmann v. Corcoran, 13 Ch. Div. 65.
[2] § 5; In re Newall, 4 C. B. N. s. 269, 293.
[3] Neilson v. Harford, 8 M. & W. 806.
[4] Penn v. Bibby, L. R. 2 Ch. 127.
[5] Neilson v. Harford, 8 M. & W. 806, Parke, B.

CHAP. VI.] INFRINGEMENT OF PATENTS, ETC. 221

workman would not be misled, but would adopt the right process. The patent granted thereon is invalid[1].

The meaning of the specification should be clearly expressed; it should not be ambiguous, or it will be bad for the purpose of the patent[2]. For example: The plaintiff files a specification for the construction of a windlass, stating the object to be 'to hold, without slipping, a chain cable of any size'. Constructions are known before the date of the patent, by which windlasses might be made to hold a single chain cable of any size. The specification does not unequivocally shew that the object is to construct a single windlass which might hold different chain cables whatever their size, and is bad[3].

But while the rule is much more exacting in regard to the final than in regard to the earlier specification, it is not unreasonable; and slight variations not touching anything of substance, or tending to mislead or to experimenting, will not be fatal. For example: The plaintiff makes a preliminary specification for a patent relating to sewing machines, which describes an instrument of the patent, and then says that 'this, or another acting therewith, acts to hold the work during the insertion of the needle'. The final specification describes only one instrument as so holding the work. The variance is not sufficient to defeat the letters patent granted thereon[4].

It matters not, either, that the specification may include an invention not new, if, omitting that, there is still enough left to constitute the ground for a patent[5].

[1] Simpson v. Holliday, L. R. 1 H. L. 315.
[2] Turner v. Winter, 1 T. R. 602; Hastings v. Brown, 1 El. & B. 450.
[3] Hastings v. Brown, supra.
[4] Thomas v. Welch, L. R. 1 C. P. 192.
[5] Frearson v. Loe, 9 Ch. D. 48, Jessel, M. R.

Further, however perfect may be the specifications in point of description, there is no valid patent of course unless the plaintiff is 'the first and true inventor'. And what this means is to be found, not necessarily in the meaning which might naturally be attached to the words, but in that meaning which the courts have given to it.

What this meaning is may be indicated by the language of a distinguished Master of the Rolls[1]. The learned judge said in substance that shortly after the first statute concerning patents, the question arose whether a man could be called a first and true inventor who in the popular sense had not invented anything, but who, having learned in some foreign country that some one had invented something, copied the invention, brought it to England, and took out a patent. It was held that he was a first and true inventor within the meaning of the statute, if the invention, being in other respects novel and useful, was not previously known in England as part of the common knowledge of the country.

Then, as the Master of the Rolls proceeded to say, this case arose: There were two people, actual inventors in England, who invented the same thing simultaneously; and the question was, whether either could be considered as the first and true inventor. The decision was that he was the first and true inventor who first took out the patent. And then this question arose: If the man who took out the patent was not, in popular language, the first and true inventor, because someone had invented the thing before, but had not taken out a patent for it, would he still be protected? It was decided that he would, provided the invention of the first inventor had been kept secret, that is, had not been made known in such a way as to

[1] Sir George Jessel in Plimpton v. Malcolmson, 3 Ch. D. 531, 551.

CHAP. VI.] INFRINGEMENT OF PATENTS, ETC. 223

become part of the common knowledge, or of the public stock of information.

The common knowledge then of the country is the test by which the question of novelty is to be applied. This obviously does not mean that everyone must know the principle of the supposed invention. What is meant, as the same judge said, is that if the thing is a manufacture connected with a particular trade, the people in that trade shall know something about it. Nor indeed need the case go so far as that. It is not necessary that the bulk, or even a large number, of those people knew the fact; if the fact be so communicated that a sufficient number may be presumed or assumed to know it, that is enough to defeat the patent.

The fact may thus be communicated in different ways; one way is by publishing it in a specification enrolled in the Patent Office; another is by printing the description in a book published and circulated in England. But the question of publication will even then turn upon the facts in the case. The mere fact that a book published in a foreign country, and containing a brief description of the invention, is found in England, is not enough. For example: The plaintiff, a citizen of the United States of America, obtains in 1865 letters patent in England for improvements in making skates. Two years before, an American book containing a brief description of the invention had been sent to the (English) Patent Office; and so had a book of drawings, containing a drawing of it, five weeks before the patent was here issued. This is not such a publication as to render that patent invalid[1].

The enrolling of the preliminary specification in the Patent Office may not amount to a publication so as to bar a claim for novelty, where part of it (or perhaps the

[1] Plimpton v. Malcolmson, supra, a case of the greatest value.

whole) contains an incomplete and insufficient description of an invention. For example: The plaintiff enrolls in the Patent Office a preliminary specification which contains an incomplete description of a patent; and that part is afterwards omitted in the final specification. Subsequently the plaintiff obtains a separate patent in respect of such part; and afterwards the defendant makes for sale an article on the principle of such patent. This is a breach of duty, the first description not being a publication[1].

Thus far of the acquisition and retention by the plaintiff of his patent right; it remains to consider what will give him a right of action, assuming the existence of the fundamental right. That is, assuming that the plaintiff has a valid patent, the question remaining relates to the act of the defendant as constituting the alleged infringement.

The statute gives to the owner of the patent liberty 'of the sole working or making' of the manufacture. This prevents all manner of 'user' in the legal sense; but it does not prevent all manner of making the patented thing by others. Patents, it has been forcibly declared from the bench, are not granted to prevent men of ingenuity from exercising their talents in a fair way. The mere making for the honest purpose of experiment, without any view of using or vending for profit, is not forbidden; it matters not that the article so made was made with a view to improving upon the patent, or with a view to see whether an improvement can be made,—that would not be an infringement[2]. Indeed, the mere exhibition of an improvement is not a user; but to expose the imitation for

[1] Stoner v. Todd, 4 Ch. D. 58. See also Oxley v. Holden, 8 C. B. N. S. 666, as to the effect of abandoning a former specification. And as to want of sufficient description in the preliminary specification see United Telephone Co. v. Harrison, 21 Ch. D. 720.

[2] Frearson v. Loe, 9 Ch. D. 48, Jessel, M. R.

CHAP. VI.] INFRINGEMENT OF PATENTS, ETC. 225

sale would be an infringement, though no sale was made[1]. And it matters not in this or any other case whether the defendant knew of the existence of the plaintiff's patent[2].

Where the patent consists, as it may, of a combination of things, an infringement of it must be an infringement of the combination as such; it would not be infringed by using some of the parts of the combination if they are not themselves patented[3]. Nor in the like case would it be an infringement to use a combination of some of the parts, less than what would be substantially necessary to constitute the subject of the patent, the combination[4]. Indeed, it is held that a patent for an entire combination will not be infringed by the use of a different combination, for the same object, of the same elements, if there is no colourable evasion or imitation of the patent[5].

But where a patent consists of and covers several parts, to imitate any one of them would be an infringement[6]. For example: The plaintiff has a patent for an improved carriage wheel; the specification stating that 'said improved wheel is manufactured wholly of bar iron, by welding iron bars together into the form of a wheel, whereof the nave, spokes, and rim, when finished, will consist of one solid piece of malleable iron. And the mode whereby the said bars of malleable iron are finished and united into the shape of a wheel is as follows:' The specification then shews by drawings how the main spoke and rim are formed and then

[1] Oxley v. Holden, 8 C. B. N. S. 666.
[2] Stead v. Anderson, 4 C. B. 806.
[3] Dudgeon v. Thomson, 3 App. Cas. 34.
[4] Clark v. Adie, 2 App. Cas. 315.
[5] Curtis v. Platt, 35 L. J. Ch. 852, H. L.
[6] Electric Tel. Co. v. Brett, 10 C. B. 838; Smith v. North-western Ry. Co., 2 El. & B. 69.

B. T. 15

welded into a wheel of one piece of malleable iron. The 'claim' states that the invention consists in the centre boss or nave, arms, and rim of the wheel being wholly composed of wrought or malleable iron, 'welded into one solid mass in manner hereinbefore described'. The defendant's wheel imitates the manner of forming the boss or nave into one piece of malleable iron with the rest of the wheel, but does not use the same mode with regard to the spokes and rim as the plaintiff's specification describes. The defendant is liable; the claim really being for the invention of the wheel as described, and the defendant's act, being an imitation of the mode of welding the nave, was an infringement of a material part of the patent[1].

Different processes, further, may be employed for reaching the same result; and the patenting of one process will not exclude the use by others of a different one, where the result to be reached is a known result[2]. So where one has obtained a patent for the use of a known substance, described by its own name, if it is afterwards discovered that the use of other known substances will produce the same effect, the use of them will not constitute an infringement of the patent; and this though the testimony of men of science may go to shew that the substances in question become, in the act of so using them, the one substance described in the patent[3].

An infringement is also committed, though, besides being equivalent to the thing patented, the later article accomplishes some other advantage beyond that effected by the patented article. The new article is still an infringement, so far as it covers the object of the patent. For

[1] Smith v. North-western Ry. Co. 2 El. & B. 69.
[2] Badische Anilin Fabrik v. Levinstein, 24 Ch. D. 156; Bovill v. Pimm, 11 Ex. 718.
[3] Unwin v. Heath, 5 H. L. Cas. 505.

CHAP. VI.] INFRINGEMENT OF PATENTS, ETC. 227

example: The defendant, for the purpose of giving signals by telegraph, uses the earth for effecting a return circuit; the plaintiffs having a patent for giving signals by means of electric currents transmitted through *metallic currents*. The machinery, aside from the return circuit, used by the defendant is the same as that covered by the plaintiff's patent, and is used without license. The defendant is liable, though the use of the earth for effecting a return circuit is an improvement in the art of telegraphing[1].

Where, however, the means employed in the later article are different, not merely in form, but in substance, and consist in combinations differing in substance, there is no infringement, though the object be to produce the same result. For example: The defendant constructs a machine for obtaining a current of air between the grinding surfaces of mill-stones, by means of a rotating vane, for effecting which the plaintiff also has a machine, protected by patent. The plan of the defendant is to remove from the centre of both stones a large circular portion, and in this space, opposite the opening between the two stones, to place a fan, by the rapid rotation of which a centrifugal motion is given to the air, driving it between the stones. The plan of the plaintiff consists of a portable ventilating machine, blowing by a screw vane, which causes a current of air parallel to the axis of the vane, being attached externally to the eye of the upper mill-stone; and the screw vane being thus set in rapid motion, the air is forced through the eye into the centre of the stones, and so finds its way out again. The defendant's machine is not an infringement upon the plaintiff's[2].

[1] Electric Tel. Co. v. Brett, 10 C. B. 838.
[2] Bovill v. Pimm, 11 Ex. 718.

§ 3. OF TRADE MARKS.

The law relating to trade marks has been changing its point of view, if not its grounds, in recent times, and becoming, as has been observed in another place[1], assimilated to the law of property[2]. The old mode of suing for deceit is falling into disuse as a remedy for infringing a trade mark, in the light of the better remedy afforded by what would formerly have been called equitable proceedings. But it is not yet clear that the law has advanced or will advance to the point of assimilating the law of trade marks so far with the law of property (as e.g. the law of patents) as to make it safe to say that, for the purpose of recovering damages, the old authorities, which make the action virtually an action for deceit, are no longer law.

The subject, with this suggestion, must then be dropped in this connection; for while an ample remedy is provided upon the footing of a property right in the trade mark where damages are not sought, it is to be borne in mind that this book is a treatise relating to actions for damages. In a word, an injunction, or nominal damages, may be had in respect of the infringement of a trade mark right, without further requirement; but can substantial damages be obtained without proof of fraud as interpreted by the courts in the law of deceit[3]? Would that not be to make a trade mark a patent?

§ 4. OF COPYRIGHTS.

Statute provides in substance that the copyright in every book published in the author's lifetime shall endure

[1] Ante p. 50, note.
[2] See 46 & 47 Vict. c. 57, §§ 62 et seq.
[3] See Singer Manuf. Co. v. Loog, 18 Ch. Div. 395; Johnston v. Ewing, 7 App. Cas. 219; s. c. 13 Ch. Div. 434; Singer Machine Manufacturers v. Wilson, 3 App. Cas. 376.

CHAP. VI.] INFRINGEMENT OF PATENTS, ETC. 229

for the natural life of the author and seven years thereafter, and shall be the property of the author and his assigns, provided that if the seven years expire before the end of forty-two years from first publication the copyright shall endure for forty-two years; and that the copyright in every book published after the author's death shall endure for forty-two years[1].

It is also provided that if any person shall in any part of the British Dominions print or cause to be printed, either for sale or exportation, any book in which there shall be a copyright, without the proprietor's consent in writing, or shall import for sale or hire any such book, so unlawfully printed beyond the sea, or knowing such book to have been so unlawfully printed or imported, shall sell, publish, or expose to sale or hire, or cause to be sold, published, or exposed to sale or hire, or shall have in his possession for sale or hire any such book, without the proprietor's consent in writing, such offender shall be liable to a special action on the case at the suit of the proprietor of the copyright, in any court of record in that part of the British dominions in which the offence shall be committed[2].

Among many other provisions penalties are fixed for unlawful importing for sale or hire of books the subject of copyright[3]; copyright in encyclopædias, reviews, magazines, periodicals, and works published in a series is provided for[4]; the provisions of earlier law are extended to musical compositions; and the term of copyright for books applied to the liberty of representing dramatic pieces and musical compositions[5]. Pirated books are to become the property of the proprietor of the copyright[6]; but no suit is

[1] 5 & 6 Vict. c. 45, § 3. [2] Id. § 15.
[3] Id. § 17. [4] Id. § 18.
[5] Id. § 20. [6] Id. § 23.

to be brought before entry of the title of the subject of copyright in the Book of Registry at Stationers' Hall[1].

It is enacted in a later statute that the author, being a British subject or resident within the dominions of the Crown, of every original painting, drawing, or photograph shall have the exclusive right of copying, engraving, reproducing, and multiplying such painting or drawing and the design thereof, or such photograph and the negative of the same, for the term of the author's life and seven years thereafter; provided that when any painting, drawing, or the negative of any photograph shall first be sold or disposed of, or shall be made for or in behalf of any other person for a good and valuable consideration, the person so selling or disposing of or making or executing the same shall not retain the copyright thereof unless it be expressly reserved to him at the time by agreement in writing signed by the vendee or assignee of such painting, drawing, or negative of photograph, but the copyright shall belong to the vendee or assignee, or to the person for or on whose behalf the same shall have been made; nor shall such vendee or assignee be entitled to any such copyright unless an agreement at the time in writing shall have been made to that effect[2].

This statute further fixes penalties for infringement of the copyright of the author of any painting, drawing, or photograph[3], and for fraudulent productions and sales of the same[4], and also gives an action for damages to the author[5].

The statute also provides with minuteness of detail the steps necessary to be taken to secure the particular kind of copyright. These cannot be entered into here. It must

---

[1] 5 & 6 Vict. c. 45, § 24.
[2] 25 & 26 Vict. c. 68, § 1.
[3] Id. § 6.   [4] Id. § 7.   [5] Id. § 11.

CHAP. VI.] INFRINGEMENT OF PATENTS, ETC. 231

suffice to say that, whatever doubts once may have existed, copyright has been determined to be a creature of statute, and hence that the author's right must stand or fall accordingly[1]; he cannot claim copyright, in the proper sense, if he has not complied with the statutes. But he may claim protection at common law against wrongful publication by others of his manuscripts, class-room lectures, and the like not printed and published by him[2]. So a painter or a buyer from him has, before, publication of the work, a right to protection against others' copying it[3].

It should be noticed, however, that the requirement of registration of title is intended only as a necessary preliminary to bringing suit, and not as a condition to the existence of copyright; hence it need not be attended to at the time of taking out the copyright. It matters not, indeed, that the plaintiff has not registered his title at the time of the infringement; enough that it is done before suit[4]. On the other hand a man cannot obtain a copyright before publishing his book by getting the title of it duly registered[5].

It is now to be considered in what the plaintiff may have copyright, where the language of the statute does not exclude all question; though this question cannot be considered in detail. Indeed, it cannot be considered even in lines of broad principle, for want of means of generalization beyond this, that real and original mental labour must have been bestowed upon the work in question. The rules laid down by the courts are in the main special, and it

[1] Jefferys v. Boosey, 4 H. L. Cas. 815; Millar v. Taylor, 4 Burr. 2303, leading case.
[2] Albert v. Strange, 1 Macn. & G. 25; Caird v. Sime, 12 App. Cas. 326. As to 'lecture', see the last case, at pp. 337, 338.
[3] Turner v. Robinson, 10 Ir. Ch. R. 121, 510.
[4] Goubaud v. Wallace, 36 L. T. N. S. 704.
[5] Maxwell v. Hogg, L. R. 2 Ch. 307.

must suffice to present only some of the more important of them, with such illustrations as may be needed.

Copyright may be had in the title of a book, if that be a material part of the book; though as a general rule the title to a book, not being in any way new or peculiar, is not a subject of copyright[1]. For example: The plaintiff publishes a book entitled 'Post Office Directory' for a certain locality; and he has taken the steps required for obtaining a copyright. The defendant afterwards publishes a book with the same title. This is no breach of duty to the plaintiff[2].

A man may have copyright in a newspaper[3]; he may have copyright in the product of his brain in the preparation even of a calendar or a catalogue, unless the same consist in a mere dry list of names[4], especially in an illustrated catalogue. For example: The plaintiffs, upholsterers, have engraved, from original drawings procured by them from artists, and publish under the copyright laws an illustrated catalogue of their wares; the catalogue containing, however, no letter-press which might be the subject of copyright. The defendants publish a catalogue containing drawings copied from those of the plaintiffs. This is a breach of duty; it does not matter that the catalogue is of things for sale[5].

A person may also have copyright in an arrangement of questions and answers in some general work, if the

[1] Dicks v. Yates, 18 Ch. Div. 76. See Jarrold v. Houlston, 3 Kay & J. 708.

[2] Kelly v. Byles, 13 Ch. Div. 682.

[3] Walter v. Howe, 17 Ch. D. 708.

[4] Matthewson v. Stockdale, 12 Ves. 270; Longman v. Winchester, 16 Ves. 269; Hotten v. Arthur, 1 H. & M. 603; Maple v. Junior Army Stores, 21 Ch. Div. 369.

[5] Maple v. Junior Army Stores, supra, overruling Cobbett v. Woodward, L. R. 14 Eq. 407.

CHAP. VI.] INFRINGEMENT OF PATENTS, ETC. 233

arrangement is the product of real mental labour[1]; he may have copyright in a book of selections and compilations from other books the copyright of which he has not thereby infringed, especially where he has added original work to the same[2], as by comment or other additions[3], or perhaps by mere arrangement of the materials[4]. A dictionary of quotations would afford an illustration. But of course no copyright could be obtained in such a case in the individual selections themselves[5]; nor will it help the case that labour has been expended upon statements made in quoted matter in the way of verifying them[6].

Copyright may be had in a translation of a book into a foreign tongue[7], if the right of translation has not been reserved, though the author himself has translated his book[8]; but not in a retranslation, i. e. a translation back again to English[9]. It may be had also in the dramatization of another man's novel, though the author himself has dramatized the same[10]. So in the piano-forte score of an opera, whether arranged by the author or not[11]; and it is held that to unite words to an old air and procure an accompaniment thereto, publishing them together, will entitle one to a copyright in the whole[12].

[1] Jarrold v. Houlston, 3 Kay & J. 708. See this case for limitations of the rule.
[2] Lewis v. Fullarton, 2 Beav. 6 ; Spiers v. Brown, 6 W. R. 352.
[3] These themselves would be the subject of copyright. Cary v. Longman, 1 East, 358.
[4] Barfield v. Nicholson, 2 Sim. & S. 1.   [5] Id.
[6] Morris v. Ashbee, L. R. 7 Eq. 34.
[7] Wyatt v. Barnard, 3 Ves. & B. 77.
[8] Semble. So held in America. Stowe v. Thomas, 2 Wall. C. C. 547.
[9] Murray v. Bogue, 1 Drew. 353.
[10] Toole v. Young, L. R. 9 Q. B. 523.
[11] Wood v. Boosey, L. R. 3 Q. B. 223, Ex. Ch.
[12] Leader v. Purday, 7 C. B. 4.

Head-notes or marginal notes to the decisions of the judges are also proper subjects of copyright[1]; and so are products of mental labour worked out of sources of general and common information[2]. Indeed, the case of maps, charts, and the like, falls within the very terms of the statute.

The plaintiff will lose his benefit of copyright by giving his book to the public, that is, ordinarily, by putting it upon the market for sale[3], before taking the steps required by the statute for securing a title. Dramatic and musical compositions, however, stand upon a different footing from ordinary books. It is held that to publish such a composition in England before representing or performing it will not deprive the author of the exclusive right, under the statute, of representing or performing it[4]; but the contrary is held if it was first represented or performed abroad[5].

Thus far of the plaintiff's title; assuming this now to exist, the remaining question is whether the defendant has infringed it.

To the author of copyrighted matter belongs the exclusive right to take all the profits of publication which the sale of the copyrighted matter may produce. And the author's exclusive right extends to the whole copy, and, in a sense, to every part of it. An infringement of a man's copyright may then be committed (1) by reprinting the whole copy, verbatim; (2) by reprinting, verbatim, a part

---

[1] Sweet *v.* Benning, 16 C. B. 459; Saunders *v.* Smith, 3 Mylne & C. 711.

[2] See Gray *v.* Russell, 1 Story, 11, 18.

[3] Selling a picture is not publication. Turner *v.* Robinson, 10 Ir. Ch. R. 121, 510. Nor is exhibiting a picture where copying is not allowed, nor exhibiting it to obtain subscribers for an engraving of it. Id.

[4] Chappell *v.* Boosey, 21 Ch. D. 232.

[5] Boucicault *v.* Chatterton, 5 Ch. Div. 267. Contra in America. Palmer *v.* Dewitt, 47 N. Y. 532.

of it; (3) by imitating the whole or a part, or by reproducing the whole or a part with colourable alterations or disguises, intended to give it the character of a new work; (4) by reproducing the whole or a part under a colourable abridgement, not fairly constituting a new work.

With regard to each of these forms of infringement, it is to be observed that the question of intention does not enter into the question of piracy[1]. The question is one of property, analogous to cases of trespass or conversion; the exclusive privilege which the law secures to authors may be equally violated whether the work complained of has been published with or without the animus furandi. The fact that a party has honestly mistaken the extent of his right to avail himself of the works of others will not excuse him from liability.

Piracies of the nature of those mentioned under the first head are seldom committed, and they may be dismissed with the observation that it matters not that much original and valuable matter, far exceeding in all respects that appropriated, may be incorporated with the reprint of the copyrighted matter. The act is still an infringement, though the public might derive great benefit from the superior value of the work.

Piracies of the second kind are more difficult to deal with. The quantity of matter cannot be a true criterion of the commission of an infringement[2], since only a small portion of a work may be pirated, and this the most important part of the work, or a very important part of it. For example: The defendant makes use, in a published volume of judicial decisions, of the head-notes, or marginal notes, of the plaintiff in a series of volumes of reports, of which

[1] Clement v. Maddick, 1 Giff. 98.
[2] Bramwell v. Halcomb, 3 Mylne & C. 737; Bradbury v. Hotten, L. R. 8 Ex. 1.

the plaintiff owns the copyright. This is an infringement of the plaintiff's rights, for which the defendant is liable; though such notes constitute but a small part of the plaintiff's work[1]. Again: The defendant publishes a book entitled, 'Napoleon III. from the popular caricatures of the last thirty years.' Amongst many other pictures, the book contains nine caricatures from Punch, a publication owned by the plaintiff. Not more than one picture is taken from a single number of Punch, and the nine taken are from numbers extending over a period of several years. This is a breach of duty to the plaintiff[2].

It may be doubtful if any part of the work of another may be taken animo furandi[3]. How much may be honestly taken, that is, taken without any purpose of supplanting the copyright work, is the difficult question. It is clear that, if so much be taken as to sensibly diminish the value of the original, an infringement has been committed[4]. It is not only quantity, but value also, that must be taken into the consideration[5].

In deciding questions of this sort, it has been observed by Mr Justice Story that the nature and objects of the selections made must be taken into account, the quantity and value of the materials used, and the extent to which the use may prejudice the sale or diminish the profits, or supersede the objects of the original work[6]. Many mixed

---

[1] See Saunders v. Smith, 3 Mylne & C. 711; Sweet v. Sweet, 1 Jur. 212; Sweet v. Benning, 16 C. B. 459; Wheaton v. Peters, 8 Peters, 591 (Supreme Court U. S.).

[2] Bradbury v. Hotten, L. R. 8 Ex. 1.

[3] Mr Godson thinks it cannot. Patents and Copyrights, 216. Mr Curtis, contra. Copyrights, 251, note.

[4] Bramwell v. Halcomb, 3 Mylne & C. 737; Saunders v. Smith, Id. 711.   [5] Id.

[6] Folsom v. Marsh, 2 Story, 100.

considerations enter into the discussion of such questions. In some cases a considerable portion of the materials of the original work may be fused into another work, so as to be indistinguishable in the mass of the latter; but yet the latter, having a distinct purpose from the copyrighted book, may not be an infringement. In other cases, the same materials may be used as a distinct feature of excellence, and constitute the chief value of the new work, and then the latter will be an infringement[1]. Be the quantity, then, large or small, if the part extracted furnish a substitute for the work from which it is taken, so as to work an appreciable injury, there is violation of copyright.

A person is entitled to make a reasonable amount of quotation from a copyrighted production by way of review or criticism; but, under the pretence of review, no one has the right to publish a material part of the author's work[2]; that is, such a part as might have a sensible effect in superseding the original[3],—not perhaps as a whole, but quoad hoc[4].

In regard to imitations of the whole or part of a copyrighted work, the difficulty of determining the question of piracy is scarcely less; a question arising generally in cases where common and general sources of information have been drawn upon, and made into a proper subject of copyright. There may be likeness without copying; and, though the copyrighted work may have suggested the new one, the imitation may not be close enough to amount to infringement. The question, however, is whether the

[1] Folsom v. Marsh, 2 Story, 100. See Bradbury v. Hotten, L. R. 8 Ex. 1; D'Almaine v. Boosey, 1 Y. & C. 288, where the taking of the airs of a copyrighted opera, and putting them into the form of quadrilles and waltzes, was held piracy.
[2] See Wilkins v. Aikin, 17 Ves. 422, 424.
[3] Roworth v. Wilkes, 1 Campb. 94.   [4] Curtis, 246, note.

variation be substantial or merely colourable[1]. For example: The defendant is alleged to have infringed the plaintiff's copyright in an Arithmetic by imitating its plan and contents. The test of the defendant's liability is whether he has in fact used the plan, arrangements, and illustrations of the plaintiff as the model of his own work, with colourable alterations and variations, only to disguise the use thereof, or whether the defendant's work is the result of his own labour, skill, and use of common materials and common sources of knowledge, open to all men, the resemblances being accidental, or arising from the nature of the work;—whether, in short, the defendant's work be quoad hoc a servile or evasive imitation of the plaintiff's work, or a bona fide original composition from other common or original sources[2].

In cases of this kind, it is considered not enough to establish a violation of duty that some parts or pages of the later work bear resemblances in methods, details, and illustrations to the copyrighted work. It must further appear that the resemblances in those parts or pages are so close, so full, so uniform, and so striking, as fairly to lead to the conclusion that the one is a substantial copy of the other, or is mainly borrowed from it[3].

The next case is that of abridgements; the rule of law in regard to which is said to be, that a fair abridgement, when the understanding is employed in retrenching unnecessary circumstances, is not a piracy of the original work. Such an abridgement is allowable as constituting a new work[4].

Digests of larger works fall under the head of abridgements. Such publications are in their nature original.

[1] Trusler v. Murray, 1 East, 363, note; Emerson v. Davies, 3 Story, 768, 793.
[2] Emerson v. Davies, supra.   [3] Id.
[4] Copinger, Copyrights, 101.

CHAP. VI.] INFRINGEMENT OF PATENTS, ETC. 239

The compiler intends to make a new use of them not intended by the original author. But such works must be real digests, and not mere colourable reproductions of the original, in whole or in an essential part. The work bestowed upon a digest must be something more than the labour of the pen and the arrangement of extracts; it must be mental labour, designed to produce a new work, the object of which must clearly appear to be consistent with the rights of the author of the original work[1].

[1] See the remarks of Lord Lyndhurst in D'Almaine *v.* Boosey, 1 Younge & C. 288, a case of infringement of a copyrighted musical composition.

CHAPTER VII.

VIOLATION OF RIGHTS OF SUPPORT.

§ 1. INTRODUCTORY.

Statement of the duty. A owes to B the duty (1) to forbear to remove, to B's detriment, the lateral support of B's land, while it lies in its natural condition, or while, under title by grant or prescription, it lies in an artificial condition; (2) to forbear to remove negligently, to B's detriment, the lateral support of B's land with the superincumbent weight of buildings or materials thereon, adjacent to the boundary; (3) to forbear to withdraw, to B's detriment, the subjacent support of his premises.

§ 2. OF LATERAL SUPPORT.

The owner of land has a right, against his neighbour, to what is termed the lateral support of the land. This right of lateral support is a right of support of the land in its natural condition, or, in case of grant or prescription, in an artificial condition; and this right of support of land in its natural condition is, prima facie, a right analogous to the right to make use of a running stream or of the air. It is not in the nature of an easement, and does not depend upon prescription or grant[1]. But of course a right to re-

---

[1] Bonomi *v.* Backhouse, El., B. & E. 622, 646; s. c. 9 H. L. Cas. 503. See Darley Colliery Co. *v.* Mitchell, 11 App. Cas. 127.

CHAP. VII.] VIOLATION OF RIGHTS OF SUPPORT. 241

move the support may be acquired by grant[1], though not by custom or prescription, because either in such a case, it is said, would be oppressive and unreasonable[2].

This right of support, unlike rights of property in general, is not infringed, for the purposes of a suit for tort, unless removing the soil cause damage[3]; but damage being caused by the removal of support, a right of action is created. For example: The defendant, owner of premises adjoining the premises of the plaintiff, which are located upon the side of a declivity, excavates the earth of his land so closely to the boundary between his own and the plaintiff's property as to cause the soil of the plaintiff's premises, of its own natural weight, to slide away into the pit. This is a breach of duty to the plaintiff, for which the defendant is liable in damages[4].

The doctrine, however, goes no further than to sustain a right of action for the sinking of land in its natural condition. The action cannot be maintained if the sinking be due to a superincumbent weight placed upon the plaintiff's premises, unless, indeed, some distinct right has been acquired against the adjoining occupant. For example: The defendant digs a gravel-pit in his premises close to the line between his own and the plaintiff's land. Within two feet of the line, on the plaintiff's land, stands a brick house, erected ten years before, and occupied by the plaintiff. By reason of the defendant's excavation, the premises being located on the side of a hill, it becomes necessary for the plaintiff to vacate his house, and to take it down, to prevent it from sliding into the defendant's pit. The defend-

[1] Rowbotham v. Wilson, 8 H. L. Cas. 348.
[2] Hilton v. Granville, 5 Q. B. 701; Wakefield v. Buccleuch, L. R. 4 Eq. 613.
[3] Bonomi v. Backhouse, supra.
[4] Thurston v. Hancock, 12 Mass. 220; s. c. L. C. Torts, 527.

ant is not liable, since it was the plaintiff's own folly to build so near the line[1].

A right to lateral support of buildings is in the nature of a right of easement, and can be acquired either by grant or by prescription which supposes a grant[2]. But even though a building may have stood upon the plaintiff's premises for the period of prescription, if its walls were improperly constructed, so as for this cause to give way, and not by reason of the excavation alone, the plaintiff cannot recover[3]. And the same would be true, if, within the period of prescription, a new storey were added to the house, whereby the pressure was so increased as to cause the sinking[4].

On the other hand, it is to be observed that the mere fact that there were buildings, recently erected, standing upon the border of the owner's land when it sank, will not prevent his recovering damages. If the soil sank, not on account of the additional weight, but on account of the operations in the adjoining close (though they were carefully conducted), and would have sunk had there been no buildings upon it, it is established law that the person sustaining the damage is entitled to redress to the extent of his loss[5]. Clearly too, if the operation in the adjoining land were conducted with a negligent disregard to the rights of the plaintiff, and the effect of such negligence were the fall of the plaintiff's building, the adjoining occupant is liable therefor[6].

[1] Thurston v. Hancock, supra; Caledonian Ry. Co. v. Sprot, 2 Macq. 449; Partridge v. Scott, 3 M. & W. 220.
[2] Dalton v. Angus, 6 App. Cas. 740; infra, p. 243.
[3] Dodd v. Holme, 1 Ad. & E. 493.
[4] See Murchie v. Black, 34 L. J. C. P. 337.
[5] Stroyan v. Knowles, 6 H. & N. 454.
[6] See Dodd v. Holme, 1 Ad. & E. 493; Bibley v. Carter, 4 H. & N 153.

But in the absence of negligence in the defendant, if the damage to the plaintiff's premises would have been slight and inappreciable had there been no superincumbent weight, the plaintiff will not be entitled to recover. For example: The defendant digs a well near the plaintiff's land, which causes the same to sink, and a building erected there within twenty years falls. If the building had not been on the plaintiff's land, the land would still have sunk, but the damage to the plaintiff would have been inappreciable. This is no breach of duty[1].

The result therefore is, (1) that the defendant is liable for the damages suffered by his neighbour from the withdrawal of the lateral support when that act, of itself, and without the fault of the neighbour, was the cause of the damage, including damage done to sound buildings built twenty years or more before; though the excavation was carefully made. (2) He is liable for all the damage suffered by withdrawing the support when he was guilty of negligence, including in the damages injuries to soundly built buildings, however recently erected. (3) He is not liable, in the absence of grant or prescription, if the subsidence was caused by the weight of buildings, or by the defective condition of the same.

The right of lateral support to contiguous buildings may be acquired by grant, reservation, or prescription[2]. Where buildings have been erected in contiguity by the same owner, and therefore require mutual support, there is, either by a presumed grant or by a presumed reservation, a right to such mutual support in favour of the original owner on a sale by him of any of the buildings. As against himself, on the other hand, there is a presumed grant of the right of support in favour of the purchaser,

[1] Smith *v.* Thackerah, L. R. 1 C. P. 564.
[2] Dalton *v.* Angus, supra; Lemaitre *v.* Davis, 19 Ch D. 281.

which right takes effect at once. And the reservation in the original owner, after one sale, of the right of support for the adjoining building, will enable a second purchaser, on buying this adjoining house, to claim against his neighbour the same right of support; since by the purchase he acquires all of his vendor's rights. It follows also that the same mutual dependency continues after subsequent alienations by the purchasers from the original owner, and this regardless of the question of time. For example: The defendant constructs a drain under his house to connect with a public sewer, and thereby weakens the support of the wall separating the defendant's house from the plaintiff's, to the injury of the latter's house. The two houses originally belonged to the same person, who had demised them both for ninety-nine years to W. The latter mortgages both to B, who assigns the mortgage to H, and H conveys (under a power) one of the houses to the plaintiff in the month of July, and the other to the defendant in September following. The defendant's act in weakening the support of the plaintiff's house is a breach of duty, and the defendant is liable[1].

But the right to such support of buildings is not a natural right; and where the adjoining buildings were erected by different owners the right of support can be acquired in favour of either of the original owners (and their successors in estate) only by grant of the other or by prescription. For example: The defendants pull down a house adjoining the plaintiff's, without shoring up the latter, and thereby cause damage to the plaintiff's property. The houses were built about the same time, but by different owners of the soil; and there is no title to support either by grant or by prescription, nor has the pulling down been negligently done. The defendants are not liable; at least

[1] Richards v. Rose, 9 Ex. 218.

CHAP. VII.] VIOLATION OF RIGHTS OF SUPPORT. 245

if the plaintiff has sufficient notice of the purpose of the defendants to enable him to take the proper precautions against the damage[1].

If there be an intervening house or store in the block, between the premises of the plaintiff and those of the defendant, the pulling down of the latter's building cannot be a breach of duty to the former in the absence of some special engagement between the parties, especially if the plaintiff's building was already in an unsafe condition[2].

There appears to be no obligation by the English law resting upon the owner of a house towards his neighbour in the adjoining tenement to keep his house in repair (further than to prevent the same from becoming a nuisance) in a lasting and substantial manner. The only duty is deemed to be to keep it in such a state that his neighbour may not be injured by its fall. The house may, therefore, be in a ruinous condition, provided it be shored up sufficiently, or the house may be demolished altogether, if this can be done without injury to the adjoining house[3].

If either of the co-tenants of a party-wall[4] should wish to improve his premises before the wall has become ruinous, or incapable of further answering the purposes for which it was built, he may underpin the foundation, sink it deeper, and increase, within the limits of his own land, the thickness, length, or height of the wall, if he can do so without injury to the building upon the adjoining close. And to avoid such injury, he may shore up and support the original wall for a reasonable time, in order to excavate and place a new underpinning beneath it; or he may pull the

[1] Peyton v. London, 9 B. & C. 725.
[2] Solomon v. Vintners' Co., 4 H. & N. 585.
[3] Chauntler v. Robinson, 4 Ex. 163, 170.
[4] For the different kinds of party-wall, see Watson v. Gray, 14 Ch. D. 192; Weston v. Arnold, L. R. 8 Ch. 1084.

wall down for the purpose of building a new one¹. To pull the wall down without intending to replace it would be evidence of an ouster, for which an action could be maintained².

It is held in America that one of the co-tenants cannot, without consent of the other, interfere with the wall unless he can do so without injury to the adjoining building. No degree of care or diligence in the performance of the work will relieve him from liability, if injury be done to the adjoining building by making the improvements. For example : The defendant, co-owner with the plaintiff of a party-wall between their premises, digs down his cellar about eighteen inches, underpinning the party-wall, and lowers the floor of his first story the same distance. In consequence of these operations, the division wall settles several inches, carrying down the plaintiff's floors, and cracking the front and rear walls of his (the plaintiff's) building. The defendant is liable to the plaintiff for the damage thus caused, though the said operation was carried on prudently and carefully³.

It follows that, if a party-wall rest upon an arch, the legs of which stand within the land of the respective owners, neither can remove one of the legs to the detriment of his neighbour, without his consent⁴. On the other hand, either may run up the wall to any height, provided no damage be thereby done to the other⁵.

The existence of a right to fix a beam or timber into the

[1] Standard Bank v. Stokes, 9 Ch. D. 68.
[2] Jones v. Read, 10 Ir. R. C. L. 315, Ex. Ch.
[3] Eno v. Del Vecchio, 6 Duer, 17; s. c. 4 Duer, 58 (N. Y.).
[4] Partridge v. Gilbert, 15 N. Y. 601; Dowling v. Hennings, 20 Md. 179.
[5] Matts v. Hawkins, 5 Taunt. 20; Brooks v. Curtis, 50 N. Y. 639, 644.

wall of a neighbour's house depends upon the situation of the wall. If it stand wholly upon the land of the owner, it is clear that no such right can exist except by grant or prescription. Any attempt by the adjoining owner to fix a timber in the wall, without consent given, would be a trespass, for which an action would lie; or (probably) it could be treated as a nuisance and abated accordingly. And a wall thus situated (the adjoining owner having acquired no right to the enjoyment of it) may be altered or removed at pleasure, provided no damage be thereby done to the adjoining premises.

If, however, the wall be a party-wall, owned in severalty to the centre thereof, or in common, by the adjoining owners, the case will of course be different; and each will be entitled to fix timbers into it, in a prudent manner, doing no damage to the wall or prejudice to the other owner[1].

Where the wall is owned in severalty to the centre, it is clear that neither owner could extend his timbers beyond the centre of the wall. To pass the line of division without permission would be as much a trespass as to make an entry upon the soil without permission.

On the other hand, the case would clearly be different if the wall were owned in common by the adjoining proprietors, since, as has elsewhere been observed[2], tenants in common are each seised of the whole common property. And it follows that such a wall may also be taken down by either owner, for the purpose of rebuilding, if necessary[3].

§ 3. OF SUBJACENT SUPPORT.

While ordinarily a man's title to land includes the underlying soil to an indefinite extent towards the centre of the

[1] See L. C. Torts, 555.
[2] Ante, p. 184.
[3] Stedman v. Smith, 8 El. & B. 1.

earth, it is settled law that there may be two freeholds in the same body of earth measured superficially and perpendicularly down towards the earth's centre; to wit, a freehold in the surface soil and enough lying beneath it to support it, and a freehold in underlying strata, with a right of access to the same, to work therein and remove the contents[1].

This right to the subjacent strata, however, as is above intimated, is not unqualified; on the contrary, it must be exercised, as in removing lateral support, in such a way as not to damage the owner of the surface freehold. If that freehold, in its natural condition, be deprived of its necessary support by underground excavation, and damage thereby ensue, the party committing the act is liable, however carefully he may have conducted the work in his own freehold. For example: The defendants, a coal mining company, lessees of a third person of coal mines underlying the plaintiff's close, upon which there are no buildings, in the careful and usual manner of working the mine so weaken the subjacent support to the plaintiff's close, without his consent, as to cause the same to sink and suffer injury. The defendants are liable for the damage sustained[2].

It is laid down that there is a difference between rights of support against a subjacent owner of land and an adjacent owner as to buildings upon the dominant tenement. The right to the support of buildings, as has been observed, depends, generally, in the absence of grant or reservation, upon the question whether they are ancient or not, that is, whether a prescriptive right has been acquired to the lateral support. But, as against an underlying free-

[1] Humphries v. Brogden, 12 Q. B. 739; s. c. L. C. Torts, 536; Wilkinson v. Proud, 11 M. & W. 33.
[2] Humphries v. Brogden, supra.

CHAP. VII.] VIOLATION OF RIGHTS OF SUPPORT. 249

hold, the owner of the surface freehold is entitled to the support of all buildings which were erected, however recently, before the title of the lower owner began and possession was taken. For example: The defendants are lessees and workers of a mine under the plaintiff's freehold. The plaintiff, at various times before the defendants began their works, and within twenty years thereof, erects buildings above the mines on ground honeycombed by the workings of another company some years before. The workings by the defendants increase the defective nature of the ground, and a subsidence of the surface follows; and from this cause and the fact that the plaintiff's buildings were not constructed with sufficient solidity, considering the state of the ground, damage ensues to the plaintiff's buildings. The defendants have violated their duty to the plaintiff by not shoring up and supporting the overlying tenement[1].

The support required, in the absence of grant or prescription, appears, however, to be merely a reasonable support. Whether the owner of the upper tenement could require the owner of the lower tenement to support structures of extraordinary weight, such as a cathedral, is doubtful. The true view seems to be that when the owner of the whole property severs it by a conveyance either of the surface, reserving the mines, or of the mines, reserving the surface, he intends, unless the contrary be made to appear by plain words, that the land shall be supported, not merely in its original condition, but in a condition suitable to any of the ordinary uses necessary or incidental to its reasonable enjoyment[2]; and that is all.

[1] Richards *v.* Jenkins, 18 Law T. N. s. 437. Of course, if the buildings would have fallen without the act of the defendants, they would not be liable for the damage to them.
[2] Richards *v.* Jenkins, supra. In this case, however, Mr. Baron

There is an analogous right of support in respect of the upper storeys of houses divided into horizontal tenements. It is laid down that if a building is divided into floors or 'flats', separately owned, the owner of each upper floor or 'flat' is entitled to vertical support from the lower part of the building, and to the benefit of such lateral support as may of right be enjoyed by the building itself[1]. The same would (probably) be true if the storeys of the building were *leased* to different persons.

Channell inclined to think that, if the buildings were erected *after* the defendants took possession, the period of prescription should elapse before a right to their support could be acquired.

[1] Dalton *v.* Angus, 6 App. Cas. 740, 793; Caledonian Ry. Co. *v.* Sprot, 2 Macq. 449.

CHAPTER VIII.

VIOLATION OF WATER RIGHTS.

§ 1. INTRODUCTORY.

Statement of the duty. A, a riparian proprietor, or mill owner, owes to B, a riparian proprietor below, on the same stream, the duty to forbear taking, except for domestic purposes or for the needs of a mill suited to the stream, anything more than a usufruct of the water thereof.

§ 2. OF USUFRUCT AND REASONABLE USE OF STREAMS.

Riparian proprietors have rights in the water of the streams flowing by or through their lands which may be thus stated: Each proprietor is entitled to the enjoyment of the water ex jure naturae, as a natural incident to the ownership of the land[1]. And the right is like ordinary property rights in this, that an action may be maintained for an infraction though no actual damage has been sustained[2]. Examples from the authorities just cited will presently appear.

There have been some expressions by the American courts, and one or two decisions, to the effect that the right to the use of a running stream is absolute, like the

[1] Embrey v. Owen, 6 Ex. 353, 369, Parke, B.
[2] Id.; Sampson v. Hoddinott, 1 C. B. N. S. 590.

right to the enjoyment of land; so that any diminution of the water by an upper proprietor is deemed actionable if he has not a right by grant or by prescription, just as an entry upon land without license is actionable[1]. And this view has been urged in England[2].

The true principle however, is that each riparian owner has a right of usufruct ('usus-fructus') in the stream, subject to the rights, whatever they may be, of the riparian owners higher up, and that no one can have any absolute right to the whole volume of water. That is, there can be no infraction of the right by any abstraction of water which does not sensibly and injuriously affect its volume. Without such an act, the usufruct is not interfered with, and the right of other proprietors has not been encroached upon[3]. It is only for an unreasonable and unauthorized use that an action will lie[4].

What amounts to an unreasonable use of a stream will vary according to the case. To take a quantity of water from a large stream for agriculture or manufacturing purposes would cause no sensible diminution of the benefit, to the prejudice of a lower proprietor; while taking the same quantity from a small brook passing through many farms would be of great and manifest injury to those below who need it for domestic or other use. This would be an unreasonable use of the water, and an action would (probably) lie therefor[5].

The same would be true if a mode of enjoyment quite

---

[1] Wheatley v. Chrisman, 24 Penn. St. 298.

[2] See the arguments in Embrey v. Owen, 6 Ex. 353.

[3] Embrey v. Owen, supra; Mason v. Hill, 2 Nev. & M. 747; s. c. 5 B. & Ad. 1; Miner v. Gilmour, 12 Moore P. C. 131; Sampson v. Hoddinott, 1 C. B. N. s. 590.

[4] Embrey v. Owen, supra.

[5] Miner v. Gilmour, supra.

CHAP. VIII.] VIOLATION OF WATER RIGHTS.   253

different from the ordinary one should be adopted, sensibly diminishing the volume of water for any considerable time¹. For example: The defendant, an upper riparian owner, diverts much water from the stream into a reservoir and delays it there to supply a factory; this being an extraordinary use of the stream. The act is a breach of duty to the plaintiff, a lower owner². Again: The defendant owns a great tract of porous land adjacent to a stream, the water of which he diverts by canals, in order to irrigate his land, sensibly diminishing the stream. This is a breach of duty to the plaintiff, an owner lower down³.

On the other hand, every riparian proprietor may use the water of the stream for his domestic purposes, including therein the needs of his animals, and this without regard to the effect it may have, in case of deficiency, upon those lower down⁴. That is, the right is not limited to the usufruct; the whole may be taken if needed.

And this leads to the remark that one criterion of liability for abstracting water from streams used for milling purposes, (probably) is whether, considering all the circumstances, the size of the stream and that of the mill-works, there has been a greater use of the stream, in abstracting or detaining the water, than is reasonably necessary and usual in similar establishments for carrying on the mill. A mill-owner is not liable for obstructing and using the water for his mill, if it appear that his dam is of such magnitude only as is adapted to the size and capacity of the stream, and to the quantity of water usually flowing there-

¹ Sampson v. Hoddinott, 1 C. B. N. S. 590.
² Wood v. Waud, 3 Ex. 748, 781.
³ Embrey v. Owen, 6 Ex. 353, 372. These two examples also illustrate the rule that the action does not require proof of damage. See p. 251. A stream may be much reduced without causing any actual loss.
⁴ Miner v. Gilmour, 12 Moore, P. C. 131; Wood v. Waud, supra.

in, and that his mode of using the water is not unusual or unreasonable, according to the general custom of the country in the case of dams upon similar streams; and this, whatever may be the effect upon the owners of land below. So at least it is held in America[1].

The water of a stream running wholly within a man's land may be diverted, if it be returned to its natural channel before reaching the lower proprietor[2]; and this could perhaps be done where the water runs between the lands of riparian occupants, so far as the rights of parties lower down are concerned. The only person entitled to complain of such an act would be the opposite proprietor.

It is to be observed, however, that the foregoing supposes that there exists no right by prescription or grant to the use of the stream by either the upper or lower proprietor. The rights and burdens of the parties may be greatly varied by grant or by prescription.

With regard to surface water running in no defined channel, the rule of law is that every occupant of land has the right to appropriate such water, though the result is to prevent the flow of the same into a neighbouring stream, or upon the land of an adjoining occupant[3]. Nor can there be any prescriptive right to such water. For example: The defendant, for agricultural and other useful purposes, digs a drain in his land, the effect of which is to prevent the ordinary rainfall, and the waters of a spring arising upon his land and flowing in no defined channel, from reaching a brook, upon which the plaintiff has for fifty years had a mill. The defendant is not liable for the diversion, however serious the inconvenience to the plaintiff[4].

[1] Springfield v. Harris, 4 Allen, 494; s. c. L. C. Torts, 506.
[2] Miner v. Gilmour, supra.
[3] Broadbent v. Ramsbotham, 11 Ex. 602.
[4] Broadbent v. Rambsbotham, supra; Rawstron v. Taylor, Ib. 369.

CHAP. VIII.] VIOLATION OF WATER RIGHTS. 255

§ 3. OF SUB-SURFACE WATER.

In regard to underground streams, if their course is defined and known, as is the case with streams which sink under ground, pursue for a short distance a subterraneous course, and then emerge again, the owner of the land lower down has the same rights as he would have if the stream flowed entirely above ground[1]. But, if the underground water be merely percolation, there can be no breach of duty in cutting it off from a lower or adjoining land-owner; and there can be no prescriptive right to the water. For example: The defendant, a land-owner adjoining the plaintiff, digs on his own ground an extensive well for the purpose of supplying water to the inhabitants of a district, many of whom have no title as land-owners to the use of the water. The plaintiff has previously for more than sixty years enjoyed the use of a stream (for milling purposes) which was chiefly supplied by percolating underground water, produced by rainfall; which water now, after the digging of the well, is cut off and fails to reach the stream. The defendant's act is no breach of duty to the plaintiff[2].

[1] Dickinson v. Grand Junc. Canal Co., 7 Ex. 282.
[2] Chasemore v. Richards, 7 H. L. Cas. 349; overruling Balston v. Bensted, 1 Campb. 463. No right to such percolating water can arise by grant or by prescription apart from the right to the land itself. Id.
As to polluting streams, see post, pp. 260, 261.

CHAPTER IX.

NUISANCE.

§ 1. INTRODUCTORY.

Statement of the duty. A owes to B the duty (1) to forbear to obstruct or impair the use of the public ways or waters in such a manner as to produce a special prejudice to B; (2) to forbear to flood the land of B with water collected upon his own land, or by changing the course of currents; (3) to forbear to cause or suffer the existence upon his own premises of anything not naturally there which produces a special prejudice to B; (4) to forbear so to use his own premises as to endanger the life or health of B, or to disturb his physical comfort in a special degree in the use of his (A's) premises.

1. Public nuisances are indictable nuisances, being committed (1) in the public ways or waters, or (2) on private premises to the prejudice of the general public.

2. Private nuisances are non-indictable nuisances, being committed on private premises to the prejudice of one person, or but a few persons, of the neighbourhood.

3. A public nuisance may become a private nuisance as well.

§ 2. OF WHAT CONSTITUTES A NUISANCE.

It appears to be of the essence of a nuisance that there should be some duration of mischief; a wrong producing damage instantaneously, as in the case of an explosion[1], could hardly be a nuisance. And then further to determine what constitutes a nuisance, so as to render the author of it liable to a neighbour in damages, a variety of other considerations must often be taken into account; especially where the act in question has been committed in a populous neighbourhood, in the prosecution of a manufacturing business. And, even if the business itself be unlawful, it does not follow that a private individual can call for redress by way of a civil action for damages. Whether he can do so or not will depend upon the question whether he has sustained a special damage, by reason of the thing alleged to be a nuisance.

Even supposing the nuisance not to be a public one, that is, not to affect seriously the rights of the public in general, much difficulty arises in determining when the business carried on upon neighbouring premises, either in itself or in the manner of conducting it, is so detrimental as to subject the proprietor or manager to liability in damages. And this difficulty was until recently increased by certain inexact terms used in the old authorities. It was said that if a business was carried on in a 'reasonable manner,' an action for damages could not be maintained, though annoyance resulted; and the term 'reasonable manner' was explained as meaning that the business was to be carried on merely in a *convenient* place. That is, a trade was not to be treated as a nuisance if carried on in the ordinary manner in a convenient locality. The result was to bestow upon a manufacturer the right to ruin his neighbour's property, provided only the business was carefully conducted in a locality convenient for its management[2].

[1] An explosion might be a *consequence* of a nuisance, however.
[2] Comyns's Digest, Action upon the Case for a Nuisance, C; Hole *v.* Barlow, 4 C. B. N. S. 334

B. T.   17

Recent authorities have, however, changed all this, by declaring that, when no prescriptive right is proved, the true meaning of the term 'convenient', used by the older authorities, lies in the consideration whether the plaintiff has suffered a visible detriment in his property by reason of the management or nature of the defendant's business: if he has, the defendant is liable. Convenience is a question for the neighbour and not for the manufacturer; and visible damage to the neighbour's property shews that the business is carried on at an inconvenient place[1]. For example: The defendants are proprietors of copper-smelting works in the plaintiff's neighbourhood, where many other manufacturing works are carried on. The vapours from the defendant's works, when in operation, are visibly injurious to the trees on the plaintiff's estate; the defendants having no prescriptive right to carry on their business as and where they do. The defendants are guilty of a breach of duty to the plaintiff, for which they are liable in damages; though, for the purposes of manufacturing, the business is carried on at a convenient place[2].

However, a person living in a populous neighbourhood must suffer some annoyance; that is part of the price he pays for the privileges which he may enjoy there. He cannot, therefore, bring an action for every slight detriment to his property which a business in the vicinity may produce. Or, to state the case in the language of judicial authority, if a man live in a town, it is necessary that he should subject himself to the consequences of those operations of trade which may be carried on in his immediate locality, which

---

[1] Bamford *v.* Turnley, 3 Best & S. 62, 66; Cavey *v.* Ledbitter, 13 C. B. N. S. 470; St Helen's Smelting Co. *v.* Tipping, 11 H. L. Cas. 642; s. c. L. C. Torts, 454.

[2] St Helen's Smelting Co. *v.* Tipping, supra. See also Broadbent *v.* Imperial Gas Co. 7 De G. M. & G. 436; s. c. 7 H. L. Cas. 600.

CHAP. IX.]　　　NUISANCE.　　　259

are actually necessary for trade and commerce, and also for the enjoyment of property, and for the benefit of the inhabitants of the town and of the public at large. If a man live in a street where there are numerous shops, and a shop be opened next door to him, which is carried on in a fair and reasonable way, he has no ground of complaint because to himself individually there may arise much discomfort from the trade carried on in that shop. But when an occupation is carried on by one person in the neighbourhood of another, and the result of that occupation is a visible injury to property, the case is different[1].

It should be observed in this connection that the plaintiff is not precluded from recovering by reason of the fact that he had notice of the existence of the nuisance when he located himself near it. If the thing complained of be unlawful—if there be no prescriptive right to do it—the doer cannot set up notice to escape liability[2]. For example: The defendant is a tallow-chandler, carrying on his business in a certain messuage, in such a manner as to convey and diffuse noxious vapours and smells over premises adjoining, which the plaintiff takes possession of while the defendant is carrying on his business. The defendant is liable[3].

Subject to any annoyance which may result from the right which every landowner has to the ordinary and natural use of his premises, no one may turn water from his own land back upon that of his neighbour without having acquired a right so to do by statute or by grant or prescription; and this though the water thrown back comes of natural rainfall[4]. Such an act might (probably) be

[1] Lord Westbury in St Helen's Smelting Co. v. Tipping.
[2] Bliss v. Hall, 4 Bing. N. C. 183; Bamford v. Turnley, 3 Best & S. 62, 70, 73; L. C. Torts, 467.
[3] Bliss v. Hall, supra.
[4] Hurdman v. North-eastern Ry. Co. 3 C. P. Div. 168. Contra, Gannon v. Hargadon, 10 Allen, 106 (Mass.).

treated as a trespass, and therefore should be redressible though no damage had been sustained; for otherwise a right to send the water there might eventually be acquired by prescription, to the substantial confiscation of the particular piece of land. For example: The defendant erects an embankment upon his land, whereby the surface-water accumulating upon the plaintiff's land is prevented from flowing off in its natural courses, and caused to flow in a different direction over his land. This is a breach of duty for which the defendant is liable to the plaintiff, though the latter suffer no damage thereby[1].

If the water of a stream be polluted, or otherwise rendered useless or perhaps materially less useful than it was before, whether it be surface or sub-surface water, and damage ensue to another riparian owner, he can maintain an action therefor, unless a right to do the thing has been acquired by statute or by grant or prescription[2]. In the case of statutory authority to pollute the waters of a stream, however, this doctrine is to be taken with qualification. It has been laid down in regard to such cases that a city is not liable for polluting by sewage the water of a stream which it has a right to use for that purpose, so far as the effect is the necessary result of the system of drainage adopted by the city; but it is otherwise if the pollution is attributable to the negligence of the city either in managing the system or in the construction of sewers[3],

[1] Tootle v. Clifton, 22 Ohio St. 247. This, it should be observed, is not the case of bringing water, as by means of a reservoir, upon one's land (Rylands v. Fletcher, L. R. 3 H. L. Cas. 330; post, ch. 12); for there the purpose is not to throw the water back but to hold it. Escape in such a case might not be a trespass.

[2] See Clowes v. Staffordshire Waterworks Co., L. R. 8 Ch. 125; Goldsmid v. Tunbridge Wells Com'rs., L. R. 1 Eq. 161; affirmed, L. R. 1 Ch. 349.

[3] Merrifield v. Worcester, 110 Mass. 216. See Blyth v. Birmingham

or if the right is exceeded. The right, whether statutory or otherwise, must be exercised in a reasonable and proper way[1].

For milling and other purposes, for which some large or special use of the water of a stream is required, statutory rights are often granted, under various restrictions, to flood the lands lying along the mill-streams, or to foul the water; for the nature of which rights reference should be made to the statutes and judicial interpretations of them.

With regard to actions for nuisances to personal enjoyment, it appears to be quite clear that for such smells or vapours proceeding from a neighbour's premises as are merely disagreeable, at least when such smells or vapours are the necessary effect of a business properly conducted there, no action is maintainable[2]. The noxious gases must produce some important sensible effect upon physical comfort. A person is, indeed, sometimes said to be entitled to an unpolluted and untainted stream of air for the necessary supply and reasonable use of himself and family; but by the terms 'untainted' and 'unpolluted' are meant, not necessarily air as fresh, free, and pure as existed before the business in question was begun, but air not rendered to an important degree less compatible, or certainly not incompatible, with the physical comfort of human existence[3].

The criterion, therefore, of liability for a supposed (private[4]) nuisance, affecting the bodily comfort of the plaintiff,

---

Waterworks Co. 11 Ex. 781, to the same effect in regard to the escape of water.

[2] Baxendale v. McMurray, L. R. 2 Ch. 790.
[2] See St Helen's Smelting Co. v. Tipping, supra.
[3] Walter v. Selfe, 4 De G. & S. 315.
[4] It is doubtful if the right of action for injury by a public nuisance would stand on different ground; but the court in Walter v. Selfe is careful to say that a private nuisance is there spoken of.

is, whether the inconvenience should be considered as more than fanciful,—more than one to mere delicacy or fastidiousness,—as an inconvenience materially interfering with the ordinary physical comfort of human existence, not merely according to elegant or dainty modes and habits of living, but according to plain and simple modes of life[1]. For example: The defendant erects upon his premises, adjoining the premises of the plaintiff, a kiln for the manufacture of bricks, and in the process of the manufacture the smoke and vapours and floating substances from the kiln are constantly directed to and within the plaintiff's house, so as to affect materially the comfort of himself and family as persons of ordinary habits of life. This is a breach of duty to the plaintiff, though it appear that the health of his family has actually been better since the erection of the kiln than before[2].

It matters not what it is that produces the discomfort: smoke alone may be sufficient; and the same is true of noxious vapour alone, or of offensive smells alone. Whatever produces a material discomfort to human life in the neighbourhood is a nuisance, for which damages are recoverable[3]. But the provisions of statute in regard to such annoyances, arising from the carrying on of a lawful business, should always be examined[4].

Thus far of private nuisances. In regard to public nuisances, it is to be observed that such become private or personal nuisances as well, by inflicting upon a particular individual any special or particular damage. For example: The defendant, without authority, moors a barge across a public

---

[1] Walter *v.* Selfe, supra. See also Crump *v.* Lambert, L. R. 3 Eq. 409; affirmed, 17 L. T. N. s. 133.

[2] Walter *v.* Selfe, supra.   [3] Crump *v.* Lambert, supra.

[4] In regard to smoke see e.g. 10 & 11 Vict. c. 34, § 108; Cooper *v.* Wooley, L. R. 2 Ex. 88; Smith *v.* Midland Ry. Co. 37 L. T. N. s. 224.

navigable stream, and harmfully obstructs the navigation thereof to the plaintiff, who at the time is floating a barge down the stream. This is a breach of duty to the plaintiff, for which the defendant is liable in damages[1].

If, however, the obstruction or invasion of the right be one of like effect upon all persons, producing no particular, actual damage to any individual, no individual can maintain an action for damages by reason of it. In other words, it is necessary to the maintenance of an action for damages for a public nuisance (and the same is true of a private nuisance) that the plaintiff should have suffered actual, specific damage thereby[2].

It matters not that the special damage sustained by the plaintiff is common to a large number of individuals, or to the whole neighbourhood; enough if there is actual damage to his property, or injury to his health, or to his physical comfort (as explained in considering private nuisances). The injury inflicted upon private interests is not merged in the wrong done to the general public. For example: The defendants carry on a large business as auctioneers near a coffee-house kept by the plaintiff in a narrow street in London. From the rear of the defendant's building, which there adjoins the plaintiff's house, the defendants are constantly loading and unloading goods into and from vans and stalling their horses. This intercepts the light of the coffee-house so as to require the plaintiff to burn gas most of the day-time, obstructs the entrance to the door, and renders the plaintiff's premises uncomfortable from stench. The nuisance is a public one, but the plaintiff suffers a special and particular damage from it for which the de-

---

[1] Rose v. Miles, 4 Maule & S. 101; s. c. L. C. Torts, 460.
[2] Benjamin v. Storr, L. R. 9 C. P. 400; Fritz v. Hobson, 14 Ch. D. 542.

fendant is liable to him[1]. Again: The defendants carry on a manufacturing business in such a way as to make themselves liable for causing a public nuisance. The plaintiff's premises are filled with smoke, and his house shaken so as to be uncomfortable for occupation. This is a breach of duty to the plaintiff, for which he is entitled to damages, though everyone else in the vicinity suffers in the same manner[2].

It is, however, a difficult matter to state what sort of detriment will amount to special damage within the law of public nuisances. It appears to be necessary in the case of obstructions of public ways or waters that a particular user had been begun by the plaintiff, and that such user was interrupted by the wrongful act of the defendant[3]. Before the complaining party has entered upon the actual enjoyment of the public easement, the wrongful act does not directly affect him, or at least does not affect him in a manner to enable a court to measure the loss inflicted upon him. If he desire to make use of the easement he can complain to the prosecuting officer, and require him to enter public proceedings against the offender; or (so it seems) he may proceed to make his particular use of the easement, and if the obstruction be not removed before he reaches it, or in time for him to have the full enjoyment of passage, he may bring an action for the damage which he has sustained in the particular case by reason of the obstruction.

This latter proposition follows from the rule of law already noticed, that the plaintiff is not barred of a recovery in damages by reason of having notice of the existence of the nuisance when he put himself in the way of suffering

[1] Benjamin v. Storr, supra.
[2] Wesson v. Washburn Iron Co., 13 Allen, 95 (Mass.).
[3] See Rose v. Miles, 4 Maule & S. 101; s. c. L. C. Torts, 460.

damage from it[1]. Such a case does not come within the principle that a consenting party cannot recover for damage sustained by reason of an act the consequences of which he has invited[2], since he has not consented to the act complained of, or invited its consequences. He may have reason to suppose that the obstruction will be removed before he reaches it; or, if not, he may well say that it is wrongful, and *must* be removed before he reaches it, on pain of damages for any loss which he may sustain by reason of its continuance.

If the obstruction of itself be insufficient to cause any actual damage, it is considered that no right of action can be derived by incurring expense in removing it. For example: The defendant obstructs a public footway, and the plaintiff on coming to the obstruction, in passing along the way, causes the obstruction to be removed; and this is repeated several times. No other damage is proved. The defendant is not liable[3].

It follows that the mere fact that the plaintiff has been turned aside by reason of the obstruction and caused to proceed, if at all, by a different route from that intended by him, is not special damage: he must have suffered some specific loss by reason of being thus defeated in his purpose. And this would (probably) be true also of obstructions to the public wagon roads. For example: The defendant obstructs a public highway leading directly to the plaintiff's farm, and the plaintiff is thereby compelled to go to his land, if at all, with his team, by a longer and very circuitous road; but no specific loss is proved. The defendant is not liable to the plaintiff[4].

[1] Ante, p. 259.
[2] 'Volenti non fit injuria.'
[3] Winterbottom *v.* Derby, L. R. 2 Ex. 316.
[4] Houck *v.* Wachter, 34 Md. 265.

CHAPTER X.

DAMAGE BY ANIMALS.

§ 1. INTRODUCTORY.

Statement of the duty. A owes to B the duty to prevent his animals, (1) from doing damage to B, if he has notice of their propensity to do damage, and (2) from straying upon B's premises.

§ 2. OF NOTICE OF PROPENSITY TO DO DAMAGE.

Whoever keeps an animal with notice that it has a propensity to do damage is liable to any person who, without fault of his own contributing to the injury, suffers an injury from such animal; and this, though the keeper be not guilty of negligence in regard to properly or securely keeping it. The gist of liability for the damage is the keeping of the animal after notice of the evil propensity. For example: The defendant has a monkey, which he knows is accustomed to bite people. The plaintiff, without fault of her own, is bitten by the animal. The defendant is liable, however careful he may have been in keeping the monkey[1].

[1] May *v.* Burdett, 9 Q. B. 101; s. c. L. C. Torts, 478. See Jackson *v.* Smithson, 15 M. & W. 563, Card *v.* Case, 5 C. B. 622.

If the animal be feræ naturæ, it will (probably) be presumed that the defendant had notice of any vicious propensity whereby the plaintiff has suffered injury, since it is according to the nature of such an animal to do damage[1]. And even if the animal be domestic, the owner will be presumed to have notice of any propensity which is secundum naturam of the animal. For example: The defendant's cattle stray into the plaintiff's garden and beat and tear down the growing vegetables. The defendant is liable, though not guilty of negligence; since it is of the nature of straying cattle to do such damage[2].

In the case of injuries committed by domestic animals contra naturam, it is clear that the owner is not liable if he had no notice of the propensity[3]. For example: The defendant's horse kicks the plaintiff, neither the plaintiff nor the defendant being at fault, and the defendant having no notice of a propensity of the horse to kick. The defendant is not liable; since it is not of the nature of horses to kick people, when not provoked to the act[4].

Statutes have been passed, declaring it unnecessary in an action against the owner of a dog to prove a previous propensity of the animal to injure sheep or cattle. In the absence of statute, however, the rule requiring notice of the vicious propensity prevails in regard to dogs as well as with regard to other domestic animals[5].

While, however, negligence in the owner of the animal

[1] If a wild animal has been tamed and domesticated, the case may be different.
[2] See Cox v. Burbridge, 13 C. B. N. S. 430, 438, Williams, J. Or, the loss is the natural consequence of the cattle's trespassing. See § 3.
[3] L. C. Torts, 490.
[4] Cox v. Burbridge, supra. The plaintiff was a boy playing in the highway at the time of the injury, but there was no evidence that he had done anything to irritate the horse.
[5] See L. C. Torts, 490.

is not necessary to constitute a breach of duty when the scienter can be proved, negligence in the care of the animal will (probably) render the owner liable, though he did not know of the propensity.

It must at the same time be understood that the right of redress of the injured person will be defeated if the injury was caused by his own fault. A person who irritates an animal, and is bitten or kicked in turn, is deemed to have proximately caused the damage sustained, and so cannot recover. But if the fault of the injured party had no necessary or natural connection with the injury, operating to produce the injury as cause produces effect, the owner of the animal will be liable. For example: The defendant keeps upon his premises a ferocious dog, and the plaintiff, having no notice that such a dog is there, trespasses in the day-time upon the premises, and the dog rushes upon him and bites him. The defendant is liable[1]; since it is not the necessary or natural and usual consequence of a person's trespassing upon a man's premises by day that he should be attacked by a savage dog.

If, however, the plaintiff had notice that the vicious animal was loose upon the premises, the case would be different, since it would be the natural and usual result of trespassing upon the land that the animal would attack the trespasser. And if a person were to venture upon another's premises in the country as a trespasser in the night-time, it might perhaps be considered that he had entered with notice of danger, since it is not unusual for people in the country to keep watch-dogs upon their lands. But, if the trespasser were not engaged in mischief or reasonably suspected of mischievous intent, the owner would have no right to set his dog upon him before giving him

---

[1] Loomis v. Terry, 17 Wend. 496 (N. Y.).

notice to leave the premises, even if he would after notice; for unnecessary injury done to a man or even to his beast, though trespassing, cannot be justified[1]. Necessary force to resist the entry, or eject the trespasser after his wrongful entry, is the utmost which the law allows the owner or occupant of the premises[2].

§ 3. OF ESCAPE OF ANIMALS.

By the common law of England the owner of land is bound to keep it fenced ; and if his animals escape and get into his neighbour's premises, he is liable for the damage done, whether the escape was owing to his negligence or not. The same is true, indeed, though the defendant's animals may not have escaped from his enclosure; if still an animal commit damage, by putting part of its body over, through, or beyond the boundary line, the defendant will be liable regardless of negligence. For example : The defendant's horse bites and kicks the plaintiff's horse through the partition fence between the plaintiff's and defendant's premises. The defendant is liable, though not guilty of negligence[3].

[1] See Loomis v. Terry, supra. Trespassing animals should not be injured unnecessarily. Janson v. Brown, 1 Campb. 41; Wright v. Ramscot, 1 Saund. 84; Murgoo v. Cogswell, 1 E. D. Smith, 359 (N. Y.); Amick v. O'Hara, 6 Blackf. 258 (Ind.). A ferocious dog at large, unattended, without muzzle, may be killed. Maxwell v. Palmerston, 21 Wend. 407 (N. Y.). See ante, p. 197.

[2] This would be another way also of explaining the right of the trespasser to recover when, having entered without notice, he is attacked and bitten by the dog without the direct command of the owner. Comp. the cases of injury by spring-guns. Bird v. Holbrook 4 Bing. 628; Ilott v. Wilkes, 3 B. & Ald. 304 ; Wootton v. Dawkins, 2 C. B. N. S. 412. But as to notice see now 24 & 25 Vict. c. 100, § 31.

[3] Ellis v. Loftus Iron Co., L. R. 10 C. P. 10.

CHAPTER XI.

ESCAPE OF DANGEROUS THINGS.

§ 1. INTRODUCTORY.

Statement of the duty. A owes to B the duty to prevent the escape of any dangerous thing, to the damage of B, brought or made upon the premises of A; the escape being due to defects within the control, though it may be not within the knowledge, of A.

§ 2. OF THE NATURE OF THE PROTECTION REQUIRED.

The duty considered in the preceding chapter of restraining animals from doing damage has been treated in England as furnishing ground for an analogous duty with reference to inanimate things of a peculiarly dangerous character, which the occupant of premises has brought or made thereon,—the duty, to wit, so to keep such things that they shall not do mischief to the occupant's neighbour; within limitations now to be stated.

In the language, substantially, of judicial authority, where the owner of land, without wilful wrong or negligence, uses his land in the ordinary manner, he will not be liable in damages, though mischief should thereby be occasioned to his neighbour[1]. But a person who, for his own

---

[1] Chasemore *v.* Richards, 7 H. L. Cas. 349

purposes, brings on his land, and collects and keeps there, anything likely to do mischief if it escapes, must keep it there at his peril; and if he does not, he will be answerable, prima facie, for all the damage which is the natural consequence of its escape; and this however careful he may have been, and whatever precautions he may have taken to prevent the damage[1]. For example: The defendants construct a reservoir on land separated from the plaintiff's colliery by intervening land. Mines under the site of the reservoir, and under part of the intervening land, have been formerly worked; and the plaintiff has, by workings lawfully made in his own colliery and in the intervening land, opened an underground communication between his own colliery and the old workings under the reservoir. It has not been known to the defendants, or to any person employed by them in the construction of the reservoir, that such communication exists, or that there have been any old workings under the site of the reservoir; and the defendants have not been personally guilty of any negligence. The reservoir is in fact, but without the defendants' knowledge, constructed over five old shafts, filled with rubbish and other loose material, and leading down to the workings; and having been filled with water, the water bursts down these shafts and flows by the underground channel into the plaintiff's mines, producing damage. The defendants are liable[2].

[1] Rylands v. Fletcher, L. R. 1 Ex. 265, Ex. Ch.; L. R. 3 H. L. 330. The decision of the Court of Exchequer (3 H. & C. 774) was reversed.

[2] Rylands v. Fletcher, supra. The general rule above stated has been the subject of great discussion on both sides of the Atlantic, since Rylands v. Fletcher was decided. It has been denied by some of the American courts, and adopted or favoured by others. It is denied e.g. by Losee v. Buchanan, 51 N. Y. 476; it is favoured e.g. by Shipley v. Fifty Associates, 106 Mass. 194. See further, L. C. Torts, 497—500. And some tendency to modify it has been shewn in

The owners of the upper tenement have, however, as has already been intimated, in such cases, a right to work their premises in the ordinary, reasonable, and proper manner, and are not liable for the effects of water which flows down into the lower tenement by mere force of gravitation. But where some unusual and extraordinary effort is put forth for effecting the occupant's purpose, the owner is liable for the injurious results which follow[1]. For example: The defendant, owner of a coal-mine above the plaintiff's mine, works out the whole of his coal, leaving no barrier between his mine and the plaintiff's, the consequence of which is, that the water percolating through the upper mine flows into the lower one, and obstructs the plaintiff in getting out his coal. This is no breach of duty by the defendant; the water having flowed down in its natural course, and the defendant being entitled to remove all of his coal[2]. Again: The defendant, under the like circumstances, does not merely suffer the water to flow through his mine in its natural way, but, in order to work his mine beneficially, pumps up quantities of water which pass into the plaintiff's mine, in addition to that which would naturally have reached it, whereby the plaintiff suffers damage. This is a breach of duty to the plaintiff, though it is done without negligence, and in the due working of the defendant's mine[3].

If the damage be produced by vis major or by the act

England, but that is as much as can be said. In substance the rule stands. See Pollock, Torts, 398—401. 'The authority of Rylands v. Fletcher is unquestioned, but Nichols v. Marsland [L. R. 10 Ex. 255, 2 Ex. Div. 1] has practically empowered juries to mitigate the rule, whenever its operation seems too harsh.' Id. p. 401.

[1] Ib.; Fletcher v. Smith, 2 App. Cas. 781; Baird v. Williamson, 15 C. B. N. S. 376.

[2] Smith v. Kenrick, 7 C. B. 515, 564.

[3] Baird v. Williamson, supra.

of God[1], or otherwise, without the intervention of acts or omission of duty by the occupant or those for whom he is responsible, the case will be different. In the example given, if the damage had been caused by lightning bursting the reservoir[2], and not by reason of the existence of the openings into the lower mines, the defendants would not have been liable. Again: The defendant's tenants, the plaintiffs, occupy the lower story of a warehouse, of which the defendant occupies the upper. A hole has been gnawed by rats through a box into which water from the gutters of the building is collected, to be thence discharged by a pipe into the drains. The water, now pouring through the hole, runs down and wets the plaintiff's goods. The defendant is not liable[3]. Again: The defendant owns premises on which stand yew-trees, which, to his knowledge, are poisonous. A third person clips some of the branches, which fall upon the plaintiff's land, and poison the latter's horses. The defendant is not liable[4].

If, too, the bringing the dangerous thing upon the occupant's land, and all the works connected therewith, be effected under sanction of legislative authority, the fact that they result in damage to the party's neighbour by purely natural escape or by authorized channels, and not by reason of negligence attributable to the occupant, will not render the occupant liable[5]. It is also certain, a fortiori, in such a case that, if the escape be caused by the act of God,

---

[1] Nichols v. Marsland, L. R. 10 Ex. 255 s. c. 2 Ex. Div. 1, shewing that this term includes events which human foresight could not *reasonably* anticipate. This case in both stages is very instructive.
[2] Id.
[3] Carstairs v. Taylor, L. R. 6 Ex. 217; Ross v. Fedden, L. R. 7 Q. B. 661.
[4] Wilson v. Newberry, L. R. 7 Q. B. 31.
[5] See Vaughan v. Taff Vale Ry. Co., 5 H. & N. 679.

no liability follows. For example: The defendant is charged by law with the duty of maintaining water tanks in his district for purposes of irrigation, as part of a national system of irrigation, for the welfare of the people. By reason of an extraordinary flood, and not by reason of the bad condition of the 'works, one of these tanks gives way, causing damage to the plaintiffs. The plaintiffs cannot recover therefor[1].

On the other hand, if the works be of a nature to require legislative sanction, the proprietor or manager, when not having it, will be liable for damage produced by any escape or breaking thereof, however occurring. For example: The defendants make use of locomotive engines, without having obtained the necessary authority of law, and the plaintiff suffers damage by reason of fire proceeding from the same. The defendants are liable, though not guilty of any negligence in the management of the engines, and though they would not have been liable had they had the proper authority[2].

The importance of the subject of this chapter and the fact that its lines may not yet be fully developed, will make it useful to refer to some of the American authorities.

It has been decided that the occupant of premises may be liable for damage caused by the fall of ice or snow from the roof of his building when the roof is so constructed as to make it substantially certain that, if the snow be not removed, accidents from snow-slides will occur; although the roof be constructed in the usual manner of the time[3]. And with regard to water collected in reservoirs, it is held

[1] Madras Ry. Co. v. The Zemindar, L. R. 1 Ind. App. 364.
[2] Jones v. Festiniog Ry. Co., L. R. 3 Q. B. 733 ; Vaughan v. Taff Vale Ry. Co., supra.
[3] Shipley v. Fifty Associates, 106 Mass. 194.

CHAP. XI.] ESCAPE OF DANGEROUS THINGS. 275

that the embankments must be so thoroughly constructed that the water cannot percolate through them[1].

The doctrine has also been laid down in the United States that where the alleged rights of adjoining land-owners conflict, it is better that one of them should yield to the other and forego a particular use of his land, rather than, by insisting upon that use, deprive the other altogether of the use of his property; which might often be the consequence of carrying on the operation. This would, of course, be an obvious principle if stated with regard to a nuisance; but it is treated as applicable to other wrongs as well. For example: The defendants, in the course of digging a canal through their land, for which purpose they are clothed with legislative authority[2], find it necessary to blast rocks by the use of gunpowder. The result of the blasting is to throw fragments of rock against the plaintiff's house, whereby the plaintiff suffers damage. The defendants are deemed liable, though not guilty of negligence[3].

A distinction has, however, been observed to exist between an injury sustained in that way and one sustained by the explosion of a boiler on the defendant's premises. For damage sustained in the latter way, it is deemed that no right of action arises unless the explosion was due to negligence of the manager[4]. The use of a boiler is not necessarily dangerous[5].

[1] Wilson v. New Bedford, 108 Mass. 261; Pixley v. Clark, 35 N. Y. 520.
[2] The work could not therefore be a nuisance when carefully conducted.
[3] Hay v. Cohoes Co., 2 N. Y. 159.
[4] Losee v. Buchanan, 51 N. Y. 476. In this case the rule in Rylands v. Fletcher, supra, is denied.
[5] Further, see Cooley, Torts, 677, 680, 2nd ed.; L. C. Torts, 496 et seq.

PART III.

BREACH OF DUTY TO REFRAIN FROM
NEGLIGENCE.

NEGLIGENCE.

§ 1. INTRODUCTORY.

Statement of the duty[1]. A owes to B the duty to forbear to inflict damage upon him by acts or omissions not in conformity with the conduct of a prudent or careful or diligent man, though damage be not actually intended.

§ 2. OF THE LEGAL CONCEPTION OF NEGLIGENCE.

The term 'negligence' as used in the law includes want of care, rashness, and thoughtlessness[2]. The law, however, regards mainly, if not entirely, the manifestation as dis-

---

[1] This statement is intended to cover all torts into which negligence may enter as an element. It should be noticed that negligence alone is not a ground of action any more than is fraud or malice; it is only an element of liability, though it is now the chief element. The specific torts in which negligence plays the chief part are mostly, it may be added, innominate.

[2] Where negligence consists in want of care, danger is adverted to, but no proper attempt is made to exert the will to avoid harm; where it consists in rashness, danger again is adverted to, but no proper attempt is made to restrain the impulse of undue confidence; where it consists in thoughtlessness, danger is not adverted to, but this because no proper attempt has been made to take notice of the situation, the case being negligent not knowing. Even 'wilful default' so-called, may, it seems, be negligence of this last kind. See Studies in Pleading, No. 18. There may be other shades of negligence, but these are certainly the chief ones.

tinguished from the mental attitude out of which the legal conception of negligence arises, as it does in cases of fraud and perhaps malice; but it will be instructive to observe that, looking at the obverse side or mental aspect of the subject, negligence consists in omission,—omission e.g. to summon the will to right action in the particular case. It is in that, in reality, that negligence consists; while the outward aspect or manifestation which the law looks to may obviously be either an act or an omission.

Liability ex delicto for the consequences of negligence as regarded by the law, arises, however, by reason only of acts, or omissions after the doing of acts. In respect of omissions not preceded at any time by overt acts, either by the defendant or by his predecessors in interest, in connection with that which occasions the damage, there may indeed be liability ex contractu (the omission being a breach of contract); there can be no liability in tort as for negligence. An innkeeper may be liable for refusing to receive a man as guest into his inn; but the liability incurred cannot properly be treated as growing out of negligence. Refusal to do a duty is one thing; negligence is another.

There can arise, indeed, no civil liability for the negligent omission to do a thing required by law, though commanded by the Legislature, unless that neglect be connected with the existence of something already done. A town may be required to build a bridge across a stream, but no one can maintain an action for damages against the town for neglect, however inexcusable, to build the bridge; though an action might be maintained for damage caused by the breaking of a bridge through failure to repair it if the town was bound to keep it in proper condition. In the latter case, there is an omission preceded (at some time) by an overt act; to wit, the building of the bridge. When it is said that no action ex delicto can be maintained for a pure non-feasance, consisting in neglect of duty, the former case is to be understood as intended.

It is conceded by all the authorities that the standard by which to determine whether a person has been guilty of negligence is the conduct of the prudent or careful or diligent man. But, if not properly understood, this standard may itself be misleading. A blacksmith finds a watch by the roadside, and on opening it and seeing that it is full of dirt, attempts to clean it, when a watchmaker is near; but in doing so, though exercising, it may be, the greatest care, he injures it by reason of his lack of skill. Now in attempting to put the watch in order, and thus perhaps preventing its ruin, he has done nothing that a prudent man might not have done; and, taking the criterion in its broadest sense, the blacksmith could not be liable to the owner of the watch for the damage which he did to it; while the law would probably be just the contrary[1].

A prudent *blacksmith*, however, would not have undertaken to put the watch in order; he would have taken it to the watchmaker. The prudent man, ordinarily, with regard to *undertaking* an act, is the man who has acquired the skill to do the act which he undertakes: a man who has not acquired that special skill is imprudent in undertaking to do the act, however careful he may be, and however great his skill in other things[2].

The criterion then of the conduct of the prudent or careful or diligent man in the *undertaking* of an act is to be understood with the limits suggested. The question to be raised with regard to a man's conduct brought in question

---

[1] It is to be noticed that as a watchmaker is near, the act could not be considered one of necessity.
[2] See Dean v. Keate, 3 Campb. 4; post, p. 289.

in such a case is, whether a prudent or careful or diligent man of his calling or business or skill would have undertaken to do the thing in question; supposing the party to have exercised due care in executing the work undertaken.

When an act has been undertaken by a person whose business or profession covers the doing of acts of the kind in question, the question to be decided is, whether that skill or care or diligence has been exercised which a prudent man of the same business would have exercised in the same situation.

In regard to omissions (after overt acts) to perform acts not distinctly and certainly required by law, the question of the duty to perform them is to be decided by the general practice of prudent or careful or diligent men of the same occupation, when such a practice exists. When no such practice exists, the question is decided upon the reasonably supposable conduct of the prudent man acting under the circumstances[1].

A remark should be made upon the question whether the conclusion or inference to be drawn from the facts in the case of an action for negligence is a matter of law or of fact. The authorities do not give any categorical answer to the question, but this appears to be the effect of them: Where the facts are found, and it is manifest that a prudent man would or would not act or omit to act as the defendant has done, the conclusion or inference may be considered as matter of law. The same is also true where the law has prescribed, as in some cases it has, the nature of the duty, and also where there exists a well-known practice in the community, of a proper character. In other

---

[1] See Dixon *v.* Bell, 5 Maule & S. 198; s. c. L. C. Torts, 568; Piggott, Torts, 220, where the authorities are well stated.

cases, and these are far more numerous, it is a matter of fact[1].

It should further be stated that a very large part of the litigation pertaining to suits for negligence turns upon the question whether the facts submitted to the court make a case which may be submitted to the jury, in jury trials, as furnishing evidence upon which negligence may properly be found. To consider such questions would require a detailed examination of the authorities beyond the purpose of this book[2].

It remains to consider the specific cases under which liability for negligence may arise; and these may be classed under two general heads, to wit, negligence in contract, and negligence not in contract. For it is to be understood, with regard to relations such as those about to be mentioned, that the negligent performance of a contract, or the unexcused neglect to perform a contract, is a breach of duty that may be treated as involving liability ex delicto or ex contractu, at the election of the injured party[3].

Under the first head, it will be proper to consider the subjects of Innkeeper and Guest, Bailor and Bailee, Professional Services, and the duties of Agents, Servants, Trustees, and the like; and, under the second head, Public

[1] See L. C. Torts, 589—596; Piggott, Torts, 220, 225 et seq.
[2] See such cases as Cotton v. Wood, 8 C. B. N. s. 568; Hammack v. White, 11 C. B., N. s. 588; Crafter v. Metropolitan Ry. Co. L. R. 1 C. P. 300; Manzoni v. Douglas, 6 Q. B. D. 145; North-eastern Ry. Co. v. Wanless, L. R. 7 H. L. 12; Metropolitan Ry. Co. v. Jackson, 3 App. Cas. 193; Dublin & Wicklow Ry. Co. v. Slattery, Id. 1155; Wakelin v. South-western Ry. Co. 12 App. Cas. 41.
[3] Marzetti v. Williams, 1 B. & Ad. 415; Brown v. Boorman, 11 Clark & F. 1: s. c. 3 Q. B. 511. These cases appear to go to the extent of allowing suit ex delicto, even when there has been no attempt to perform the contract. The distinction between the two modes of suit is still less under the Judicature Acts.

Bodies and Public Officers, and the Use of Premises. These, though by no means all the subjects in which the law of negligence might be instructively considered, will still serve to create a clear conception of the subject as an element of liability.

§ 3. OF INNKEEPER AND GUEST.

With regard to the duties of innkeepers, it will be almost sufficient in the present connection to say that, though it has sometimes been considered that for loss or damage to the goods of guests liability depends upon the question of negligence in the host, or in his servants acting for him[1], it is now more generally considered that an innkeeper's liability for the failure to keep the goods of his guest safely, when once delivered into the former's custody, arises independently of the question of negligence. The host is now held liable for damage to or loss of the goods put in his custody, though he exercised the greatest diligence in the care of them, unless the loss occur by the guest's negligence, or by vis major, inevitable accident, or the act of God[2].

It follows, a fortiori, that the innkeeper is liable in case of loss sustained by reason of his own negligence, or that of his servants; but, inasmuch as the question of his liability does not turn upon the question of negligence, the subject of negligence need not be here pursued.

It is proper, however, to mark the fact in this connection that a question of contributory negligence[3] may arise in

[1] Dawson v. Chamney, 5 Q. B. 164.
[2] Armistead v. Wilde, 17 Q. B. 261; Cashill v. Wright, 6 El. & B. 891; Morgan v. Ravey, 6 H. & N. 265; Oppenheim v. White Lion Hotel Co., L. R. 6 C. P. 515. See 26 & 27 Vict. c. 41, as to restrictions of liability.
[3] Post, § 10.

considering cases of innkeeper and guest, as well as in other cases. If the negligence of the guest occasion the loss in such a way that it would not have happened if the guest had exercised the usual care that a prudent man might reasonably be expected to have taken under the circumstances, the innkeeper is not liable[1].

§ 4. Of Bailor and Bailee.

So much of the subject of bailment as relates to breaches of duty by common carriers may be dismissed with a brief word. The liability of a common carrier is similar to that of an innkeeper, and does not turn upon the question of negligence, the subject of the present chapter. And there are other cases in which the bailor of an article for special use, as a job-master of carriages, while not for all purposes an insurer, is still liable for loss happening without negligence in the ordinary sense[2]. These too fall without the present subject.

It was long considered a settled doctrine of the English law that the duty of bailees was to be distributed under three heads, having reference respectively to the nature of the bailment; to wit, (1) the duty to observe very great care, (2) the duty to observe ordinary care, and (3) the duty to observe slight care only. Conversely, therefore, the bailee was deemed to be liable for loss sustained by the bailor, under the first head, if the bailee were guilty of slight negligence; under the second head, if he were guilty

[1] Cashill v. Wright, 6 El. & B. 891; Oppenheim v. White Lion Hotel Co., L. R. 6 C. P. 515.

[2] See e.g. Hyman v. Nye, 6 Q. B. D. 685. The liability of one whose business is to let carriages is here put upon the footing of coach proprietors and railway companies. 'He is an insurer against all defects which care and skill can guard against.' Id., Lindley, J. He is not an insurer against all defects absolutely. Id.

of 'ordinary negligence', or rather of negligence of an intermediate grade; and, under the third head, if he were guilty of gross negligence[1].

The application of these three degrees of negligence was thus explained: If the bailment were gratuitous, by the bailor, that is, for the sole benefit of the bailee, the bailee was deemed to be liable for loss or damage to the subject of the bailment occasioned even by slight negligence on his part. If the bailment were for hire, that is, for the mutual benefit of the bailor and the bailee, he was deemed to be liable for the consequences of negligence of an intermediate grade only. If the bailment were without benefit to the bailee, that is, if the bailor had requested the bailee to take care of his, the former's, goods without reward, the bailee was deemed to be liable for the result of gross negligence only[2].

This doctrine arose from a misconception, apparently, of the Roman law, the doctrines of which were resorted to in order to assist in the solution of a question which arose in England in the eighteenth century[3]. But it remained in the English law unchallenged for so long a time that it has not been readily abandoned, and it may be still considered as retaining some faint vitality in England and in various parts of the United States.

The tendency of authority for a considerable time has been to break away from this division of negligence, and to accept the true doctrine of the Roman law in regard to bailments as well as in relation to other subjects covered by the title Negligence. The effect is to make the criterion of

[1] Coggs v. Bernard, 2 Ld. Raym. 909; 1 Smith's L. C. 188 (7th ed.). [2] Id.
[3] Coggs v. Bernard, supra. Lord Holt took his Roman law mainly from the mediæval jurists, or glossarists. See Wharton, Negligence, § 57 et seq.; Smith, Negligence, 11 et seq., 2nd ed.

SECT. 4.] NEGLIGENCE. 287

liability to depend upon the consideration already adverted to, whether the party complained of conducted himself in the particular situation as a man of prudence or carefulness or skill, of the same business, would have conducted himself, or as prudent or careful or skilful men, of the same business, generally do conduct themselves in the like situation [1].

This criterion indeed will often if not generally be found to be the real test applied in those cases in which the old terms are used. For example: The defendant, a bailee of money to keep without reward, gives the following account of himself: He was a coffee-house keeper, and had placed the money in question in his cash-box in the tap-room, which had a bar in it, and was open on Sunday; and on a Sunday the cash-box was stolen. The defendant's liability turns upon the question whether he has taken such care of the plaintiff's money as a reasonable man would ordinarily take of his own; if not, he is deemed to be guilty of 'gross negligence' and liable for the loss [2]. Again: The defendants receive a deposit from a stranger, S, to be kept without reward. Subsequently another stranger calls for and gets the bonds, representing himself to be S, the depositor. The judge instructs the jury that, if the defendants are guilty of want of 'ordinary care' under all the circumstances,

[1] As indicating the tendency to discard the old theory of the three degrees of negligence, see Wilson *v.* Brett, 11 M. & W. 113; Hinton *v.* Dibdin, 2 Q. B. 646; Grill *v.* General Colliery Co., L. R. 1 C. P. 600; Beal *v.* South Devon Ry. Co., 3 H. & C. 337; Giblin *v.* McMullen, L. R. 2 P. C. 317, 328; The New World, 16 How. 469 (Sup. Court U. S.); Milwaukee Ry. Co., *v.* Arms, 91 U.S. 489, 494; Cass *v.* Boston & L. R. Co., 14 Allen, 448 (Mass.); Lane *v.* Boston & A. R. Co., 112 Mass. 455; Briggs *v.* Taylor, 28 Vt. 180.

[2] Doorman *v.* Jenkins, 2 Ad. & E. 256. The question, it will be seen, was not whether the defendant had taken the same care of the money that he took of his own.

they are liable, otherwise not. The instruction is correct, being equivalent to a ruling that the defendants are liable for gross negligence only[1]. Again: The defendants receive a deposit of debentures to be kept without reward, and the cashier of the bank fraudulently abstracts the same and makes away with them. The defendants are liable if they have failed to exercise 'ordinary care', which means a failure to exercise that ordinary diligence which a reasonably prudent man takes of his own property of the like description[2].

The result, therefore, is, that the terms 'gross negligence', or 'negligence', are, with regard to goods bailed, now used to prescribe liability where the defendant or his servants have not taken the same care of the property intrusted to them as a prudent man would have taken of his own in the same situation[3]. Or, as it has recently been laid down by judicial authority: For all practical purposes the rule may be stated to be, that the failure to exercise reasonable care, skill, and diligence, is 'gross negligence'. What is reasonable, varies in case of a gratuitous bailee and that of a bailee for hire. From the former are reasonably expected such care and diligence as persons ordinarily use (that is, careful persons) in their own affairs, and such skill as he has. From the latter are reasonably expected care and diligence such as are exercised in the ordinary and proper course of similar business, and such skill as he ought to have; namely, the skill usual and requisite in the business for which he receives payment[4].

[1] Lancaster Co. Bank *v.* Smith, 62 Penn. St. 47.
[2] Giblin *v.* McMullen, L. R. 2 P. C. 317.
[3] See also Duff *v.* Budd, 3 Brod. & B. 177; Riley *v.* Horne, 5 Bing. 217; Batson *v.* Donovan, 4 B. & Ald. 21.
[4] Beal *v.* South Devon Ry. Co., 3 H. & C. 337, Ex. Ch., Crompton, J. speaking for the court.

On the other hand, to leave the side of the bailee's duty, there may be a case of negligence on the part of the bailor, resulting in harm to the bailee or to others. This may happen in many ways, as in the careless handling of the goods by the bailor; it may also happen by reason of the failure of the bailor to give notice of the nature of the articles delivered. It is a general principle that wherever a person employs another to carry an article which from its dangerous nature requires more than ordinary care, he must give reasonable notice to him of the nature of the article; otherwise he will be liable for the natural consequences of the neglect[1]. For example: The defendant delivers a carboy of nitric acid to the plaintiff, servant of a Croydon carrier, to be taken to Croydon, without indicating to him the nature of the article; and there is nothing in its appearance to indicate its nature. While carrying it, the carboy bursts from some unexplained cause, and the plaintiff is injured. The defendant is liable[2].

Thus far of a bailment for custody (locatio custodiæ), or for hire (locatio rei), or the like. Where the bailment requires the performance of services upon chattels (locatio operis), the rule with regard to diligence is still similar. The bailee is bound to exercise ordinary diligence; to wit, the diligence of a prudent man of the same occupation, and under the same circumstances. He is also bound to exercise a fair average degree of skill in relation to the business which he undertakes; to do his work in a workmanlike manner; and to be possessed of sufficient skill to execute it. He will therefore be liable if he should either make an engagement without sufficient skill to execute it, or if, possessing the adequate skill, he should not exercise it.

Willes, J. in Farrant v. Barnes, 11 C. B. N. s. 553, 564.
Farrant v. Barnes, supra. See Brass v. Maitland, 6 El. & B. 470.

For example: The defendant hires a horse of the plaintiff which becomes slightly sick. The defendant, not being a farrier, thereupon prescribes improperly for the horse, and the medicine kills it. This is a breach of duty to the plaintiff, a farrier being near at hand at the time[1]. Again: The defendant, a builder of houses, undertakes for the plaintiff to rebuild a good and substantial front to his house, but he builds the same so out of perpendicular that it must be taken down. The defendant is liable in an action for negligence[2].

The degree of skill and diligence which is required rises in proportion to the value, the delicacy, and the difficulty of the operation. A workman employed to repair the works of a very delicate instrument would be expected to exercise more care and skill than would be required about an ordinary undertaking[3]. The criterion of liability, however, still remains the same: if all things are done by the workman which a diligent and skilful workman in the same situation and business would do, he will be exonerated from liability though the instrument be broken[4].

It should be observed, however, with regard to cases requiring the exercise of skill, that a bailee is not to be required to possess extraordinary skill, such as is possessed by but few persons only in the particular business, but only a fair average, or ordinary, degree of skill; unless, indeed, he engage to possess extraordinary ability. In the absence of agreement or false representation, reasonable skill constitutes the measure of the engagement of the workman in regard to the thing undertaken[5].

On the other hand, a bailee employed to do work

[1] Dean v. Keate, 3 Campb. 4.
[2] Farnsworth v. Garrard, 1 Campb. 38.
[3] Story, Bailments, § 432. [4] Id.
[5] Ib. § 433.

unfamiliar to him is not liable, it seems, for failing to possess the requisite skill, if he has not held himself out as possessing it. It is the bailor's fault if he intrust a work requiring the exercise of skill to one whom he knows to be without that skill. For example: The defendant, a matter, is employed by the plaintiff, with notice, to embroider a fine carpet, and the defendant, from want of skill, spoils the materials put into his hands by the plaintiff for the purpose. This is no breach of duty, the defendant not having represented himself as competent for such work[1].

It is further to be observed that if the loss or ill execution be not properly attributable to the fault or unskilfulness of the workman, or of his servants, but arise from an inherent defect in the thing upon which the work is done, the bailor, having furnished the materials, cannot treat the bailee as guilty of negligence[2]. But if the materials were furnished by the bailee, and the result were a failure to perform the contract altogether, or a failure to perform it within the time agreed upon, the bailee would be liable; unless perhaps the materials required by the bailor were such as he (the bailee) was not familiar with, and he had exercised such skill as he possessed in the management of them, the risk being taken by the bailor[3].

§ 5. OF PROFESSIONAL SERVICES.

The only difference between the case presented in the present section and that in the last half of the preceding is that there is now no bailment of goods to be wrought upon. The rules of law with regard to the duty of the person employed are not materially different from those above pre-

[1] Ib. § 435.   [2] Ib. § 428 a.
[3] In the latter case, the bailor might himself be liable to the bailee; as in case of injury from dangerous materials ordered by the bailor.

sented.. To render a professional man liable for negligence, it is not enough that there has been a less degree of skill than some other professional men might have shewn. Extraordinary skill is not required unless professed or contracted for: a fair average degree of skill is all that can be insisted on. Or, as it has been laid down, a person who enters a learned profession undertakes to bring to the exercise of his business simply a reasonable degree of skill and care. He does not undertake, if an attorney, that he will gain a cause at all events, or, if a physician, that he will effect a cure[1].

For special illustration of the application of this doctrine, the nature of the liability of lawyers and of doctors of medicine for negligence may be taken.

Every client has a right to expect the exercise, on the part of his attorney[2], of care and diligence in the performance of the business intrusted to him, and of a fair average degree of professional skill and knowledge; and if an attorney have not as much of these qualities as he ought to possess, or if, having them, he neglect to use them without valid excuse, the law makes him liable for any loss which may have been sustained thereby by his client[3].

Hence an attorney possessed of a reasonable amount of information and skill, according to the duties which he undertakes to perform, and exercising what he possesses with reasonable care and diligence in the affairs of his client, is not liable for errors in judgment, whether in matters of law or of discretion, unless he profess to have a high order of skill.

It is clear, however, that, when an injury has been sus-

[1] Lamphier v. Phipos, 8 Car. & P. 475, Tindal, C. J.; Hart v. Frame, 6 Clark & F. 193, 210.
[2] 'Attorney' here = lawyer of any grade or name.
[3] Saunders, Negligence, 155.

tained which could not have happened except from the want of reasonable skill and diligence on the part of the attorney, the law will hold him liable. To take proceedings upon a wrong statute, when there is no question of doubtful construction involved, would be evidence of negligence under this rule. For example: The defendant, an attorney, is employed to take statutory proceedings on behalf of the plaintiffs against their apprentices for misconduct. The defendant proceeds upon a section of the statute relating to servants and not to apprentices. This is deemed such a want of skill or diligence as to render the attorney liable to repay to the plaintiffs the damages and costs incurred by his mistake[1].

If an attorney has doubt in regard to the legal effect of an instrument in which his client is concerned, and submits the question to counsel for advice on which to act, he must state the facts correctly and with fulness. If, instead of laying the case and facts fully before the counsel, he attempt to state inferences from the facts, he acts at his peril. The counsel should be permitted to draw his own inferences. For example: The defendant, a lawyer, employed by the plaintiff, seeking counsel of another lawyer, misstates the legal effect of certain deeds not accompanying the case, whereby he (the defendant) receives and acts upon incorrect advice, to the damage of his client. This is evidence of negligence for which he is liable[2].

In the like exercise of due care and skill, an attorney employed to investigate the title to an estate, or to seek out a good investment and obtain security for money advanced, must examine the title to and extent of the security offered; and even then if the title prove obviously

[1] Hart v. Frame, 6 Clark & F. 193.
[2] Ireson v. Pearman, 3 B. & C. 799.

defective, or the security prove evidently bad or insufficient, he will be liable[1].

The authorities finally appear to establish the rule that an attorney is liable for the consequences of ignorance or non-observance of the rules of practice of court, for the want of care in the preparation of a cause for trial, or of attendance thereon with his witnesses, and for the mismanagement of so much of the conduct of the cause as is usually allotted to his department of the profession. On the other hand, he is not answerable for error in judgment upon points of new occurrence, or of nice or doubtful construction, or of such as are usually submitted to one in the highest walks of the legal profession[2].

To render a doctor of medicine liable for negligence, there must likewise appear to have been a failure to exercise such diligence or skill as a prudent practitioner of fair ability would have exercised under the same circumstances. The degree of diligence required will be proportionate to the nature of the case; and, in some cases, nothing short of the highest degree of diligence can be excusable.

As regards the *skill* to be exercised, however, nothing more than a fair and reasonable degree can be insisted upon; the law does not require the exercise of the highest order of medical ability, unless the party has held himself out as possessed of it. For example: The defendant, a physician, is retained as accoucheur to attend the plaintiff's wife, and the plaintiff charges that he failed to use due and proper care and skill in the treatment of the lady, whereby she was injured. The judge instructs the jury that it is not enough to make the defendant liable that some medical men, of far greater experience or ability, might have used

[1] Knights *v.* Quarles, 4 Moore, 532; Whitehead *v.* Greetham, 10 Moore, 183; Donaldson *v.* Haldane, 7 Clark & F. 762.
[2] Godefroy *v.* Dalton, 6 Bing. 460.

SECT. 6.] NEGLIGENCE. 295

a greater degree of skill, nor that even he might possibly have used some greater degree of care. The question to be decided is, whether there has been a want of competent care and skill to such an extent as to lead to the bad result[1]. Again: The defendant, a surgeon, is employed by the plaintiff to treat an injury done to his hand and wrist; and the plaintiff charges that he conducted himself in the business in such a careless, negligent, and unskilful manner, that the plaintiff's hand became withered, and was likely to become useless. The judge instructs the jury that the question for them to decide is, whether they are satisfied that the injury sustained is attributable to the want of a reasonable and proper degree of care and skill in the defendant's treatment. The defendant's business did not require him to undertake to perform a cure, nor to use the highest possible degree of skill[2].

If the patient, by refusing to adopt the remedies of the physician, frustrate the latter's endeavours, or if he aggravate the case by his own misconduct, he, of course, cannot hold the physician liable for the consequences attributable to such action. Still if, after such misconduct, the physician continue to treat the patient, he will be liable for any injury sustained by reason of his own negligence in such subsequent treatment[3].

§ 6. OF THE LIABILITY OF AGENTS, SERVANTS, TRUSTEES, AND THE LIKE.

The test of the liability of an agent to his principal for damage done by reason of alleged negligence is, speaking

[1] Rich v. Pierpont, 3 Fost. & F. 35.
[2] Lamphier v. Phipos, 8 Car. & P. 475. These two cases, though at nisi prius, are often referred to as authority.
[3] Hibbard v. Thompson, 109 Mass. 286; Wharton, Negligence, § 737.

generally, the conduct of a prudent or careful or skilful agent in the like situation. If the agent's action conform to this standard, he will be exempt from liability; otherwise not. But it is important to look into this rule closely.

In accordance with the general rule it is in America held not necessary, in order to fix the liability of a factor to his principal for damage, to prove that the factor has been guilty of fraud or of such gross negligence as would carry with it a presumption of fraud. The factor is required to act with reasonable care and prudence in his employment, exercising his judgment after proper inquiry and precautions[1]. If the exercise of ordinary diligence on his part would have prevented the loss, he will be liable; otherwise not. For example: The defendants, factors, are directed by the plaintiff, their principal, to remit in bills the amount of funds in their hands. They do so in the bills of persons who at the time are in good credit in the place in which the factors reside, though not in the place of residence of the plaintiff. If they have not notice of the latter fact, the defendants are not liable; due diligence not requiring them to make inquiry of the credit of the parties to the bills at the place of residence of the principal, when they are of good credit at the place of residence of the factors[2]. Again: The defendants, factors, are requested to remit to the plaintiff, their principal, in bills 'on some good house' in New York, the plaintiff's place of residence. They remit in the bills of R and B, partners, drawn upon and accepted by B, the former residing at the place of residence of the defendants, the latter at the place of residence of the plaintiff, to the defendants' knowledge. R and B have houses of business at both places. R (the resident party) is in good credit at the defendants' place of residence, but B

[1] Story, Agency, § 186.
[2] Leverick v. Meigs, 1 Cowen, 645 (N. Y.).

(the New York party) is not. The defendants are liable whether they knew B's standing or not; being bound to make inquiry in regard to him[1].

Extraordinary emergencies may arise in which a person who is an agent may, from the very necessities of the case, be justified in assuming extraordinary powers; and his acts fairly done under such circumstances will be deemed lawful[2]. On the other hand, it seems clear that the presence of such emergencies may not only justify, but, in the light of prudence, even demand the resort to extraordinary measures. Ordinarily, it is proper and (probably) necessary for an agent to deposit the funds of his principal in bank[3]; but if a hostile army were approaching the place at the time, to the knowledge of the agent, prudence would require him to make some other and unusual disposition of the funds[4].

The duty of an agent employed to procure insurance is to take care that the policy is executed so as to cover the contemplated risk; and to this end he is, of course, bound to possess and use reasonable skill. The agent is also to take care that the underwriters are in good credit; though it is enough that they are at the time in good repute[5].

What is the proper exercise of due diligence and skill in such cases is sometimes a matter of great nicety. On the one hand, an agent who acts bona fide in effecting insurance for his principal, using reasonable skill and diligence, is not liable to be called to account, though the insurance might possibly have been procured from other underwriters on better terms, or so as to include additional risks, by which the principal might, in the event of loss by those risks,

[1] Id.
[2] Story, Agency, § 141; Bailments, § 83.
[3] Heckert's Appeal, 69 Penn. St. 264.
[4] See Wood v. Cooper, 2 Heisk. 441 (Tenn.).
[5] Story, Agency, § 187.

have been indemnified[1]. On the other hand, an agent in the like case is bound to have inserted in the policy all the ordinary risks commonly covered; and if he omit to have them inserted when a reasonable attention to his business and the objects of the insurance would have induced other agents, of reasonable skill and diligence, to have them inserted, he will be liable for negligence in case of loss[2]. And the same will be true if he negligently or wilfully conceal a material fact or make a material misrepresentation whereby the policy is afterwards avoided[3].

In any case, if it should appear that, even if the duty expected had been performed with proper care, the principal could have derived no benefit therefrom either because the result would have been contrary to express law or to public policy or to good morals, the negligence of the agent or other party acting in the matter is not a breach of duty[4].

Servants also are bound to take due care of their master's interests, so far as intrusted to them. If a servant be guilty of a failure to exercise such care or skill or prudence as a diligent servant would exercise under the circumstances, and the master suffer damage thereby, the servant will be liable for a breach of duty. On the other hand, the servant is not bound to prevent loss to his master at all hazards: he is only required to use the care or skill of a diligent servant. For example: The defendant, a servant, loses by theft of another the goods of the plaintiff, his master and a carrier; but there is no proof of negligence on the part of the defendant. The plaintiff must bear the loss[5]. Again: The defendant, treasurer of the plaintiffs,

[1] Story, Agency, § 191; Moore v. Mourgue, Cowp. 479.
[2] Id. § 191; Park v. Hammond, 6 Taunt. 495.
[3] Maydew v. Forrester, 5 Taunt. 615.
[4] Story, Agency, § 238.
[5] Savage v. Walthew, 11 Mod. 135, coram Lord Holt.

is charged with a failure to pay over to the plaintiffs specific money in his possession. He pleads that after receiving the money, and before the time when he ought to have paid it or could have paid it to the plaintiffs, he was robbed by violence of the whole amount without any default or want of due care on his part. The plea shews that the defendant has not violated his duty to the plaintiffs[1].

If too it should appear that the principal or master, upon a full knowledge of the circumstances, has deliberately ratified the acts or omissions complained of, he will then be compelled to overlook the breach of duty, and cannot recall his condonation of the offence[2].

A trustee is not liable for a loss which has occurred, if he exercised ordinary skill, prudence, and caution[3]. In considering whether a trustee has made himself liable for a loss, such as one arising by reason of a failure to collect and convert into money the trust assets, regard must be had to the nature of the trust. A guardian is not in ordinary cases held to such prompt action in enforcing the collection of securities as an executor, administrator, or assignee acting for the benefit of creditors. The duty of a guardian is to hold and retain; of an executor, to collect and prepare for distribution. But it is the duty of a trustee to be active in reducing to his possession any debt forming part of the trust fund; for the consequences of neglect he would be liable[4].

An administrator or executor or assignee of an insolvent should within a reasonable time make proper efforts to convert all the assets and securities of the estate into money for distribution; failing to make such effort, the

[1] Walker v. British Guarantee Assoc., 18 Q. B. 277.
[2] Story, Agency, § 239.
[3] Charitable Corp. v. Sutton, 2 Atk. 400, Lord Hardwicke.
[4] Caffrey v. Darby, 6 Ves. 488.

party is liable for any loss to the estate thereby sustained. For example : The defendant, an executor, fails for several years after the death of the testator to call in part of the personal estate left out on personal security by the testator himself. The debtor becomes bankrupt, but down to that time pays his interest regularly. Eight months afterwards, the plaintiffs, cestuis que trust, request the defendant to call in the money, but nothing can be found. The defendant is liable[1].

If the business of the trustee be such as to involve questions of law, or such as to suggest the aid of legal counsel, due care and diligence will (probably) require him to obtain legal advice. But having done so, and having no reason to suppose that the advice given is incompetent, the trustee will be exonerated in acting thereon. For example: The defendants, executors of an estate, under directions to invest the moneys of the estate on loan well secured, apply to a lawyer of good standing in another town concerning the security of a mill in that place, offered by a person desiring to borrow money of the defendants, and are told that the security is good; and a mortgage of the borrower's interest therein is accordingly taken. The mill, however, is owned by the borrower and another in partnership, and is liable for the firm debts. The owners become insolvent, and the note of a third person, well secured, is offered the defendants on condition of a release of the mortgage. By advice of the same lawyer, the offer is declined, and the mill security is lost. The defendants are not liable, having acted with the prudence of men of ordinary diligence, care, and prudence in the matter[2].

[1] Powell v. Evans, 5 Ves. 839. See post, p. 354; also Johnston's Estate, 9 Watts & S. 107 (Penn.), stated at p. 282 of the Am. ed. of this work.

[2] Miller v. Proctor, 20 Ohio St. 442.

Directors of corporations are bound to exercise all the ordinary diligence of persons in the same situation[1]; and that may vary according to the nature of the business[2]. In speculative ventures, so understood by all parties concerned, a less rigid rule of prudence would be applied than in transactions not speculative; and it is laid down that in cases of the first kind 'crassa negligentia' must be shewn, if the directors acted within their powers, in order to impose liability upon them[3]. Directors are not in ordinary cases expected to devote their whole time and attention to the corporation over whose interests they have charge, and are not guilty of negligence in failing to give constant superintendence to the business. Other officers, to whom compensation is paid for their whole time in the affairs of the corporation, have the immediate management. But the duties may be such as to require all the time of the directors; and whatever the office, if they undertake it they must perform it fully and entirely[4].

In relation to those officers, the duties of directors are those of control; and the neglect which would render them liable for not exercising that control properly must depend upon circumstances. They are simply to exercise common diligence over such officers. If nothing, in the exercise of such diligence, has come to their knowledge to awaken suspicion concerning the conduct of the managing officers, the directors are not guilty of negligence, and hence are not liable for losses sustained by reason of the misconduct of such officers. Those officers are the agents or servants of the corporation, not of the directors.

If, however, the directors become acquainted with any

[1] Overend v. Gibb, L. R. 5 H. L. 480, 494, Lord Hatherley.
[2] Ib.   [3] Ib.
[4] York & North Midland Ry. Co. v. Hudson, 16 Beav. 485, 491, Romilly, M. R.

fact concerning the officers of the body, calculated to put prudent men on their guard, a degree of care commensurate with the evil to be avoided is, it seems, required; and a failure to exercise such care, resulting in damage to the corporation or to its customers, will (probably) render the directors personally liable[1]. And the same rule (probably) applies to all trustees or general officers having the oversight of subordinate officers.

§ 7. OF PUBLIC BODIES AND PUBLIC OFFICERS.

The fact that public bodies or public officers may have contracted with or assumed some duty to the Crown or a municipal government to perform a service faithfully does not imply that they may not also owe special duties to individuals in the performance of their business[2]. Their duties in this respect are like those of private individuals transacting similar business; and whether they receive emoluments or not is immaterial[3]. Such officers are bound to exercise the diligence which the nature of their position reasonably demands; and for a failure, resulting in special damage to any individual, they are liable to him[4]. For example: The defendant, a municipal corporation, accepts

[1] Quære if 'crassa negligentia' would be necessary to create liability in such a case? But after all 'crassa negligentia' is only negligence in the particular situation; it is 'crassa' only as compared with what might be negligence in a different situation. See Beal v. South Devon Ry. Co. 3 H. & C. 337, ante, p. 288. The want of that prudence which in the same circumstances a prudent man would exercise in his own behalf is 'crassa negligentia'. Lord Hatherley in Overend v. Gibb, L. R. 5 H. L. 480, 494.

[2] Henley v. Lyme Regis, 5 Bing. 91; s. c. 1 Bing. N. C. 222. See Clothier v. Webster, 12 C. B. N. S. 790; Mersey Docks v. Gibbs, L. R. 1 H. L. 93.

[3] Mersey Docks v. Gibbs, supra.

[4] See Story, Agency, §§ 320, 321; Hayes v. Porter, 22 Maine, 371.

SECT. 7.] NEGLIGENCE. 303

a grant from the Crown conveying a borough, by which it is directed to keep in repair certain sea walls. The corporation fails in this duty, and the plaintiff, a private citizen, is injured thereby. This is a breach of duty to the plaintiff[1]. Again: the defendant, a public inspector of meat, undertakes, in accordance with his official duty, to cut, weigh, pack, salt, and cooper, for export, a quantity of beef belonging to the plaintiff, and does the same so negligently that the meat becomes spoiled and worthless. This is a breach of duty to the plaintiff, and the defendant is liable to him in damages[2].

An individual cannot, however, for his own benefit, in his own name, maintain a suit against another for negligence in the discharge of a public duty where the damage is solely to the public[3]. The reason sometimes given for this is, that great inconvenience would follow if a person violating a trust of this kind could be sued by each person in the community[4]. A better reason, possibly, is, that as the right infringed belongs to the sovereign, as representing the public at large, so the correlative duty is one for the breach of which the sovereign alone can sue.

Officers of the courts are liable for the injurious consequences of such official acts of their own or of their servants as are attributable to want of the care of prudent men in the same situation. For example: The defendant levies upon a quantity of coal on board a vessel. The coal is left on the vessel, with the master's consent, in charge of a keeper of the defendant, and while so held the vessel is sunk during a gale, with the coal on board, to the damage of the plaintiff, for whom the levy is made. The de-

[1] Henley v. Lyme Regis, supra.
[2] Hayes v. Porter, supra.
[3] 1 Black. Com. 220.
[4] Wharton, Negligence, § 286; Ashby v. White, Ld. Raym. 938.

fendant is liable if he has failed to take such steps for the safety of the coal as a careful, prudent man, well acquainted with the condition of the vessel and its location with regard to exposure to storms, might reasonably be expected to take if the coal belonged to himself[1].

A judge, however, while acting in a judicial capacity, within his jurisdiction, is not liable for negligence[2]; and the same is true even of a person acting in a situation which makes him virtually a private arbitrator[3]. Having submitted a dispute to the decision of an arbitrator, neither party can require him to exercise the skill or care of an expert, unless he has held himself out to possess it, or has agreed to exercise it. For example: The defendant, as broker, makes a contract for the plaintiff, as follows: "Sold by order and for account of P, to my principal S, to arrive, 500 tons Black Smyrna raisins—1869 growth—fair average quality in opinion of selling broker, to be delivered here in London—at 22s. per cwt.," &c. This contract makes the defendant virtually an arbitrator, to determine between the parties any difference arising between them as to the quality of the raisins tendered in fulfilment of the contract, not stipulating for care or skill on the part of the defendant; and he is not liable for failing to exercise reasonable care and skill in coming to a decision, if he act in good faith, to the best of his judgment[4].

§ 8. OF THE USE OF PREMISES.

In this section the duty of the owner or occupant of

[1] Moore v. Westervelt, 27 N. Y. 234.
[2] See Bradley v. Fisher, 13 Wall. 335, 350 (Sup. Court U. S.).
[3] Pappa v. Rose, L. R. 7 C. P. 32, 525; Tharsis Sulphur Co. v. Loftus, L. R. 8 C. P. 1. See Hoosac Tunnel Co. v. O'Brien, 137 Mass. 424.
[4] Pappa v. Rose, supra.

premises to persons who have sustained damage thereon, by reason of the condition of the premises, is to be stated. The question of the existence and nature of this duty turns upon the consideration of the occasion which brought the injured person there; that is whether the plaintiff was a trespasser, a bare licensee, an invited licensee, a customer, or a servant. The question must, therefore, be considered with reference to each of these situations.

The owner or occupant of premises owes no duty to keep his premises in repair for the purposes of trespassers. In other words, it is no breach of duty to a trespasser that a man's premises were in a dangerous state of disorder, whatever the consequences to the former. But this rule of law must not be understood as declaring that the occupant or owner owes *no* duty to trespassers with regard to the management of his premises. He has no right even towards such persons to maim them, as by letting off hidden guns or by setting savage beasts upon them. For example: The defendant sets a spring-gun in his grounds to catch persons entering thereon without permission, and fails to give notice of the particular danger. The plaintiff while trespassing on the premises is injured by the gun, having no notice of danger. The defendant is liable[1].

A bare licensee, as the term is here used, is one who enters another's premises, or is upon some particular part of the same[2], without right or actual grant of permission, but still under circumstances from which he has come to suppose a permission; as in the case of persons accustomed, without interference, to cross a portion of the line of a railway in no definite track[3], or possibly of persons crossing

[1] Bird *v.* Holbrook, 4 Bing. 628. As to notice now see 24 & 25 Vict. c. 100, § 31.

[2] See Batchelor *v.* Fortescue, 11 Q. B. Div. 474.

[3] Harrison *v.* North-eastern Ry. Co. 29 L. T. N. s. 844.

an open field on a foot-path, commonly used by the neighbours, but without any right of way. A person so doing, though not in a position to require the owner or occupant of the land to exercise care in regard to the management or the state of the premises[1], occupies (probably) a more favourable position than a trespasser. He can, of course, insist that the occupant shall let loose no savage beast upon him, and set no traps in his way without giving him fair notice. But, further, it should seem that, if it were usual for people to pass over the occupant's premises in the night-time, he could require the occupant to exercise reasonable care with regard to the keeping of vicious animals, of whose propensity to do harm the occupant has notice.

And it may be that some special duty has been assumed by the occupant, or has been imposed by law upon him, as in the case of a railway company to sound a whistle at certain places, or to keep gates shut while trains are passing; this would modify the question of liability[2]. For example: The defendant, a railway company, has a rule that a whistle shall be sounded by express trains at a certain point where, with the acquiescence of the company, persons are accustomed to cross its track. The plaintiff's intestate attempts to cross at the point in the night, while a train is standing still in such a position, according to some of the evidence, as to prevent anyone from seeing an approaching express train, and is run over and killed. There is evidence,

---

[1] Batchelor *v.* Fortescue, 11 Q. B. Div. 474; Harrison *v.* North-eastern Ry. Co., 29 L. T. N. S. 844; Tolhausen *v.* Davies, 57 L. J. Q. B. 392; Sweeny *v.* Old Colony R. Co., 10 Allen, 368; s.c. L. C. Torts, 660.

[2] Dublin & Wicklow Ry. Co. *v.* Slattery, 3 App. Cas. 1155; North-eastern Ry. Co. *v.* Wanless, L. R. 7 H. L. 12, as to open gates; Williams *v.* Great Western Ry. Co., L. R. 9 Ex. 157, open gates.

but it is contradicted, that a whistle was duly sounded, and there is evidence that the train carried lights. A jury may find the defendant guilty of breach of duty to the deceased[1].

A bare licensee can insist upon the occupant's keeping his premises in a safe condition in another particular. A man has no right to render the highway dangerous or less useful to the public than it ordinarily is; if he should do so, he is liable as for a nuisance to anyone who has suffered damage thereby[2]. And a bare licensee on the wrong-doer's premises will be entitled to recover for any damage sustained thereby. For example: The defendant digs a pit adjoining the highway, and fails to fence it off from the street. The plaintiff, while walking along the street, in the dark, accidentally steps a little aside in front of the pit, and falls into it, thereby sustaining bodily injury. The defendant's act in leaving the place unguarded makes it a public nuisance, and he is liable for the injury received by the plaintiff[3].

If, however, the pit, though near, were not substantially adjoining the highway, so that the plaintiff must have been a trespasser before reaching it, he could not treat the omission of the defendant to fence as a breach of duty. For example: The defendants, being possessed of land near to an ancient common and public footway, construct a reservoir for receiving the back-wash of water at the lock of a canal owned by them. The plaintiff's intestate

[1] Dublin & Wicklow Ry. Co. v. Slattery, supra. See also Davey v. South-western Ry. Co., 12 Q. B. Div. 70, affirming 11 Q. B. D. 213; Gray v. North-eastern Ry. Co., 48 L. T. N. s. 904.
[2] Ante, p. 256.
[3] Barnes v. Ward, 9 C. B. 392. See Pigott, Torts, 235. But see contra, Howland v. Vincent, 10 Met. 371 (Mass.), in which, however, the point appears to have been overlooked that the defendant's act amounted to a public nuisance.

sets out by night along this footpath for Sheffield. The path runs alongside of the canal for about three hundred yards to a point at which it is bounded on one side by a lock, and on the other by the reservoir. At this point, the pathway turns to the right over a bridge, crossing the by-wash. A person continuing straight on in the direction of the pathway, and not turning to the right to go over the bridge, would find himself (if not prevented by the arm of a lock) upon a grassy plat about five yards long by seven broad, between the lock and the by-wash, level with, but somewhat distant from, the footpath; the plat being unfenced, and having a fall of about three yards to the water. On the morning following the setting out of the deceased, he is found drowned at this point. The defendants are not guilty of a breach of duty in not fencing the place, since it is not substantially adjoining the highway, and the deceased must have become a trespasser before reaching the reservoir[1].

The same will be true of injury sustained by straying cattle or horses[2]. For example: The defendant digs a pit in his waste land within thirty-six feet of the highway, and the plaintiff's horse escapes into the waste and falls into the pit and is killed. The defendant has violated no duty to the plaintiff[3].

If the licensee were invited, either expressly or by active conduct, by the occupant, the situation becomes entirely changed. In such a case, the occupant owes a duty to the invited licensee, not merely to restrain his ferocious animals, and to prevent injury from dangerous concealed

[1] Hardcastle v. South Yorkshire Ry. Co., 4 H. & N. 67. See Dinks v. South Yorkshire Ry. Co., 3 Best & S. 244; Hounsell v. Smyth, 7 C. B. N. S. 731; Pigott, Torts, 236.
[2] Blyth v. Topham, Croke Jac. 158.
[3] Blyth v. Topham, supra.

SECT. 8.] NEGLIGENCE. 309

engines, and to guard against nuisances adjoining the highway, but also to keep his premises in reasonable repair, and to refrain from negligence generally; otherwise, he will be liable for any injury sustained by the licensee, not caused by the latter's own act. In other words, the owner or occupant[1] is bound to exercise reasonable care to prevent damage from unusual danger, of which he has, or ought to have, knowledge. For example: The defendants, a railroad corporation, have a private crossing on their land over their railroad, at grade, in a city, which crossing they have constructed for the accommodation of the public; and they keep a flagman stationed there to prevent persons from crossing when there is danger. The plaintiff coming down the way to the crossing with horse and wagon is signalled by the flagman to cross, and on proceeding, according to the signal, to cross the track, is run against by one of the defendants' engines; the flagman having been guilty of carelessness in giving the signal. This is a breach of duty, and the defendants are liable for the damage sustained[2]. Again: The defendant, owner of land, having a private road for the use of persons coming to his house, gives permission to a builder engaged in erecting a house on the land, to place materials on the road. The plaintiff, having occasion to use the road in the night, for

[1] A lessor of premises is liable for their condition if their unsafe condition was due to his negligence; if due to the negligence of the tenant, the latter is liable, unless the lessor has expressly assumed the duty to keep in repair, or unless he is in possession with his tenant. See Nelson *v.* Liverpool Brewery Co., 2 C. P. D. 311; Todd *v.* Flight, 9 C. B. N. s. 377; Fisher *v.* Thirkell, 21 Mich. 1; s. c. L. C. Torts, 627.

[2] Sweeny *v.* Old Colony R. Co., 10 Allen, 368 (Mass.); s. c. L. C. Torts, 660. See Clarke *v.* Midland Ry. Co., 43 L. T. N. s. 381. As to the discontinuance of a gate-keeper see Cliff *v.* Midland Ry. Co., L. R. 5 Q. B. 258. Further, see the cases stated in Pigott, Torts, 238—244.

the purpose of going to the defendant's residence, runs against the materials and sustains damage, without fault of his own. The defendant is liable; having held out an inducement to the plaintiff to go to the place in question[1].

The gist of the liability in such cases consists in the fact that the person injured did not act merely for his own convenience and pleasure, and from motives to which no act or sign of the owner or occupant contributed, but that he entered the premises because he was led to believe that they were intended to be used by visitors or passengers, and that such use was not only acquiesced in by the owner or person in possession and control of the premises, but that it was in accordance with the intention and design with which the way or place was adapted and prepared, or allowed to be so used[2]. The real distinction, therefore, is this: A mere passive acquiescence by an owner or occupier in a certain use of his land by others, involves no liability for negligence; but, if he, directly or by implication, induce persons to enter upon his premises, he thereby assumes an obligation to keep them in a safe condition, suitable for such use, and for a breach of this obligation he is liable in damages to a person injured thereby[3].

It was urged in the authority in which this doctrine was laid down (a point worthy of notice here) that, if the defendants were liable in such a case, they would be made to suffer by reason of the fact that they had taken precautions to guard against accident at a place which they were not bound to keep open for use at all, and that the case would thus present the singular aspect of a party liable for neglect in the performance of a duty voluntarily assumed,

[1] Corby v. Hill, 4 C. B. N. s. 556.
[2] Sweeny v. Old Colony R. Co., supra, Bigelow, C. J.
[3] Id. See also Bolch v. Smith, 7 H. & N. 736, 741.

SECT. 8.] NEGLIGENCE. 311

and not imposed by law. The answer was, that this was no anomaly. If a person, it was observed, undertake to do an act, or to discharge a duty, by which the conduct of others may properly be regulated, he is bound to perform it in such a manner that those who are rightfully led to a course of conduct or action on the faith that the act or duty will be properly performed shall not suffer loss or injury by reason of his negligence[1]. The liability in such cases does not depend upon the motives or considerations which induced a party to take on himself a particular duty, but on the question whether the legal rights of others have been violated by the mode in which the charge assumed has been performed[2].

In case the injury arise by reason of a defective condition of the occupant's premises, it is necessary to the liability of the party to a licensee that he had notice of the defect before the damage was sustained[3]. For example: The defendant is proprietor of a hotel, containing in one of the passage-ways a glass door, the glass in which has gradually become loosened and insecure; but the defendant is not aware of the fact, nor is he in fault for not knowing it. The glass falls out as the plaintiff opens the door, and the plaintiff, a visitor merely, is injured. The defendant is not liable[4].

The case of a person entering upon the premises of another as a customer, on purposes of business, is (probably) still stronger against the occupant. It should seem that a

[1] See Dublin & Wicklow Ry. Co. v. Slattery, 3 App. Cas. 1155, supra; Cliff v. Midland Ry. Co., L. R. 5 Q. B. 258.

[2] Sweeny v. Old Colony R. Co., Bigelow, C. J.

[3] Welfare v. London & B. Ry. Co., L. R. 4 Q. B. 693; Southcote v. Stanley, 1 H. & N. 247.

[4] Southcote v. Stanley, supra. Had the plaintiff been a guest, the defendant would (probably) have been liable.

greater degree of care ought to be taken to protect such a person than one to whom a mere tacit inducement was held out to enter, since it may be the *duty* of the customer to enter, and not merely his convenience. A master may require his servant to go to a neighbouring shop for provisions; and an officer may be required to enter upon premises to make a levy. And the right to protection covers both entering and leaving the premises[1].

It is clear that customers stand upon a more favourable plane than bare licensees, and that the owner or occupant of the premises owes a duty to them to keep the premises in such repair or condition as to enable them to go thereon for the transaction of their business in the usual manner of customers; and that, if injury happen by reason of the improper state of the premises, of which fact the occupant has notice, he will be liable. Or, as the rule has been stated in America, the owner or occupant of premises is liable in damages to those who come to it, using due care, at his invitation or inducement, express or implied, on any business to be transacted with or permitted by him for an injury occasioned by the unsafe condition of the premises or of the access thereto, which is known by him and not by them, and which he has negligently suffered to exist, and has given them no notice of[2]. For example: The defendant, proprietor of a brewery, leaves a trap-door in a passage-way within his premises, leading to his office, open and unguarded by night, and the plaintiff's wife, in going through the passage-way by night for purposes of business with the proprietor, falls, without fault of her own, down the hole and is killed. The defendant is liable[3].

---

[1] Chapman *v.* Rothwell, El. B. & E. 168, infra.
[2] Carleton *v.* Franconia Iron Co., 99 Mass. 216, Gray, J.
[3] Chapman *v.* Rothwell, El. B. & E. 168.

In accordance with the principle stated, the proprietors of a wharf, established for the use of the public, are (probably) liable for injury sustained by a vessel by reason of the dangerous condition of the place of landing, known to the proprietors of the wharf and carelessly allowed to remain, and not known to the plaintiff. For example: The defendants, owners of a wharf at tide-water, procure the plaintiff to bring his vessel to it to be there discharged of its cargo, and suffer the vessel to be placed there, at high tide, over a rock sunk and concealed in the adjoining dock. The defendants are aware of the position of the rock and of its danger to vessels; but no notice of its existence is given, and the plaintiff is ignorant of the fact. With the ebb of the tide, the vessel settles down upon the rock and sustains injury. The defendants are guilty of a breach of duty, and are liable for the damage [1].

The question of the occupant's liability in cases like this, will be affected by the consideration whether the injured party was fairly authorized under the circumstances to go upon the particular part of the premises at which the accident happened. If the place was one which customers usually frequent without objection, it will (probably) be assumed that the party is authorized to go there. For example: The defendants, owners of a shop, situated upon a public street, let the upper stories thereof to another; and an entrance directly in front of the stairs which lead above is so constructed and kept constantly open that it is used for passage for persons going upstairs. There is a trap-door between the entrance and the stairs; and the plaintiff entering the place on business, and in the exercise of due care, falls through the trap, the same being open, and is injured. The defendant is guilty of a breach

---

[1] Carleton v. Franconia Iron Co., supra.

of duty in leaving the trap-door open, and is liable to the plaintiff[1].

If, however, a customer is injured by reason of the bad condition of a portion of the premises not open to the public, and no invitation or inducement has been held out to him by the owner or occupant to go there, he cannot recover for injury sustained there, though the place be frequented by the servants of the occupant. For example: The defendants are owners of a foundry, on the front door of the outer part of which is placed the sign 'No admittance.' The plaintiff enters the outer building to inquire after certain castings of his, and the defendant tells him that they are nearly ready, and sends a workman into the foundry part of the building to see about them. The plaintiff follows the workman, though not invited, and though none but persons employed there go into the foundry, falls into a scuttle, and is injured. The defendant is not liable[2].

This duty to customers, however, requires the occupant to use due care over all parts of his premises and their appurtenances to which the customer has need of access in the performance of the business. For example: The defendants, owners of a dock, provide a gangway for passage from the plaintiff's vessel; the gangway being in an insecure position, to the knowledge of the defendants, but not to the knowledge of the plaintiff. The plaintiff is injured while properly passing over the same. The defendants are liable[3].

Workmen too on ships in dock, though not the servants of the dock-owner, are deemed to be invited by him to use

---

[1] Elliott v. Pray, 10 Allen, 378 (Mass.).
[2] Zoebisch v. Tarbell, 10 Allen, 385 (Mass.).
[3] Smith v. London Docks Co., L. R. 3 C. P. 326.

the dock and all appliances provided by him as incident to the use of the dock¹. Indeed, the owner of premises may be liable, though the business was not transacted by the plaintiff in the usual way or place, provided he could not so do it conveniently, and was not prohibited from doing it as he did; the defendant or his servant seeing him at the time. The plaintiff is not deemed a bare licensee in such a case².

Where the injury has been sustained, not by reason of any improper condition of the defendant's premises, but by a fall down an ordinary stairway, or the like, the defendant is not guilty of negligence in leaving a door open or in failing to give notice of the place where danger may happen³.

In regard to this class of cases, it is to be observed that, if there be no actual invitation to the injured person to go upon the premises in question, in order to recover damages for injury sustained, he must have gone upon the premises for business with the occupier⁴. But this is not enough.

---

¹ Heaven v. Pender, 11 Q. B. Div. 503, 515. A broad rule of liability in negligence cases was laid down at p. 509 by Lord Esher, broader than the other judges were willing to accept. But it was considered correct in Thrussell v. Handyside, 20 Q. B. D. 359, 363. The rule of Lord Esher was thus stated: 'Whenever one person is by circumstances placed in such a position with regard to another that everyone of ordinary sense who did think would at once recognize that if he did not use ordinary care and skill in his own conduct with regard to those circumstances he would cause danger of injury to the person or property of the other, a duty arises to use ordinary care and skill to avoid such danger.' See Pollock, Torts, 354 note, 418 note. For what Heaven v. Pender decides, see Cann v. Willson, 39 Ch. D. 39, 42.

² Holmes v. North-eastern Ry. Co., L. R. 4 Ex. 254; s. c. L. R. 6 Ex. 123, Ex. Ch.

³ Wilkinson v. Fairrie, 1 H. & C. 633.

⁴ Collis v. Selden, L. R. 3 C. P. 495; Tebbutt v. Bristol & E. Ry. Co., L. R. 6 Q. B. 73, 75.

A man has no right to intrude himself upon another, even for purposes of business. The business which will justify an entry upon the premises, and entitle the party to damages for injury sustained, must, in the absence of an express invitation, or an engagement for services, be the business of the *occupant*, or business which he is bound to attend to. The ground of liability is that an invitation is implied; and an invitation can be implied only when the entry is made in connection with business of the occupant. A retail dealer is bound to use due diligence to keep his premises in fit condition for persons who go to him to buy, but not (probably) for peddlers who go to sell; unless, indeed, they are persons with whom he is accustomed to deal and whom he expects to come into his shop. So likewise, under the same circumstances, he would (probably) be liable for injury to a creditor, or his servant, who went into his shop to demand payment of a debt due, but not to a beggar.

It remains to consider the nature of the duty which a master owes to his servants with regard to the condition of his premises, his machinery, tackle, and the like. It is settled law that the master is liable for injury sustained by reason of his negligence; and this is doubtless to be understood as the failure to exercise such care of his premises or machinery as a prudent or careful master would exercise.

If the apparatus to be made use of by the servant be unsafe to the knowledge of the master, and not to the knowledge of the servant, and the servant be liable to sustain damage thereby, a prudent master would give warning of the fact or procure proper apparatus; one who should fail to do either would be liable for any damage sustained thereby by the servant without the latter's fault. For example: The defendants employ the plaintiff to lay bricks for them, which must be carried up over a scaffold, erected by the defendants. The materials of the scaffold

SECT. 8.]　　　　NEGLIGENCE.　　　　317

are in bad condition to the knowledge of the defendants; but they direct the use of them, as being good enough. By reason of the bad condition of the materials, the scaffold falls, and the plaintiff is injured. The defendants are liable[1].

The nature and extent of this duty of the master have, however, been the subject of some conflict and doubt. It has sometimes been supposed that the duty grows out of the contract of service[2]; but the contrary has with better appearance of soundness been maintained[3]. In other cases, and very commonly, it is said that the servant undertakes the ordinary risks incident to the business, and that the master therefore is not liable for damage sustained by the servant by reason of accidents arising from such risks; supposing the master not to have been personally guilty of negligence[4]. This may be considered the usual way of stating the nature of the master's duty. It has, however, been strongly argued that this does not truly state his duty; and that, apart from the dicta of some of the judges, there is no final authority for drawing a distinction between the duty which a master owes to his servant, with regard to the care of premises or machinery, and that which he owes to other persons who have gone upon his premises by invitation or for business[5].

In accordance with this latter view, it is urged that it is the duty of all who occupy land to which others have the right to resort upon business with the occupier to take care that those resorting there are not exposed to hidden dan-

[1] Roberts v. Smith, 2 Hurl. & N. 213, Ex. Ch.; s. c. L. C. Torts, 684.

[2] See Albro v. Jaquith, 4 Gray, 99 (Mass.); Coombs v. New Bedford Cordage Co., 102 Mass. 572.

[3] Riley v. Baxendale, 6 H. & N. 445, Martin, B.

[4] Priestley v. Fowler, 3 M. & W. 1; Farwell v. Boston & W. R. Co., 4 Met. 49 (Mass.): s. c. L. C. Torts, 688.

[5] Story, Agency, § 453 d, note, 8th ed.

gers. Such persons have the right to expect that the occupier will use reasonable care to guard them from dangers of the existence of which he is or ought to be aware, and of the existence of which they are ignorant; provided he has no good reason to presume that they have equal knowledge upon the subject with himself. A servant may be as well acquainted as his master with the danger of premises or the defects of machinery. If he is, he cannot recover, unless assured by the master that everything not directly before his own eyes is safe, or unless directed to do the work. But the same may be true of customers[1]. The difference between the two cases may be only a matter of presumptive knowledge of the premises in the case of a servant.

This view is intended merely to point out the (supposed) fact that *personal* negligence in the occupant of premises towards a customer would be negligence towards a servant; assuming that there is no difference between the two in point of familiarity with the post of danger. It does not touch the question of the liability of a master for the negligence of a servant, where the master himself is not negligent.

Whatever the true doctrine concerning the relative positions of customer and servant, it is a well-settled rule in regard to servants that the master's duty requires him to take all reasonable precautions for the safety of his men, and that when he knows or ought to know that his premises, his machinery, or his apparatus are unsafe, the servant being ignorant of the fact, and the master having no sufficient cause to presume his knowledge, he will be liable for damage to his servant thereby sustained[2].

[1] Story, Agency, supra.
[2] Id.; Paterson *v.* Wallace, 1 Macq. 748; Williams *v.* Clough, 3 H. & N. 258; Mellors *v.* Shaw, 1 Best & S. 437; Bartonshill Coal

In the absence of personal negligence on the part of the master, the master's duty, at common law, was not defined, with reference to injuries sustained by a servant through the negligence of a fellow-servant, by his duty to customers. A man is liable to customers for damage sustained by reason of the negligence of his servants in the course of their business; but, in the absence of personal negligence on the part of the master, he was not liable at common law for injuries sustained by a servant by reason of the negligence of a fellow-servant[1]. For example: The switch-tender of the defendants, a railroad company, negligently leaves his switch open, whereby the plaintiff, an engineer of one of the defendant's locomotives, is caused, without fault of his own, to run his engine off the track, from which he suffers bodily injury. The defendants are not liable at common law, the evidence shewing that they are not guilty of personal negligence; the switchman being shewn to have been theretofore a careful and trustworthy servant[2].

This doctrine was commonly put upon the ground above mentioned with reference to cases of master and servant, to wit, that he who engages in the employment of another for the performance of specified duties and services for compensation takes upon himself the natural and ordinary risks and perils incident to the performance of such services. And the negligence of fellow-servants was deemed one of these ordinary risks[3].

Co. v. Reid, 3 Macq. 266; Watling v. Oastler, L. R. 6 Ex. 73; Coombs v. New Bedford Cordage Co., 102 Mass. 572, 586.

[1] Farwell v. Boston & W. R. Co., 4 Met. 49 (Mass.); s. c. L. C. Torts, 688; Bartonshill Coal Co. v. Reid, 3 Macq. 266; Bartonshill Coal Co. v. McGuire, Id. 300; Morgan v. Vale of Neath Ry. Co., L. R. 1 Q. B. 149, Ex. Ch.

[2] Farwell v. Boston & W. R. Co., supra.

[3] Id.; Priestley v. Fowler, 3 M. & W. 1.

Within this exemption of the master from liability for the consequences to one servant of negligence by another servant, the generally received rule appears to have been that the term 'fellow-servant' included all who served the same master, worked under the same control, derived authority and compensation from the same source, and were engaged in the same general business, though it might be in different grades or departments of it[1]; though some of the American courts have strongly maintained that the parties are not fellow-servants if the person through whose negligence the injury was sustained is superior in authority and rank to the person injured[2].

In the year 1880, an important statute was passed to extend and regulate the liability of employers to make compensation for personal injuries suffered by workmen in their service[3]. This statute enacts, in its first section, that where personal injury is caused to a workman (1) by reason of any defect in the condition of the ways, works, machinery, or plant connected with or used in the business of the employer[4]; or (2) by reason of the negligence of any person in the service of the employer who has any superintendence entrusted to him whilst in the exercise of such superintendence[5]; or (3) by reason of the negligence of any person in the service of the employer to whose orders or directions the workman at the time of the injury was bound to conform, and did conform, where such injury resulted from

[1] Story, Agency, § 453 d, note, 8th ed.
[2] Pittsburgh R. Co. v. Devinney, 17 Ohio St. 197, 210; Chicago Ry. Co. v. Ross, 112 U. S. 377.
[3] Employers' Liability Act, 43 & 44 Vict. c. 42.
[4] See McGiffin v. Palmer's Shipbuilding Co., 10 Q. B. D. 5, as to ways; Walsh v. Whiteley, 21 Q. B. Div. 371, and cases cited, as to machinery and the whole clause; Howe v. Finch, 17 Q. B. D. 187, as to the whole clause.
[5] See Kellard v. Rooke, 21 Q. B. Div. 367.

SECT. 8.] NEGLIGENCE. 321

his having so conformed[1]; or (4) by reason of the act or omission of any person in the service of the employer in obedience to the rules or by-laws of the employer, or in obedience to particular instructions given by any person delegated with the authority of the employer in that behalf; or (5) by reason of the negligence of any person in the service of the employer who has the charge or control of any signal, points, locomotive engine, or train upon a railway;—the workman, or in case the injury results in death, the legal personal representatives of the workman, and any persons entitled in case of death, shall have the same right of compensation and remedies against the employer as if the workman had not been a workman of nor in the service of the employer, nor engaged in his work.

The second section of the Act makes in effect the following exceptions: There is to be no action against the employer under (1) supra, unless the defect arose from, or had not been discovered or remedied owing to, the negligence of the employer, or of some person in the service of the employer, and entrusted by him with the duty of seeing that the ways, works, machinery, or plant were in proper condition; nor under (4) supra, unless the injury resulted from some impropriety or defect in the rules, by-laws, or instructions therein contained, provided that where a rule or by-law has been approved or accepted by one of her Majesty's Principal Secretaries of State, or by the Board of Trade or any other department of the Government, under any Act of Parliament, it shall not be deemed an improper or defective rule or by-law; nor in any case where the workman knew of the defect or negligence which caused the injury, and failed within reasonable time to give, or cause to be given, information thereof to the employer or some person superior to himself in the service, unless he

[1] Id.; Millward v. Midland Ry. Co., 14 Q. B. D. 68.

was aware that the employer or such superior already knew of the defect or negligence[1].

Other sections regulate the sum recoverable[2], subject to certain possible deductions[3], the serving notice of the injury[4], and define terms used in the Act[5]. In regard to definitions, the 'person who has superintendence entrusted to him' means one whose sole or principal duty is superintendence, and who is not ordinarily engaged in manual labour[6]; 'employer' includes a body of persons corporate or unincorporate; 'workman' means a railway servant and any person to whom a certain prior statute[7] concerning employment applies.

The Act itself appears to have been intended to be experimental, for it declares that it shall continue in force until the end of the year 1887, and to the end of the then next session of Parliament, and no longer, unless Parliament shall otherwise determine[8]. Another bill is now pending.

§ 9. Of Notice.

It is a well-settled rule of law that if facts are brought to the knowledge of a person which would put him, as a man of common prudence, upon inquiry, he is bound to inquire; and, if he fail to do so, he will be chargeable with notice of what he might have learned upon examination[9].

---

[1] See Weblin v. Ballard, 17 Q. B. D. 122; Thomas v. Quartermaine, id. 414, affirmed, 18 Q. B. Div. 685, Lord Esher diss.
[2] § 3.   [3] § 5.
[4] § 7.   [5] § 8.
[6] See Kellard v. Rooke, 21 Q. B. Div. 367.
[7] Employers and Workmen Act, 1875, 38 & 39 Vict. c. 90.
[8] A workman may contract with his employer not to claim compensation under *this* Act. Griffiths v. Dudley, 9 Q. B. D. 357.
[9] Kennedy v. Green, 3 Mylne & K. 699; 1 Story's Equity, pp. 404, 405, note, 13th ed.

There may, it should be remembered, be negligence in not knowing, as well as in knowing and not avoiding danger[1]. In general, therefore, where a defendant's liability for negligence depends upon his knowledge of a particular fact, it is enough that facts have been brought to his attention of such a nature as, if reasonably pursued, would have led to a knowledge of the matter in question. A failure to make inquiry under such circumstances will be evidence of negligence, unless the person has been misled by the opposite party[2].

§ 10. Of Contributory Negligence, or Negligence as Defence.

Generally speaking, it is a defence to an action of tort that the negligence of the plaintiff 'contributed' to produce the damage of which he complains. The reason of this lies in the consideration that a man is not liable for damage which he has not caused[3]; or, conversely, the law holds men liable for those wrongs alone which they have caused. If the defendant did not, either personally or by another under his express or implied authority, cause the damage, he is not liable; and it is part of the plaintiff's case to shew that the defendant caused the damage of which he complains[4]. Now, if there intervened between the act or omission of the defendant and the damage sustained an independent act or omission which, in the sense of a cause, contributed to effect the damage, it follows that the misfortune might not have happened but for that act or

[1] See Mersey Docks *v.* Gibbs, L. R. 1 H. L. 93; ante, p. 302.
[2] See ante, pp. 38—42.
[3] The word 'cause' when used alone = 'proximate cause'.
[4] The liability of a master for the (in fact) unauthorized torts of his servant, or of a principal for the like torts of his agent, stands on special grounds.

omission; and hence the plaintiff cannot shew that the defendant caused the harm[1].

But an act or an omission may be said to 'contribute' to a result as well when it does not stand in the relation of a cause to that result as when it does; and the word 'contribute' or 'contributory' is in fact often used of situations in which there is no connection of cause and effect recognized by law, that is in cases in which the contributory act or omission is not 'causa proxima' as it must be to have any legal consequences, but is only 'causa remota'. 'Causa proxima, non remota, spectatur.' When the term in question is used in this broader sense, it will then be necessary to understand that only such contributory act or omission as may be considered a proximate cause[2] of the misfortune complained of can bar the action. But the stricter use of the term as causa proxima is the more common and better use.

In some cases, the situation may be such that the plaintiff cannot recover even when the defendant's fault was adequate to produce the injury without the plaintiff's negligence, as in certain cases of collision where the fault on each side is contemporaneous. But in no case can the plaintiff recover where the evidence falls *short* of shewing that the defendant's act or omission proximately caused the injury.

On the other hand, conditions (remote causes) must not be confounded with proximate causes. The mere fact that a person or his property is in an improper position, when, if he had not been there, no damage would have been done to him, does not preclude him from recovering. Such

---

[1] With this doctrine of contributory negligence the Admiralty rule dividing the loss in cases of mutual negligence may be contrasted. See Judicature Act, 1873, § 25, subs. 9.

[2] Not necessarily as the only one.

circumstance is only a condition to the happening of the damage, not a cause of it. The misfortune may have been a very unnatural and extraordinary result of the situation, not to be foreseen in the light of ordinary events; and, when that is the case, the fact that the person or property was in the particular situation is not in contemplation of law a cause of the damage. A man may in the day-time fall asleep in the country highway, or leave his goods there, and recover for injury by another's driving carelessly over him or them; since, though the position occupied is a condition to the damage, the damage is not the natural result of the act[1].

The law therefore considers whether the conduct of the plaintiff had a natural tendency, such as exists between cause and effect, to place the party or his property in the direct way of the danger which resulted in the disaster. If it had not, it did not, in the sense of a cause, contribute to the injury. For example: The defendant sails a vessel in such a careless manner as to cause a collision with another vessel on which the plaintiff is a passenger; the plaintiff at the time standing in an improper place for passengers, to wit, near the anchor, which is struck by the defendant's boat and caused to fall upon the plaintiff's leg, breaking it. The defendant is liable; the plaintiff's standing in the improper position not contributing, in the stricter sense, to the injury, since it would not be the natural and probable result that one standing there would be hurt by a collision[2]. Again: The defendant driving carelessly along

[1] See the remarks of Parke, B. in Davies *v.* Mann, 10 M. & W. 546, 549.
[2] Greenland *v.* Chaplin, 5 Ex. 243. Or, as Pollock, C. B. suggested, the plaintiff could not have foreseen the consequences of standing where he did; that is, such consequences were unusual,— not the common effect of such an act.

the highway runs against and injures the plaintiff's donkey, straying improperly therein, and fettered in his forefeet so as not to be able to move with freedom. This is a breach of duty to the plaintiff; the latter's act not contributing (in the same sense) to the damage[1].

In accordance with the same principle, a traveller may be riding a horse or in a carriage which he had no right to take or use, or on a turnpike without payment of toll, or with a speed forbidden by law, or upon the wrong side of the road; or his horses may be standing in the street of a town, without his attending by them and keeping them under his command as the law requires; and in none of these cases is his right of action for any injury he may sustain by the negligent conduct of another affected by these circumstances. He is none the less entitled to recover, unless it appear that his own negligence or fault contributed as a proximate cause to the damage[2].

And the same is equally true though the plaintiff, instead of being guilty of negligence merely, is a positive trespasser, as the examples elsewhere given of parties injured by savage dogs or spring-guns while trespassing by day upon the defendant's premises clearly shew[3]; for it is not the natural or usual effect of trespassing in the day-time (not feloniously) that the party should be bitten by a savage dog not seen before the entry, or maimed by the discharge of a hidden gun. Wrongful acts or omissions cannot be set off against each other, so as to make the one excuse the other, unless they stand respectively in the situation of true causes to the damage.

In this connection attention may be called instructively to certain American cases of injury sustained on Sunday

---

[1] Davies v. Mann, 10 M. & W. 546.
[2] Norris v. Litchfield, 35 N. H. 271, Bell, J.
[3] Bird v. Holbrook, 4 Bing. 628; ante, p. 305.

through the defendant's negligence by a plaintiff engaged in acts neither of necessity nor of charity; in other words, in acts rendered unlawful by statute. By many of the courts it is held that the plaintiff is not thereby precluded from recovering for damage sustained, in the absence of explicit language to that effect in the statute; and this on the ground that the mere doing of the illegal act is not, or may not be, contributory in the proper sense to the damage sustained[1]. For example: The defendant, a town, bound to keep a certain bridge in repair, negligently allows it to get out of good order; and the plaintiff, without notice of the condition of the bridge, in attempting to drive cattle over it to market on Sunday breaks through the bridge, several of his cattle being killed and others hurt thereby. The defendant is guilty of a breach of duty to the plaintiff, and liable to him for the damage sustained; the violation of the Sunday law not properly contributing to the result, since it is not the natural or usual result of travelling on Sunday that damage should follow[2].

This is clearly correct in principle, in the absence of language of the statute plainly intended to prohibit all actions for damage sustained on Sunday, except such as is caused without any violation of law by the injured party; but the contrary rule prevails in some of the American States[3]. This contrary rule, however, is considerably narrowed by the courts which adhere to it. It is considered not to apply to cases in which the defendant has misused property of the plaintiff hired on Sunday[4]. So too it is

[1] Sutton v. Wauwatosa, 29 Wis. 21; s. c. L. C. Torts, 711; Mohney v. Cook, 26 Penn. St. 342; Corey v. Bath, 35 N. H. 530; Carroll v. Staten Island R. Co., 58 N. Y. 126.

[2] Sutton v. Wauwatosa, supra.

[3] Bosworth v. Swansea, 10 Met. 363 (Mass.); Connolly v. Boston, 117 Mass. 64. But see Newcomb v. Boston Protective Dept., 146 Mass. 596.

[4] Hall v. Corcoran, 107 Mass. 251.

held that one who is walking on the highway on Sunday, simply for exercise and fresh air, may recover against a town for negligence whereby he has sustained damage[1].

It is laid down in certain cases that, if the plaintiff could have avoided the disaster by the exercise of reasonable care, he is not entitled to complain of the negligence of the defendant[2]. This is not intended, however, to suggest a general test of liability. In the case of the fettered donkey above stated, the plaintiff might have avoided the effect of the defendant's negligence by keeping his animal at home, but he was still held entitled to recover. The meaning of the rule in question is that in the moment of actual peril, the plaintiff must not be guilty of failing to exercise such reasonable care under the circumstances as he can, to protect himself against damage. Being at hand at the moment, the plaintiff might be able to prevent harm, and must govern himself accordingly.

One who, however, in a sudden emergency loses his presence of mind through the misconduct of the defendant, and while in such loss, and owing to it, falls into danger and is hurt, is not thereby guilty, it should seem, of contributory negligence[3]. The defendant's unlawful act has caused the loss of presence of mind, and what happens afterwards is but the natural effect of the act. For example: The defendant is carelessly driving an express wagon along the side-walk of the street of a city, at a rapid rate, which suddenly comes up behind the plaintiff, when she instinctively springs aside to escape danger, and in so

[1] Hamilton v. Boston, 14 Allen, 475 (Mass.).
[2] Butterfield v. Forrester, 11 East, 60; Bridge v. Grand Junc. Ry. Co., 3 M. & W. 244; Davies v. Mann, 10 M. & W. 546; Tuff v. Warman, 5 C. B. N. s. 573, Ex. Ch.; Caswell v. Worth, 5 El. & B. 849, see Pigott, Torts, 248.
[3] Comp. The Bywell Castle, 4 P. Div. 219.

SECT. 10.] NEGLIGENCE. 329

doing strikes her head against the wall of a building, and
is hurt. The defendant is liable[1]. Again: The defendant,
a railway company, negligently leaves the gates of a level-
crossing open, and the plaintiff is thereby misled into
crossing, supposing it to be safe to cross, but not using
his faculties as well as he might have done under other
circumstances; and he is hurt by a passing train. The
defendant is liable[2].

On the other hand, it is laid down in certain cases that
the plaintiff may be entitled to recover, if the *defendant*
might, by the exercise of care on his part, have avoided the
consequences of the negligence of the plaintiff[3]. This too
cannot be intended to suggest a general test of liability.
In the case of one who in the want of due care has fallen
through a trap-door left open by the defendant negligently,
the defendant clearly might have avoided the consequence
of the plaintiff's negligence by having closed the door; and
yet he is not liable. The meaning of the rule is that where
the plaintiff was not at hand, so as to prevent the damage,
the defendant will be liable if by due care he might have
prevented the harm and did not exercise it. The question
would be proper in a case like that of the fettered donkey[4].

[1] Coulter *v.* American Exp. Co., 56 N. Y. 585.
[2] North-eastern Ry. Co. *v.* Wanless, L. R. 7 H. L. 12. See Davey
v. South-western Ry. Co., 12 Q. B. Div. 70. Dublin & Wicklow Ry. Co.
v. Slattery, 3 App. Cas. 1155; ante, p. 306. Comp. cases of actual invitation, Sweeny *v.* Old Colony Ry. Co., ante, p. 309.
[3] Tuff *v.* Warman, 5 C. B. N. S. 573, Ex. Ch., leading case.
[4] See also Radley *v.* London and North-western Ry. Co., 1 App.
Cas. 754, reversing L. R. 10 Ex. 100, and restoring L. R. 9 Ex. 71, a
very instructive case. See especially p. 760, Lord Penzance, quoted
in Pollock, Torts, p. 378. It is there stated that if the defendant
'might at this stage of the matter [the actual emergency] by ordinary
care have avoided all accident, any previous negligence of the plaintiffs
would not preclude them from recovering.'

Again : The defendant is pilot of a steamer on the Thames, which runs down the plaintiff's barge. There is no look-out on the barge, but there is evidence that the steamer might easily have cleared her. It is proper to leave it to the jury to say whether the want of a look-out is negligence in the plaintiff, and if so, whether it directly contributed to the damage done; the negligence of the plaintiff, if found, not barring his action if the defendant might have avoided the consequences of it by the exercise of due care[1]. If the rule referred to were applied to cases of simultaneous negligence at the moment of disaster either party to a collision caused by their joint carelessness might be entitled to recover against the other; when, in truth, neither can recover.

Closely connected with the subject of contributory negligence in the plaintiff, but yet distinct from it, is the case of the plaintiff's consent to the risk. 'Volenti non fit injuria.' But to know of the existence of danger is not necessarily to consent to the exposure with its consequences. 'Scienti' is not equivalent to 'volenti'[2]. For example: The defendants are contractors doing work above the floor where the plaintiff is by his employer directed to work, the place of the plaintiff being one of exposure by reason of the nature of the work which the defendants are doing, and the plaintiff being aware of the exposure but not incurring it voluntarily. By the defendants' negligence a piece of iron is dropped upon and injures the plaintiff. The defendants are liable, the plaintiff's knowledge not amounting to consent[3].

[1] Tuff v. Warman, 5 C. B. N. s. 573. See Pigott, Torts, 248.

[2] Thrussell v. Handyside, 20 Q. B. D. 359, 364; Thomas v. Quartermaine, 18 Q. B. Div. 685, 692; Yarmouth v. France, 19 Q. B. Div. 647, 659; Osborne v. North-western Ry. Co., 21 Q. B. D. 220.

[3] Thrussell v. Handyside, supra, distinguishing Woodley v. Metropolitan Ry. Co. 2 Ex. Div. 384, and other cases. Thrussell v. Handyside

§ 11. OF INTERVENING FORCES.

Thus far of the contributory acts or omissions of the plaintiff. But it may be that, between the wrongful act of the defendant and the damage sustained by the plaintiff, there intervened an act or agency of a third person, in no way probable[1], and not in fact anticipated, which directly produced the damage. If this be the case, and the misfortune would not have followed without it, the defendant, similarly it seems, will not be liable. For example: The defendant wrongfully sells gunpowder to the plaintiff, a boy eight years old, who takes it home and puts it into a cupboard, where it lies for more than a week, with the knowledge of the child's parents. The boy's mother now gives some of the powder to him, which he fires off with her knowledge. This is done a second time, when the child is injured by the explosion. The defendant is not liable[2].

Indeed, the defendant can never be liable when anything out of the natural and usual course of events unexpectedly arises and operates in such a way as to make the defendant's negligence, otherwise harmless, productive of injury. A whirlwind does not usually arise on a quiet day, and hence, though a person should build a small fire in a country road, contrary to law, on a mild day, he would not (probably) be liable for the consequences of a whirlwind sud-

---

is further important as adopting the broad ground of liability for negligence laid down by Lord Esher in Heaven *v.* Pender, 11 Q. B. Div. 503, 509.

[1] See Clark *v.* Chambers, 3 Q. B. D. 327, as to damage resulting from removal by a third person of obstructions unlawfully put in the highway by the defendant, he being held liable.

[2] Carter *v.* Towne, 103 Mass. 507.

denly springing up and scattering the fire, to the damage of another[1].

The case will be different if the party acted with a real or a presumable knowledge of the intervening act, agency, or force of nature. In this case he will be liable. For example: The defendant shoots a pistol against a polished surface in a thoroughfare, at such an angle as to render it likely that the ball will glance and hit someone. It does glance and hits the plaintiff. The defendant has caused the injury and is liable[2]. Again: The defendant throws a lighted squib into a market-house on a fair-day, which strikes the booth of A, who instinctively throws it out, when it strikes the booth of B. The latter casts it out in the same manner, and it now strikes the plaintiff in the face, injuring him. The defendant is liable[3]. Again: The defendant wrongfully sells a mischievous hair-wash to the plaintiff's husband, knowing that it is intended for the plaintiff's use, and the plaintiff is injured in using it. The defendant is liable[4]. Again: The defendant, a manufacturer of drugs, negligently labels a jar of belladonna, put up by him, as dandelion, the former a poisonous, and the latter a harmless, drug. The jar passes from the defendant to a wholesale dealer, then to a retail dealer, and a portion of it then to the plaintiff, who buys and takes it as dande-

---

[1] Comp. Insurance Co. v. Tweed, 7 Wall. 44 (Sup. Court U. S.). For all that happens in the regular course of things, under the conditions as they exist at the time of the act or omission in question, the defendant will be liable, though the particular harm resulting may have been altogether improbable. See the important case of Smith v. South-western Ry. Co. L. R. 5 C. P. 98, and 6 C. P. 14, Ex. Ch.

[2] This example is fairly borne out by Scott v. Shepherd, 3 Wils. 403. [3] Scott v. Shepherd, supra.

[4] George v. Skivington, L. R. 5 Ex. 1. See Cann v. Willson, 39 Ch. D. 39, 43.

lion. The defendant is (probably) liable; the intermediate parties have only carried out, in the sale, the intention of the defendant[1].

In cases, however, where the alleged breach of duty is directly involved in a breach of contract, the courts qualifiedly deny the liability of the defendant to anyone except to the party with whom he made the contract, a point elsewhere noticed[2]. The authorities are not altogether consistent, but there appears to be an agreement in regard to cases of intended harm; and the general result may be stated to be, that if the defendant intended or perhaps can fairly be assumed to have intended the acts of the intermediate agency, he will be liable, though his act was a breach of contract with another[3]. The fact of the existence of a duty to the person with whom he contracted is not inconsistent with the existence of another duty respecting the same thing. The duty to forbear to do negligently a thing obviously harmful, if not properly done, preceded the forma-

---

[1] Thomas *v.* Winchester, 6 N. Y. 397; s. c. L. C. Torts, 602. The reason given by the court, however, was that the defendant, being engaged in a very dangerous business, acted at his own peril. Comp. Farrant *v.* Barnes, 11 C. B. N. S. 553, and Brass *v.* Maitland, 6 El. & B. 470; ante, p. 289. The subject is well discussed in 2 Law Quarterly Review, 63—65; Pollock, Torts, 411—414. It is not clear by any means that this case would be followed in England on the ground adopted in it; but on the ground of intention, not indeed to harm, but to sell to the plaintiff a preparation improperly put up, it seems to come within the rule of Langridge *v.* Levy, 2 M. & W. 519; s. c. 4 M. & W. 337, Ex. Ch. and of George *v.* Skivington, L. R. 5 Ex. 1. See Collins *v.* Selden, L. R. 3 C. P. 495; Piggott, Torts, 230—232.

[2] Ante, p. 128. See L. C. Torts, 617—619.

[3] See Langridge *v.* Levy, Collis *v.* Selden, and George *v.* Skivington, above cited. Further see Heaven *v.* Pender, 11 Q. B. Div. 503, 514, a case of great value, and Piggott, Torts, 241, where the subject is discussed at length.

tion of the contract; and it is difficult to see how that duty, owed to all persons, could, by a contract made with one or several, be abrogated as to others[1].

The difficulty is with cases short of intention, that is, with cases of negligence only. It has been supposed that if, by the negligence of A, a contract is broken between B and C, the injured party cannot maintain any action against A; it being declared that no duty is infringed or exists except that created by the contract. For example: The defendant, a railway company, contracts with the plaintiff's servant to carry him safely to a certain place, but negligently injures him on the way. This is deemed no breach of duty to the plaintiff[2].

There is grave doubt, however, both in principle and upon authority, whether, apart from the special facts in the case just referred to, the rule itself upon which the decision is founded can be supported. A railway company or other person would not (probably) be liable to a master for an injury wrongfully done to a servant, without notice of the relation of master and servant[3]. But if there is a duty to refrain from intentional wrong, it is not easy to see why there may not be a duty to refrain from negligence, where

[1] See 1 Wms. Saund. 474.
[2] Alton v. Midland Ry. Co., 19 C. B. N. s. 213. Doubted by Sir E. V. Williams and by Mr Pollock, 1 Wms. Saund. 474; Pollock, Torts, 445, 446. But see Fairmount Ry. Co. v. Stutler, 54 Penn. St. 375, to the same effect with the case first cited; Playford v. United Kingdom Tel. Co., L. R. 4 Q. B. 706. Mr Pollock (Torts, 449) has pointed out the fact, commonly overlooked, that in Winterbottom v. Wright, 10 M. & W. 109, and Longmeid v. Holliday, 6 Ex. 761, generally relied upon for the rule under consideration, there was no negligence on the part of the defendant; in the one case knowledge of the defect not being alleged, in the other not being proved. See also Collis v. Selden, L. R. 3 C. P. 495.
[3] Comp. such cases as Blake v. Lanyon, 6 T. R. 221.

that is attended with notice of the contract, that is, of the rights of the plaintiff.

As a question of authority there are cases of negligence entitled to great weight which are quite inconsistent with the view that the contract creates the only duty that exists in such situations. For example: The defendant, a railway company, contracts with the plaintiff's master, with whom the plaintiff is to travel in the defendant's coaches, to carry the plaintiff's luggage to a certain place, which the defendant, through negligence, fails to do. This is a breach of duty to the plaintiff[1]. Again: The defendant, a railway company, receives the plaintiff into one of its coaches, on a ticket bought from another railway company, with which the defendant shares the profits of traffic. The steps of the defendant's coaches are too high for persons to alight easily at the station, which is owned by the other company; and in alighting with due care the plaintiff is hurt. The defendant is liable, without regard to the question whether the plaintiff had contracted with the other company[2].

If the duty resting upon the defendant be that of common carrier of passengers or of goods, the carrier or bailee will be liable for the damage produced by a breach of his contract, due to his own negligence, even though the negligence of a third person should contribute to the damage sustained; for the party was bound to exercise due care, and has not done so[3]. For example: The defendant, a

[1] Marshall v. York and Newcastle Ry. Co., 11 C. B. 655; Austin v. Great Western Ry. Co., L. R. 2 Q. B. 442. The first of these cases was before Alton v. Midland Ry. Co., supra, but the second was afterwards, and in it Marshall's case was cited with approval by Blackburn, J. See also Foulkes v. Metropolitan Ry. Co., 5 C. P. Div. 157; Ames v. Union R. Co., 117 Mass. 541; and cases like Henley v. Lyme Regis, 5 Bing. 91, and 1 Bing. N. C. 222; ante, p. 303.
[2] Foulkes v. Metropolitan Ry. Co., supra.
[3] Compare Burrows v. March Gas Co., L. R. 7 Ex. 96, Ex. Ch.

railroad company, contracts to carry the plaintiff to W, but on the way the train carrying the plaintiff is brought into collision with the train of another railroad company, at a crossing, through the negligence of the managers of both roads, and the plaintiff suffers injury thereby. The defendant has violated its duty to the plaintiff, and is liable for the damage sustained by him[1].

The same doctrine would, indeed, apply to cases arising under any ordinary absolute contract for the performance of a specific duty. For example: The defendants contract to supply the plaintiffs with proper gas-pipe. Gas escapes in a certain room from a defect in the pipe provided, a third person negligently enters the room with a lighted candle, and an explosion takes place. The defendants are liable for the loss thereby caused[2].

The rule formerly prevailed in England that a passenger in a stage or railway coach, or other vehicle, became by the act of obtaining passage 'identified' in law with the driver or manager of the vehicle. The effect of this doctrine was, that in an action by the passenger against a third person for negligence, whereby the former suffered damage in the course of the ride or journey, negligence on the part of the driver or manager of the vehicle in which the plaintiff has taken passage, contributing to the misfortune, was the negligence of the plaintiff. The plaintiff, therefore, was not entitled to recover, though he might himself have been free from fault[3]. For example: The defendant, owner of a stage-coach, by her driver's negligence, runs over and kills the plaintiff's intestate, while he is alighting from another

[1] Eaton v. Boston & L. R. Co., 11 Allen, 500 (Mass.).
[2] Burrows v. March Gas Co., L. R. 7 Ex. 96, Ex. Ch.
[3] Thorogood v. Bryan, 8 C. B. 115; Armstrong v. Lancashire Ry. Co., L. R. 10 Ex. 47; Cleveland R. Co. v. Terry, 8 Ohio St. 570; Puterbaugh v. Reasor, 9 Ohio St. 484; Lockhart v. Lichtenthaler, 46 Penn. St. 151; Smith v. Smith, 2 Pick. 621.

stage-coach; which latter coach, by the negligence of the driver, has stopped at an improper place for alighting. The latter's negligence is properly contributory, but the deceased was not personally at fault. The defendant is deemed not liable[1].

This doctrine was much criticised and often denied by other courts[2]; and in the form above presented it was recently overruled[3]. It was hard to understand how the plaintiff could be considered identified with the driver of the carriage when the driver was wholly under the control of another. The driver could not be the passenger's servant in any accurate sense in such a case; since the essential element of the relation of master and servant is wanting, to wit, authority over the supposed servant. And, for the same reason, the driver could not be considered as the passenger's agent. The passenger could not contract directly with the driver in the first instance, or require him to go or to stay; nor could he compel him to stop by the way, or direct him to take a particular road, or how to drive, or how to pass a coach or an obstruction[4]. Instead of an identification between passenger and driver, the driver himself would be liable, with the other wrong-doer, to the passenger[5].

[1] Thorogood v. Bryan, supra.
[2] The Milan, Lush. 388; Brown v. McGregor, Hay (Scotl.) 10; Little v. Hackett, 116 U. S. 366; Chapman v. New Haven R. Co., 19 N. Y. 341; Coleman v. New York & N. H. R. Co., 20 N. Y. 492; Webster v. Hudson River R. Co., 38 N. Y. 260; Danville Turnp. Co. v. Stewart, 2 Met. (Ky.) 119.
[3] The Bernina, 12 P. Div. 58, affirmed, nom. Mills v. Armstrong, 13 App. Cas. 1.
[4] Identification, in any such sense as making the driver or manager of the vehicle the servant or agent of the passenger, had been already repudiated by Pollock, B. in Armstrong v. Lancashire Ry. Co., L. R. 10 Ex. 47, 52.
[5] See The Bernina, supra.

If, however, the passenger were himself at fault, as by participating in the negligent conduct of the driver, or by directing it in advance, it is clear that he could not recover; supposing the negligence to have contributed to the misfortune. In such a case as this, he makes the driver, pro hac vice, his servant, and may therefore be said to be 'identified' with him.

Upon views not unlike those in regard to the supposed 'identification' of passenger and carrier, the negligence of the parent or guardian or other person in charge of a young child, in allowing the child to fall into danger, has sometimes been deemed 'imputable' to the child, so as to affect the child with contributory negligence in all cases in which the parent or guardian would in the same situation be barred of a right of action[1]. For example: The defendants, a railroad company, by the negligence of their servants in the course of their employment and the contributory negligence of a person in charge of the plaintiff, a child too young to take care of himself, injure the plaintiff. They are deemed not liable for the misfortune[2].

This doctrine, however, is not accepted by all the American courts, and has often been met with the same answer that has been given to the doctrine of imputing to passengers the negligence of their carriers. The negligence of a parent or custodian of a child, it is well said, cannot properly be imputed to the child; and, supposing the child

[1] See Mangan v. Atterton, L. R. 1 Ex. 239; Clark v. Chambers, 3 Q. B. D. 327; Waite v. North-eastern Ry. Co., El. B. & E. 719; Hughes v. Macfie, 2 H. & C. 744; Wright v. Malden R. Co., 4 Allen, 283 (Mass.); Holly v. Boston Gas Co., 8 Gray, 123 (Mass.); Callahan v. Bean, 9 Allen, 401 (Mass.); Pittsburgh Ry. Co. v. Vining, 27 Ind. 513; Lafayette R. Co. v. Huffman, 28 Ind. 287. The doctrine would, so far as it may be sound, be equally applicable of course to the case of any helpless or imbecile person.

[2] Wright v. Malden Ry. Co., supra.

incapable of negligence, the conclusion is reached that he can recover for injuries sustained by the negligence of another, though the negligence of the child's parent or guardian contributed to the misfortune[1].

It is clear that if the child himself be guilty of contributory negligence (supposing him capable of negligence), apart from the negligence of his parent or guardian, there can be no recovery; and whether the child be capable of personal negligence is a question of fact, depending upon his age and ability to take proper care of himself[2]. It has sometimes been said that the same discretion is necessary in a child that is required of an adult[3]. This, however, could only be true, it should seem, in those cases in which the child is sufficiently mature to be able to take good care of himself. In other cases, the better rule is that, so far as the question of the *child's* negligence is concerned, it is only necessary that he should exercise such care as he reasonably can, or as children of the same capacity generally exercise[4].

In the case of a child too young to take care of himself, it is clear that, if the negligence of the parent or person in charge is the sole proximate cause of the misfortune, the defendant cannot be liable. For example: The defendant, a railway company, is negligent in moving a train along one of its tracks. The plaintiff's grandmother, who has bought of the defendant a ticket of passage for herself and the plaintiff, a child, negligently attempts to cross the track in charge of the child, and the child is injured by

[1] Bellefontaine & I. R. Co. *v.* Snyder, 18 Ohio St. 399; North Penn. R. Co. *v.* Mahoney, 57 Penn. St. 187; Louisville Canal Co. *v.* Murphy, 9 Bush, 522 (Ky.).
[2] Lynch *v.* Nurdin, 1 Q. B. 29; Lynch *v.* Smith, 104 Mass. 52.
[3] Burke *v.* Broadway R. Co., 49 Barb. 529 (N. Y.).
[4] Lynch *v.* Smith, supra.

the train. The defendant is deemed not liable; the defendant having the right to expect that the lady would take due care of herself and of the plaintiff[1].

It is equally clear that if the fault of the person in charge of the child was not a proximate cause of the misfortune, the defendant, being negligent, will be liable[2]. The parent or other person in charge could recover for an injury done to himself by the defendant's negligence; and a fortiori should a young child, incapable of negligence, be entitled to recover in such a case. And the same would be true of negligence on the part of the child (supposing him capable of negligence) when such fault did not contribute as a proximate cause to the injury. For example: The defendant, a hackman, carelessly runs over a child five years of age, in a city, while the child is crossing a street alone, on his way home from school. The child is not guilty of any negligence further than may be implied from his going alone; in regard to this the child's parent may be negligent. The defendant is liable; the negligence of the child, if there was any in his going alone, and of the parent, if found to exist, not contributing in the stricter sense to the misfortune, since it is not the natural and usual effect of a child's crossing the street that he should be run over[3].

Indeed, it is not clear that the rule should not be, that a child of tender years, that is, incapable of negligence,

---

[1] Waite v. North-eastern Ry. Co., El. B. & E. 719, approved in The Bernina, supra, by Lord Esher, 12 P. Div. at pp. 71—75. See 13 App. Cas. 10, 16, 19. And see Pollock, Torts, 381, 382. This assumes that the defendant's negligence was not also a proximate cause of the injury, as it might be, as where the person in charge of the child, and the defendant, were driving negligently and came into collision. But there is ground for doubt still in regard to Waite's case.

[2] Ihl v. Forty-second St. R. Co., 47 N. Y. 317, 323.

[3] Lynch v. Smith, supra.

should be able to maintain an action for the injury he has sustained in cases of this kind, though the person in charge was guilty of contributory negligence. It might be considered enough that the defendant's act or omission was (though not the sole) a proximate cause of the damage. And the principle of the recent decisions above referred to in regard to passenger and carrier appears to sustain the view that if the negligence of each of the persons concerned is, as it might well be, a proximate cause of the injury to the plaintiff, both of them are liable.

If the parent sue for himself, upon the relation of master and servant, for loss of service, the question is somewhat different. If the child be incapable of negligence, the question will be whether the parent's negligence contributed (in the stricter sense) to the misfortune; but if the child were capable of negligence, and were in fact negligent, it would still be doubtful in principle whether any negligence of his could bar an action against another by the parent, as a master, for loss of service caused, though in part only, by the defendant's negligence[1].

The result is, that whatever particular phase a case may present, be it contributory negligence or an intervening agency, the question upon which the defendant's liability turns must be whether his conduct was the (or was a) proximate cause of the damage, or only a condition thereto.

[1] Compare the action for seduction, ante, pp. 157 et seq.

STUDIES IN PLEADING,

BASED UPON

STATEMENTS OF CLAIM.

STUDIES IN PLEADING,

BASED UPON STATEMENTS OF CLAIM.

THE Rules of the Supreme Court, 1883, Order XIX., rule 5, declare: The Forms in Appendices *C, D*, and *E*, when applicable, and where they are not applicable Forms of the like character, as near as may be, shall be used for all pleadings; and where such Forms are applicable and sufficient, any longer forms shall be deemed prolix, and the costs occasioned by such prolixity shall be disallowed to or borne by the party so using the same, as the case may be.

The Forms here given are taken from Appendix *C* above referred to; and it is suggested that the student be called upon to frame special statements of claim on the model of these Forms, from various of the examples given throughout the text of this book, and to defend the same by shewing how they fulfil the rules of the law, not merely by falling within the prescribed Forms, but by meeting the requirements of the doctrines of the law itself. The Forms themselves may be profitably studied in regard to the last-named particular.

DECEIT.

1. Fraudulent Prospectus. (No. 13, § 6.)

1. On 31st January, 1883, the defendant issued a prospectus to the public relating to the *AB* Company, Limited.

2. On February 1st, 1883, the plaintiff received a copy of this prospectus.

3. The plaintiff subscribed for 100 shares in the company on the faith of this prospectus.

4. The prospectus contained misrepresentations, of which the following are particulars :—

    (*a*) The prospectus stated ...... whereas in fact ......
    (*b*) The prospectus stated ..... whereas in fact ......
    (*c*) The prospectus stated ...... whereas in fact ......

5. The defendant knew of the real facts as to the above particulars.

6. The following facts, which were within the knowledge of the defendant, are material, and were not stated in the prospectus :—

    (*a*)
    (*b*)

7. The plaintiff has paid calls to the company to the extent of £1,000. The plaintiff claims :—

    (1) Repayment of £1,000 and interest.
    (2) Indemnity.

                  (Signed)

                     Delivered

    2. Fraudulent Sale of Lease. (No. 14, § 6.)

The plaintiff has suffered damage from the defendant inducing the plaintiff to buy the goodwill and lease of the 'George' public-house, Stepney, by fraudulently representing to the plaintiff that the takings of the said public-house were £40 a week, whereas in fact they were much less, to the defendant's knowledge.

Particulars of special damage :—

    (Fill them in).

The plaintiff claims £

                  (Signed)

                     Delivered

STUDIES IN PLEADING. 347

MALICIOUS PROSECUTION.

3. (No. 15, § 6.)

The defendant maliciously and without reasonable and probable cause preferred a charge of larceny against the plaintiff before a justice of the peace, causing the plaintiff to be sent for trial on the charge and imprisoned thereon, and prosecuted the plaintiff thereon at the Middlesex Quarter Sessions, where the plaintiff was acquitted.

Particulars of special damage :—

Messrs L. & L.'s bill of costs, £65.

Loss in business from January 1st, 1883, to February 18th, 1883, £100.

The plaintiff claims £500.

Place of trial,

(Signed)
Delivered

TRESPASS, CONVERSION, DETINUE.

4. Possession. Mesne Profits. (No. 2, § 7.)

1. The plaintiff is entitled to the possession of Blackacre in the parish of   [*or*, of No. 2, Bridge-street, Bristol] in the county of

2. On or before the   day of   , 188 , AB was seised in fee and in possession of the premises.

3. On the   day of   , 188 , the said AB died so seised, whereupon—

4. The estates descended to the plaintiff, his eldest son and heir-at-law.

5. After the death of the said AB the defendant wrongfully took possession of the premises.

348   LAW OF TORTS.

The plaintiff claims
(1) Possession of the premises.
(2) Mesne profits from the   of   .
Place of trial,
     (Signed)
       Delivered

5. Possession. Co-tenancy. (No. 5, § 3.)

The plaintiff is owner of 32-64th parts or shares, and master of the vessel 'Lady of the Lake', and the defendant, who is owner of the remaining 32-64th parts, withheld possession of the said vessel from the plaintiff.

The plaintiff claims
(1) Possession of the said vessel.
(2) The condemnation of the defendant in all losses and damages occasioned by the withholding possession of the vessel from the plaintiff.
     (Signed)
       Delivered

6. Conversion. (No. 1, § 6.)

The plaintiff has suffered damage by the defendant wrongfully depriving the plaintiff of two casks of oil by refusing to give them up on demand [*or*, throwing them overboard out of a boat in the London Docks, &c.]

[If any special damage is claimed, add]
Particulars [fill them in].
The plaintiff claims £100.
Place of trial, London.
     (Signed)
       Delivered

7. Detinue. (No. 2, § 6.)

The defendant detained from the plaintiff the plaintiff's goods and chattels, that is to say, a horse, harness, and gig.

The plaintiff claims a return of the said goods and chattels or their value, and £10 for their detention.

Place of trial, Lincolnshire.

(Signed)

Delivered

INFRINGEMENT OF PATENT, COPYRIGHT, TRADE MARK.

8. Patent. (No. 6, § 6.)

The defendant has infringed the plaintiff's patent, No. 14,084, granted for the term of fourteen years, from the 21st of May, 1880, for certain improvements in the manufacture of iron and steel, whereof the plaintiff was the first inventor.

The plaintiff claims an injunction to restrain the defendant from further infringement, and £100 damages.

Particulars of breaches are delivered herewith.

Place of trial, Durham.

(Signed)

Delivered

9. Copyright. (No. 7, § 6.)

The defendant has infringed the plaintiff's copyright in a book entitled 'The History of Rome', registered on the   day of

Particulars of special damage are as follows:—

	£
Loss of sale of 50 copies	50
Loss of profit in the copyright	50
	100

The plaintiff claims £100.
Place of trial, Surrey.

(Signed)

Delivered

10. Trade Mark. (No. 8, § 6.)

1. The defendant has infringed the plaintiff's trade mark.

2. The trade mark is [describe it].

[If the plaintiff is not the original proprietor of the trade mark, shew shortly how his title is derived.]

3. The following are the acts complained of, viz.:—
[Set them out.]

The plaintiff claims an injunction to restrain the defendant, his servants, and agents, from infringing the plaintiff's said trade mark, and in particular from [stating any particular injunction sought].

The plaintiff also claims an account or damages.

(Signed)

Delivered

SEDUCTION.

11. (No. 9, § 6.)

The plaintiff has suffered damage from the seduction and carnally knowing by the defendant of *G H* the [daughter and] servant of the plaintiff.

	£	s.	d.
Loss of service from the 1st of March to the 30th of November, 1882	100	0	0
Nursing and medical attendances	10	10	0
	110	10	0

The plaintiff claims £500.
Place of trial, Berkshire.

(Signed)
Delivered

Nuisance.

12. By Smells. (No. 11, § 6.)

The plaintiff has suffered damage from offensive and pestilential smells and vapours caused by the defendant in the plaintiff's dwelling-house, No. 15, James-street, Durham.

The plaintiff claims :—

(1) £50.

(2) An injunction to restrain the defendant from the continuance or repetition of the said injury, or the committal of any injury of a like kind in respect of the same property.

Place of trial, Yorkshire, West Riding.

(Signed)
Delivered

13. By Pollution of Water. (No. 12, § 6.)

1. The plaintiff is the owner [or lessee] and occupier of a farm known as   , through which there runs a river known as   .

2. The defendant, or persons in his employ, pollute the water in the said river by passing into the same the refuse

of the defendant's dye works, situate higher up the said river.

The plaintiff claims an injunction to restrain the defendant, his servants and agents, from sending from the said dye works into the said river any matter so as to pollute the waters thereof, or to render them unwholesome or unfit for use, to the injury of the plaintiff [or as the case may be].

The plaintiff will also claim damages in respect of the said nuisance.

Place of trial,

      (Signed)
       Delivered

NEGLIGENCE.

14. Personal Injury caused by Railway Company.

(No. 7, § 5.)

The plaintiff has suffered damage from the defendants' negligence in carrying the plaintiff as a passenger by railway from London to Brighton, causing personal injuries to the plaintiff, in a collision near Hayward's Heath, on the 15th January, 1882.

Particulars of expenses, &c.:—

	£	s.	d.
Loss of fifteen weeks' salary as clerk at £2 per week	30	0	0
Dr. Smith	10	10	0
Nurse for six weeks	3	0	0
	43	10	0

The plaintiff claims £500.

Place of trial, Sussex.

      (Signed)
       Delivered

STUDIES IN PLEADING. 353

15. Client against Solicitor. (No. 8, § 5.)

1. The plaintiff has suffered damage from the defendant's negligence in his conduct for the plaintiff, as his solicitor, of business undertaken by the defendant on the plaintiff's retainer.

2. The negligence was in making an application under Order XIV., Rule I., in the case of *A B* (the plaintiff) *v. C D*, where the case was one of unliquidated damages and not of debt.

Particulars of damage :—
    Taxed costs paid to defendant on dismissal of summons, £
The plaintiff claims £
Place of trial,
                  (Signed)
                  Delivered

16. Negligent Driving. (No. 3, § 6.)

The plaintiff has suffered damage from personal injuries to the plaintiff and damage to his carriage, caused by the defendant or his servant on the 15th of January, 1882, negligently driving a cart and horse in Fleet Street.

Particulars of expenses, &c. :—

	£	s.	d.
Charges of Mr Smith, surgeon	10	10	0
Charges of Mr Jones, coachmaker	14	5	6
	24	15	6

The plaintiff claims £150.
Place of trial, London.
                  (Signed)
                  Delivered

17. Lord Campbell's Act. (No. 4, § 6.)

The plaintiff, as executor of *C D*, deceased, brings this action for the benefit of Eva the widow, and William and

Margaret and Dorothea the children of *C D* [as the case may be], who have suffered damage from the defendant's negligence in carrying the said *C D* by omnibus, whereby the said *C D* was killed in Cornhill on the 15th of January, 1882.

Particulars pursuant to statute are delivered herewith.

The plaintiff claims £500.

Place of trial, London.

(Signed)

Delivered

18. Wilful Default of Executors[1]. (No. 2, § 2.)

1. The plaintiff is residuary legatee of *A B*, of the city of Bath, who died March 3, 1882, having made his will dated March 2, 1882, and appointed the defendants his executors, who proved his will April 6, 1882.

2. The defendants have been guilty of wilful default in not getting in certain property of the testator.

3. The wilful default on which the plaintiff relies is as follows:—

C D owed to the testator £1000, in respect of which no interest had been paid or acknowledgement given for five years before the testator's death. The defendants were aware of this fact, but never applied to *C D* for payment until more than a year after testator's death, whereby the said sum was lost.

The plaintiff claims :—

(1) Account of testator's personal estate on footing of wilful default.

(3) Administration of the testator's personal estate.

(Signed)

Delivered

---

[1] The 'wilful default' appears to be only neglect on advertence, ante, pp. 279, 299.

INDEX.

[The italic lines indicate the titles to sections.]

A.

ABRIDGEMENTS,
 when infringement of copyright, 238.
ABUSE OF PROCESS,
 effect of, 70, 71.
ACCIDENT,
  (*See* NEGLIGENCE.)
 as an excuse of a battery, 121.
ACTIO PERSONALIS MORITUR CUM PERSONA, 129.
 Lord Campbell's Act, 129 n.
 Employers' Act, 321.
ADMINISTRATORS AND EXECUTORS,
 liability for negligence, 299.
AGENTS,
 liability of, to third persons, 36.
 possession of, 181, 203, 204.
 liability to principals for negligence, 295-298.
AMBIGUITY,
 in misrepresentation, 23.
ANIMALS,
 having contagious disease—deceit, 21, 22.
 Notice of Propensity to do Damage, 266-269.
 wild animals, 266.
 domestic animals, 267.
 negligence of owner, 267, 268.
 injury from irritating animal, 268.
 injured party having notice, 268.
 Escape of Animals, 269.
 duty to provide fences, 269.

23—2

ANIMALS,—*continued.*
    right to kill trespassing animals, 269.

ARBITRATORS,
    not liable for negligence, 304.

ARRESTS,
           (*See* FALSE IMPRISONMENT.)

ASSAULT AND BATTERY,
    Assault, 115–118.
    what constitutes, 115.
    intention, 116, 117.
    distance of parties from each other, 117.
    damage, 118.
    Battery, 118–123.
    what constitutes, 118.
    contact, 118, 119.
    intention, 120, 121.
    negligence, 121.
    accident, 121.
    acts done in sport, 122.
    hostile acts, 122.
    taking property, 122, 123.
    *Son Assault Demesne: Justifiable
        Assault: Self Defence:* 123–126.
    what amounts to, 123.
    acts of parents and schoolmasters, 123.
    self defence, 123, 124.
    protection of property, 124, 125.
    amount of force which may be used, 124, 125.
    wrongful entry upon another's land, 125.
    defence of family, 125.
    defence of master, 125.
    defence of servant, 126.
    quelling a riot, 126.
    Violence to another's Servants, 126–129.
    double right of action, 126.
    servant's right, 126.
    master's right, 127.
    parent's right, 128.
    breaches of contract, 128.
    death of servant or wrong-doer, 129.
    Felony, 129, 130.

ASSIGNEES,
    liability for negligence, 299.

ATTORNEY,
    liability of, for false imprisonment, 145.
    for negligence, 292–294, 300.

INDEX.

B.

BAILOR AND BAILEE,
  duties of bailee, 285-291.
    (*See* NEGLIGENCE.)
BLASTING,
  damage from, 275.

C.

CARRIER,
  identification of passenger with, 336-338.
CERTAINTY,
  in misrepresentation, 22-24.
CHILDREN,
  negligence of, 338-341.
CLERK OF COURT,
  improper writ issued by, 141, 142, 145.
CONCEALMENT,
    (*See* DECEIT.)
CONFIDENTIAL RELATIONS,
  dealings between parties to, 43, 299-302.
  in actions for defamation, 106, 107.
CONSPIRACY,
  distinguished from malicious prosecution, 72, 73.
  action for, much narrowed in modern times, 72, 73.
  present phases, 74.
  Malice and the Combination, 74-76.
  participation in, 74, 75.
  overt acts, 75.
  silent observation of, 75.
  no benefit derived, 75.
  intention to make profit, 75.
CONSTRUCTIVE NOTICE,
  by failing to inquire, 322, 323.
CONTRACT,
  malicious interference with, 77-80.
  torts growing out of breaches of, 128, 333-336.
CONTRIBUTORY NEGLIGENCE,
    (*See* NEGLIGENCE.)
CONVERSION,
  trover and detinue explained, 198, 199.
  Possession, 199-204.
  actions by purchasers and lessors, 199.
  right of possession, 199-204.

CONVERSION,—*continued.*
  special property, 198, 200.
  jus tertii, 201.
  possession wrongfully taken, 201, 202.
  finding, 202, 203.
  possession of servant, 203, 204.
  What constitutes Conversion, 204–216.
  intention, 204, 213.
  sale without authority, 204, 205.
  knowledge of title, 205, 206.
  liability of purchaser, 206.
  effect of fraud in sale, 206, 207.
  sale with right of repurchase, 207, 208.
  conditional sale, 208.
  sale of pledge, 208, 209.
  sale of qualified interest, 209, 210.
  sale of part, 210.
  permitting another to sell one's goods, 211.
  appropriating article to use not intended, 211.
  injury of chattel, 211, 212.
  mere assertion of dominion, 212.
  intention to convert, 213.
  co-owners, 214.
  demand and refusal, 214–216.
COPYRIGHTS,
    (*See* PATENTS AND COPYRIGHTS.)
CORPORATIONS,
  torts of directors, 36, 301, 302.
CRITICISM, 109–111.
CUSTOMERS,
  injuries to, by condition of premises, 311–315, 317, 318.

D.

DAMAGE,
  what constitutes, in general, 12, 13.
  in deceit, 17, 46, 47.
  in malicious prosecution, 52, 68, 69.
  in conspiracy, 72, 76.
  in interference with contract, 79, 80.
  in slander, 81, 84–86.
  in assault and battery, 115, 118.
  in false imprisonment, 131.
  in enticement and seduction, 157, 161, 163, 169, 170.
  in trespass, 176, 189.
  in conversion, 198, 211, 212.
  in infringements of patents and copyrights, 217.

INDEX. 359

DAMAGE,—*continued.*
in violation of rights of support, 240.
in violation of water rights, 251.
in nuisance, 256, 262–265.
escape of animals, 266, 269.
escape of dangerous things, 270.
negligence, 279.

DANGEROUS THINGS, ESCAPE OF,
protection against, 270–275.

DEATH,
Lord Campbell's Act—assault and battery, 129 n.
Employers' Act—negligence, 321.

DECEIT,
elements of action for, 18.
The Representation, 18–32.
distinguished from warranty, 18, 19.
warranty a question of intention, 19.
warranty treated as misrepresentation, 19, 20.
representation requires an act, 20.
silence, 20, 21.
passive concealment, 20, 21.
clearness and certainty, 22.
need not be in words, 22, 23.
vagueness and ambiguity, 23, 24.
terms of art, 24.
words of different meaning in different places, 24.
should justify a prudent man in acting, 24.
statements of opinion, 25–28.
statements of value, 25, 26.
of rental receipts and the like, 26.
statements concerning a man's pecuniary condition, 26.
representation should relate to present or past facts, 27.
implied statements in opinion or prediction, 27, 28.
must be matter of fact, not of law, 29.
exception, 29.
must be material, 30.
must be false, 30–32.
Defendant's Knowledge of Falsity, 32–37.
honest statement of fact generally not actionable, 32.
rescission of contract for innocent misrepresentation, 32.
fraud probable in one of three ways, 32.
'the scienter,' 33.
statements known to be false, 33.
not known to be true or false, 33 n.
duty to know the facts, 33–37.
implied warranty in last case, 35, 36.

DECEIT,—*continued.*
    Ignorance of the Plaintiff, 37–43.
    knowledge of facts by plaintiff fatal to action, 37.
    belief in defendant's statements, 37.
    making investigation, 37.
    when plaintiff bound to know the facts, 38–42.
    means of knowledge, 38–42.
    plaintiff prevented from investigation, 39.
    knowledge of contents of writing, 40.
    doctrine of means of knowledge examined and explained, 41, 42.
    sales at buyer's risk, 42.
    acceptance of goods, 43.
    Intention that Representation should be acted on, 43–45.
    explanation of this expression, 44.
    reasonable inference of such intention, 44.
    intent to injure, 45.
    Acting on Representation, 45–47.
    damage, 45, 46.
    preventing one from attaching property, 46.
    when plaintiff entitled to act on representation, 47.
    Trade Marks, 47, 48.
    elements of action for, 48.
    Slander of Title, 48–51.
    elements of action for, 50.

DEMAND AND REFUSAL,
    when necessary to constitute conversion, 214–216.

DIGESTS,
    when infringements of copyright, 238, 239.

DIRECTORS OF CORPORATION,
    misrepresentations by, 36.
    liability of, for negligence, 301, 302.

DOCTORS OF MEDICINE,
    negligence of, 294, 295.

DURESS, 71.

E.

EFFIGY,
    defamation by, 81, 93.

EMPLOYERS' ACT, 320–322.

ENTICEMENT AND SEDUCTION,
    elements of action, 157.
    Master and Servant ex Contractu, 158–160.
    procuring servant to leave his master, 158.
    service not begun, 158, 159.

ENTICEMENT AND SEDUCTION,—*continued.*
 notice, 159.
 harbouring servant, 159, 160.
 persons not servants, 160.
 breaches of contract, 160.
 Master and Servant ex Gratia, 160–162.
 the relation protected, 160, 161.
 servant under obligation to another, 161.
 harbouring gratuitous servant, 161, 162.
 Parent and Child, 162–168.
 ground of parent's rights of action, 162, 163.
 child of age, 162, 164.
 seduction of daughter away from home, 162, 163.
 animus revertendi, 162, 163.
 fraud on parent, 163.
 acts of service, 163.
 majority of daughter, 164.
 pregnancy and disease, 164, 165.
 willingness of daughter, 165.
 mother's right of action, 166, 167.
 action by daughter, 168.
 consent or misconduct of parent, 168.
 Guardian and Ward, 168, 169.
 suit by guardian, 168, 169.
 ground of action, 169.
 Husband and Wife, 169–175.
 gist of action by husband or wife, 169, 170.
 liability of parent for enticing daughter from husband, 170, 171.
 harbouring wife, 171, 172.
 action for criminal conversation abolished, 173.
 substituted remedy, 173, 174.
 seduction after wife's separation, 174.
 infidelity of husband, 174, 175.
 consent or misconduct of husband, 175.
 condonation, 175.

ESCAPE OF ANIMALS,
 (*See* ANIMALS.)

ESCAPE OF DANGEROUS THINGS,
 Nature of Protection required, 270–275.
 reservoirs, 271.
 effect of gravitation, 272.
 extraordinary efforts, 272.
 vis major and act of God, 272, 273.
 legislative authority, 274.
 fall of snow or ice, 274, 275.

ESCAPE OF DANGEROUS THINGS,—*continued.*
    damage from blasting, 275.
    explosion of boiler, 275.

EXECUTORS AND ADMINISTRATORS,
    liability for negligence, 299.

EXPLOSION,
    damage from, 275.

F.

FALSE IMPRISONMENT,
    Nature of Restraint, 130–134.
    submission to restraint, 133.
    partial restraint, 133.
    Arrest with Warrant, 134–150.
    officer's justification, 134.
    arrest of wrong person, 134, 135.
    misleading officer, 135.
    description in writ of person intended, 135.
    misnomer, 135, 136.
    acts in excess of authority, 136.
    oppressive conduct, 136.
    detention after writ has expired, 136, 137.
    detention on other writs, 137, 138.
    retaking escaped prisoner, 138, 139.
    in civil cases, 138.
    in criminal cases, 138, 139.
    invalidity of writ, and effect on officer, 139.
    writ void or not, when, 139, 140.
    officer's liability restated, 140, 141.
    liability of clerk, 141, 142.
    liability of judge, 142–144.
    summary, 145.
    liability of plaintiff and his attorney, 145–148.
    distinction between civil and criminal cases, 148, 149.
    setting aside the writ, 149.
    malicious prosecution, 150.
    Arrests without Warrant, 150–156.
    when proper, 150, 151.
    arrest on the spot, 151.
    on suspicion of felony by officer, 151, 152.
    reasonable cause, 152.
    misdemeanour, 153, 154.
    arrest after termination of breach of peace, 154, 155.
    right of private citizen to arrest, 155, 156.

FALSE REPRESENTATIONS,
              (*See* DECEIT.)

FELLOW-SERVANTS,
    injury by negligence of, 319-322.
    who are, 320.
    Employers' Act, 320-322.
FINDING,
    gives right of possession against wrong-doer, 202, 203.
FRAUD,
    (*See* DECEIT.)
    makes sale voidable, 206, 207.

G.

GUARDIAN AND WARD,
    seduction of ward, 168, 169.

H.

HIGHWAYS,
    obstructing, 256, 307.
HUSBAND AND WIFE,
    seduction or enticement of wife, 169-175.
    harbouring wife, 171, 172.
    infidelity of husband, 174, 175.
    condonation of offence, 175.

I.

IDENTIFICATION,
    of passenger with carrier, 336-338.
IMPRISONMENT,
    (*See* FALSE IMPRISONMENT.)
IMPUTABILITY,
    of negligence of parent or guardian to child, 338-341.
INNKEEPERS,
    general duties of, 284, 285.
INTENTION,
    in deceit, 43-45.
    in assault and battery, 116, 117.
    in conversion of goods, 204, 213.
INTERPRETATION OF LANGUAGE,
    in deceit, 24.
    in cases of slander, 82, 83.

J.

JUDGE,
    liability of, for false imprisonment, 142-144.
    not liable for negligence, 304.

K.

KNOWLEDGE OF FALSITY,
  in cases of misrepresentation, 32-37.

L.

LANDLORD AND TENANT,
  landlord's right of action for injury to reversion, 181, 199.
LATERAL SUPPORT,
  (*See* SUPPORTS.)
LAWYERS,
  (*See* ATTORNEY; MALICIOUS PROSECUTION; SLANDER AND LIBEL; TRUSTEES.)
LIBEL,
  (*See* SLANDER AND LIBEL.)
LICENSE,
  to enter,—trespass, 177, 178, 190-194.
LICENSEES,
  injuries to, by condition of premises, 305-311.

M.

MACHINES,
  infringement of patents of, 217-227.
MALICE, 5.
(*See* CONSPIRACY; MALICIOUS INTERFERENCE WITH CONTRACT; MALICIOUS PROSECUTION; SLANDER AND LIBEL.)
MALICIOUS INTERFERENCE WITH CONTRACT,
  a tort of recent development, 77.
  Malice, 77, 78.
  Damage, 79, 80.
  Contract not Property, 80.
MALICIOUS PROSECUTION,
  elements of the action, 52, 53.
  criminal and civil prosecutions, 53.
  Termination of the Prosecution, 53-58.
  acquittal of party prosecuted, 53-55.
  civil suit terminated, how, 55.
  dismissal of action, 55.
  discontinuance, 55.
  criminal suit terminated, how, 56, 57.
  dismissal by prosecuting officer, 56.
  return of 'not found', 56.
  prosecution before magistrate, 56, 57.
  dismissal of, 57.
  jeopardy of prisoner, 57.

MALICIOUS PROSECUTION,—*continued*.
   Statute of Malicious Appeals, 57 n.
   summary, 58.
   Want of Probable Cause, 58–67.
   meaning of term, 59.
   slight circumstances of suspicion, 59.
   belief in guilt of accused, 59, 60.
   how probable cause to be determined, 59, 60.
   subsequent facts, 60–64.
   judgment of conviction, 61.
   conviction, 61.
   action of magistrate, 62–64.
   abandonment of prosecution, 62.
   advice of lawyer, 64–66.
   evidence of malice not proof of want of probable cause, 66.
   a question for the judge, 67.
   Malice, 67, 68.
   meaning of, 68.
   Damage, 68, 69.
   when to be proved, 69.
   Analogous Wrongs, 69–71.
   action for slander, 70.
   abuse of process, 70.

MAINTENANCE,
   recent cases on the law of maintenance, 71.

MASTER AND SERVANT,
      (*See* ENTICEMENT AND SEDUCTION.)
   charges by master affecting servant's character, 105, 106.
   defence of master, 125.
   defence of servant, 126.
   servant's right of action for battery, 126, 127.
   master's right of action for battery of servant, 127.
   death of servant, 129.
   servant has no possession, 181, 203, 204.
   servant's liability to master, 298, 299.
   injuries to servants by condition of master's premises or machinery, 317–322.
   negligence of fellow-servant, 319–322.
   Employers' Act, 320–322.

MEANS OF KNOWLEDGE,
      (*See* DECEIT.)

MEDICINE, DOCTORS OF,
   negligence of, 294–295.

MILLS,
      (*See* WATERCOURSES.)

366 LAW OF TORTS.

MISDEMEANOUR,
   false charge of committing, 82 n.
   arrests for, 154–156.

MISREPRESENTATION,
          (*See* DECEIT.)

N.

NEGLIGENCE,
   meaning of term 'negligence', 279, 280.
   of owner of animals, 268.
   acts or omissions may constitute, 280.
   standard of the prudent man, 281, 282.
   province of court and jury, 282, 283.
   Innkeeper and Guest, 284, 285.
   innkeeper an insurer, 284.
   negligence of guest, 284, 285.
   Bailor and Bailee, 285–291.
   common carriers, 285.
   degrees of negligence, 285–289.
   the true criterion, 287.
   ordinary care, and 'gross negligence', 288.
   bailment for services, 289–291.
   exercise of skill, 289, 290.
   inherent defect in goods to be wrought upon, 291.
   Professional Services, 291–295.
   extraordinary skill not required, 292.
   duties of attorneys, 292–294.
   duties of medical men, 294, 295.
   acts of patient, 295.
   Liability of Agents, Servants, Trustees, and the like, 295–302.
   agent's liability to principal, 296–298.
   extraordinary emergencies, 297.
   agents for insurance, 297, 298.
   servant's liability to master, 298, 299.
   ratification, 299.
   liability of trustee, 299–302.
   executors, administrators, and assignees, 299, 300.
   obtaining legal advice, 300.
   directors of corporations, 301, 302.
   Public Bodies and Public Officers, 302–304.
   public officers, 302–304.
   officers of government, 303.
   officers of the courts, 303, 304.
   judges and arbitrators, 304.
   Use of Premises, 304–322.

NEGLIGENCE,—*continued.*
    duty of occupant to trespassers, 305.
    to bare licensees, 305–308.
    pits adjoining highway, 307, 308.
    invited licensees, 308–311.
    customers, 311–315.
    place where injury happened, 313–316.
    business of the occupant, 315, 316.
    duty of master to servant, 316–322.
    defective apparatus, 316–318.
    personal negligence of master, 318.
    negligence of fellow-servant, 319–322.
    who are fellow-servants, 320.
    Employers' Liability Act, 320–322.
    Notice, 322, 323.
    failing to make inquiry, 322, 323.
    Contributory Negligence, 323–331.
    term explained, 323, 324.
    unlawful acts not per se contributory, 325–328.
    violations of Sunday law, 326–328.
    party paralyzed by fear, 328, 329.
    Intervening Forces, 331–341.
    knowledge and intention of defendant, 331–333.
    cases growing out of breach of contract, 333–336.
    'identification' of passenger with carrier, 336–338.
    'imputability' of parent's negligence to child, 338–341.
    negligence of child, 339–341.
NEWSPAPER,
    libels by, 92, 95, 97, 99–101, 103, 104, 110, 111.
    may be subject of copyright, 232.
NOTICE,
    of vicious propensity of animals, 266–269.
    by failure to inquire, 322, 323.
NUISANCE,
    What constitutes, 256–265.
    locality, 257.
    'convenient' place, 257, 258.
    slight detriment to property, 258, 259.
    notice of nuisance, 259.
    flooding a neighbour's land, 259, 260.
    polluting streams, 260, 261.
    milling operations, 261.
    smells and gases, 261, 262.
    public nuisances, 262–265.
    special damage, 262–265.
    removing obstructions, 265.

O.

OFFICERS,
(*See* ASSAULT AND BATTERY; DIRECTORS OF CORPORATIONS
FALSE IMPRISONMENT; PUBLIC OFFICERS.)
OPINION, .
(*See* DECEIT.)

P.

PARENT AND CHILD,
protection of child from battery, 128.
seduction of child, 162–168.
(*See* ENTICEMENT AND SEDUCTION.)
injury of child by parent's negligence, 338–341.
PATENTS AND COPYRIGHTS,
general questions as to infringement, 216, 217.
Patents for Invention, 218–227.
statutory provisions, 218, 219.
provisional specification, 219.
complete specification, 219, 220.
rigid rules concerning the latter, 220, 221.
'first and true inventor,' 222, 223.
'common knowledge of the country,' 223.
publication abroad, 223.
defendant's acts of infringement, 224.
'sole working or making,' 224.
combinations, 225.
different processes, 226.
difference in substance, 227.
Trade Marks, 228.
law of, becoming assimilated to property, 228.
old mode of suing for, 228.
Infringement of Copyright, 228–239.
statutory provisions, 228–231.
in what copyright may be had, 231.
newspapers, 232.
catalogues, 232.
compilations, 233.
translations, 233.
dramatizing another's novel, 233.
score of an opera, 233.
head-notes of law reports, 234, 235, 236.
maps, charts, and the like, 234.
publishing before obtaining copyright, 234.
dramatic or musical composition, 234.
selling pictures not publication, 234 n.
different ways of pirating, 234, 235.

PATENTS AND COPYRIGHTS,—*continued.*
animus furandi, 235, 236.
quantity of matter taken, 235.
quotation for criticism, 237.
imitations of copyrighted matter, 237, 238.
common sources of information, 238.
abridgements, 238.
digests, 238, 239.

PERJURY,
false charges of, 83.

PHYSICIANS AND SURGEONS,
negligence of, 294, 295.

PLEDGE,
sale of, 208, 209.

POLLUTION OF STREAM,
(*See* NUISANCE.)

POSSESSION,
(*See* CONVERSION ; TRESPASS.)

PREMISES,
use and condition of, 304–322.
(*See* NEGLIGENCE.)

PRINCIPAL AND AGENT,
(*See* AGENTS.)

PRIVILEGED COMMUNICATIONS,
in slander and libel, 93–109.
(*See* SLANDER AND LIBEL.)

PROBABLE CAUSE, 58–67, 152–154.

PROFESSIONAL SERVICES,
duties by persons rendering, 292–295.
(*See* NEGLIGENCE.)

PROSECUTION,
termination of, 53–58.

PUBLICATION,
of slander or libel, 84.
of invention, 223.
of book or picture, 234, 234 n.

PUBLIC OFFICERS,
criticism of, 109–111.
liability for negligence, 302–304.

PUBLISHERS OF BOOKS AND PAPERS,
liable for defamation, 92, 95, 97, 99–101, 103, 104, 110, 111.

R.

REASONABLE CAUSE, 58-67, 152-154.
RECAPTION,
 in civil cases, 138.
 in criminal cases, 138, 139.
REPORTS,
 of trials, when privileged, 99, 100.
 copyrights of, 234-236.
RESERVOIRS,
 breaking of, 271.
RIOT,
 acts done in quelling, 126.

S.

SALES,
   (*See* CONVERSION; DECEIT.)
SCIENTER,
   (*See* DECEIT.)
SEDUCTION,
   (*See* ENTICEMENT AND SEDUCTION.)
SELF DEFENCE,
 protection of person and property, 123-125.
SILENCE,
 effect of, in cases of supposed deceit, 20, 21.
SERVANT,
   (*See* MASTER AND SERVANT; NEGLIGENCE.)
SLANDER AND LIBEL,
 kinds of actionable defamation, 82.
 Interpretation of Language, 82, 83.
 doctrine of mitiori sensu, 82.
 perjury, 83.
 natural meaning, 83.
 Publication and Special Damage, 84, 85.
 what constitutes publication, 84, 85.
 meaning of 'special damage', 84, 85.
 sickness and distress of mind, 84, 85.
 loss of marriage, 85.
 loss of consortium, 85.
 Criminal Offence charged, 86, 87.
 degradation, the criterion, 86, 87.
 Contagious and disgraceful Disease charged, 87.
 charge of having *had* same, 87.

SLANDER AND LIBEL,—*continued.*
Charge affecting Plaintiff in his Occupation, 88-90.
natural tendency of charge, 88, 89.
charges affecting servants, 89.
positions of mere honour, 89, 90.
party not in exercise of his occupation, 90.
Charge tending to Disherison, 90, 91.
bastardy, 90, 91.
Libel, 91, 92.
of wider extent than slander, 91.
publishers, editors, and booksellers, 92.
Truth of Charge, 92, 93.
a good defence, 92.
belief in truth, 93.
effigy, picture, or sign, 93.
Malice and Privileged Communications, 93-110.
malice in law, 94.
malice in fact, 94.
occasion of publication, 95.
absolute privilege, 95-98.
statements in judicial proceedings, 95-97.
arguments of counsel, 96.
allegations in pleadings, 96.
affidavits, 96.
statements of witnesses, jurors, and judges, 96, 97.
proceedings in Parliament, 97, 98.
prima facie privilege, 98-110.
proceedings before church organizations, 98, 99.
reports of trials, 99, 100.
headings to, 100.
ex parte proceedings, 100.
matters of public interest, 101.
publication of legislative proceedings, 101.
communications to public authorities, 102.
persons acting for the public weal, 102, 103.
use of public prints, 103.
vindicating character, 103, 104.
voluntary communications, 104-107.
communications by master concerning his servant, 105.
near relationship, 106.
confidential relations, 106, 107.
statements on inquiry, 107, 108.
summary of doctrine of privileged communications, 109.
repeating defamation, 109.
criticism, 109-111.
conduct of public officers, 110, 111.
defamatory accusation prosecuted, 111.

SLANDER OF TITLE,
    in nature of deceit, 48–51.
SMELLS, DISAGREEABLE,
    when nuisance, 261, 262.
SNOW AND ICE,
    injury by fall of, from building, 274, 275.
SON ASSAULT DEMESNE,
    what amounts to, 123–126.
SPECIAL DAMAGE,
            (See DAMAGE.)
SPECIAL PROPERTY,
            (See CONVERSION; TRESPASS.)
SPORT,
    acts done in, 122.
SUNDAY LAW,
    injury while in violation of, 326–328.
SUPPORTS,
    lateral support, 240–247.
    natural condition of soil, 240, 241.
    superincumbent weight, 241–243.
    lateral support of buildings, 242–245.
    depends on grant or prescription, 242.
    subsidence not caused by weight of buildings, 242, 243.
    lateral support of contiguous buildings, 243–245.
    depends on grant, reservation, or prescription, 243.
    keeping house in repair, 245.
    party-walls, 246, 247.
    Subjacent Support, 247–250.
    freehold beneath surface, 247, 248.
    nature of right of support, 248.
    buildings, 249.
    support of upper tenements, 250.
SURFACE WATER,
            (See WATERCOURSES.)
SURGEONS,
    negligence of, 294, 295.

T.

TENANTS,
            (See LANDLORD AND TENANT.)
    in common, 184–186, 214.
TERMINATION OF PROSECUTION,
            (See MALICIOUS PROSECUTION.)

TRADE MARKS,
   infringements of, 47, 48, 228.

TRANSLATION,
   infringement of copyright by, 233.

TRESPASS,
   general meaning of, 176.
   Possession, 176–189.
   necessity of, 177.
   without title, 177, 178.
   several in possession adversely to each other, 178, 179.
   possession of personalty, 179, 180.
   special property, 180.
   possession wrongfully obtained, 180.
   agent, bailee for hire, or tenant at will, 181.
   injury to reversion, 181, 182.
   waste, 182.
   personalty in hands of a bailee or lessee, 182, 183.
   extent of possession, 183, 184.
   possession of co-tenants, 184–186.
   ouster, 185.
   withholding possession from co-tenant, 185.
   mesne profits, 187–189.
   recovery of possession, 187.
   successor by descent or purchase to disseisor, 187–189.
   What constitutes Trespass, 189–197.
   trespass to land, 189.
   entry justifiable when, 189–194.
   trespass ab initio, 194–196.
   definition of trespass, 196, 197.
   property in animals, 197.

TRESPASS AB INITIO,
   meaning of, 194–196.

TRESPASSERS,
   duties of occupants of premises towards, 305.

TRUSTEES,
   liability of, for negligence, 299–302.
   obtaining legal advice, 300.
   dealings between trustees and their cestuis que trust, 43.

U.

USUFRUCT,
   (*See* WATERCOURSE.)

V.

VALUE,
　misrepresentations of, 25, 26.

VIS MAJOR,
　breaking of reservoirs by, 271.
　other cases of, 284, 297.

W.

WANT OF PROBABLE CAUSE,
　　　　(*See* MALICIOUS PROSECUTION.)

WARRANTY,
　distinguished from representation—deceit, 18, 19.
　implied warranty, 33–37.

WASTE, 182.

WATERCOURSES,
　Usufruct and Reasonable Use, 251–254.
　water in defined channels, 251.
　what amounts to reasonable use, 252, 253.
　milling operations, 253, 261.
　diverting stream within one's land, 254.
　grant or prescription, 254.
　surface water running in no defined channel, 254.
　Sub-surface Water, 254, 255.
　percolating water, 255.
　underground stream, 255.
　flooding neighbour's land, 259, 260.
　surface water diverted, 260.
　pollution of stream, 260, 261.
　legislative authority, 261.

WRIT,
　　　　(*See* FALSE IMPRISONMENT.)

SELECT PUBLICATIONS OF

THE CAMBRIDGE UNIVERSITY PRESS.

The Commentaries of Gaius and Rules of Ulpian.
With a Translation and Notes, by J. T. ABDY, LL.D., late Regius Professor of Laws in the University of Cambridge, and BRYAN WALKER, M.A., LL.D., late Law Lecturer of St John's College, Cambridge. *New Edition* by BRYAN WALKER. Crown 8vo. 16s.

The Institutes of Justinian, translated with Notes by J. T. ABDY, LL.D., and the late BRYAN WALKER, M.A., LL.D. Crown 8vo. 16s.

Selected Titles from the Digest, annotated by the late B. WALKER, M.A., LL.D.

Part I. Mandati vel Contra. Digest XVII. 1. Crown 8vo. 5s.

Part II. De Adquirendo rerum dominio and De Adquirenda vel amittenda possessione. Digest XLI. 1 and 2. Crown 8vo. 6s.

Part III. De Condictionibus. Digest XII. 1 and 4—7 and Digest XIII. 1—3. Crown 8vo. 6s.

The Fragments of the Perpetual Edict of Salvius
Julianus, corrected, arranged and annotated by the late BRYAN WALKER, M.A., LL.D. Crown 8vo. 6s.

An Introduction to the Study of Justinian's
Digest. Containing an account of its Composition and of the Jurists used or referred to therein. By HENRY JOHN ROBY, M.A., formerly Professor of Jurisprudence, University College, London. Demy 8vo. 9s.

Justinian's Digest. Lib. VII., Tit. I. De Usufructu, with a Legal and Philological Commentary. By H. J. ROBY, M.A. Demy 8vo. 9s.
Or the Two Parts complete in One Volume. Demy 8vo. 18s.

An Analysis of Criminal Liability. By E. C. CLARK, LL.D., Regius Professor of Civil Law in the University of Cambridge. Crown 8vo. 7s. 6d.

Practical Jurisprudence, a Comment on AUSTIN. By E. C. CLARK, LL.D. Crown 8vo. 9s.

Grotius de Jure Belli et Pacis, with the Notes of Barbeyrac and others; accompanied by an abridged Translation of the Text, by W. WHEWELL, D.D., late Master of Trinity College. 3 Vols. Demy 8vo. 12s. The Translation separate, 6s.

A Selection of the State Trials. By J. W. WILLIS-BUND, M.A., LL.B., Professor of Constitutional Law and History, University College, London. Crown 8vo. Vols. I. and II. In 3 parts. **Now reduced to** 30s. (*originally published at* 46s.)

The Influence of the Roman Law on the Law of England. Being the Yorke Prize Essay for 1884. By T. E. SCRUTTON, M.A. Demy 8vo. 10s. 6d.

Land in Fetters. Being the Yorke Prize Essay for 1885. By T. E. SCRUTTON, M.A. Demy 8vo. 7s. 6d.

Commons and Common Fields, or the History and Policy of the Laws relating to Commons and Enclosures in England. Being the Yorke Prize Essay for 1886. By T. E. SCRUTTON, M.A. Demy 8vo. 10s. 6d.

History of the Law of Tithes in England. Being the Yorke Prize Essay for 1887. By W. EASTERBY, B.A., LL.B., St John's College and the Middle Temple. Demy 8vo. 7s. 6d.

Bracton's Note Book. A Collection of Cases decided in the King's Courts during the reign of Henry the Third, annotated by a Lawyer of that time, seemingly by Henry of Bratton. Edited by F. W. MAITLAND of Lincoln's Inn, Barrister at Law, Downing Professor of the Laws of England. 3 vols. Demy 8vo. Buckram. £3. 3s. *Net.*

A Selection of Cases on the English Law of Contract. By GERARD BROWN FINCH, M.A., of Lincoln's Inn, Barrister at Law. Royal 8vo. 28s.

Complete Catalogues forwarded on application.

London: C. J. CLAY AND SONS,
CAMBRIDGE UNIVERSITY PRESS WAREHOUSE,
AVE MARIA LANE.

UNIVERSITY PRESS, CAMBRIDGE.
November, 1888.

PUBLICATIONS OF

The Cambridge University Press.

THE HOLY SCRIPTURES, &c.

The Cambridge Paragraph Bible of the Authorized English
Version, with the Text revised by a Collation of its Early and
other Principal Editions, the Use of the Italic Type made uniform,
the Marginal References remodelled, and a Critical Introduction,
by F. H. A. SCRIVENER, M.A., LL.D. Crown 4to., cloth gilt, 21s.

THE STUDENT'S EDITION of the above, on *good writing paper*, with
one column of print and wide margin to each page for MS. notes.
Two Vols. Crown 4to., cloth, gilt, 31s. 6d.

The Lectionary Bible, with Apocrypha, divided into Sections adapted to the Calendar and Tables of Lessons of 1871.
Crown 8vo., cloth, 3s. 6d.

The Old Testament in Greek according to the Septuagint.
Edited by H. B. SWETE, D.D. Vol. I. Genesis—IV Kings.
Crown 8vo. 7s. 6d. Vol. II. By the same Editor. [*In the Press.*

The Book of Ecclesiastes. Large Paper Edition. By the
Very Rev. E. H. PLUMPTRE, Dean of Wells. Demy 8vo. 7s. 6d.

Breviarium ad usum insignis Ecclesiae Sarum. Juxta Editionem
maximam pro CLAUDIO CHEVALLON et FRANCISCO REGNAULT
A.D. MDXXXI. in Alma Parisiorum Academia impressam : labore
ac studio FRANCISCI PROCTER, A.M., et CHRISTOPHORI WORDS-
WORTH, A.M.

FASCICULUS I. In quo continentur KALENDARIUM, et ORDO TEM-
PORALIS sive PROPRIUM DE TEMPORE TOTIUS ANNI, una cum
ordinali suo quod usitato vocabulo dicitur PICA SIVE DIRECTORIUM
SACERDOTUM. Demy 8vo. 18s.

FASCICULUS II. In quo continentur PSALTERIUM, cum ordinario
Officii totius hebdomadae juxta Horas Canonicas, et proprio
Completorii, LITANIA, COMMUNE SANCTORUM, ORDINARIUM
MISSAE CUM CANONE ET XIII MISSIS, &c. &c. Demy 8vo. 12s.

FASCICULUS III. In quo continetur PROPRIUM SANCTORUM quod
et Sanctorale dicitur, una cum Accentuario. Demy 8vo. 15s.

FASCICULI I. II. III. complete £2. 2s.

Breviarium Romanum a FRANCISCO CARDINALI QUIGNONIO
editum et recognitum iuxta editionem Venetiis A.D. 1535 impressam curante JOHANNE WICKHAM LEGG. Demy 8vo. 12s.

The Pointed Prayer Book, being the Book of Common
Prayer with the Psalter or Psalms of David, pointed as they are
to be sung or said in Churches. Embossed cloth, Royal 24mo, 2s.

The same in square 32mo. cloth, 6d.

The Cambridge Psalter, for the use of Choirs and Organists.
Specially adapted for Congregations in which the "Cambridge
Pointed Prayer Book" is used. Demy 8vo. cloth, 3s. 6d. Cloth
limp cut flush, 2s. 6d.

The Paragraph Psalter, arranged for the use of Choirs by
B. F. WESTCOTT, D.D., Canon of Westminster. Fcp. 4to. 5s.

The same in royal 32mo. Cloth, 1s. Leather, 1s. 6d.

London : Cambridge Warehouse, Ave Maria Lane.

PUBLICATIONS OF

The Authorised Edition of the English Bible (1611), its Subsequent Reprints and Modern Representatives. By F. H. A. SCRIVENER, M.A., D.C.L., LL.D. Crown 8vo. 7s. 6d.

The New Testament in the Original Greek, according to the Text followed in the Authorised Version, together with the Variations adopted in the Revised Version. Edited by F. H. A. SCRIVENER, M.A., D.C.L., LL.D. Small Crown 8vo. 6s.

The Parallel New Testament Greek and English. The New Testament, being the Authorised Version set forth in 1611 Arranged in Parallel Columns with the Revised Version of 1881, and with the original Greek, as edited by F. H. A. SCRIVENER, M.A., D.C.L., LL.D. Crown 8vo. 12s. 6d. (*The Revised Version is the joint Property of the Universities of Cambridge and Oxford.*)

Greek and English Testament, in parallel columns on the same page. Edited by J. SCHOLEFIELD, M.A. *New Edition, with the marginal references as arranged and revised by* DR SCRIVENER. 7s. 6d.

Greek and English Testament. THE STUDENT'S EDITION of the above on *large writing paper.* 4to. cloth. 12s.

Greek Testament, ex editione Stephani tertia, 1550. Small Octavo. 3s. 6d.

The Gospel according to St Matthew in Anglo-Saxon and Northumbrian Versions. By Rev. Prof. SKEAT, Litt.D. New Edition. Demy Quarto. 10s.

The Gospels according to St Mark—St Luke—St John, uniform with the preceding. Edited by the Rev. Prof. SKEAT. Demy Quarto. 10s. each.

The Missing Fragment of the Latin Translation of the Fourth Book of Ezra, discovered and edited with Introduction, Notes, and facsimile of the MS., by Prof. BENSLY. M.A. Demy 4to. 10s.

Codex S. Ceaddae Latinus. Evangelia SSS. Matthaei, Marci, Lucae ad cap. III. 9 complectens, circa septimum vel octavum saeculum scriptvs, in Ecclesia Cathedrali Lichfieldiensi servatus. Cum codice versionis Vulgatae Amiatino contulit, prolegomena conscripsit, F. H. A. SCRIVENER, A.M., LL.D. Imp. 4to. £1. 1s.

The Origin of the Leicester Codex of the New Testament. By J. R. HARRIS, M.A. With 3 plates. Demy 4to. 10s. 6d.

THEOLOGY—(ANCIENT).

Theodore of Mopsuestia's Commentary on the Minor Epistles of S. Paul. The Latin Version with the Greek Fragments, edited from the MSS. with Notes and an Introduction, by H. B. SWETE, D.D. Vol. I., containing the Introduction, and the Commentary upon Galatians—Colossians. Demy Octavo. 12s.

Volume II., containing the Commentary on 1 Thessalonians—Philemon, Appendices and Indices. 12s.

The Greek Liturgies. Chiefly from original Authorities. By C. A. SWAINSON, D.D., late Master of Christ's Coll. Cr. 4to. 15s.

Sayings of the Jewish Fathers, comprising Pirqe Aboth and Pereq R. Meir in Hebrew and English, with Critical Notes. By C. TAYLOR, D.D., Master of St John's College. 10s.

London: Cambridge Warehouse, Ave Maria Lane.

Sancti Irenæi Episcopi Lugdunensis libros quinque adversus Hæreses, edidit W. WIGAN HARVEY, S.T.B. Collegii Regalis olim Socius. 2 Vols. Demy Octavo. 18s.

The Palestinian Mishna. By W. H. LOWE, M.A., Lecturer in Hebrew at Christ's College, Cambridge. Royal Octavo. 21s.

M. Minucii Felicis Octavius. The text newly revised from the original MS. with an English Commentary, Analysis, Introduction, and Copious Indices. By H. A. HOLDEN, LL.D. Cr. 8vo. 7s. 6d.

Theophili Episcopi Antiochensis Libri Tres ad Autolycum. Edidit, Prolegomenis Versione Notulis Indicibus instruxit GULIELMUS GILSON HUMPHRY, S.T.B. Post Octavo. 5s.

Theophvlacti in Evangelium S. Matthæi Commentarius. Edited by W. G. HUMPHRY, B.D. Demy Octavo. 7s. 6d.

Tertullianus de Corona Militis, de Spectaculis, de Idololatria with Analysis and English Notes, by GEORGE CURREY, D.D. Master of the Charter House. Crown Octavo 5s.

Fragments of Philo and Josephus. Newly edited by J. RENDEL HARRIS, M.A. With two Facsimiles. Demy 4to. 12s. 6d.

The Teaching of the Apostles. Newly edited, with Facsimile Text and Commentary, by J. R. HARRIS, M.A. Demy 4to. 21s.

THEOLOGY—(ENGLISH).

Works of Isaac Barrow, compared with the original MSS. A new Edition, by A. NAPIER, M.A. 9 Vols. Demy 8vo. £3. 3s.

Treatise of the Pope's Supremacy, and a Discourse concerning the Unity of the Church, by I. BARROW. Demy 8vo. 7s. 6d.

Pearson's Exposition of the Creed, edited by TEMPLE CHEVALLIER, B.D. Third Edition revised by R. SINKER, M.A., Librarian of Trinity College. Demy Octavo. 12s.

An Analysis of the Exposition of the Creed, written by the Right Rev. Father in God, JOHN PEARSON, D.D. Compiled by W. H. MILL, D.D. Demy Octavo. 5s.

Wheatly on the Common Prayer, edited by G. E. CORRIE, D.D. late Master of Jesus College. Demy Octavo. 7s. 6d.

The Homilies, with Various Readings, and the Quotations from the Fathers given at length in the Original Languages. Edit. by G. E. CORRIE, D.D. late Master of Jesus College. Demy 8vo. 7s. 6d.

Two Forms of Prayer of the time of Queen Elizabeth. Now First Reprinted. Demy Octavo. 6d.

Select Discourses, by JOHN SMITH, late Fellow of Queens' College, Cambridge. Edited by H. G. WILLIAMS, B.D. late Professor of Arabic. Royal Octavo. 7s. 6d.

De Obligatione Conscientiæ Prælectiones decem Oxonii in Schola Theologica habitæ a ROBERTO SANDERSON, SS. Theologiæ ibidem Professore Regio. With English Notes, including an abridged Translation, by W. WHEWELL, D.D. Demy 8vo 7s. 6d.

Cæsar Morgan's Investigation of the Trinity of Plato, and of Philo Judæus. 2nd Ed., revised by H. A. HOLDEN, LL.D. Cr.8vo. 4s.

London: Cambridge Warehouse, Ave Maria Lane.

PUBLICATIONS OF

Archbishop Usher's Answer to a Jesuit, with other Tracts on Popery. Edited by J. SCHOLEFIELD, M.A. Demy 8vo. 7s. 6d.

Wilson's Illustration of the Method of explaining the New Testament, by the early opinions of Jews and Christians concerning Christ. Edited by T. TURTON, D.D. Demy 8vo. 5s.

Lectures on Divinity delivered in the University of Cambridge. By JOHN HEY, D.D. Third Edition, by T. TURTON. D.D. late Lord Bishop of Ely. 2 vols. Demy Octavo. 15s.

S. Austin and his place in the History of Christian Thought. Being the Hulsean Lectures for 1885. By W. CUNNINGHAM, B.D. Demy 8vo. Buckram, 12s. 6d.

GREEK AND LATIN CLASSICS, &c.
(See also pp. 13, 14.)

Sophocles: the Plays and Fragments. With Critical Notes, Commentary, and Translation in English Prose, by R. C. JEBB, Litt. D., LL.D., Professor of Greek in the University of Glasgow.
Part I. The Oedipus Tyrannus. Demy 8vo. *New Edit.* 12s. 6d.
Part II. The Oedipus Coloneus. Demy 8vo. 12s. 6d.
Part III. The Antigone. Demy 8vo. 12s. 6d.
Part IV. Philoctetes. [*In the Press.*

Select Private Orations of Demosthenes with Introductions and English Notes, by F. A. PALEY, M.A., & J. E. SANDYS, Litt.D.
Part I. Contra Phormionem, Lacritum, Pantaenetum. Boeotum de Nomine, de Dote, Dionysodorum. Cr. 8vo. **New Edition.** 6s.
Part II. Pro Phormione, Contra Stephanum I. II., Nicostratum, Cononem, Calliclem. Crown 8vo. **New Edition.** 7s. 6d.

The Bacchae of Euripides, with Introduction, Critical Notes, and Archæological Illustrations, by J. E. SANDYS, Litt.D. New Edition, with additional Illustrations. Crown 8vo. 12s. 6d.

An Introduction to Greek Epigraphy. Part I. The Archaic Inscriptions and the Greek Alphabet. By E. S. ROBERTS, M.A., Fellow and Tutor of Gonville and Caius College. Demy 8vo. 18s.

Aeschyli Fabulae.—ΙΚΕΤΙΔΕΣ ΧΟΗΦΟΡΟΙ in libro Mediceo mendose scriptae ex vv. dd. coniecturis emendatius editae cum Scholiis Graecis et brevi adnotatione critica, curante F. A. PALEY, M.A., LL.D. Demy 8vo. 7s. 6d.

The Agamemnon of Aeschylus. With a translation in English Rhythm, and Notes Critical and Explanatory. **New Edition, Revised.** By B. H. KENNEDY, D.D. Crown 8vo. 6s.

The Theætetus of Plato, with a Translation and Notes by the same Editor. Crown 8vo. 7s. 6d.

P. Vergili Maronis Opera, cum Prolegomenis et Commentario Critico pro Syndicis Preli Academici edidit BENJAMIN HALL KENNEDY, S.T.P. Extra fcp. 8vo. 5s.

Demosthenes against Androtion and against Timocrates, with Introductions and English Commentary by WILLIAM WAYTE, M.A. Crown 8vo. cloth. 7s. 6d.

Essays on the Art of Pheidias. By C. WALDSTEIN, Litt.D., Phil. D. Royal 8vo. With Illustrations. Buckram, 30s.

London: Cambridge Warehouse, Ave Maria Lane.

M. Tulli Ciceronis ad M. Brutum Orator. A Revised Text.
Edited with Introductory Essays and Critical and Explanatory
Notes, by J. E. SANDYS, Litt.D. Demy 8vo. 16s.

M. Tulli Ciceronis pro C. Rabirio [Perduellionis Reo] Oratio
ad Quirites. With Notes, Introduction and Appendices. By W.
E. HEITLAND, M.A. Demy 8vo. 7s. 6d.

M. T. Ciceronis de Natura Deorum Libri Tres, with Introduction and Commentary by JOSEPH B. MAYOR, M.A. Demy 8vo.
Vol. I. 10s. 6d. Vol. II. 12s. 6d. Vol. III. 10s.

M. T. Ciceronis de Officiis Libri Tres with Marginal Analysis,
an English Commentary, and Indices. New Edition, revised, by
H. A. HOLDEN, LL.D. Crown 8vo. 9s.

M. T. Ciceronis de Officiis Libri Tertius, with Introduction,
Analysis and Commentary by H. A. HOLDEN, LL.D. Cr. 8vo. 2s.

M. T. Ciceronis de Finibus Bonorum libri Quinque. The
Text revised and explained by J. S. REID, Litt. D. [*In the Press.*
Vol. III., containing the Translation. Demy 8vo. 8s.

Plato's Phædo, literally translated, by the late E. M. COPE.
Fellow of Trinity College, Cambridge. Demy Octavo. 5s.

Aristotle. The Rhetoric. With a Commentary by the late
E. M. COPE, Fellow of Trinity College, Cambridge, revised and
edited by J. E. SANDYS, Litt.D. 3 Vols. Demy 8vo. 21s.

Aristotle.—ΠΕΡΙ ΨΥΧΗΣ. Aristotle's Psychology, in Greek
and English, with Introduction and Notes, by EDWIN WALLACE,
M.A., late Fellow of Worcester College, Oxford. Demy 8vo. 18s.

ΠΕΡΙ ΔΙΚΑΙΟΣΥΝΗΣ. The Fifth Book of the Nicomachean Ethics of Aristotle. Edited by HENRY JACKSON, Litt. D.
Fellow of Trinity College, Cambridge. Demy 8vo. 6s.

Pindar. Olympian and Pythian Odes. With Notes Explanatory and Critical, Introductions and Introductory Essays. Edited
by C. A. M. FENNELL, Litt. D. Crown 8vo. 9s.

— The Isthmian and Nemean Odes by the same Editor. 9s.

The Types of Greek Coins. By PERCY GARDNER, Litt. D.,
F.S.A. With 16 plates. Impl. 4to. Cloth £1. 11s. 6d, Roxburgh
(Morocco back) £2. 2s.

SANSKRIT, ARABIC AND SYRIAC.

The Divyâvadâna, a Collection of Early Buddhist Legends,
now first edited from the Nepalese Sanskrit MSS. in Cambridge
and Paris. By E. B. COWELL, M.A. and R. A. NEIL, M.A.
Demy 8vo. 18s.

Nalopakhyánam, or, The Tale of Nala; containing the Sanskrit Text in Roman Characters, with Vocabulary. By the late
Rev. T. JARRETT. M.A. Demy 8vo. 10s.

Notes on the Tale of Nala, for the use of Classical Students,
by J. PEILE, Litt. D., Master of Christ's College. Demy 8vo. 12s.

The History of Alexander the Great, being the Syriac version
of the Pseudo-Callisthenes. Edited from Five Manuscripts, with an
English Translation and Notes, by E. A. BUDGE, M.A. [*In the Press.*

London: Cambridge Warehouse, Ave Maria Lane.

The Poems of Beha ed din Zoheir of Egypt. With a Metrical Translation, Notes and Introduction, by the late E. H. PALMER, M.A. 2 vols. Crown Quarto.
Vol. I. The ARABIC TEXT. 10s. 6d.; cloth extra, 15s.
Vol. II. ENGLISH TRANSLATION. 10s. 6d.; cloth extra, 15s.

The Chronicle of Joshua the Stylite edited in Syriac, with an English translation and notes, by W. WRIGHT, LL.D., Professor of Arabic. Demy Octavo. 10s. 6d.

Kalīlah and Dimnah, or, the Fables of Bidpai; with an English Translation of the later Syriac version, with Notes, by the late I. G. N. KEITH-FALCONER, M.A. Demy 8vo. 7s. 6d.

MATHEMATICS, PHYSICAL SCIENCE, &c.

Mathematical and Physical Papers. By GEORGE GABRIEL STOKES, M.A., LL.D. Reprinted from the Original Journals and Transactions, with additional Notes by the Author. Vol. I. Demy 8vo. 15s. Vol. II. 15s. [Vol. III. *In the Press.*

Mathematical and Physical Papers. By Sir W. THOMSON, LL.D., F.R.S. Collected from different Scientific Periodicals from May, 1841, to the present time. Vol. I. Demy 8vo. 18s. Vol. II. 15s. [Vol. III. *In the Press.*

A History of the Theory of Elasticity and of the Strength of Materials, from Galilei to the present time. Vol I. GALILEI TO SAINT-VENANT, 1639–1850. By the late I. TODHUNTER, D. Sc., edited and completed by Prof. KARL PEARSON, M.A. Demy 8vo. 25s. Vol. II. By the same Editor. [*In the Press.*

A Treatise on the General Principles of Chemistry, by M. M. PATTISON MUIR, M.A. Demy 8vo. 15s.

Elementary Chemistry. By M. M. PATTISON MUIR, M.A., and CHARLES SLATER, M.A., M.B. Crown 8vo. 4s. 6d.

Practical Chemistry. A Course of Laboratory Work. By M. M. PATTISON MUIR, M.A., and D. J. CARNEGIE, B.A. Cr. 8vo. 3s.

A Treatise on Geometrical Optics. By R. S. HEATH, M.A. Demy 8vo. 12s. 6d.

An Elementary Treatise on Geometrical Optics. By R. S. HEATH, M.A. Crown 8vo. 5s.

Lectures on the Physiology of Plants, by S. H. VINES, M.A., D.Sc., Fellow of Christ's College. Demy 8vo. 21s.

A Short History of Greek Mathematics. By J. Gow, Litt. D., Fellow of Trinity College. Demy 8vo. 10s. 6d.

Notes on Qualitative Analysis. Concise and Explanatory. By H. J. H. FENTON, M.A., F.C.S. New Edit. Crown 4to. 6s.

Diophantos of Alexandria; a Study in the History of Greek Algebra. By T. L. HEATH, M.A. Demy 8vo. 7s. 6d.

A Catalogue of the Portsmouth collection of Books and Papers written by or belonging to SIR ISAAC NEWTON. Demy 8vo. 5s.

London: Cambridge Warehouse, Ave Maria Lane.

The Collected Mathematical Papers of ARTHUR CAYLEY, M.A., F.R.S., Sadlerian Professor of Pure Mathematics in the University of Cambridge. Demy 4to. [*In the Press.*

A Treatise on Natural Philosophy. Part I. By Professors Sir W. THOMSON, LL.D., D.C.L., F.R.S., and P. G. TAIT, M.A., Demy 8vo. 16s. Part II. Demy 8vo. 18s.

Elements of Natural Philosophy. By Professors Sir W. THOMSON and P. G. TAIT. *Second Edition.* Demy 8vo. 9s.

An Elementary Treatise on Quaternions. By P. G. TAIT, M.A. *Second Edition.* Demy 8vo. 14s.

A Treatise on the Theory of Determinants and their Applications in Analysis and Geometry. By ROBERT FORSYTH SCOTT, M.A., Fellow of St John's College. Demy 8vo. 12s.

Counterpoint. A practical course of study. By the late Prof. Sir G. A. MACFARREN, Mus.D. 5th Edition, revised. Cr. 4to. 7s. 6d.

The Analytical Theory of Heat. By JOSEPH FOURIER. Translated, with Notes, by A. FREEMAN, M.A. Demy 8vo. 12s.

The Scientific Papers of the late Prof. J. Clerk Maxwell. Edited by W. D. NIVEN, M.A. Royal 4to. [*Nearly ready.*

The Electrical Researches of the Honourable Henry Cavendish, F.R.S. Written between 1771 and 1781. Edited by J. CLERK MAXWELL, F.R.S. Demy 8vo. cloth, 18s.

Practical Work at the Cavendish Laboratory. Heat. Edited by W. N. SHAW, M.A. Demy 8vo. 3s.

Hydrodynamics, a Treatise on the Mathematical Theory of Fluid Motion, by HORACE LAMB, M.A. Demy 8vo. 12s.

The Mathematical Works of Isaac Barrow, D.D. Edited by W. WHEWELL, D.D. Demy Octavo. 7s. 6d.

Illustrations of Comparative Anatomy, Vertebrate and Invertebrate. Second Edition. Demy 8vo. 2s. 6d.

A Catalogue of Australian Fossils. By R. ETHERIDGE, Jun., F.G.S. Demy 8vo. 10s. 6d.

The Fossils and Palæontological Affinities of the Neocomian Deposits of Upware and Brickhill. With Plates. By W. KEEPING, M.A., F.G.S. Demy 8vo. 10s. 6d.

A Catalogue of Books and Papers on Protozoa, Coelenterates, Worms, etc. published during the years 1861–1883, by D'ARCY W. THOMPSON, M.A. Demy 8vo. 12s. 6d.

An attempt to test the Theories of Capillary Action, by F. BASHFORTH, B.D., and J. C. ADAMS, M.A., £1. 1s.

A Catalogue of the Collection of Cambrian and Silurian Fossils contained in the Geological Museum of the University of Cambridge, by J. W. SALTER, F.G.S. Royal Quarto. 7s. 6d.

Catalogue of Osteological Specimens contained in the Anatomical Museum of the University of Cambridge. Demy 8vo. 2s. 6d.

Astronomical Observations made at the Observatory of Cambridge from 1846 to 1860, by the late Rev. J. CHALLIS, M.A.

Astronomical Observations from 1861 to 1865. Vol. XXI. Royal 4to., 15s. From 1866 to 1869. Vol. XXII. [*Nearly Ready.*

London: Cambridge Warehouse, Ave Maria Lane.

LAW.

Elements of the Law of Torts. A Text-book for Students. By MELVILLE M. BIGELOW, Ph.D. Crown 8vo. [*In the Press.*

A Selection of Cases on the English Law of Contract. By GERARD BROWN FINCH, M.A. Royal 8vo. 28s.

The Influence of the Roman Law on the Law of England. Being the Yorke Prize Essay for the year 1884. By T. E. SCRUTTON, M.A. Demy 8vo. 10s. 6d.

Land in Fetters. Being the Yorke Prize Essay for 1885. By T. E. SCRUTTON, M.A. Demy 8vo. 7s. 6d.

Commons and Common Fields, or the History and Policy of the Laws of Commons and Enclosures in England. Being the Yorke Prize Essay for 1886. By T. E. SCRUTTON, M.A. Demy 8vo. 10s. 6d.

History of the Law of Tithes in England. Being the Yorke Prize Essay for 1887. By W. EASTERBY, B.A., LL.B. Demy 8vo. 7s. 6d.

An Introduction to the Study of Justinian's Digest. By HENRY JOHN ROBY. Demy 8vo. 9s.

Justinian's Digest. Lib. VII., Tit. I. De Usufructu with a Legal and Philological Commentary by H. J. ROBY. Demy 8vo. 9s. The Two Parts complete in One Volume. Demy 8vo. 18s.

Practical Jurisprudence. A comment on AUSTIN. By E. C. CLARK, LL.D., Regius Professor of Civil Law. Crown 8vo. 9s.

An Analysis of Criminal Liability. By the same Editor. Crown 8vo. 7s. 6d.

A Selection of the State Trials. By J. W. WILLIS-BUND, M.A., LL.B. Crown 8vo. Vols. I. and II. In 3 parts. 30s.

The Fragments of the Perpetual Edict of Salvius Julianus, Collected, Arranged, and Annotated by the late BRYAN WALKER, M.A., LL.D. Crown 8vo. 6s.

The Commentaries of Gaius and Rules of Ulpian. Translated and Annotated, by J. T. ABDY, LL.D., and BRYAN WALKER, M.A., LL.D. New Edition by Bryan Walker. Crown 8vo. 16s.

The Institutes of Justinian, translated with Notes by J. T. ABDY, LL.D., and BRYAN WALKER, M.A., LL.D. Cr. 8vo. 16s.

Grotius de Jure Belli et Pacis, with the Notes of Barbeyrac and others; an abridged Translation of the Text, by W. WHEWELL, D.D. Demy 8vo. 12s. The translation separate. 6s.

Selected Titles from the Digest, by BRYAN WALKER, M.A., LL.D. Part I. Mandati vel Contra. Digest XVII. 1. Cr. 8vo. 5s.

Part II. De Adquirendo rerum dominio, and De Adquirenda vel amittenda Possessione, Digest XLI. 1 and 2. Crown 8vo. 6s.

Part III. De Condictionibus, Digest XII. 1 and 4—7 and Digest XIII. 1—3. Crown 8vo. 6s.

Bracton's Note Book. A Collection of Cases decided in the King's Courts during the Reign of Henry the Third, annotated by a Lawyer of that time, seemingly by Henry of Bratton. Edited by F. W. MAITLAND. 3 vols. Demy 8vo. £3. 3s. (nett.)

HISTORICAL WORKS.

Life and Times of Stein, or Germany and Prussia in the Napoleonic Age, by J. R. SEELEY, M.A. With Portraits and Maps. 3 vols. Demy 8vo. 30s.

London: Cambridge Warehouse, Ave Maria Lane.

The Architectural History of the University of Cambridge
and of the Colleges of Cambridge and Eton, by the late Professor
WILLIS, M.A., F.R.S. Edited with large Additions and a Continuation to the present time by JOHN WILLIS CLARK, M.A.
Four Vols. Super Royal 8vo. £6. 6s.

Also a limited Edition of the same, consisting of 120 numbered Copies only, large paper Quarto; the woodcuts and steel engravings mounted on India paper; of which 100 copies are now offered for sale, at Twenty-five Guineas net each set.

The University of Cambridge from the Earliest Times to the
Royal Injunctions of 1535. By J. B. MULLINGER, M.A. Demy 8vo. 12s.
—— Part II. From the Royal Injunctions of 1535 to the Accession of Charles the First. Demy 8vo. 18s.

History of the College of St John the Evangelist, by THOMAS BAKER, B.D., Ejected Fellow. Edited by JOHN E. B. MAYOR, M.A., Fellow of St John's. Two Vols. Demy 8vo. 24s.

Scholae Academicae: some Account of the Studies at the
English Universities in the Eighteenth Century. By CHRISTOPHER WORDSWORTH, M.A. Demy Octavo, 10s. 6d.

Studies in the Literary Relations of England with Germany
in the Sixteenth Century. By C. H. HERFORD, M.A. Crown 8vo. 9s.

The Growth of English Industry and Commerce. By W. CUNNINGHAM, B.D. With Maps and Charts. Crown 8vo. 12s.

Chronological Tables of Greek History. By CARL PETER.
Translated from the German by G. CHAWNER, M.A. Demy 4to. 10s.

Travels in Northern Arabia in 1876 and 1877. By CHARLES M. DOUGHTY. With Illustrations. Demy 8vo. 2 vols. £3. 3s.

History of Nepāl, edited with an introductory sketch of the Country and People by Dr D. WRIGHT. Super-royal 8vo. 10s. 6d.

A Journey of Literary and Archæological Research in Nepal
and Northern India, 1884—5. By C. BENDALL, M.A. Demy 8vo. 10s.

MISCELLANEOUS.

Kinship and Marriage in early Arabia, by W. ROBERTSON SMITH, M.A., LL.D. Crown 8vo. 7s. 6d.

Chapters on English Metre. By Rev. JOSEPH B. MAYOR, M.A. Demy 8vo. 7s. 6d.

A Catalogue of Ancient Marbles in Great Britain, by Prof. ADOLF MICHAELIS. Translated by C. A. M. FENNELL, Litt.D. Royal 8vo. Roxburgh (Morocco back). £2. 2s.

From Shakespeare to Pope. An Inquiry into the causes and phenomena of the Rise of Classical Poetry in England. By E. GOSSE, M.A. Crown 8vo. 6s.

The Literature of the French Renaissance. An Introductory Essay. By A. A. TILLEY, M.A. Crown 8vo. 6s.

A Latin-English Dictionary. Printed from the (Incomplete) MS. of the late T. H. KEY, M.A., F.R.S. Demy 4to. £1. 11s. 6d.

Epistvlae Ortelianae. ABRAHAMI ORTELII (Geographi Antverpiensis) et virorvm ervditorvm ad evndem et ad JACOBVM COLIVM ORTELIANVM Epistvlae. Cvm aliqvot aliis epistvlis et tractatibvs (1524—1628). Ex avtographis edidit JOANNES HENRICVS HESSELS. Demy 4to. £3. 10s. *Net.*

London: Cambridge Warehouse, Ave Maria Lane.

Contributions to the Textual Criticism of the Divina Commedia. Including the complete collation throughout the *Inferno* of all the MSS. at Oxford and Cambridge. By the Rev. EDWARD MOORE, D.D. [*Nearly ready.*

The Despatches of Earl Gower, English Ambassador at the court of Versailles, June 1790 to August 1792, and the Despatches of Mr Lindsay and Mr Monro. By O. BROWNING, M.A. Demy 8vo. 15s.

Rhodes in Ancient Times. By CECIL TORR, M.A. With six plates. 10s. 6d.

Rhodes in Modern Times. By the same Author. With three plates. Demy 8vo. 8s.

The Woodcutters of the Netherlands during the last quarter of the Fifteenth Century. By W. M. CONWAY. Demy 8vo. 10s. 6d.

Lectures on Teaching, delivered in the University of Cambridge. By J. G. FITCH, M.A., LL.D. Cr. 8vo. 5s.

Occasional Addresses on Educational Subjects. By S. S. LAURIE, M.A., F.R.S.E. Crown 8vo. [*Immediately.*

A Grammar of the Irish Language. By Prof. WINDISCH. Translated by Dr NORMAN MOORE. Crown 8vo. 7s. 6d.

A Catalogue of the Collection of Birds formed by the late HUGH EDWIN STRICKLAND, now in the possession of the University of Cambridge. By O. SALVIN, M.A., F.R.S. £1. 1s.

Catalogue of the Hebrew Manuscripts preserved in the University Library, Cambridge. By Dr SCHILLER-SZINESSY. 9s.

Catalogue of the Buddhist Sanskrit Manuscripts in the University Library, Cambridge. Edited by C. BENDALL, M.A. 12s.

A Catalogue of the Manuscripts preserved in the Library of the University of Cambridge. Demy 8vo. 5 Vols. 10s. each.

Index to the Catalogue. Demy 8vo. 10s.

A Catalogue of Adversaria and printed books containing MS. notes, in the Library of the University of Cambridge. 3s. 6d.

The Illuminated Manuscripts in the Library of the Fitzwilliam Museum, Cambridge, by W. G. SEARLE, M.A. 7s. 6d.

A Chronological List of the Graces, etc. in the University Registry which concern the University Library. 2s. 6d.

Catalogus Bibliothecæ Burckhardtianæ. Demy Quarto. 5s.

Graduati Cantabrigienses: sive catalogus exhibens nomina eorum quos usque gradu quocunque ornavit Academia Cantabrigiensis (1800—1884). Cura H. R. LUARD, S. T. P. Demy 8vo. 12s. 6d.

Statutes for the University of Cambridge and for the Colleges therein, made, published and approved (1878—1882) under the Universities of Oxford and Cambridge Act, 1877. Demy 8vo. 16s.

Statutes of the University of Cambridge. 3s. 6d.

Ordinances of the University of Cambridge. 7s. 6d.

Trusts, Statutes and Directions affecting (1) The Professorships of the University. (2) The Scholarships and Prizes. (3) Other Gifts and Endowments. Demy 8vo. 5s.

A Compendium of University Regulations. Demy 8vo. 6d.

Admissions to Gonville and Caius College in the University of Cambridge March 1558—9 to Jan. 1678—9. Edited by J. VENN, Sc.D., and S. C. VENN. Demy 8vo. 10s.

London: Cambridge Warehouse, Ave Maria Lane.

The Cambridge Bible for Schools and Colleges.

GENERAL EDITOR: J. J. S. PEROWNE, D.D., DEAN OF PETERBOROUGH.

"It is difficult to commend too highly this excellent series."—*Guardian*.

"The modesty of the general title of this series has, we believe, led many to misunderstand its character and underrate its value. The books are well suited for study in the upper forms of our best schools, but not the less are they adapted to the wants of all Bible students who are not specialists. We doubt, indeed, whether any of the numerous popular commentaries recently issued in this country will be found more serviceable for general use."—*Academy*.

"Of great value. The whole series of comments for schools is highly esteemed by students capable of forming a judgment. The books are scholarly without being pretentious: information is so given as to be easily understood."—*Sword and Trowel*.

Now Ready. Cloth, Extra Fcap. 8vo.

Book of Joshua. By Rev. G. F. MACLEAR, D.D. With Maps. 2s. 6d.
Book of Judges. By Rev. J. J. LIAS, M.A. 3s. 6d.
First Book of Samuel. By Rev. Prof. KIRKPATRICK, M.A. With Map. 3s. 6d.
Second Book of Samuel. By Rev. Prof. KIRKPATRICK, M.A. With 2 Maps. 3s. 6d.
First Book of Kings. By Rev. Prof. LUMBY, D.D. 3s. 6d.
Second Book of Kings. By Prof. LUMBY, D.D. 3s. 6d.
Book of Job. By Rev. A. B. DAVIDSON, D.D. 5s.
Book of Ecclesiastes. By Very Rev. E. H. PLUMPTRE, D.D., Dean of Wells. 5s.
Book of Jeremiah. By Rev. A. W. STREANE. M.A. 4s. 6d.
Book of Hosea. By Rev. T. K. CHEYNE, M.A., D.D. 3s.
Books of Obadiah and Jonah. By Arch. PEROWNE. 2s. 6d.
Book of Micah. Rev. T. K. CHEYNE, M.A., D.D. 1s. 6d.
Books of Haggai and Zechariah. By Arch. PEROWNE. 3s.
Gospel according to St Matthew. By Rev. A. CARR, M.A. With 2 Maps. 2s. 6d.
Gospel according to St Mark. By Rev. G. F. MACLEAR, D.D. With 4 Maps. 2s. 6d.
Gospel according to St Luke. By Archdeacon FARRAR. With 4 Maps. 4s. 6d.
Gospel according to St John. By Rev. A. PLUMMER, M.A., D.D. With 4 Maps. 4s. 6d.
Acts of the Apostles. By Prof. LUMBY, D.D. 4 Maps. 4s. 6d.
Epistle to the Romans. Rev. H. C. G. MOULE, M.A. 3s. 6d.
First Corinthians. By Rev. J. J. LIAS, M.A. With Map. 2s.

London: Cambridge Warehouse, Ave Maria Lane.

Second Corinthians. By Rev. J. J. LIAS, M.A. With Map. 2s.
Epistle to the Ephesians. Rev. H. C. G. MOULE, M.A. 2s. 6d.
Epistle to the Hebrews. By Arch. FARRAR, D.D. 3s. 6d.
General Epistle of St James. By Very Rev. E. H. PLUMPTRE, D.D. 1s. 6d.
Epistles of St Peter and St Jude. By Very Rev. E. H. PLUMPTRE, D.D. 2s. 6d.
Epistles of St John. By Rev. A. PLUMMER, M.A., D.D. 3s. 6d.

Preparing.

Book of Genesis. By Very Rev. the Dean of Peterborough.
Books of Exodus, Numbers and Deuteronomy. By Rev. C. D. GINSBURG, LL.D.
Books of Ezra and Nehemiah. By Rev. Prof. RYLE, M.A.
Book of Psalms. By Rev. Prof. KIRKPATRICK, M.A.
Book of Isaiah. By W. ROBERTSON SMITH, M.A.
Book of Ezekiel. By Rev. A. B. DAVIDSON, D.D.
Epistle to the Galatians. By Rev. E. H. PEROWNE, D.D.
Epistles to the Philippians, Colossians and Philemon. By Rev. H. C. G. MOULE, M.A.
Epistles to the Thessalonians. By Rev. W. F. MOULTON, D.D.
Book of Revelation. By Rev. W. H. SIMCOX, M.A.

THE CAMBRIDGE GREEK TESTAMENT
FOR SCHOOLS AND COLLEGES

with a Revised Text, based on the most recent critical authorities, and English Notes, prepared under the direction of the General Editor,

J. J. S. PEROWNE, D.D., DEAN OF PETERBOROUGH.

Gospel according to St Matthew. By Rev. A. CARR, M.A. With 4 Maps. 4s. 6d.
Gospel according to St Mark. By Rev. G. F. MACLEAR, D.D. With 3 Maps. 4s. 6d.
Gospel according to St Luke. By Archdeacon FARRAR. With 4 Maps. 6s.
Gospel according to St John. By Rev. A. PLUMMER, M.A. With 4 Maps. 6s.
Acts of the Apostles. By Prof. LUMBY, D.D. 4 Maps. 6s.
First Epistle to the Corinthians. By Rev. J. J. LIAS, M.A. 3s.
Second Epistle to the Corinthians. By Rev. J. J. LIAS, M.A.
[Preparing.
Epistle to the Hebrews. By Archdeacon FARRAR, D.D.
[In the Press.
Epistle of St James. By Very Rev. E. H. PLUMPTRE, D.D.
[Preparing.
Epistles of St John. By Rev. A. PLUMMER, M.A., D.D. 4s.

London: Cambridge Warehouse, Ave Maria Lane.

THE PITT PRESS SERIES.

I. GREEK.

Platonis Apologia Socratis. With Introduction, Notes and Appendices by J. ADAM, M.A. *Price* 3s. 6d.
—— **Crito.** With Introduction, Notes and Appendix. By the same Editor. *Price* 2s. 6d.
Herodotus, Book VIII., Chaps. 1—90. Edited with Notes and Introduction by E. S. SHUCKBURGH, M.A. *Price* 3s. 6d.
Herodotus, Book IX., Chaps. 1—89. By the same Editor. 3s. 6d.
Homer. Oydssey, Book IX. With Introduction, Notes and Appendices by G. M. EDWARDS, M.A. *Price* 2s. 6d.
Sophocles.—Oedipus Tyrannus. School Edition, with Introduction and Commentary by R. C. JEBB, Litt.D., LL.D. 4s. 6d.
Xenophon—Anabasis. With Introduction, Map and English Notes, by A. PRETOR, M.A. Two vols. *Price* 7s. 6d.
—— —— **Books I. III. IV. and V.** By the same Editor. *Price* 2s. each. **Books II. VI. and VII.** *Price* 2s. 6d. each.
Xenophon—Cyropaedeia. Books I. II. With Introduction and Notes by Rev. H. A. HOLDEN, M.A., LL.D. 2 vols. *Price* 6s.
—— —— **Books III. IV. and V.** By the same Editor. 5s.
Xenophon—Agesilaus. By H. HAILSTONE, M.A. 2s. 6d.
Luciani Somnium Charon Piscator et De Luctu. By W. E. HEITLAND, M.A., Fellow of St John's College, Cambridge. 3s. 6d.
Aristophanes. Aves—Plutus—Ranae. By W. C. GREEN, M.A., late Assistant Master at Rugby School. *Price* 3s. 6d. each.
Euripides. Hercules Furens. With Introduction, Notes and Analysis. By A. GRAY, M.A., and J. T. HUTCHINSON, M.A. 2s.
Euripides. Heracleidæ. With Introduction and Critical Notes by E. A. BECK, M.A., Fellow of Trinity Hall. *Price* 3s. 6d.
Euripides. Hippolytus. By W. S. HADLEY, M.A. [*In the Press.*
Plutarch's Lives of the Gracchi.—Sulla. With Introduction, Notes and Lexicon by H. A. HOLDEN, M.A., LL.D. 6s. each.
Plutarch's Life of Nicias. By the same Editor. *Price* 5s.

II. LATIN.

Horace. Epistles, Book I. With Notes and Introduction by E. S. SHUCKBURGH, M.A., late Fellow of Emmanuel College. 2s. 6d.
Livy. Book XXI. With Notes, Introduction and Maps. By M. S. DIMSDALE, M.A., Fellow of King's College. *Price* 3s. 6d.
P. Vergili Maronis Aeneidos Libri I.—XII. Edited with Notes by A. SIDGWICK, M.A. *Price* 1s. 6d. each.
P. Vergili Maronis Georgicon Libri I. II. By the same Editor. *Price* 2s. **Libri III. IV.** By the same Editor. *Price* 2s.
P. Vergili Maronis Bucolica. With Introduction and Notes by the same Editor. *Price* 1s. 6d.
Caesar. De Bello Gallico Comment. I. With Maps and Notes by A. G. PESKETT, M.A. *Price* 1s. 6d.
—— **Comment. I. II. III.** *Price* 3s. **Com. IV. V.**, and **Com. VII.** *Price* 2s. each. **Com. VI.** and **Com. VIII.** *Price* 1s. 6d. each.

London: Cambridge Warehouse, Ave Maria Lane.

M. Tulli Ciceronis Oratio Philippica Secunda. With Introduction and Notes by A. G. PESKETT, M.A. *Price* 3s. 6d.
M. T. Ciceronis de Amicitia. Edited by J. S. REID, Litt. D., Fellow of Gonville and Caius College. Revised edition. 3s. 6d.
M. T. Ciceronis de Senectute. By the same Editor. 3s. 6d.
M. T. Ciceronis Oratio pro Archia Poeta. By the same. 2s.
M. T. Ciceronis pro Balbo Oratio. By the same. 1s. 6d.
M. T. Ciceronis pro Sulla Oratio. By the same. 3s. 6d.
M. T. Ciceronis in Q. Caecilium Divinatio et in C. Verrem Actio. By W. E. HEITLAND, M.A., and H. COWIE, M.A. 3s.
M. T. Ciceronis in Gaium Verrem Actio Prima. With Notes by H. COWIE, M.A., Fellow of St John's Coll. *Price* 1s. 6d.
M. T. Ciceronis Oratio pro L. Murena, with English Introduction and Notes. By W. E. HEITLAND, M.A. *Price* 3s.
M. T. Ciceronis Oratio pro Tito Annio Milone, with English Notes, &c., by JOHN SMYTH PURTON, B.D. *Price* 2s. 6d.
M. T. Ciceronis pro Cn. Plancio Oratio, by H. A. HOLDEN, LL.D. Second Edition. *Price* 4s. 6d.
M. T. Ciceronis Somnium Scipionis. With Introduction and Notes. Edited by W. D. PEARMAN, M.A. *Price* 2s.
Quintus Curtius. A Portion of the History (Alexander in India). By W. E. HEITLAND, M.A. and T. E. RAVEN, B.A. 3s. 6d.
M Annaei Lucani Pharsaliae Liber Primus. Edited by W. E. HEITLAND, M.A., and C. E. HASKINS, M.A. 1s. 6d.
P. Ovidii Nasonis Fastorum Liber VI. With Notes by A. SIDGWICK, M.A., Tutor of Corpus Christi Coll., Oxford. 1s. 6d.
Beda's Ecclesiastical History, Books III., IV. Edited by J. E. B. MAYOR, M.A., and J. R. LUMBY, D.D. Revised Edit. 7s. 6d

III. FRENCH.
Le Philosophe sans le savoir. Sedaine. Edited with Notes by Rev. H. A. BULL, M.A., late Master at Wellington College. 2s.
Recits des Temps Merovingiens I—III. Thierry. Edited by the late G. MASSON, B.A. and A. R. ROPES, M.A. Map. *Price* 3s.
La Canne de Jonc. By A. DE VIGNY. Edited with Notes by Rev. H. A. BULL, M.A., late Master at Wellington College. *Price* 2s.
Bataille de Dames. By SCRIBE and LEGOUVÉ. Edited by Rev. H. A. BULL, M.A. *Price* 2s.
Jeanne D'Arc. By A. DE LAMARTINE. Edited by Rev. A. C. CLAPIN, M.A. New Edition. *Price* 2s.
Le Bourgeois Gentilhomme, Comédie-Ballet en Cinq Actes. Par J.-B. Poquelin de Molière (1670). By the same Editor. 1s. 6d.
L'École des Femmes. MOLIÈRE. With Introduction and Notes by GEORGE SAINTSBURY, M.A. *Price* 2s. 6d.
La Picciola. By X. B. SAINTINE. The Text, with Introduction, Notes and Map. By Rev. A. C. CLAPIN, M.A. *Price* 2s.
La Guerre. By MM. ERCKMANN-CHATRIAN. With Map, Introduction and Commentary by the same Editor. *Price* 3s.

London: Cambridge Warehouse, Ave Maria Lane.

Le Directoire. (Considérations sur la Révolution Française. Troisième et quatrième parties.) Revised and enlarged. With Notes by G. MASSON, B.A. and G. W. PROTHERO, M.A. *Price 2s.*

Lettres sur l'histoire de France (XIII—XXIV). Par AUGUSTIN THIERRY. By the same. *Price 2s. 6d.*

Dix Années d'Exil. Livre II. Chapitres 1—8. Par MADAME LA BARONNE DE STAËL-HOLSTEIN. By G. MASSON, B.A. and G. W. PROTHERO, M.A. New Edition, enlarged. *Price 2s*

Histoire du Siècle de Louis XIV. par Voltaire. Chaps. I.—XIII. Edited by GUSTAVE MASSON, B.A. and G. W. PROTHERO, M.A. 2s. 6d. Chaps. XIV.—XXIV. 2s. 6d. Chap. XXV. to end. 2s. 6d.

Lazare Hoche—Par ÉMILE DE BONNECHOSE. With Three Maps, Introduction and Commentary, by C. COLBECK, M.A. 2s.

Le Verre D'Eau. A Comedy, by SCRIBE. Edited by C. COLBECK, M.A. *Price 2s.*

M. Daru, par M. C. A. SAINTE-BEUVE (Causeries du Lundi, Vol. IX.). By G. MASSON, B.A. Univ. Gallic. *Price 2s.*

La Suite du Menteur. A Comedy by P. CORNEILLE. With Notes Philological and Historical, by the same. *Price 2s.*

La Jeune Sibérienne. Le Lépreux de la Cité D'Aoste. Tales by COUNT XAVIER DE MAISTRE. By the same. *Price 2s.*

Fredégonde et Brunehaut. A Tragedy in Five Acts, by N. LEMERCIER. By GUSTAVE MASSON, B.A. *Price 2s.*

Le Vieux Célibataire. A Comedy, by COLLIN D'HARLEVILLE. With Notes, by the same. *Price 2s.*

La Métromanie. A Comedy, by PIRON, by the same 2s.

Lascaris ou Les Grecs du XVᴱ **Siècle, Nouvelle Historique,** par A. F. VILLEMAIN. By the same. *Price 2s.*

IV. GERMAN.

Mendelssohn's Letters. Selections from. Edited by JAMES SIME, M.A. *Price 3s.*

Benedix. Doctor Wespe. Lustspiel in fünf Aufzügen. Edited with Notes by KARL HERMANN BREUL, M.A. *Price 3s.*

Selected Fables. Lessing and Gellert. Edited with Notes by KARL HERMANN BREUL, M.A. *Price 3s.*

Zopf und Schwert. Lustspiel in fünf Aufzügen von KARL GUTZKOW. By H. J. WOLSTENHOLME, B.A (Lond.). *Price 3s. 6d.*

Die Karavane, von WILHELM HAUFF. Edited with Notes by A. SCHLOTTMANN, PH. D. *Price 3s. 6d.*

Hauff, Das Wirthshaus im Spessart. By A. SCHLOTTMANN, Ph.D., late Assistant Master at Uppingham School. *Price 3s. 6d.*

Hauff, Das Bild des Kaisers. By KARL HERMANN BREUL, M.A., Ph.D. [*Nearly Ready.*

Culturgeschichtliche Novellen, von W. H. RIEHL. Edited by H. J. WOLSTENHOLME, B.A. (Lond.). *Price 4s. 6d.*

Uhland. Ernst. Herzog von Schwaben. With Introduction and Notes. By the same Editor. *Price 3s. 6d.*

Goethe's Knabenjahre. (1749—1759.) **Goethe's Boyhood.** Arranged and Annotated by W. WAGNER, Ph. D. *Price 2s.*

London: Cambridge Warehouse, Ave Maria Lane.

Goethe's Hermann and Dorothea. By W. WAGNER, Ph. D.
Revised edition by J. W. CARTMELL. *Price* 3s. 6d.

Der Oberhof. A Tale of Westphalian Life, by KARL IMMERMANN. By WILHELM WAGNER, Ph.D. *Price* 3s.

Der erste Kreuzzug (1095—1099) nach FRIEDRICH VON RAUMER. THE FIRST CRUSADE. By W. WAGNER, Ph. D. *Price* 2s.

A Book of German Dactylic Poetry. Arranged and Annotated by WILHELM WAGNER, Ph.D. *Price* 3s.

A Book of Ballads on German History. Arranged and Annotated by WILHELM WAGNER, PH. D. *Price* 2s.

Der Staat Friedrichs des Grossen. By G. FREYTAG. With Notes. By WILHELM WAGNER, PH. D. *Price* 2s.

Das Jahr 1813 (THE YEAR 1813), by F. KOHLRAUSCH. With English Notes by the same Editor. *Price* 2s.

V. ENGLISH.

An Elementary Commercial Geography. A Sketch of the Commodities and the Countries of the World. By H. R. MILL, Sc.D., F.R.S.E. 1s.

Theory & Practice of Teaching. By E. THRING, M.A. 4s. 6d.

The Teaching of Modern Languages in Theory and Practice. By C. COLBECK, M.A. *Price* 2s.

John Amos Comenius, Bishop of the Moravians. His Life and Educational Works, by S. S. LAURIE, A.M., F.R.S.E. 3s. 6d.

Outlines of the Philosophy of Aristotle. Compiled by EDWIN WALLACE, M.A., LL.D. Third Edition, Enlarged. 4s. 6d.

The Two Noble Kinsmen, edited with Introduction and Notes by the Rev. Professor SKEAT, Litt.D. *Price* 3s. 6d.

Bacon's History of the Reign of King Henry VII. With Notes by the Rev. Professor LUMBY, D.D. *Price* 3s.

Sir Thomas More's Utopia. By the same. 3s. 6d.

More's History of King Richard III. Edited with Notes, Glossary, Index of Names. By J. RAWSON LUMBY, D.D. 3s. 6d.

Cowley's Essays. By Prof. LUMBY, D.D. 4s.

Locke on Education. With Introduction and Notes by the Rev. R. H. QUICK, M.A. *Price* 3s. 6d.

A Sketch of Ancient Philosophy from Thales to Cicero, by JOSEPH B. MAYOR, M.A. *Price* 3s. 6d.

Three Lectures on the Practice of Education. I. On Marking, by H. W. EVE, M.A. II. On Stimulus, by A. SIDGWICK, M.A. III. On the Teaching of Latin Verse Composition, by E. A. ABBOTT, D.D. *Price* 2s.

General aims of the Teacher, and Form Management. Two Lectures by F. W. FARRAR, D.D. and R. B. POOLE, B.D. 1s. 6d.

Milton's Tractate on Education. A facsimile reprint from the Edition of 1673. Edited by O. BROWNING, M.A. *Price* 2s.

London: C. J. CLAY AND SONS,
CAMBRIDGE WAREHOUSE, AVE MARIA LANE.
Glasgow: 263, ARGYLE STREET.
Cambridge: DEIGHTON, BELL AND CO. **Leipzig:** F. A. BROCKHAUS.

www.ingramcontent.com/pod-product-compliance
Lightning Source LLC
Chambersburg PA
CBHW030547300426
44111CB00009B/891